THE CIVILIZATION OF THE AMERICAN INDIAN

THE INDIAN AND THE HORSE

THE INDIAN
and the
HORSE

by
FRANK GILBERT ROE

UNIVERSITY OF OKLAHOMA PRESS
NORMAN

BY FRANK GILBERT ROE

*The North American Buffalo: A Critical Study
of the Species in Its Wild State*
(Toronto, 1951)

The Indian and the Horse
(Norman, 1955)

LIBRARY OF CONGRESS CATALOG CARD NUMBER: 55–6359

COPYRIGHT 1955 BY THE UNIVERSITY OF OKLAHOMA PRESS
PUBLISHING DIVISION OF THE UNIVERSITY
MANUFACTURED IN THE U.S.A.
FIRST EDITION, APRIL, 1955
SECOND PRINTING, BY OFFSET, APRIL, 1962

TO D. M. R.

PREFACE

In relation to the appearance and influence of the historic horse among the Plains tribes, there have been many excellent monographs written, dealing with individual tribes. Some of these I have been able to utilize; others I have had no opportunity to see. In general, however, the writers have dealt with only one tribe as the central thesis, and the comparative aspects of the question have occupied a secondary place. Since Clark Wissler's admirable study of forty years ago (1914),[1] there has been no sufficiently detailed attempt to discuss the many phases of this important historical question as a whole. The present book, which is an amplification of an earlier and much slighter paper,[2] was planned in the hope of remedying this deficiency in some measure. This is at least partly due to the kind encouragement received by the author from Wissler himself, on the appearance of the earlier effort.[3]

The present work can lay no claim to exhaustiveness. But in this particular field, where *direct* evidence concerning this or that tribe is almost invariably lacking, and where our conclusions, however cautious and rational they may be, are necessarily inferential, no possible scrap of information can safely be neglected. I have therefore striven to present as much as I could obtain on the various aspects of our topic. The study itself is in its nature controversial.

[1] Clark Wissler, "The Influence of the Horse in the Development of Plains Culture," *American Anthropologist*, Vol. XVI (1914), 1–25.
[2] Frank Gilbert Roe, "From Dogs to Horses among the Western Indian Tribes," *Proceedings and Transactions of the Royal Society of Canada*, 3rd Series, Vol. XXXIII (1939), Section II, 209–75.
[3] Correspondence to the author, February 26, 1940.

For this reason (as I view such questions), it is essential that all statements of extraneous or objective fact be carefully documented. It would obviously be intolerable in scientific discussion for any critic to dissect, depreciate, or demolish the arguments of another, without most particularized authority for his own assertions. A proposition may or may not be logically self-evident, but it can never be historically self-evident, in an unfamiliar and little-cultivated field, on anyone's mere word that it is or was thus and thus.

I have no apology to offer for the introduction of personal reminiscence into a study of the present character. Much has been said about the writing of Western history by Westerners, even though one encounters work at times that adds little force to that contention. Whatever may be the ultimate critical verdict upon the arguments of which reminiscent matter forms a part, I shall not acknowledge that such reminiscent matter is irrelevant per se. I regard this attitude as being the more sound since evidence of this precise character is clearly considered admissible in severely scientific publications;[4] and this, too, despite the fact of its being presented at second hand, and (ultimately) from nonliterate witnesses, very frequently in extreme old age. Critics are certainly entitled to demand that such testimony shall be presented in good faith and with reliable accuracy. Since a witness can cite no other authority for such matter than his own, it becomes additionally incumbent upon him to observe those conditions. I can only say that I have striven to do so at all times, and not by reliance upon memory alone.

Much of the research work for this volume was carried out in connection with an earlier publication, and the majority of the acknowledgments mentioned there are applicable here also.[5] To those I must add my grateful thanks to Willard E. Ireland, Provincial archivist of British Columbia, and also to Miss Madge Wolfenden, Miss Mitchell, and every other member of the Provincial Archives Library staff, for permission to avail myself of its treasures and for their ungrudging kindness to a somewhat troublesome visitor.

[4] See Bibliography for John C. Ewers' two important essays, frequently cited in these pages; and compare with Appendix B.
[5] Frank Gilbert Roe, *The North American Buffalo*, v–vi.

I particularly must acknowledge assistance received from several American friends, some of whom I have never met. I have mentioned the late Clark Wissler. The others include some outstanding specialists in Hispano-American history. From some I have received gifts of important additional material that might otherwise have been missed, and from all of them kind encouragement and valued criticism. Among these are included Arthur S. Aiton of the University of Michigan; Charles Julian Bishko of the University of Virginia; Merrill G. Burlingame of the University of Montana; Robert M. Denhardt of Arbuckle, California; my friend J. Frank Dobie of Austin, Texas; John C. Ewers of the Smithsonian Institution, Washington, D. C.; my friend Francis Haines of the Oregon College of Education; R. Leslie Jones of Marietta College, Marietta, Ohio; Erik K. Reed of the U. S. Forest Service, Santa Fé, New Mexico; Francis A. Riddell of the University of California; my friend Vilhjalmur Stefansson of New York and Dartmouth College, Hanover, New Hampshire; Laurence H. Snyder of the University of Oklahoma; and finally, my earliest and most patient counsellor and critic, my wife.

In respect to the illustrations, I should like to acknowledge a deep indebtedness to many sources for the gift or loan of highly valuable material from public or private collections in their care. In each case there was a cordial and instant response to our requests for assistance, and every effort was made to meet our wishes. These include: Donald Cameron, director of the Banff School of Fine Arts in the University of Alberta and head of the Extension Department in the same institution. The Bureau of Indian Affairs, Washington, D. C., in conjunction with the Smithsonian Institution; particularly John C. Ewers, of the latter organization, for the ready assistance of an expert. Francis Haines of the Oregon College of Education, Monmouth, an incomparable authority on the early horse culture of the Northwestern area. Edward S. King of the Walters Art Gallery, Baltimore. Patrick Patterson, director of the Woolaroc Museum, Bartlesville, Oklahoma. John Porter (then of Banff), an exceptionally skilled expert in artistic photography. The Public Archives of Canada, Ottawa; and my friend W. Kaye Lamb, Dominion archivist, for his personal interest in rendering assistance. The Cultural Activities Department of the Province of Alberta for the use of very valuable early photographic material from the Ernest Brown Collection; also my friend Miss Gladys Reeves of Edmonton, curator of the collection (and a niece of the late Mr. Brown), for her personal interest in securing these considerations on our behalf. Perry Rathbone, director of the City Art Museum of St. Louis; Don Rickey, Jr., librarian of the Frank Phillips Collection, the University of Oklahoma; and Will G. Robinson of the South Dakota State Historical Society. Miss Marjorie Sherlock, librarian of the University of Alberta, and Lewis H. Thomas of Regina, Saskatchewan, archivist of that province. K. Ross Toole, director, and Michael Kennedy of the Historical Society of Montana; Stanley Vestal; and Miss Muriel H. Wright and Mrs. C. E. Cook of the Oklahoma Historical Society.

These names do not exhaust the list. There are several others (prominent among whom are Robert Leslie Jones, professor of history, Marietta College, Marietta, Ohio; and Dick Spencer III, editor of *The Western Horseman*, Colorado Springs, Colorado) whose response was equally generous—and in some cases involved much time and trouble—who should not go unthanked, even if it did not prove practicable to use their contributions.

I must add in conclusion that the responsibility for any statements made in this work is mine alone.

FRANK GILBERT ROE

Cadboro Bay, Victoria, B. C.
July 15, 1954

CONTENTS

ILLUSTRATIONS

xv

THE INDIAN AND THE HORSE

INTRODUCTION

In entering upon the examination of this problem, one is struck by the attitude of virtual despair that has always prevailed among scholars at the hopelessness of our ever attaining any really precise knowledge of the relationship of the Indian and the horse. The additional data which have been accumulated by many scholars have done much to throw light upon a multitude of secondary details, but it is still possible for one of the very latest of them to write: ". . . it is impossible to say in just what year, at just what place, this tribe and that obtained its first horse."[1]

It is unlikely that this condition will ever be remedied in any really definitive sense. An authentic *detailed* history of the process and its chronology could come only from the Indians themselves; and this, in the nature of things, must be considered an impossibility for peoples having no written records. This is not one of those cases where one can entertain any hopes of some fortunate discovery in neglected archives that may dispel our ignorance. We shall have occasion to note later in this volume a variation on the "stray Spanish horse" theme, which in this instance is "said

[1] J. Frank Dobie, *The Mustangs*, 28. Compare this with Clark Wissler, "The Influence of the Horse in the Development of Plains Culture," *American Anthropologist*, Vol. XVI (1914), 1–25. Francis Haines, "How did the Indians Get Their Horses?" *ibid.*, Vol. XL (1938), 112–17, 429–37. G. P. de T. Glazebrook, "Roads in New France," *Canadian Historical Association Annual Report*, 1934, 49. Richard M. Saunders, "The First Introduction of European Plants and Animals into Canada," *Canadian Historical Review*, Vol. XVI (1935), 403. Edmund H. Oliver, "The Beginnings of Agriculture in Saskatchewan," *Proceedings and Transactions of the Royal Society of Canada* (1935), Section II, 1–32. D. E. Worcester, "The Spread of Spanish Horses in the Southwest," *New Mexico Historical Review*, Vol. XIX (1944), 225–32. Robert Moorman Denhardt, *The Horse of the Americas*.

to be fortified by documents in Jalapa."[2] In this relationship, "documents" are generally taken to signify official records. We shall find ourselves compelled to ask what inherent value such documents can necessarily possess in cases such as the one in question. The mere fact that a notarial official attached a seal or a signature to some unknown person's declaration cannot in itself authenticate that affirmation. Numbers of palpable or demonstrable impossibilities have been recorded in print with fully as much emphasis as any oath is supposed to confer, and we shall find that this particular field presents a rich collection of this type of "evidence."

Our source material relating to Indian usages or characteristics groups itself naturally in two principal classes. These are, of course, the recitals of contemporary contacts with the tribes in their various historic habitats from the earliest eras of European association with them; and, in later times, the critical investigations of more strictly scientific students, culminating in the learned anthropologists of our day. The first of these categories subdivides again into two rather sharply contrasting types. One of these comprises material like the *Jesuit Relations* and the individual recitals of men of education such as the various early missionaries in general, or intelligent (and often, in part, scientific) travelers such as Lewis and Clark, Zebulon M. Pike, Prince Maximilian of Wied, and Josiah Gregg. With these we may associate such early residents as David Thompson, the younger, Alexander Henry, Daniel Williams Harmon, and others who took the trouble to write up their own journals or experiences. Such men more commonly exhibit some degree of quasi-scientific caution, and at least a literary conscience—factors which are frequently revealed and vindicated by the more exacting comparative critic of later times.

The westward expansion of settlement, and particularly the great trek beyond the Mississippi, which dates roughly from the era of the Santa Fé and Oregon Trails, brought another type of "publicist" into the picture. This was the "plainsman," frequently so called, it would seem, for the lack of any other distinctive term. As purveyors of historical source material, these men were certainly picturesque, as they were in most other relations. Their reliability is another question. They were commonly illiterate and

[2] See Chapter VII.

completely destitute of any vestige of self-criticism. Their years on the Plains were supposed to consecrate any tale they chose to tell. They were spiritually—and in an overwhelming degree lineally —the descendants of the trans-Alleghenian pioneers of the Revolutionary era, against the implicit acceptance of whose reminiscences Theodore Roosevelt warns his readers again and again, and above all things in the province of numbers.[3] The plain truth is that much of this last class of material is personal chronicle rather than document. It comes from witnesses who at the time were in a more or less chronic condition of open-mouthed amazement. Caution and exactitude were completely foreign to their habits of thought or of speech. It is extremely doubtful whether they recognized such defects—except in other people—and virtually certain that they would have made no efforts to amend them. It was probably of much more vital importance to put up a bigger yarn and beat the other fellow to it.

The second of the two principal categories into which our material divides itself is that of the modern investigations of anthropological scholars. Here we can rest well-assured beforehand that the presentation at least will be authentic; what is given, for example, as native testimony will be such, and not merely the interpolated opinion of the recorder. At the present time their evidence is scattered in very widely diffused and varied forms. Much of the most valuable of all is buried from sight in a vast periodical literature, principally the abstruse and not always accessible publications of learned societies. This has been accumulated during many years by the labors of many patient investigators, both in the examination of ancient chronicles, and in field work among the tribes affected by the horse. The latter type of student in particular has often dwelt for years among the people he studied, and whose language he had first to master before he could get much further. Trained observers of this caliber are commonly completely and successfully objective in their approach to the cultural study of their chosen tribes. It is recognized that such scholars can be implicitly accepted as *recorders* of the information that has been given them.

Yet in certain respects the modern anthropologist works under a disadvantage. The stream cannot rise higher than its source.

[3] Theodore Roosevelt, *The Winning of the West*, I, 259, *et passim*.

3

While the transmission of the data into documentary form can be implicitly accepted as authentic, we cannot be equally sure of the authenticity of the native informant. In the course of years, changes have taken place in many of the tribes. Certain things may not have been remembered accurately or may have dropped from memory altogether—so completely that their former prevalence affirmed by one is doubted or denied altogether by another. While we accept the laws of numbers or of probability, a given case affords no *absolute* guarantee that the one may not be right and the many wrong. Other usages asserted by observers of past times, which have long been outgrown and discarded in the gradual climb to a relatively higher level, have sometimes apparently come to be regarded as rather childish or perhaps even indecent and degrading.

Numerous early eyewitnesses (1809–1870) describe the buffalo as running round and round in the "simple" (non-jumping) buffalo pound, and "always the way of the sun," following the direction of the decoy, or "bringer-in."[4] A modern Blackfoot (born about 1900) considered the sun-turning absurd.[5] The Blackfoot strenuously denied to the same inquirer (Kenneth E. Kidd) that the tribe had ever eaten dogs, but Kidd felt dubious none the less.[6] An extreme form of this supersensitive attitude is found in Hawaii. The Hawaiians, who have long been Christians, do not merely deny the former prevalence of cannibalism among them, they vehemently repudiate it, evidently as a moral stigma. Yet to an anthropologist such an obsolete practice would be merely a historic cultural usage and nothing more. In such disagreements, whichever argument ultimately wins adoption, the inquirer and the reader are inevitably left with a sense of disquietude concerning other assertions from the informant who has been proved in error. A critical historian writes concerning a certain half-legendary figure of the eighteen thirties, Markhead, that the famous Joe Meek said this man was a Shawnee, "but this is unlikely since everyone else speaks of him as white."[7] The same author tells us elsewhere: "The Little Chief . . . was a great man among the Flatheads. He was tall or

[4] Frank Gilbert Roe, *The North American Buffalo*, App. AA, 880–84.
[5] Kenneth E. Kidd, "Blackfoot Ethnography" (unpublished thesis), 98.
[6] *Ibid.*, 103–104.
[7] Bernard De Voto, *Across the Wide Missouri*, 193.

4

short, fat or lean, old or middle-aged, depending on whose diary you were reading."[8] Yet the Joe Meeks and the diarists of this description constitute a considerable part of our historical material for the Plains area, and are treated by many as authoritative.

There is another phase in this question of testimony that we need to look squarely in the face. Such colloquialisms as "two or three," "six or eight," "twelve or fifteen" are used by every one of us, and nobody can fling the first stone. Actually, of course, if taken literally they add from 25 to 50 per cent to any given number we may suggest. Even then no great harm is done so long as we are merely dealing with units. But when these easy idioms are applied to thousands, the additional masses assume serious proportions. Whether the raconteurs themselves always expected to be taken seriously in spite of their emphatic insistence is not altogether certain. But for historical critics to do this without anything like an adequate sifting of the evidence, and to reproduce it under the aegis of their own scientific authority as though such aggregates were those of trained census enumerators, is highly unwise. To proceed to elaborate calculations or dogmatic conclusions based upon such material is in my judgment inadmissible.

One cannot but note the testimony concerning horse numbers in particular which many authorities have presented, both from early printed sources and from later *viva voce* contacts with living informants. In the case of the Cree, for example, where it is obviously impossible to give precise figures, we find early commentators giving them as "well supplied," while later ones instance "few," and in some cases insist that this latter was always the Cree condition. We have no means of judging what constituted a good supply to Edward Umfreville in 1790,[9] or a poor one to later observers or tribesmen;[10] whether intervening epidemics had depleted their horse stocks; or even whether at the time of the observation in question the approximately full strength was on view, or a large proportion absent on some raid or expedition. Of one thing we may be tolerably sure. Such descriptions cannot safely be used as a basis for definitive pronouncements on Cree horse numbers dur-

[8] *Ibid.*, 199.
[9] Edward Umfreville, *The Present State of Hudson's Bay*, 188–89.
[10] See Chapters V, XV.

ing a century and a half. Mandelbaum describes the Cree buffalo-pound "markers" as leading in toward the pound from a mile or more back on the plain, or "ten miles, according to Maskwa," one of his Cree informants.[11]

An item which is palpably absurd, or physically or logically impossible, may be queried; but there are no means in many cases of finally assaying those assertions which *could* be true, but possibly are *not*. For example, there is nothing inherently incredible in either of the two following statements, taken separately: The Cree sought to remedy their poverty in horses by stealing from the wealthier Blackfoot;[12] the Blackfoot in the same era sought to remedy their poverty in horses by stealing from the wealthier Cree.[13] When brought together it is obvious that both statements cannot be equally sound and acceptable as fixed and unqualified generalizations. Yet they both rest upon precisely the same type of authority; the same kind, moreover, from which all our modern knowledge of those tribes is and must be derived. We cannot demand that either scholar discard his mass of acquired information. If we could, which is it to be? Again, a critical student on the authority of Zenas Leonard (1839), mentions that seven hundred buffalo were slain in a single surround by the Crow.[14] This may or may not have been the case, but another critical student finds Zenas Leonard almost invariably exaggerating or positively wrong, and "to be used with caution."[15] Similarly, we find the following: "Colonel [Charles] Goodnight was firmly convinced that at least 300,000 head of Texas cattle had been stolen and sold or traded to New Mexicans during the Civil War. John Hitson, another Texas ranchman, writing in 1873, was more conservative, estimating the loss of Texas cattle during the two preceding decades [1853–1873] at 100,000 head."[16] Goodnight's estimate (or guess, for there could

[11] David G. Mandelbaum, "The Plains Cree," *Anthropological Papers of the American Museum of Natural History*, Vol. XXXVII (1940), 153–316.

[12] *Ibid.*, 184, 195; Chapters V, XV *infra*.

[13] John C. Ewers, "Were the Blackfoot Rich in Horses?" *American Anthropologist*, Vol. XLV (1943), 602–10.

[14] Robert H. Lowie, "Material Culture of the Crow Indians," *Anthropological Papers of the American Museum of Natural History*, Vol. XXI (1922), 212.

[15] De Voto, *Across the Wide Missouri*, 76, 422, 432.

[16] Rupert Norval Richardson, *The Comanche Barrier to South Plains Settlement*, 310.

be no calculation from figures) is three times as many in one-fifth of the time, equal to *fifteen times* the smaller ratio. Yet many scholars cite Charles Goodnight's utterances on any Plains subject as final. In another place we find a certain Curly Hatcher making sundry assertions. On the following page Andy Mather stigmatizes Curly Hatcher as a liar, only to be discounted himself (and his victim vindicated) on the next one.[17] In such circumstances a critic who is endeavoring to discover the facts says, "A plague o' both your houses!" It should perhaps be said in extenuation that the *casus belli* in this case is the Great White Horse.[18] What reliance can one place upon any testimony from such sources?

It is in such conditions that comparative evidence assumes its highest value. Even this cannot solve these questions completely and finally, but it can at least indicate contradictory or variable data that must be examined in attempting to form approximately final conclusions. The present essay is an attempt to draw these scattered comparative data together from their various resting places, and to summarize in a conveniently co-ordinated form the existent evidence—or the main currents of its findings—concerning the impact of the historic horse upon the principal horse-using tribes of the North American continent in the predominating aspects of chronology, geography, and tribal reactions. While no student can hope to exhaust the subject, it is none the less possible to present a sufficient volume of evidence in relation to the numerous phases of the problem to furnish a fairly clear conception of the probabilities of the case and the essential factors that must be considered.

[17] Dobie, *The Mustangs*, 155–57.
[18] See Chapter VIII.

PART I
THE ACQUISITION OF THE HORSE

A Note to the Reader: The use of single quotation marks throughout this work denotes a paraphrasing of quotations which required some syntactical alteration to fit them into their context. Double quotation marks of course indicate the exact language of the document quoted, or certain expressions for which a distinctive marking other than italics was desired.

I

FROM DOGS TO HORSES

Prior to their acquisition of the horse, the Indian tribes of North America possessed only the dog as a beast of burden.[1] This important fact must necessarily have had a great bearing upon the development of the supposed "network of trails" with which the continent has been thought by many to have been covered from remote times.

Unfortunately this concept has not received the attention it merits from students of archaeological problems. In relation to our present topic of dog transport, there is only one method of dog traction used by the Indian tribes that could make any kind of visible trail sufficiently distinct to be followed up later if need arose, and thereby develop into a permanent trackway. This, of course, is the dog sled. A careful modern investigator of one of the principal Northern Indian nations, whose conclusions are based very largely upon native informants, states that the dog sled is not of aboriginal origin, but was taken over from the fur traders.[2] When we reflect upon its construction and post-European use as a winter vehicle for long journeys with relatively heavy loads and for the provisioning of whose dogs some systematic organization was essential, such as the fur-trading economy brought into being, we can recognize its inapplicability to aboriginal Indian life. Prior

[1] Joseph D. McGuire, in *Handbook of American Indians North of Mexico* (ed. by Frederick Webb Hodge), Bureau of American Ethnology, *Bulletin 30* (cited hereafter as Hodge, *Handbook*), II, 799–801; Otis T. Mason, in *ibid.*, II, 802; Clark Wissler, *The American Indian*, 30–34.

[2] David G. Mandelbaum, "The Plains Cree," *Anthropological Papers of the American Museum of Natural History*, Vol. XXXVII (1940), 198.

to the fur-trading era the Indian had practically no heavy winter loads to convey, nor was he much given to travel at that season.

Factors of this character have been almost completely ignored. Trails of known Indian use in what are relatively modern times have been hastily assumed to be of very early—even remotely early[3]—Indian origin; and the purely relative term "old" has often been gratuitously invested with the meaning it might more reasonably convey in England or on the European continent. It is needless in the present essay to discuss this traditional conception in detail. Its tenets in general are well known to historical and archaeological students on this continent and elsewhere.[4] I should like, however, to quote a passage from an authoritative Canadian anthropologist, who presents very concisely some of the factors which stand in the way of too loose and hasty an acceptance of a "general network of trails" theory. Diamond Jenness writes as follows:

In Canada . . . the tribe . . . was too small numerically, too self-contained, and in most cases too migratory to demand or require specially-built highways for communication and transport, particularly when there were no vehicles save sleds and toboggans to drive over them, and no pack-animal except the dog. So from east to west, and from north to south, throughout the whole Dominion, there was not a single mile of road before the coming of the Europeans, nothing except a few narrow trails that led past rapids and canyons, or through forest, plain, or upland from one valley or lake to another, trails that were often so overgrown with brush or lichens that they could hardly be distinguished from those of the bison or deer.[5]

The foregoing conclusions could be supported abundantly from such early sources as the history of New France by Lescarbot, the travels of Champlain, and the *Jesuit Relations*. Yet another

---

[3] It is difficult to find a term which really conveys one's meaning. On this continent "prehistoric" does not necessarily imply remote antiquity. On the present topic, it merely means prior to 1492, 1530–1540, 1607–1608, 1689, etc.

[4] See on this, among others, John Fiske, *The Discovery of America*, I, 249; II, 501, etc.; Ernest Thompson Seton, *Life Histories of Northern Animals*, I, 300; also his *Lives of Game Animals*, III, 701; J. E. Thorold Rogers, *A History of Agriculture and Prices*, IV, 692; also his *Economic Interpretation of History*, 490. Above all, Archer Butler Hulbert, *The Historic Highways of America*. Hulbert's first two volumes are a mass of contradictions. Later, when his topics are really historical instead of prehistorical speculation, he is of high value.

[5] Diamond Jenness, *The Indians of Canada*, National Museum of Canada, *Bulletin 15*, 100.

enthusiastic archaeologist, citing no authority whatever, pushes his buffalo-and-Indian trails "from the Gulf of Mexico to the country of the Eskimo."[6] The present writer discusses this question in detail elsewhere. It is sufficient to say here that the unanimous testimony of missionaries, fur traders, explorers, engineers, geographers, geologists, and historians is hopelessly fatal to any such contention.[7]

The researches of many years lead me to the conclusion that topographical considerations were the dominant factor in trail-making. Where the Indian was independent of these, he preferred, temperamentally, to make no trail at all, if possible. It is completely inadmissible to extend wholesale into the Plains regions the supposed trailmaking predilections that are inferred from the presence of what are termed "old Indian trails" in certain portions of the eastern woodland territories. In the Plains area there was no such thing for hundreds of miles as the "topographical compulsion" of rapid or canyon, as indicated by Jenness. There were the incessant workings of an almost petulantly individualistic tribal spirit, which appears to have differentiated this very characteristic most conspicuously among a host of others, in a virtually identical environment, rendering the term "Indian trail" meaningless without further (tribal) definition.[8] There were also such potent factors

6 Hulbert, *Historic Highways*, II, 80. The passage is from a contributor, G. H. Harris, but Hulbert's tacit endorsement makes it his own.

7 This is well summed up in G. P. de T. Glazebrook's two important chapters, "Water Transport in the French Regime," and "Roads in the Old Provinces," in *A History of Transportation in Canada*, 1–24, 101 ff.

8 For some of the tribal diversities in camping and trail customs, see Lawrence J. Burpee (ed.), "The Journal of Antony Hendry [Henday], 1754–1755," *Proceedings and Transactions of the Royal Society of Canada*, 3rd Series (1907), Section II, 337–39; Capt. Thomas Morris, *Journal, 1764*, in *Early Western Travels, 1748–1846* (ed. by Reuben Gold Thwaites; cited hereafter as Thwaites, *Travels*), I, 306; Edwin James, *An Account of the Expedition from Pittsburg to the Rocky Mountains, Performed in the Years 1819, 1820; under Major Stephen H. Long*, in Thwaites, *Travels*, XV, 203; XVI, 247; Elliott Coues (ed.), *New Light on the Early History of the Greater Northwest: The Henry-Thompson Journals* (1799–1814), I, 244, 307; John C. Frémont, *Narrative of the Exploring Expedition to the Rocky Mountains . . . and to Oregon and North California. . . .* (1842–44), 14; Francis Parkman, *The Oregon Trail* (1846), 74, 219; Col. Richard I. Dodge, *Our Wild Indians* (1849, et seq.), 241, 557; (Rev.) John McDougall, *Forest, Lake, and Prairie* (Alberta, 1862 et seq.), 183; *Saddle, Sled, and Snowshoe*, 69; *Pathfinding on Plain and Prairie*, 152. Henry Inman, *The Old Santa Fé Trail*, 238; Clark Wissler, "Material Culture of the Blackfoot Indians," *Anthropological Papers of the American Museum of Natural History*, Vol. V (1910), 87–98, 108–17; George Bird Grinnell, *The Fighting*

as hard, sun-baked soil, short grass, frequent firings, and the practically incessant prairie winds, which obliterated horse and wagon tracks.[9] These of themselves would reduce trailmaking of any lasting character by a small, light animal such as the dog to the negligible point.

This conclusion finds additional emphasis from another incidental circumstance, which is clearly of pre-equestrian antiquity. Dogs were taken by Cree war parties to carry extra moccasins, etc.[10] The many feints and deceptions practiced to hide the passing of a war party are well known. While the warriors might no doubt control their own trailmaking, it would be difficult to control that of their dogs, if the latter made any trail. It is the general conclusion of travelers and observers that the Indian dogs are descendants of domesticated wolves, and any other origin, indeed, seems highly improbable. Speaking generally, the more southerly "wolf" is the coyote (*Canis latrans*),[11] while the more northern one is the huge timber wolf (*C. occidentalis*),[12] perhaps a principal ancestor of the big northern Malemutes. One of Mandelbaum's Cree informants had seen a bitch mating with a wolf.[13] To a resident of

Cheyennes, 185, 254, 396; Robert H. Lowie, "Material Culture of the Crow Indians," *Anthropological Papers of the American Museum of Natural History*, Vol. IV (1909), 222; Gilbert L. Wilson, "The Horse and the Dog in Hidatsa Culture," *Anthropological Papers of the American Museum of Natural History*, Vol. XV (1924), 181–93, 196–230, 275–85; Diamond Jenness, *The Sarcee Indians of Alberta*, National Museum of Canada, *Bulletin 90*, 12–14. Compare all these with the so-called "Indian" habit of marching in single file, as in Hulbert, *Historic Highways*, XI, 17–22; and McGuire, in Hodge, *Handbook*, II, 799–801.

9 Compare Juan Martínez de Montoya (1602): "The greatest obstacles to travel are the large hills of very fine sand. It was considered a miracle to be able to find a way between two mountains . . . where the people were able to cross, not without fear of being buried under the sand, as sometimes happens in the desert of Arabia." (George P. Hammond and Agapito Rey [eds.], *New Mexico in 1602*, 41.) See also Walter Prescott Webb, *The Great Plains*, 21–25; and Archer Butler Hulbert (ed.), *Forty-Niners*, 18, 84, where the sand is drifting around their feet while they are actually discussing it! In Hulbert's editorial remarks there is no allusion whatever to his earlier great work, nor to his thesis. The same silence is also maintained by his chroniclers.

10 Mandelbaum, "The Plains Cree," 198. The Blackfoot carried their own (Clark Wissler, "The Social Life of the Blackfoot Indians," *Anthropological Papers of the American Museum of Natural History*, Vol. VII (1911), 33.

11 Wilson, "Horse and Dog in Hidatsa Culture," 196–99, 205.

12 David Thompson, *Narrative of Explorations in Western America, 1784–1812* (ed. by J. B. Tyrrell), 75, editor's note.

13 Mandelbaum, "The Plains Cree," 197.

the Cree country, the term "wolf" signifies the timber wolf; hence the Plains "trail area" is that of the smaller and fainter trail maker, the coyote.

In spite of much vague general assertion about the use of the Santa Fé Trail "dating from time immemorial"[14]—which finds very scanty support from the earliest European and English-speaking travelers over its supposed route[15]—it is a familiar historical fact that Zebulon M. Pike and his comrades could find no such defined route on their journey to Santa Fé in 1806. Otherwise they would scarcely have exhibited the virtual panic which their journals clearly indicate whenever they lost their only guidance—the track of the Spanish party which immediately preceded them—in a maze of buffalo paths. Neither could they very logically have professed to have "lost their way" on their journey to the precise objective to which the supposedly immemorial highway led. It requires little imagination to conceive the effect of such a clumsy tale upon the already hostile Spanish authorities at Santa Fé had there actually been a permanently visible road. It may be pointed out also that when the Spanish governor released Pike from his imprisonment,

14 Thwaites, *Travels,* XVI, 230, editor's note.

15 Cabeza de Vaca, circa 1530: "All through that country there are no trails. . . ." (*The Journey of Alvar Nuñez Cabeza de Vaca and His Companions from Florida to the Pacific, 1528–1536* [translated and edited by Fanny and Adolf F. Bandelier], 97, 102, 128.) See also George P. Winship (ed.), *The Journey of Coronado, 1540–1542,* 67, 70, 75–76, 83, 110, 140, 145, 195, 215, 217, 231. Note especially Pedro de Castañeda's description of the Indian's way-methods: selecting a direction and holding it by arrows shot ahead of them (*ibid.,* 75–76). This was thought by Winship (in his introduction) to be along the route of the later Santa Fé Trail. His conclusion has been disputed; and Coronado has been thought by some 'never to have been off Texan soil.' Webb is justly dubious about this (*The Great Plains,* 95–103); and Herbert E. Bolton rejects it altogether (*Coronado, Knight of Pueblos and Plains,* 285–95, 340). For the present purpose, this does not matter. As described by Castañeda and Jaramillo (Winship [ed.], *Journey of Coronado*), they were returning under Indian guidance from "Quivira" to "Cíbola," the two most important centers in that country. Wherever these were situated, *there was no visible road!* See Chapter III *infra.*

I strongly suspect that many critics (as apparently Inman, *Old Santa Fé Trail,* Chap. I) are really referring to the *route* of the later trail-highway. If they actually intend to signify a visible, *made* trackway, existing in 1541, it would be of interest to learn their authority for so doing. Cleve Hallenbeck (*The Journey and Route of Alvar Nuñez Cabeza de Vaca,* 75, 165) insists that Cabeza de Vaca and his comrades everywhere followed permanently visible trails, but offers no proof of their existence about 1530, beyond emphatic reiteration of his contention. 'Losing the trail in an all-day rainstorm' is intelligible enough with a *route;* it is preposterous with a *road!* I do not speak without considerable Plains experience.

15

no attempt was made to send him home again by the way he had come. Yet this would have been by far the safest course from the military or political standpoint, since it would have shown Pike little of the Spanish territories that he had not already seen. Instead he was escorted over the roundabout route by way of the *Camino Real* and the Natchitoches Trace, with its inevitable opportunities to reveal yet more of the nakedness of the land to a keen observer.[16]

It is a further fact that across a most important section of the Santa Fé Trail, the dreaded Cimarron Cut-off, no trustworthy visible trail was made even by the great Santa Fé caravans for thirteen years after its inception in 1821 until the excessively wet season of 1834, when the wheels cut through the softened surface, and left a permanent track.[17] A Southwestern scholar writes more convincingly: "William Becknell and his associates proved that it was practicable to go by wagon . . . to Santa Fé, and the famous Santa Fé Trail came into existence."[18] The relation of these matters to the history of Indian dog transport lies in the fact that neither the presence nor the absence of trails possesses any significance in the attempt to estimate the geographical or topographical range of this phase of dog culture. The same possibly applies in large measure to horse culture also.

In dealing with the general topic of Indian dog transport at large, I do not of course refer to the quite familiar winter use of dog traction, which has remained in continuous practice to our own day. We have seen that this is considered to be an essentially modern innovation, and it requires no further comment here. What may be termed the two aboriginal methods of utilizing the dog for such services were the well-known travois, afterwards adapted on a larger and heavier scale to the horse, and packing by dogs. By the latter method the burden—again like the later pack pony—was secured saddle-wise on the dog's back, or with some types of load,

---

[16] See Elliott Coues (ed.), *The Expeditions of Zebulon Montgomery Pike, 1805–1807*, II, 400–546; and particularly the editor's invaluable notes.
[17] Josiah Gregg, *Commerce of the Prairies*, in Thwaites, *Travels*, XX, 91–93; Hiram M. Chittenden, *The History of the American Fur Trade of the Far West*, II, 531, 541, 775.
[18] Rupert Norval Richardson, *The Comanche Barrier to South Plains Settlement*, 78.

such as firewood in the Hidatsa practice, the weight was divided into two parts, which balanced over the dog's shoulders on either side, and was cut into short lengths of two feet or less.[19]

A profound student of the Blackfoot (Siksika) people, who is also an adopted member or "son" of the tribe, considers "the true travois" to have been a horse litter made of poles.[20] A critic with a much less intimate knowledge of Indian life must feel some diffidence in dissenting from that or any kindred assertion coming from so authoritative a source, but one would surely think that the true travois would be the primitive one used with dogs. This last would obviously be somewhat impracticable as a litter for carrying weights of any material amount, because of the limited strength of dogs, and any attempt to spread the load by the use of longer poles would necessitate stronger and consequently heavier ones. These (particularly in the litter proper, as distinct from the later travois—following McClintock's classification) would materially increase the dead weight to be carried. The use of a litter slung between two animals, whether dogs or ponies, would be far more troublesome in rough scrub or forest country than any single burden, and much more so for dogs than for ponies, because there was less clearance from the ground. I have encountered no further suggestion to that effect.

The dimensions and even the constructional details of the travois apparently varied with different tribes, as did most other Indian techniques. Clark Wissler(1910) found that the Assiniboin dog travois did not follow the X form over the dog's shoulders, but terminated in the apex ∧. They were the only tribe doing this, to his knowledge,[21] but Gilbert L. Wilson later found the same practice among the Hidatsa of the Missouri, though none other are mentioned, in so far as I am aware. The Hidatsa dog travois was described by Wilson's native informants (who also stated that sleds were "never used" by the tribe) as being about eight

[19] Wilson, "Horse and Dog in Hidatsa Culture," 206–209.

[20] Walter McClintock, The Old North Trail, 518. Since first adopting my conclusions which follow, I am glad to find myself in agreement with Clark Wissler. He derives the travois itself from the tipi, as a modification of the tipi poles dragged by dogs ("The Influence of the Horse in the Development of Plains Culture," American Anthropologist, Vol. XVI [1914], 11–12).

[21] Wissler, "Material Culture of the Blackfoot Indians," 89, 92.

feet long.[22] Catlin (1832–1840) gave dog-travois poles as "about fifteen feet,"[23] but Wissler noted Blackfoot lodgepoles as fifteen feet and apparently used as both tipi and travois poles.[24] Catlin may have seen a similar practice in some other tribe.

Rupert N. Richardson writes: "Journeys were shorter in the era before the horse; lodge poles were lighter, if they were transported at all, and the tepees smaller and flimsier."[25] As a generalization this would be unexceptionable (if it were possible to generalize about Indians), as Richardson himself well knew.[26] But the inescapable Indian diversity thrusts itself into the picture. An observer among tribes that never became "horse Indians" notes the common usage of twenty-five, thirty, or forty lodgepoles, "according to size."[27] Possibly supply governed demand, as it did in cases among Plains tribes having to obtain their lodgepoles by trade. Edwin James found the "Bad Hearts" (Kiowa-Apache[28] or possibly Wichita[29]) along the Arkansas River doing this in 1820. They had to give a horse for five poles, and consequently could afford only "six or eight poles to a lodge."[30] These poles were twenty to thirty feet long, as allowance was made for them to wear down considerably shorter. In 1852 Randolph B. Marcy found the Comanche with only eight or ten (imported) poles per lodge.[31] Among the tribes farther north, however, the number ranged from thirteen for the "very smallest" lodge to as many as twenty-six for the larger ones.[32]

The Hidatsa preferred poplar for their tipi poles.[33] This must

---

[22] Wilson, "Horse and Dog in Hidatsa Culture," 211–24.

[23] George Catlin, *Letters and Notes on the North American Indians*, I, 45.

[24] Wissler, "Material Culture of the Blackfoot Indians," 88–92.

[25] Richardson, *Comanche Barrier*, 25.

[26] "The general policy . . . (if we may speak of a general policy where every warrior did about as he pleased). . . ." (*Ibid.*, 209.)

[27] Alanson Skinner, "Notes on the Eastern Cree and Northern Saulteaux," *Anthropological Papers of the American Museum of Natural History*, Vol. IX (1911), 12.

[28] Hodge, *Handbook*, I, 701; II, 1070.

[29] Richardson, *Comanche Barrier*, 49.

[30] James, *Account of the Expedition under Long*, in Thwaites, *Travels*, XVI, 110.

[31] Marcy, *Exploration of the Red River of Louisiana, in the Year 1852*, 25; *The Prairie Traveller*, 141.

[32] See figures collected in Frank Gilbert Roe, *The North American Buffalo*, 874–76.

[33] Wilson, "Horse and Dog in Hidatsa Culture," 193.

have been white poplar or aspen, as no other poplar would be suitable, either in weight or form. This preference could only be valid, in all probability, when lodgepole pine or spruce was not obtainable. The dimensions suggested (eight to fifteen feet long, about one inch in diameter at the small end to less than two inches at the large end) would not bear a very heavy concentrated weight. The practice among the Hidatsa (and perhaps among other tribes) of tapering off the butt ends of the poles to make them slide over the ground more easily[34] would certainly ease the load on the dogs, but could do little or nothing to increase the weight-carrying capacity of the poles.

In respect of the territory in which these general techniques prevailed, with their various tribal modifications in detail, Wissler states that dog travois and dog-packing covered the entire "bison area," and the latter in particular "is a concomitant of those hunting tribes following a regular migratory circle."[35] It appears to have prevailed far beyond those limits.

While no doubt subject to local modifications, such as might arise from various temporary or characteristic circumstances, the broad influence of topography seems unmistakable. The travois was apparently more common in the open Southern Plains area, and the dog-packing in the more northern territory.[36] Even here, however, we note one of those tribal exceptions from which no phase of Indian life seems exempt. The Crow, while surrounded on all sides by tribes that used the dog travois, within the nineteenth-century period covered by Lowie's informants and their immediate ancestors, confined their dog transport exclusively to packing, although they had formerly utilized the travois.[37]

The historical notices that I have encountered between the sixteenth and the nineteenth centuries are not numerous, but they

[34] *Ibid.*, 208–209, 216, 227.
[35] Wissler, *The American Indian*, 31.
[36] See on this, Wissler, "Material Culture of the Blackfoot Indians," 90–92; Robert H. Lowie, "The Assiniboin," *Anthropological Papers of the American Museum of Natural History*, Vol. IV (1909), 220; Wilson, "Horse and Dog in Hidatsa Culture," 212.
[37] Lowie, "The Assiniboin," 220.

are at least consistent. In their travels in the Southwest, Coronado's party in 1541 did not fail to notice the presence of "packs of dogs," and also the use to which they were put as pack animals.[38] In 1724, De Bourgmont from New Orleans found some three hundred warriors and their families of the "Canzas" (Kanzas or Kansas) on the lower Missouri. They were moving camp. They had no horses, and their possessions were loaded on dog travois and on the backs of their women.[39] In 1738, La Vérendrye writes of the Prairie Assiniboin of the Red River region in Manitoba: "They make the dogs even carry wood to make the fires, being often obliged to camp in the open prairie [camper en plaine prairie], from which the clumps of wood may be at a great distance. . . . The women and the dogs carry all the baggage."[40]

A striking feature is the persistence, or at least the survival, down to very late times, of dog transport among tribes possessing an apparent abundance of horses. While the earliest instances of this joint practice may possibly belong to an era when horses were still scarce in the tribe in question, the evidence also appears in part to indicate the conflict of the two ideas, with the horse at first the aristocrat of the community, perhaps kept principally for buffalo hunting. We find the famous "buffalo runners" at a fairly early date in the far north of the horse area. Duncan McGillivray (a Northwest Company fur trader) thought them, from their superiority, to be stallions, which may have been the case.[41] For many of the tribes apparently preferred to retain their superior horses as *enteros;* in fact, practically all the tribes, in the opinion of some scholars. J. Frank Dobie writes: "Geldings, it was believed, gave out more quickly than stallions, especially in mud or snow."[42] Curiously enough, the Hidatsa castrated for precisely the opposite reason: because castrated horses "did not tire so easily"![43] Incidentally, McGillivray's observation would indicate that the local Assiniboin

[38] Castañeda, the *Traslado de las Nuevas,* the *Relacion del Suceso,* and Coronado to Charles V, in Winship (ed.), *Journey of Coronado,* 70, 112, 196, 211, 215.

[39] Cited by J. Frank Dobie, *The Mustangs,* 39.

[40] Lawrence J. Burpee (ed.), *The Journals and Letters of Pierre Gaultier de Varennes, Sieur de la Vérendrye, and His Sons,* 317, 318.

[41] Arthur S. Morton (ed.), *The Journal of Duncan McGillivray,* xlix, 29.

[42] Dobie, *The Mustangs,* 55.

[43] Wilson, "Horse and Dog in Hidatsa Culture," 147.

and Cree must have had enough horses (at least in 1794) to lead an onlooker to draw such a distinction.

The earliest notice I have found of the use of dogs and horses together is in the same general region, and at an even earlier date. A fur-trader's journal at Hudson House, some distance above the modern city of Prince Albert on the North Saskatchewan River, records the arrival there on April 20, 1779, of a band of "Southern" Indians "with upwards of Thirty Horses well Loaded and a great number of Dogs."[44] Duncan McGillivray once again perhaps reveals another not infrequent reason for the dogs' still being utilized. He records the following at Fort George, farther up the same river and about 140 miles northeast of Edmonton, April 9, 1795: "This morning a Band of about 30 Blood Indians and 10 Blackfeet arrived they have carried all their comodities [sic] on dogs their horses being too much exhausted by hunger to undergo the fatigues of the journey."[45]

This factor of limited resources in horseflesh may even have been much more of a normal condition than has commonly been thought to be the case with the tribes of the Blackfoot Confederacy. A learned and critical contemporary scholar is of the opinion that the very generally accepted wealth of the Blackfoot in horses, based upon the numbers given by(or to)Maximilian in 1833, has been misunderstood or misinterpreted, and that in consequence their possessions in horseflesh have been vastly overestimated. This concept will require detailed examination in a later chapter. At the moment we may note that Matthew Cocking, over twenty years before McGillivray(December, 1772) observed that the Blackfoot were able to, and did, use horses instead of their women for packing.[46] And nearly twenty years before that, Antony Henday encountered and described the Blackfoot(1754–55) in circumstances which certainly seem to indicate a completely habit-

[44] *Cumberland and Hudson House Journals, 1775–1782*, 1st. Series, 330.

[45] McGillivray, *Journal* (ed. by Morton), 69. Fort George was at the mouth of Middle Creek, east of St. Paul des Métis; about 140 miles northeast of Edmonton. See L. R. Masson, *Les Bourgeois de la Compagnie du Nord-Ouest*, II, 17; Coues (ed.), *Henry-Thompson Journals*, II, 560.

[46] Lawrence J. Burpee (ed.), "The Journal of Matthew Cocking, 1772–1773" *Proceedings and Transactions of the Royal Society of Canada*, 3rd Series (1908), Section II, 111.

uated horse Indian society.[47] The use of dog travois by tribes possessing horses cannot in itself constitute evidence of poor or insufficient resources in horseflesh. The same contemporary scholar to whom I have referred writes thus:

The continued use of the dog travois among the nomadic tribes of the northern plains in the latter half of the nineteenth century might, at first thought, seem to be an index of poverty in horses. Undoubtedly, poverty in horses was an important factor in the reliance of numerous Assiniboine and Plains Cree bands on dog transport. But what of the Blackfoot? Informants said that poor people, owners of few or no horses, who were unable to borrow a sufficient number of horses to transport their belongings in moving camp placed their effects on dog travois. Nevertheless, people with plenty of horses also made some use of the dog travois in moving camp for carrying small, light household articles such as skin dressing tools and pemmican pounders encased in rawhide containers. The dogs could move along at a rapid pace and keep up with the more heavily laden horse travois if their own burdens were light. Therefore, the presence of dog travois in the moving camp was not necessarily a sign of poverty in horses. The dog travois was also valuable for light work near camp. It was commonly used for collecting wood, and also roots or berries. More than a century after the Blackfoot began to acquire horses the dog travois had not outlived its usefulness. For the desperately poor, the dog travois stood between them and the necessity of packing their belongings on their own backs or leaving them behind. For the other people of the tribe, it afforded an auxiliary transport particularly useful for light work near camp, and an insurance against the evil day when an enemy raiding party, a severe storm, or some other misfortune might set them too afoot.[48]

As a general illustration of Ewers' contention we may note that in 1834 George Catlin found dog travois still in use among such well-supplied and inveterate horsemen as the Comanche.[49] The inquiries of a tireless investigator of the Hidatsa throw some light upon what we may term the psychological reactions toward the old

[47] Henday, "Journal" (ed. by Burpee), 338–51.
[48] John C. Ewers, "Were the Blackfoot Rich in Horses?" *American Anthropologist,* Vol. XLV (1943), 602–10. I am greatly indebted to the author's kindness for a copy of this important essay.
[49] Catlin, *Letters and Notes,* II, 55.

and the new. The Indian was essentially a conservative. The indications really appear to suggest that the dog travois was preferred whenever practicable, and somewhat unwillingly abandoned when necessity dictated. Wilson's Hidatsa informants stated that the dog travois was "very ancient" in their minds, while the horse travois carried a sense of being "very recently introduced." The dog travois were in use almost daily; horse travois were used less frequently. Both remained in regular use until wagons were issued to the tribe in 1879, when both were abandoned.[50]

Concerning the Assiniboin of Canada ("Stoneys"), the early trade: John McDonnell notes their use of dog travois in Manitoba, in the Portage la Prairie country west of Winnipeg, in 1793.[51] As late as 1808, the younger Alexander Henry remarks respecting the Assiniboin and Cree: "Transportation of their baggage is mostly performed by dogs, as their horses are generally kept for hunting buffalo . . . often horses are tackled [to travois] in the same manner in winter."[52]

In addition to the tribes already mentioned, we have several notices concerning others. The Sioux were found on the upper Mississippi in 1774 by the fur trader Peter Pond to be using their horses and dogs for "carrying their baggage."[53] Dog and horse transport were noted together among various subdivisions of the Dakota Sioux by Catlin in 1832;[54] by Maximilian in 1833–34, both among the Sioux and their kindred, the Missouri River Assiniboin;[55] by Samuel Hancock, the old Oregon pioneer, in 1845;[56] and by Francis Parkman in 1846.[57] Farther south, we have noted Catlin in 1834. John C. Frémont records meeting with Sioux and Cheyennes along the upper Arkansas River in 1844, with pack ponies and "dog-trains carrying baggage."[58] This might signify either

[50] Wilson, "Horse and Dog in Hidatsa Culture," 219–20.
[51] Charles M. Gates (ed.), Five Fur Traders of the Northwest, 114.
[52] Coues (ed.), Henry-Thompson Journals, II, 518.
[53] Harold A. Innis, Peter Pond, Fur Trader and Adventurer, 58.
[54] Catlin, Letters and Notes, II, 66.
[55] Maximilian, Prince of Wied, Travels in the Interior of North America, 1832–1834, in Thwaites, Travels, XXII, 310, 391; XXIII, 202.
[56] A. D. Howden Smith (ed.), The Narrative of Samuel Hancock, 1845–1860, 15–16.
[57] Parkman, Oregon Trail, 127, 279.
[58] Frémont, Narrative, 317.

travois or packs.[59] A Southwestern archaeologist, however, sums up the general Indian relationship towards the dog as follows: "The dog among the natives was chiefly a companion of the chase, excepting at the far north and in some parts of the great plains, where he was a passable beast of burden."[60] The late Clark Wissler, perhaps a better-known authority, takes a somewhat wider view: "We should expect no one to doubt the assumption that dog traction, one of the most distinctive traits of Plains culture was fully diffused over the area before the horse was known." Later in the same volume, however, Wissler's general conclusion is not noticeably different from that of A. J. Fynn's given above. He states that dog domestication was universal, but that the dog was *used* only in limited areas; for example, there was no dog transport among the Pueblo tribes.[61]

Among the Northern Indians, the practice varied, and it is not always easy to decide in a given instance whether the allusion bears reference to packing or travois. Sir John Franklin uses the latter term at Carlton, 1819–20, but may even have intended it for "sled."[62] Daniel W. Harmon, a Northwest Company trader, about the same time (and in the same broad region), merely speaks of the Indians of the "woody country'" using their dogs as beasts of burden.[63] Captain John Palliser mentions both dog and horse travois as being in use together in the Saskatchewan country, 1857–60;[64] and his colleague, Hector, records his having to organize "dog-travails" from Fort Pitt to Carlton when the snow thawed somewhat unexpectedly in April, 1858.[65]

[59] On the Sioux, see Cyrus Thomas and John R. Swanton, in Hodge, *Handbook*, II, 577–79; also see Joseph Jablow, *The Cheyenne in Plains Indian Trade Relations, 1795–1840*.

[60] A. J. Fynn, *The American Indian as a Product of Environment*, 38.

[61] Wissler, "Influence of the Horse," 11; "Material Culture of the North American Indians," *American Anthropologist*, Vol. XVI (1914), 477–505.

[62] Sir John Franklin, *Narrative of a Journey to the Shores of the Polar Sea in the Years 1819, 1820, 1821, and 1822*, 112.

[63] *A Journal of Voyages and Travels in the Interior of North America* (1820), 290.

[64] *Journals, Detailed Reports, and Observations, Relative to Palliser's Exploration of British North America, 1857, 1858, 1859, 1860*, 202.

[65] *Ibid.*, 81.

The Earl of Southesk observed dog travois at Fort Qu'Appelle in the summer of 1859;[66] and John McDougall, the pioneer Western missionary, noted them along the Saskatchewan below Edmonton in the winter of 1864–65.[67] Father A. G. Morice found dog-packing among the Northern Déné;[68] and George M. Douglas has recorded it among the Great Bear Lake tribes.[69] Jenness states that none of the tribes in the Mackenzie River basin used dogs for dragging the toboggans except the Chipewyan, and these but rarely.[70] He also remarks that dog travois are still in use among the Eskimo. This is quite logical, from his own description: "The treeless prairies and the plains of the Arctic and sub-Arctic offered so few obstacles that definite paths were needless. . . ."[71] In the same scholar's *The Copper Eskimo*,[72] he speaks of "packing everything we needed for the summer on our backs, and on the backs of the dogs."[73] This expression could apply, in the strictest sense, to packs, or, figuratively, to a travois, in which the poles that carry the weight rest upon the back or shoulders of the dog. Elsewhere Jenness prints a photograph of an "Eskimo woman and her dog, both carrying packs." In this print two long poles are shown, which clearly appear to suggest a travois.[74] With these exceptions, all other references to transport indicate sleds.[75] A hastily improvised means of conveying caribou meat home in the spring, when the snow had melted from the hillsides, was to wrap the meat in a polar bear skin, which was then dragged home by the dogs.[76] The treeless appearance of the terrain makes it evident that only in certain restricted localities *could* a travois be made, whatever the abstract preferences of the residents might be.

The explicit mention of toboggans by Jenness[77] would seem

[66] The Earl of Southesk, *Saskatchewan and the Rocky Mountains* (1859–1860), 63.

[67] McDougall, *Saddle, Sled, and Snowshoe*, 121.

[68] A. G. Morice, *Fifty Years in Western Canada*, 58. The Déné are identical with the "Tinné" of many writers.

[69] George M. Douglas, *Lands Forlorn*, 141, 142, 193.

[70] Jenness, *Indians of Canada*, 104, 386.

[71] *Ibid.*, 100. See also Wissler on the use of dogs in summer for packing and dragging tent poles among the Eskimo west of Hudson Bay ("Material Culture of the North American Indians," 494–95).

[72] Diamond Jenness, *The Copper Eskimo* (*Report of the Canadian Arctic Expedition, 1913–1918*, Vol. XII).

[73] *Ibid.*, 133. [74] *Ibid.*, 234; cf. 139. [75] *Ibid.*, 88, 118, 120, 124, etc.

[76] *Ibid.*, 130. [77] See note 5, this chapter.

to justify the inference that by "travois" he signifies the usual appliance of that name: two long poles dragging behind the dog, as heretofore described, with cross-poles constituting a light framework upon which the load rests. His description appears to leave this somewhat uncertain: "The dog-travois of pre-European times, however, was small and low, capable of bearing not more than thirty-five or fifty pounds."[78] These are exactly the (presumably conjectural) limits mentioned for dog-travois loads by one of Coronado's chroniclers in the Southwest.[79] In the Northland, the few figures I have been able to glean suggest much greater weights. These discrepancies may indicate the difference between the northern Malemutes, the sometimes really superb Huskies, and the dogs of the Southern Indians, frequently more of the "cur" species. Although there were "large" and "small" dogs among the Hidatsa, as a whole their dogs were noted as "biting like coyotes," and their cry was a howl rather than a bark, leaving the present-day investigator doubtful as to their true state—whether semiferal or domesticated.[80] (The almost invariable cry of a coyote is three single rapid, but well-divided, barks—I do not think I have ever heard more—in the lower half of the octave, followed by a long howl on a higher note.)[81]

[78] Jenness, *Indians of Canada*, 103; cf. 310.

[79] Winship (ed.), *Journey of Coronado*, 196. Catlin's drawing No. 166 (*Letters and Notes*, II, 65) exhibits various Southwestern styles of transport for dogs and horses. See also dog and horse travois in Marvin C. Ross ed.), *The West of Alfred Jacob Miller*, Plate 66.

[80] Wilson, "Horse and Dog in Hidatsa Culture," 196–99, 205. Edmonton's dogs bore an evil reputation in the old days. Alexander Ross described them (1825) as being of the wolf breed, and the terror of every woman and child after dark (*Fur Hunters of the Far West*, II, 211, 212). Paul Kane mentions a horse being torn by them, and five being shot by Chief Trader Harriott before they would desist from their attack. They attacked Rundle the missionary one night and got him down; and would have killed him but for an Indian woman's help (Kane, *Wanderings of an Artist among the Indians of North America*, 388). Henry shot two for destroying meat, and six for killing a colt, and another "for attempting to bite my little girl" (Coues, [ed.], *Henry-Thompson Journals*, II, 615, 619, 620). John Mc-Dougall speaks of children devoured by dogs in Indian camps (*On Western Trails in the Early Seventies*, 129). See also Southesk, *Saskatchewan and the Rocky Mountains*, 152.

[81] The howl of the coyote (with female, or perhaps immature voices an octave higher) is shown here. I owe the musical definition to the kindness of Charles Palmer, Esq., A.R.C.O., of Victoria, B. C. This was taken by Mr. Palmer from my own rendering of the cry. Any errors in this are mine.

Moreover, it is not entirely clear whether the northern loads may not in some instances be snow loads. Even with a travois proper—as specifically distinct from a sled—this made a considerable difference; and in more than one tribe the variation between summer and winter loads was "formally" recognized.[82] However this may be, the weights given by Jenness are elsewhere indicated as being approximately the weights *carried*—and sometimes widely exceeded—by dogs bearing packs. There may have been certain local conditions that governed transportation techniques, since Jenness is very closely corroborated by George M. Douglas. The latter states that among the Great Bear Lake Indians pack loads varied from some fifty pounds for a strong and willing dog down to as low as thirty for a dog lacking either of these qualities.[83]

Such figures as I can find respecting dog loads among the Plains tribes are anything but uniform. In chronological order, the earliest of all is from a Spanish captain, about 1600. This man, Gaspar Pérez de Villagrá, describes dog and horse travois as he saw them in New Mexico, and he states that the dogs carried or dragged seventy-five to eighty pounds.[84] John McDonnell, of the Northwest Company (1793), gives fifty to one hundred pounds as the load on the Assiniboin dog travois.[85] A modern student of the same tribe, referring approximately to the mid-nineteenth century, says that "each family had from six to twelve dogs, which could carry from thirty to fifty pounds apiece."[86] In what was roughly the same era, the dog-travois load among the Teton Sioux was reckoned at seventy pounds,[87] while Hidatsa loads were even heavier.[88] There were any number from four to twenty dogs in a family. They naturally varied in strength, but were "all willing." A good dog could bring in nearly one hundred pounds of firewood, or an eighty-

---

[82] Wilson, "Horse and Dog in Hidatsa Culture," 208–209, 227; Mandelbaum, "The Plains Cree," 198.

[83] Douglas, *Lands Forlorn*, 141, 142, 193. Horse pack-loads represented roughly the weight of a man. David Thompson, 1810: "We loaded our horses in proportion to their strength from 180 to 240 pounds weigh each Horse." (*Narrative* [ed. by Tyrrell], 441.)

[84] Gaspar Pérez de Villagrá, *History of New Mexico* (translated by Gilberto Espinosa; ed. by Frederick Webb Hodge), 160–61.

[85] Gates (ed.), *Five Fur Traders*, 114.

[86] Lowie, "The Assiniboin," 15.

[87] Wissler, "Material Culture of the Blackfoot Indians," 91.

[88] Wilson, "Horse and Dog in Hidatsa Culture," 206–15, 227, 252.

pound green buffalo hide. A dog could carry a cowskin bullboat, but not a bullhide one.[89]

These figures show conclusively that there is no confusion of any kind with *sled,* for the Reverend Egerton Young mentions a sled load(in the Lake Winnipeg wooded country)of six hundred pounds, including one hundred twenty pounds of fish alone for the dogs, for a trip of one week.[90] I have heard old Hudson's Bay Company men speak of "four hundred pounds" as a typical sled load; not, however, in answer to any specific questioning. Bulk must have some bearing on the case; it certainly loomed large in Copper Eskimo camp movements. Jenness gives a most informative description of the loading and trail methods followed by the Copper Eskimo sled drivers, but makes no mention of any approximate estimates of weight.[91] An old Hudson Bay man, discussing horse and dog travois about 1867, speaks of "pack dogs" bearing burdens "mountain high."[92] Such language is hopelessly vague and indefinite. An informative historian gives sled loads as "up to five hundred pounds." The regulation loads of the Hudson's Bay Company were four hundred pounds, with blankets, dog food(fish), and provisions extra.[93] In difficulties, David Thompson (1810) mentions having to reduce the weights of dog loads to "less than two-thirds." Two dogs were given one hundred twenty pounds per sled; one dog was reckoned at seventy pounds. This was in very rough country.[94]

Any contrivance, however fashioned, must of course be suited to the stature of an Indian or Eskimo dog. We must make allowance for the difference in a dog's hauling capacity in relation to a winter toboggan(dog sled)with its long bearing surface, in addition to its snow surface, and a travois, where the weight ultimately devolves upon two points with their inevitable joltings over rough

[89] *Ibid.,* 285. Surely this could only have been the original type bullboat of a single hide. Bernard De Voto mentions one of three hides stitched together (*Across the Wide Missouri,* 116–17); and reproduces a painting of one by Alfred Jacob Miller (Plate XXII) which looks more like a crowded excursion boat than any description of a bullboat I have ever encountered.

[90] Egerton R. Young, *By Canoe and Dog Train,* 92–93, 122.

[91] Jenness, *The Copper Eskimo,* 116–19.

[92] Isaac Cowie, *The Company of Adventurers,* 322–23.

[93] Harold A. Innis, *The Fur Trade in Canada,* 365.

[94] Thompson, *Narrative* (ed. by Tyrrell), 443.

country. We must also allow for tribal diversities, wherein, as we have seen, one tribe's dogs *carried* more than another tribe's dogs *hauled*. Despite all these factors, however, one would surely think the hauling limit should exceed the carrying limit more noticeably.

There are certain social (or what we may term psychological) phenomena arising from the dog culture of various tribes which deserve notice at this point, particularly since we shall have occasion to note their repercussions in the later horse culture. In the pre-equestrian economy, the ownership of the dogs was vested in the women in several tribes, perhaps half-contemptuously, since the dogs—unlike the horse—could be used for nothing but labor, which was the woman's province. The Blackfoot women owned their own dogs and travois as their personal property.[95] Among the Hidatsa, at least in the family of Gilbert Wilson's principal informant, Wolf-chief(born about 1869), the ownership of the dogs ("four to twenty in a family") was not divided; the dogs belonged to all the women of the household collectively.[96] Whether Wolf-chief used the term *family* in our narrow sense or in that of some wider body embracing more of the tribe is not indicated. The Cree women had broadly similar rights. They too owned their dogs, but whether individually or in joint possession like the Hidatsa family is not specified.[97] Ownership of dogs by the women apparently did not include the Crow. Robert H. Lowie, the most penetrating investigator of the tribe, makes no mention of this. He says instead: "In pre-equestrian days, I heard a wealthy man was one who owned many dogs. One Crow of old was said to have owned as many as a hundred."[98] Unless the customary practice of an alien tribe was *ipso facto* a thing of scorn to any and every Indian, the Crow belief may in course of time have contributed to raise the Hidatsa women and others in their men's estimation, for they owned what men considered wealth!

[95] *Ibid.*, 361. This was confirmed by Kidd's native Siksika or Piegan informant (Kenneth E. Kidd, "Blackfoot Ethnography," [unpublished master's thesis], 149–50).
[96] Wilson, "Horse and Dog in Hidatsa Culture," 206.
[97] Mandelbaum, "The Plains Cree," 197.
[98] Robert H. Lowie, *The Crow Indians*, 91.

Wolf-chief told Wilson that his father would assist in felling cottonwoods, which the women brought home with their dogs;[99] the bark was for the horses and the wood for the fires. It is extremely unlikely that his father was the only man in the village to do this.

The Indian dog played a part in sacrificial rites, both before and after the coming of the horse. White dogs are thought to have been the prototype of the Illinois white buffalo sacrifice.[100] George Bird Grinnell considers that in pre-equestrian times dogs probably performed the spirit functions of the horses that were later slain when a Blackfoot warrior died.[101] Lewis and Clark mention the custom among the Assiniboin, Mandan, and Hidatsa, of sacrificing the favorite horse and dogs of a deceased owner.[102] One would like to know a little more in the case of the Hidatsa communal ownership (or of women's ownership in general): just *whose* dogs were being sacrificed?

If it were possible to discover a basic reason, common to more than one or two nations, for *any* Indian tribal practice, one might suppose that the eaters of dogs would be the later eaters of horses. Among some twenty tribes I can find only five who ate both. Wissler states that the Bannack, Crow, Flathead, Nez Percé, Snake, and Ute did not eat dogs. The Apache, Arapaho, Dakota, Kiowa, and Pawnee did.[103] To the first list we may very conspicuously add the Comanche. Dogs were nauseating to them, according to a learned investigator.[104] Other related tribes of the same (Shoshonean) family ate dogs, however; one northern branch was known as the "Shirrydika" or "dog-eaters."[105] Quite probably the southerly Comanche were aware of this, but it did not prevent them from applying the name "dog-eaters" to the Arapaho as a

[99] Wilson, "Horse and Dog in Hidatsa Culture," 172–80.

[100] Hodge, *Handbook*, II, 403, 939–44.

[101] *Ibid.*, I, 571.

[102] *The Original Journals of the Lewis and Clark Expedition* (ed. by Reuben Gold Thwaites), I, 323.

[103] Wissler, "Material Culture of the Blackfoot Indians," 44: citing W. P. Clark, *The Indian Sign Language* (1885), which I have not seen.

[104] E. Adamson Hoebel, "The Political Association and Law-ways of the Comanche Indians," *Memoirs of the American Anthropological Association, No. 54* (1940), 17.

[105] Alexander Ross, *Fur Hunters*, I, 249; Coues (ed.), *Henry-Thompson Journals*, II, 818; Hodge, *Handbook*, I, 130, 743.

term of contempt.[106] We have a typical instance of the vague and ambiguous use of the tribal name of "Snake" when we find the Snake listed among those who did *not* eat dogs, for the Shirrydika were a subdivision of the Snake.

We may add two more tribes to the dog-eaters. It has been stated (1910) that the eating of dogs in festival uses had been introduced among the Crow in more recent times.[107] Kenneth E. Kidd's native informants denied strenuously that the Blackfoot had ever eaten dogs, though Kidd himself is dubious.[108] Maximilian stated in 1833 that some Blackfoot had learned the habit from the Sioux, though it was "only rarely" practiced.[109] With the Cree, dog-eating (the "dog feast") was more of a ritual.[110] Sometimes, however, it became a necessity. The Hudson House journal mentions the "Beaver" being driven to eat their dogs and horses from sheer want, in February, 1781, about the time of the devastating smallpox epidemic.[111] These would seem to be the "Beaver Hills Cree," who were described to Mandelbaum as being the "richest in horses" in the earlier nineteenth century.[112] The true "Beaver" of Peace River (Tsattine) are impossible, and Edmonton (from which the Beaver Hills are visible to the eastward) was long known as Beaver Hills House, at least as late as 1862.[113] Devouring sacrificial victims for food is comparable to David and his men eating the shewbread;[114] in both instances the act must have demanded moral courage.

Although cruelty to dogs was apparently regarded as almost characteristic (perhaps particularly among half-bloods),[115] it is of interest to note that the Assiniboin, who had a rather poor repu-

---

[106] Hugh Lenox Scott, "Early History and Names of the Arapaho," *American Anthropologist*, Vol. IX (1907), 545–60; citing 551.

[107] Maximilian, *Travels*, in Thwaites, *Travels*, XXII, 352; Lowie, *The Crow Indians*, 91, 228.

[108] Kidd, "Blackfoot Ethnography," 103–104.

[109] Maximilian, *Travels*, in Thwaites, *Travels*, XXIII, 104.

[110] Mandelbaum, "The Plains Cree," 197, 286.

[111] *Cumberland and Hudson House Journals*, 2nd. Series, 181.

[112] Mandelbaum, "The Plains Cree," 167.

[113] See Coues (ed.), *Henry-Thompson Journals*, II, 611; for 1862, see McDougall, *Forest, Lake, and Prairie*, 218.

[114] I Samuel, 21:1–6.

[115] See Thompson, *Narrative* (ed. by Tyrrell), 210, 239, 444, 446; cf. Viscount Milton and W. B. Cheadle, *The North-West Passage by Land*, 151.

tation as horsemasters,[116] were wont to carry water in buffalo paunches for their dogs on long dry journeys.[117] Perhaps in this and in the well-known winter "dog shoes," humanity and self-interest combined. I have not found it recorded of any other tribe, though it may have been practiced.

[116] See Chapter XIII, "The Indians as Horse Masters."
[117] Wilson, "Horse and Dog in Hidatsa Culture," 225, 243.

II

THE "STRAY" LEGEND

It seems to have been quite commonly (and perhaps still is, almost conventionally) taken more or less for granted that the historic horse on the North American continent appeared very much by accident in the beginning, from De Soto's "lost or abandoned horses," or even from those stolen from De Soto, Coronado, or other *Conquistadores.* Putting aside writers who may be considered critically negligible on such questions, later historians are much more cautious. Even as competent and critical a student as the late Clark Wissler could write as recently as 1914: "It is generally considered that horses abandoned by De Soto's men in 1541 gave rise to the wild horses later found west of the lower Mississippi."[1] A careful investigation of the evidence has relegated the expression of this concept to the realms of poetry and fiction. In the first of these fields, the poet himself is not ignorant of the truth. Mark Van Doren, in a prefatory note to his poem *The Distant Runners,* outlines the legend: "Six great horses of Spain, set free after his death by De Soto's men, ran west and restored to America the wild race there lost some thousands of years ago.—A legend."

The Western fictionist H. H. Knibbs belongs to a literary province in which the picturesque takes precedence over the authentic. In his book *The Barb of Spain,* a lone stallion survivor from Coronado's expedition encounters a young Spanish mare from another expedition (which could only be De Soto's force) "somewhere, somewhen, somehow," and the first mustang is born! J. Frank Dobie's caustic comment sums up the situation completely: "If

[1] Wissler, "Influence of the Horse," 9–10.

33

another fable had placed Adam in Asia and Eve in Africa, the chances of mating would have been about as high."[2]

In relation to these mythical "strays" from De Soto, Coronado, or any other early explorer, that hypothesis or belief awaits evidence to support it. Its exponents or defenders have thus far offered nothing beyond supposition. The evidence we actually possess points to conclusions quite the contrary. One of the latest critical scholars to discuss the subject summarizes in a paragraph the main features of the problem we have to consider in detail. Herbert Eugene Bolton writes as follows:

> . . . in the accounts of the Spanish expeditions to the Southwest and Kansas in the later sixteenth and early seventeenth centuries, no mention is made of horses or mounted Indians, which, if encountered, would have been certain to attract attention. It would seem, therefore, that the horses ridden by the Plains Indians in the eighteenth century as far north as the prairies of Canada were descended from stock which strayed or was obtained from the Spanish settlements after the permanent colonization of New Mexico and Texas in the seventeenth century.[3]

So much has been said about De Soto and Coronado that we are apt to forget that the first of these was not the earliest Spanish explorer to land upon the Atlantic seaboard of what was later to be the United States. A careful investigator of our own day has noted that Ponce de León took (or landed) fifty horses on his expedition of 1521. Similarly, Vásquez de Ayllon took eighty-nine horses, probably to some point in Carolina, in 1526. The same scholar has searched the records diligently for any traces they might present of strayed horses from their respective expeditions, or any possibility of progeny therefrom. He pronounces that there is no discoverable evidence to support any such suppositions.[4] With such a people as the medieval Spaniards—their "horse psychology" being what it was—the negative testimony of silence is only one degree less strong than positive testimony of affirmation.

For it so chances that the early Spanish relations are quite noticeably full on the subject of their horses, as indeed might be

[2] Dobie, *The Mustangs*, 34–35.
[3] Bolton, *Coronado*, 399–400.
[4] Thornton Chard, "Did the First Spanish Horses Landed in Florida and Carolina Leave Progeny?" *American Anthropologist*, Vol. XLII (1940), 91–92.

expected from an outdoor equestrian nation whose common term of politeness—even to their very beggars—was *caballero*.[5] This partiality toward their horses is noted among the very earliest of the *Conquistadores* in Mexico. "When anything happened to a horse, he [Cortés] does not fail to notice it."[6] This appears to be equally true of the two great early expeditions of De Soto and Coronado. Any circumstances reasonably to be inferred from any of their allusions may fairly be considered broadly applicable to all of these explorers.

The mount of a Spanish *hidalgo* in medieval or later times was quite commonly (even preferably) a stallion. Richard Ford states that the use of stallions (*caballos enteros* or "entire horses") was general in Spain, an unchanging land, about 1830;[7] and his even better-known contemporary, George Borrow, corroborates this.[8] Both men possessed an exceptionally intimate knowledge of the country. Obviously, of course, for the "stray" theory to possess any possibility the Spaniards must have brought stallions with them to America. The fact that they did is substantiated by an incident in Cortés' advance on Mexico.[9] Such high-spirited creatures were no doubt more impatient of the tether and less easily recaptured in event of escape. None the less, the somewhat facile assumptions of the "escape" theory need to be examined in the light of known facts.

A leader's horse might be "lost," that is to say, strayed away, or may have disappeared from sight in battle without its fate being positively known. But such losses *by leaders* would be events of immense importance to the average medieval chronicler, Castilian or otherwise. Losses of this accidental character occurred in Coronado's expedition, horses 'falling into ravines fully saddled and bridled' among stampeding buffalo, and never being seen again.[10]

[5] Richard Ford, *Gatherings from Spain*, 40; also Thomas Okey, in the introduction, *xiv*.

[6] R. B. Cunninghame Graham, *The Horses of the Conquest*, 15.

[7] Ford, *Gatherings from Spain*, 101.

[8] George Borrow, *The Bible in Spain*, 174, 334.

[9] Cunninghame Graham, *Horses of the Conquest*, 58–59. William H. Prescott notes a common national preference for mules, and several stringent edicts (1495–1598) forbidding any but ecclesiastics to ride them (*History of the Reign of Ferdinand and Isabella*, II, 340; III, 249, 482). Some further data on this in Robert Moorman Denhardt, *The Horse of the Americas*, 22–24, 30.

[10] Castañeda, and the *Traslado de Las Nuevas*, in Winship (ed.), *Journey of Coronado*, 66, 195.

This in itself proves nothing. Although the recorded incidents of this nature between buffalo and horses are erratic and irregular, the preponderance of evidence is against the probabilities of survival on the part of the horse. Another of Coronado's scribes tells us that the buffalo killed and wounded many horses.[11] James Kipp, the well-known Missouri River fur trader, lost his horse saddled and bridled; it joined a herd of buffalo and was never seen again.[12] Paul Kane, the Canadian artist, mentions an occurrence at Fort Pitt, the Hudson's Bay Company post on the North Saskatchewan River, January, 1848:

They [the buffalo] killed with their horns twenty or thirty horses in their attempt to drive them off from the patches of grass which the horses had pawed the snow from with their hoofs for the purpose of getting at the grass, and severely gored many others, which eventually recovered.[13]

Conversely, Alexander Henry, the younger, notes the following at Rocky Mountain House, 350 miles farther up the Saskatchewan, November 27, 1810: "A small herd of [wood buffalo] cows was found among our horses near the fort."[14] He makes no mention of any difficulty. And F. A. Larocque instances a case of a hunted buffalo cow taking refuge among their horses.[15] But the sex of the casualties in the Coronado cavalcade is not mentioned, nor is anything said of their being leaders' mounts. In regard to that, however, J. Frank Dobie says "the early Spaniards brought no geldings."[16]

In so far as the general fortunes of war were concerned, the leaders' horses, like their riders, naturally ran greater risks. In some cases few except the leaders were horsed; this attracted attention and drew the main Indian attack upon such men.[17] On other occa-

---

[11] *Ibid.*, 206.

[12] Maximilian, *Travels*, in Thwaites, *Travels*, XXIV, 45.

[13] Kane, *Wanderings of an Artist*, 396.

[14] Coues (ed.), *Henry-Thompson Journals*, II, 666.

[15] Lawrence J. Burpee (ed.), "The Journal of Francois Antoine Larocque," *Publications of the Canadian Archives, No. 3*, p. 34.

[16] J. Frank Dobie, *Tales of the Mustang*, 15; also his *The Mustangs*, 22.

[17] See Cunninghame Graham, *Horses of the Conquest* (citing several sources), 32–40, 49–52, 58–59, 63–65, 71, 77, 106, 113, 146, etc.; also Denhardt, *Horse of the Americas*, 48–63.

sions nothing but the awe-inspiring prowess of a mounted leader saved some hard-pressed comrade—as with De Soto and Rodrigo Ranjel at Maubila[18]—or perhaps retrieved the day. The very precise accounts of leaders' horses slain on such occasions,[19] as well as deaths of horses from other causes,[20] compel us to conclude that such animals as our hypothetical strays, missing and unaccounted for, would not escape mention.

With respect to the horses of the common troops, their chances of escape and of producing offspring—sex conditions even permitting—were virtually nonexistent. In this connection, Francis Haines draws attention to some vital considerations that might easily be overlooked in glib generalization about "strayed Spanish horses."[21] The hypothetical strays must wander away (or be lost in battle, hunting, or what not) in combinations of not less than two *together,* and necessarily be of both sexes on each of such occasions. Haines furthermore points out that while a pair, sire and dam could *mathematically* produce some three hundred or so progeny in the course of twenty years or thereabouts, in actual conditions in an unfamiliar environment this would not be possible. He very pertinently emphasizes the fact that it would be precisely in the very earliest years of such a reproductive cycle or period, when even a single loss might endanger or preclude the successful survival of the potential "dynasty," that such losses would be most likely to occur. For in those earlier years their chances of surviving the various adverse or positively hostile influences of the environment would be at their most precarious stage. By an inversion of the "vicious circle," the extraneous perils would progressively diminish in the precise ratio to which their presence would cease to seriously affect the situation.

The initial panic of the Indians upon their first contact with

---

[18] E. G. Bourne (ed.), *Narratives of the Career of Hernando De Soto, in the Conquest of Florida, 1539–1542,* II, 125.

[19] *Ibid.,* I, 42; II, 74. De Soto's own horse was slain at Napetaca. Another case in Morris Bishop, *The Odyssey of Cabeza de Vaca,* 219.

[20] Compare the account of *El Morzillo,* Cortés' black charger, which had to be left behind in the Honduras expedition of 1525, with a splinter in its foot, and died: Cunninghame Graham, *Horses of the Conquest,* 32–40.

[21] Francis D. Haines, "How Did the Indians Get Their Horses?" *American Anthropologist,* Vol. XL (1938), 113.

the horse was little more than momentary. Cortés,[22] Coronado,[23] and De Soto[24] all speedily found their horses to be objects of hatred instead of simple dread. The immense number of horses killed in the fight at Mabila (Maubila or Mauvila)[25] are variously given. We find 7 killed, 29 wounded;[26] 12 killed, 70 wounded;[27] 35 killed or captured;[28] 45 killed or captured;[29] and 59 "burned and captured."[30] Whatever the actual total may be, the mention of such numbers testifies to a considerable aggregate and also to a passionate hate little likely to spare the strange beasts. Even allowing for such as they could heal of their wounds by "grease from dead Indians" or other expedients,[31] there must have been a great mortality among the earliest Spanish horses. De Soto's expedition left Cuba (1539) with 243 horses on board, of which 20 died on the voyage, leaving 223 to be landed on the coast of Florida.[32] Within

[22] See note 17, this chapter.

[23] See Winship (ed.), *Journey of Coronado*, 34 (Tiguex), 49–50, 56, 124 (Suya: "more than twenty killed"). Suya is perhaps to be identified with the modern Puaray, where a considerable quantity of horses' bones have been found, agreeing with the accounts of Coronado's men (*ibid.*, 131). I am indebted for this local information to W. P. Bliss (1937), then of the University of New Mexico. Horses were also killed at Cíbola (*ibid.*, 171, 188).

[24] See Bourne (ed.), *Narratives of De Soto*, for eyewitness accounts of Napetaca, Cayas, Pacaha, Chicaca, etc., I, 42, 49, 97, 138; II, 22, 33, 68, 74, 80, 126–27, 134, 148. See also Chard, "Did the First Spanish Horses Leave Progeny?" 92–93; Bolton, *Coronado*, 278.

[25] The letters "v" and "b" are interchangeable in Spanish: Havana=Habana, Cíbola=Cívola, Obando=Ovando, Quivira=Quibira, Valparaiso=Balparaiso, etc., litter the pages of Hakluyt and Purchas. Maubila is one of the places thought to furnish some clue to De Soto's route (hence Mobile, Alabama?). See on this, among others, Fiske, *Discovery of America*, II, 509; Hodge, *Handbook*, I, 916; Cunninghame Graham, *Horses of the Conquest*, 75–76; Bishop, *Odyssey of Cabeza de Vaca*, 30–32.

[26] Bourne (ed.), *Narratives of De Soto*, II, 216–17.

[27] *Ibid.*, I, 97. The same witness, Elvas, also gives "fifty" (*ibid.*, I, 106). His first figure is cited by Bolton (*Coronado*, 277) without reference to the discrepancies.

[28] Cunninghame Graham, *Horses of the Conquest*, 75–76, 103 (citing the Inca, Garcilaso de la Vega, on the Indians' pulling off the saddles); cf. a similar incident in Mexico (*ibid.*, 60). See also Bishop, *Odyssey of Cabeza de Vaca*, 31.

[29] Denhardt, *Horse of the Americas*, 80.

[30] Bourne (ed.), *Narratives of De Soto*, II, 134.

[31] The Indians were 'opened to obtain it' (Cunninghame Graham, *Horses of the Conquest*, 15, 50, 57). Luys Hernandez de Biedma describes its use for human casualties (Bourne [ed.], *Narratives of De Soto*, II, 21). Ford mentions this (*unto del hombre*) as a famed specific in Spain, doubtless of ancient standing (*Gatherings from Spain*, 254). One horse of Cortés was cured by bathing him in the sea (Cunninghame Graham, *Horses of the Conquest*, 15–16, 50, 57).

[32] Two hundred and forty-three is Ranjel's figure, in Bourne (ed.), *Narratives of De Soto*, II, 55. Ranjel gives the figure again as 223, as does Biedma (*ibid.*, II, 1).

three years, 150 of these had perished.[33] This number includes 50 slain at Pacaha (which is perhaps the same place as Thornton Chard's "50 killed at Chicaca"[34]), in March, 1541. In March, 1542 —which covers a lesser period than three years—the Gentleman of Elvas states that only 40 remained.[35]

When the remnants of the force launched their brigantines on the lower Mississippi in July, 1543, twenty-two horses—"the only good ones" (out of how many?)—were put aboard; the remainder were "jerked" (made into *charqui*) for food. Later, all were slain but four or five, which are stated by Garcilaso de la Vega, the Inca, to have been all stallions.[36] The Indians there appeared to be afraid of them, according to a contemporary chronicler who was present.[37] These were turned adrift in a region where every other Indian tribe very speedily mastered the fear of the horse and slew rather than shunned it. Quite apart from any adverse possibilities of sex, this leaves some "four or five" out of an original total of 223. And these four or five constitute the case for abandonment as the probable original source of Indian supply.

In the case of De Soto's horses at least, even this extremely slender possibility is in itself not merely questionable; it is denied as a fact by some scholars. Francis Haines quotes a modern (nineteenth century) writer, who has possibly utilized Spanish contemporary historical material which I have had no opportunity to consult. The author in question states that the "four or five" horses which were left behind by Luis de Moscoso (who had succeeded to the command of the expedition after De Soto's death) "were slain before the Spanish boats were out of sight."[38] Thornton Chard considers that the first fear of the Indians indicates that they had never seen the animal before.[39] While he is doubtless correct, in such a huge territory as that covered by De Soto's party, this

Denhardt gives round numbers: 'about 300,' and 'more than 100 lost' by 1542 (*Horse of the Americas*, 76, 81); 300 also in Cunninghame Graham, *Horses of the Conquest*, 73.

[33] The Gentleman of Elvas, in Bourne (ed.), *Narratives of De Soto*, I, 142, 154.

[34] For Chicaca and Pacaha, see Chard, "Did the First Spanish Horses Leave Progeny?" 92–93.

[35] Elvas in Bourne (ed.), *Narratives of De Soto*, I, 142, 154.

[36] Cited by Dobie, *The Mustangs*, 34.

[37] Elvas, in Bourne (ed.), *Narratives of De Soto*, I, 146, 154, 192, 200–201.

[38] Haines, "How Did the Indians Get Their Horses?" 115.

[39] "Did the First Spanish Horses Leave Progeny?" 110.

would scarcely constitute evidence in itself for any region beyond that of their broad locality at the time (1543).

The identification of the precise route followed by De Soto has baffled many inquirers. Thomas Nuttall (1819) thought the exploration of the "immemorial trails" (if there are any!) might facilitate this, but the difficulty was as great as ever down to 1931. Most of the earlier commentators confined themselves to taking the party through Florida, Georgia, Alabama, Louisiana, Mississippi, Arkansas, and Texas, which is fairly safe. The problem is now apparently considered solved. Herbert E. Bolton takes them through southern North Carolina and eastern Tennessee, and thence across to Arkansas, where he thinks, contrary to opinion hitherto, they even saw the buffalo, at Coligua, near Little Rock.[40]

The question would scarcely be relevant to the present essay, but for one important consideration. The localization of the route (as by Bolton) widens immensely the geographical area in which wild horses might be encountered or their existence—alleged or actual—learned by later explorers, since horses could be lost anywhere. I have found no evidence of any such character. Perhaps the earliest Europeans (of record) on the lower Mississippi to cross De Soto's route would be La Salle's party in 1680. Henri de Tonty mentions that the "Cadodaquis" had horses, which they called *cavalis*.[41] This term clearly proves the Spanish source of the horses in question. It would be impossible for untouched tribes utilizing wild horses to have a Spanish name for them. We may note that apparently no Spanish (or other) "loan-word" names are found among the early Northern or Eastern Indians. Their horse terms are native etymons or faunal adaptations, such as the dog names.

We have another indication of the extremely slender likelihood of accidental survival. Cabeza de Vaca has recorded that the ex-

---

[40] Bolton, *Coronado*, 275–81. See on this, Thomas Nuttall, *A Journal of Travels into the Arkansas Territory, 1819*, in Thwaites, *Travels*, XIII, 145; J. G. Shea, in Justin Winsor (ed.), *A Narrative and Critical History of America*, II, 250–54; Fiske, *Discovery of America*, II, 509; Alfred Brittain, *Discovery and Exploration*, in *The History of North America* (ed.) by Guy Carlton Lee and Francis Newton Thorpe), I, 361; Bourne (ed.), *Narratives of De Soto*, II, 54, editor's note; Webb, *The Great Plains*, 111–14.

[41] Tonty, in Isaac Joslin Cox (ed.), *The Journeys of Robert René Cavelier, Sieur de la Salle*, I, 47–50, 55, 60.

pedition of Pánfilo de Narváez in 1528—of which he and his fellow castaways were the only survivors—originally embarked eighty horses, of which only forty-two were put ashore in Florida.[42] During the five months or more which passed before the final overwhelming of their miserable "barges" in the stormy Gulf of Mexico, all their horses were either slain in battle or devoured for food, with the exception of one animal only, whose fate or sex is not mentioned.[43] Even were this one a pregnant mare, the chances of propagating a family from one only are almost mathematically nil. The skulls of Narváez' horses were shown to De Soto's party by their Indian guides in 1539; the place, Ochete, was described as "The Bay of the Horses" (*Bahia de Los Caballos*).[44] It may be noted that in 1539–1543, nothing was heard even of any tradition of that sole surviving animal. Thornton Chard denies any survivor whatever from Narváez' horses.[45]

There is one other recorded instance of the "escape"—if one can call it that—of a lone animal; in this case it was specified by Castañeda to be a mare, though his comrade Jaramillo described it as a horse. A certain Do Campo, who is variously described as a Spaniard or a Portuguese, deserted from Coronado's force, or at any rate fled from the camp "on a mare" and got away.[46] He turned up again a year or two later by way of Panuco, Mexico, apparently in company with De Soto's returning expedition, but without the mare. Castañeda's competence is commented on by Bolton, who states: "Castañeda, writing with a knowledge of the explorations of both Coronado and De Soto gives us an unmistakable clue to Do Campo's route."[47] To almost any other chronicler, writing at the time, the loss of the mare would be a mere incident in the

---

[42] Bishop, *Odyssey of Cabeza de Vaca*, 33, 38, 43.

[43] *Ibid.*, 43–47, 50–52, 65; Cunninghame Graham, *The Conquest of the River Plate*, 91, 97. Poor Cabeza de Vaca, despite the unspeakable things he ate later on, could not stomach horseflesh (Bandelier [ed.], *Journey of Cabeza de Vaca*, 58).

[44] Bourne (ed.), *Narratives of De Soto*, I, 47–48; II, 7; Bishop, *Odyssey of Cabeza de Vaca*, 53.

[45] "Did the First Spanish Horses Leave Progeny?" 92.

[46] Castañeda and Jaramillo, in Winship (ed.), *Journey of Coronado*, 114, 144, 212, 239. There is some confusion here. Arthur S. Aiton's roll call gives three Portuguese in the muster: Aorta, Gaspar Alvarez, and Andres Martin. Bartolomé del Campo (the only one of the name) is presumably a Spaniard (Aiton, "The Muster-Roll of Coronado," *American Historical Review*, Vol. XLIV [1938], 556–70).

[47] Bolton, *Coronado*, 360.

fortunes of war. But by the time Castañeda was writing, things must surely have been different. If there be any historic authenticity to those bands—or even *one* band—of wild horses from the truants of Coronado or De Soto, it is incredible that no word would penetrate through to the Spaniards from Indian sources; or that Castañeda, writing "at a time when many men are still living who saw" these wonders,[48] would not have heard of and mentioned such reports. Here again, nothing more ever appears to have been heard of the mare.

The case of Pedro de Castañeda is of immense interest. Unlike his chronicler-comrades of Coronado's famous expedition, whose accounts were principally written at or near the time in the form of letters or reports, Castañeda's work is a history, composed at a much later date. In regard to this, Bolton observes that possibly "there were men whose deaths he had awaited before finishing his book."[49] This could of course serve a sinister purpose, as with Hennepin toward La Salle, but it could also indicate an honorable intention to tell the truth. Castañeda's history bears every mark of having been written by an honest man, and has won commendation from modern critics for its accuracy of description in the light of later knowledge.[50] It seems reasonable to suppose that if anybody's "lost horses" were—or had even been rightly or wrongly thought to be—the ancestors of any wild herds then ranging in *Nueva España* (if there were such) he would surely have mentioned the belief.

We know that the economic potentialities of the Southwestern Plains region as a whole from "Cíbola" (identified by common critical consent as Zuñi, New Mexico) onward attracted the attention of Coronado and his companions at the outset,[51] as they had

[48] Castañeda, in Winship (ed.), *Journey of Coronado*, 139.

[49] Bolton, *Coronado*, 255.

[50] Castañeda, in Winship (ed.), *Journey of Coronado*, 139. See also on him, Henry Inman (ed.), *Buffalo Jones' Forty Years of Adventure*, 6–11; Fynn, *The American Indian as a Product of Environment*, 100, 171. Aiton, "Muster-Roll of Coronado," 556–70; also his "The Later Career of Coronado," *American Historical Review*, Vol. XXX (1924), 298–304. Bolton, *Coronado*, 69, 195, 238, 255, 360. Re the authenticity of our two earliest sources for the Plains at large, see Bandelier (ed.), *Journey of Cabeza de Vaca*, 89, 92, 100, 113, 154–55, 174–75; Winship (ed.), *Journey of Coronado, ix–xii*, 64, 113, 209. W. P. Bliss of the University of New Mexico (1937) endorses these (correspondence to the author).

[51] Coronado to Viceroy Mendoza; also Jaramillo, in Winship (ed.), *Journey of*

previously done over the same broadly identical ecological environment with Cabeza de Vaca, who writes thus, in the quaint version of old Purchas, probably the earliest in English: "Throughout the whole Countrie there are many great and goodly fences [defenses: meaning probably as a soldier, 'defensible places'] and of excellent pasture for flockes and herds of cattle, and it would be a very fruitful Countrie if it were manured and inhabited by a people which had reason and knowledge."[52] Yet we must consider the very dubious chances inseparable from the "accidental" hypothesis: the right animals escaping, and surviving the numerous perils inevitable at first in a totally strange environment. These include human foes, savage carnivores of more than one species, venomous reptiles, and possibly poisonous vegetation and bad water. The last causes may have been responsible for the mysterious deaths among Coronado's horses en route from Tiguex (on the Río Grande) to Cíbola, and thence to Culiacán.[53]

Having regard for these physical impedimenta, which to an outdoor critic at least lie upon the surface and are not the result of any ingenious theorizing, it seems in my view more logical and probable to ascribe the earliest introduction of the historic horse to a deliberate course of policy on the part of the Spaniards, who were not improbably struck by a measure of resemblance of certain regions to the high plains and arid tablelands characteristic of portions of Spain.[54] A learned contemporary scholar in Hispano-American history shows that these were not the idle or superficial impressions of mere "tourists." He presents a wealth of testimony showing the age-old prevalence in medieval Spain and Portugal of the characteristic Western American ranching technique, the detailed usages and terminology of which did not "evolve" on this continent, but were *brought* here.[55] The judgment of the *Con-*

Coronado, 182, 236; cf. an apparently later colonizing project mentioned by Castañeda (*ibid.*, 139–40).

[52] Samuel Purchas, *Hakluytus Posthumus, or Purchas His Pilgrimes*, XVII, 480; a modern rendering in Bandelier (ed.), *Journey of Cabeza de Vaca*, 97; Bishop, *Odyssey of Cabeza de Vaca*, 102.

[53] Castañeda and Coronado, in Winship (ed.), *Journey of Coronado*, 128, 166, 198.

[54] See Webb, *The Great Plains*, 85–139; Ford, *Gatherings from Spain*, 1–43.

[55] Charles Julian Bishko, "The Peninsular Background of Latin-American Cattle Ranching," *Hispano-American Historical Review*, Vol. XXXII (1952), 491–515. I am much indebted to Mr. Bishko's kindness for a copy of this most important paper.

quistadores was doubtless in many cases that of experienced observers. I am happy to find that the general conclusions I formed years ago—even before they were so enormously reinforced by Bishko's researches—are broadly in agreement with those of a competent Southwestern archaeologist with a very wide and intimate knowledge of the region.[56] Certainly, in face of the foregoing considerations, the point of view summarized by Wissler many years ago (and to which reference has been made above) must be regarded as still awaiting substantiation, and likely to remain waiting indefinitely. Several notable specialists in Hispano-American history describe the concept as a "pretty legend."[57] These all refer to the De Soto–Coronado era. Thornton Chard has applied the critical process to various later expeditions to Florida, 1549–1565, but with equally barren results.[58]

The scholars' conclusion finds strong support in the historical circumstance that the deliberate policy was actually pursued in South America. A Spanish voyager or chronicler has recorded that Pedro de Mendoza—another of the powerful clan to which Coronado's patron and correspondent belonged[59]—"left behind in the place called Buenos Ayeres," about 1540, thirty mares and seven horses.[60] The number has elsewhere been given as "five horses and seven mares,"[61] "seven horses and five mares,"[62] "seven horses," "seven horses and mares," or "five mares and two horses."[63] There appears to be no contemporary

---

[56] W. P. Bliss (notes 23, 50 *supra*).

[57] Bishop, *Odyssey of Cabeza de Vaca*, 31; similarly, D. E. Worcester, "The Spread of Spanish Horses in the Southwest," *New Mexico Historical Review*, Vol. XIX (1944), 225; Denhardt, *Horse of the Americas*, 224; Dobie, *The Mustangs*, 34.

[58] "Did the First Spanish Horses Leave Progeny?" 93ff.

[59] For Pedro de Mendoza, see Cunninghame Graham, *Conquest of the River Plate*, 43–71; Bishop, *Odyssey of Cabeza de Vaca*, 179–85. Coronado's viceroy, Antonio de Mendoza (*el bueno*—"the good"), was governor of *Nueva España* only (Bishop, *ibid.*, 154–58); for its precise limits, see Coues's note, *Expeditions of Pike*, II, 718.

[60] Lopez Vaz, in Richard Hakluyt, *The Principal Navigations, Voyages, Traffiques and Discoveries of the English Nation*, VIII, 175.

[61] Cunninghame Graham, *Conquest of the River Plate*, 71, 267, 290 (citing Azara, 1790).

[62] Denhardt, *Horse of the Americas*, 34.

[63] All three in Cunninghame Graham, *Horses of the Conquest*, 112, 113, 143.

account of this abandonment; and it is doubtful if it could correctly be termed such—even if the governor was leaving the country, for learned Spanish scholars in the historical literature of the Americas note that the early leading *Conquistadores* were bound by their agreement (*asiento*) with the Sovereign to take so many horses and mares with them.[64] In accordance with this provision, it is stated that Mendoza took "100 horses and 100 mares,"[65] or "72 horses and mares"[66] with him on his voyage to the River Plate in 1535.[67] Their high value in official estimation—partly at least for breeding purposes, we must assume from what follows—may be inferred from the fact that when two starving soldiers killed a horse (the unpardonable "sin against the Holy Ghost") they were hanged on the spot.[68] A later, very careful student gives three culprits and states that their death was not for any sacrilege but for stealing the horse and eating it secretly while their comrades were starving.[69]

Cabeza de Vaca, on his appointment as Governor of Paraguay in 1540, took out with him thirty, or thirty-six, or forty-six horses (or "forty-six horses and mares").[70] These included several stallions for breeding purposes, which cost him a very considerable sum of money.[71] Of the total, twenty-six landed there.[72] There was at this

[64] *Ibid.*, 110. Some details on this in Denhardt, *Horse of the Americas,* 30–33, 160–63.

[65] Cunninghame Graham, *Conquest of the River Plate,* 44.

[66] Denhardt, *Horse of the Americas,* 161.

[67] Cunninghame Graham, *Conquest of the River Plate,* 44 (who says "1534"). This is clearly a misdating, of which there are several, since on p. 50 he lands them 'early in 1536,' as also do Bishop, *Odyssey of Cabeza de Vaca,* 180, and Denhardt, *Horse of the Americas,* 161.

[68] Cunninghame Graham, *Conquest of the River Plate,* 62; Bishop, *Odyssey of Cabeza de Vaca,* 180.

[69] Madaline W. Nichols, "The Spanish Horse of the Pampas," *American Anthropologist,* Vol. XLI (1939), 119–29, who discredits the "twelve" left behind by Mendoza. She cites Juan de Rivadeneyra, 1581, to the effect that Mendoza left forty-four horses and mares; which agrees broadly with Lopez Vaz (note 60 *supra*).

[70] Cunninghame Graham, *Conquest of the River Plate,* 113, has thirty; Bishop, *Odyssey of Cabeza de Vaca,* 189, has thirty-six; Denhardt, *Horse of the Americas,* 165, has forty-six horses and mares. The last gives the departure from San Lucar, November 2, 1540; arrival in southern Brazil, March 29, 1541, and at Asunción, March 2, 1542.

[71] Cunninghame Graham, *Conquest of the River Plate,* 117; see also Denhardt, *Horse of the Americas,* 165.

[72] *Ibid.* John J. Johnson estimates that 30 per cent of the live stock imported into the Indies was lost in transportation ("The Spanish Horse in Peru before 1550,"

time, it would seem, no direct communication overland between Paraguay (whose capital was the city of Asunción) and the deserted "city" or district of Buenos Aires. We have early accounts of horse numbers in Paraguay which must either be exaggerations, or else there had been importations on some rather extensive scale. Domingo Martínez de Irala led an expedition in 1550 with six hundred horses, all of which perished. In 1551, the same Irala paid "4,000 gold dollars" for one horse; and at his death in 1557, he possessed twenty-four.[73] But from just how large a parent stock, or whether augmented by purchase or otherwise from outside, we are not informed.

The afore-mentioned conditions of isolation between Paraguay and the River Plate region, and the (then) commonly northwestward trend of exploration from the former province, together with the ravages of rebellion and civil war, producing such losses as the six hundred horses, might leave little reason to suppose that Paraguay contributed much or anything to any general increase in the horse population beyond her own borders. Yet in 1580, at the second foundation of Buenos Aires, Don Juan Garay "found the whole province full."[74] We are not told just what "full" signified to Garay, nor whether he reached this conclusion immediately on landing or after some further experience. A contemporary researcher, who has given special attention to this particular phase, considers that the numbers of 1580 were probably *not* descendants of Mendoza's horses. Certainly on her showing they were not necessarily such. The scholar in question, Madaline W. Nichols, states that in Chile, Peru, and perhaps in Brazil, the Indians were stealing, riding, and breeding horses from 1540 onward. In her opinion the horses of the Pampas were actually from Chile and Tucumán. The loss of one thousand horses in the civil war era from hostilities and famine presupposes numbers to be lost.[75] At the same time another scholar

---

Greater America [Essays in Honor of Herbert Eugene Bolton], 20). Narváez' virtual 50 per cent, De Soto's 8 per cent, and Cabeza de Vaca's 33 per cent (from the mean figure of 38), almost exactly agree with Johnson's estimate.

[73] Cunninghame Graham, *Conquest of the River Plate*, 182–83, 292; Denhardt, *Horse of the Americas*, 35.

[74] Cunninghame Graham, *Conquest of the River Plate*, 121, 238–43, 267–73, 290; see also his *Horses of the Conquest*, 113.

[75] Nichols, "Spanish Horse of the Pampas," 119–29.

instances 3,000 to 4,000 pesos as the price of a horse in Peru before 1550.[76] We need further data on local prices to elucidate such values. This could indicate either fewness of horses per se, or Indian depredations so great that originally large numbers were very heavily depleted.

Certain incidental items of evidence appear to substantiate both a considerable (relative) degree of numbers and the spread of the South American horses to the southeastward in comparatively early times. In 1587, English voyagers noted a "great store of horses" on the mainland near Concepción (Chile), and in such evident quantities that the very "neteherds" were mounted at their tasks.[77] In 1579, according to Madaline Nichols, the Patagonian Indians were riding.[78] Another very competent scholar says the same with reference to 1590, and adds that they "hardly stirred a step on foot."[79] Perhaps these were the first generation—they were certainly an early one—of the world-famous Gauchos of the Pampas.

According to at least one notable Spanish scholar, the wild cattle of the country were even then in large numbers, which in itself must have stimulated the horse-breeding situation, precisely as in the ranching areas of the northern continent. R. B. Cunninghame Graham speaks of Garay's loading a ship with sugar and hides in 1580, ". . . hides from the great herds of cattle that had descended from those Don Pedro de Mendoza had abandoned only fifty years before."[80] There seems no warrant for this assertion. Robert Moorman Denhardt, discussing this, mentions Garay's finding wild horses, but says nothing about wild cattle or shipments of hides.[81] Another most critical scholar states that the first horned cattle in South America were seven cows and a bull, driven overland from Santa Catalina to Asunción by Ciprian de Goes in 1554–55, with which Cunninghame Graham himself agrees.[82] There seems to be no evidence of any early overland communication between

[76] Johnson, "Spanish Horse in Peru," 19–37. On Chile, see Denhardt, *Horse of the Americas,* 156–60.

[77] Hakluyt, *Voyages,* VIII, 218.

[78] "Spanish Horse of the Pampas," 127–28.

[79] Denhardt, *Horse of the Americas,* 35.

[80] Cunninghame Graham, *Conquest of the River Plate,* 274.

[81] Denhardt, *Horse of the Americas,* 34, 163.

[82] Bishop, *Odyssey of Cabeza de Vaca,* 189; cf. Cunninghame Graham, *Horses of the Conquest,* 112; also his *Conquest of the River Plate,* 196 ('eight and a bull').

the two provinces, as I have remarked. The statement must therefore be regarded as one of its author's historical exuberances, which his immense knowledge did not always curb.

From such beginnings, in all probability, arose the historic horse of the western regions of the North American continent, the "maroon," as it was often termed in the old days.[83] Doubtless the process was aided by the day-to-day accidents of flood and field. If later times furnish any analogy, this would be frequently much against the will of the nominal owners of such fugitives. John K. Townsend, along the Columbia River below Fort Walla Walla, in 1833, noted herds of wild horses, on which he commented:

Large bands . . . as wild as deer . . . seldom permitting an approach to within a hundred yards or more. They generally have owners, as we observe upon many of them strange hieroglyphic looking characters, but there are no doubt some that have never known the bit, and will probably always roam the prairie uncontrolled.[84]

An almost exact parallel came within the present writer's personal experience. In the Elbow River foothills, southwest of Calgary, Alberta, in August, 1902, I saw bands of horses (of which

[83] So, Pierre-Jean De Smet, *Letters and Sketches, with a Narrative of a Year's Residence among the Indian Tribes of the Rocky Mountains*, in Thwaites, *Travels*, XXVII, 180. According to Coues, the Cimarron (river) is the same word, meaning "wild," "lost," or "unreclaimed"; the verb "to maroon" is of buccaneering ill-fame (Coues [ed.], *Expeditions of Pike*, II, 438). So also Cunninghame Graham, who cites the term for wild horses, *los caballos cimarrones*, from Azara, about 1790 (*Horses of the Conquest*, 115; also his *Conquest of the River Plate*, 29). Vast as were the hosts of wild horses (and cattle) in South America, they would have been even greater but for the destructive ravages of a navel-haunting fly in Paraguay (Charles Darwin, *On the Origin of Species by Means of Natural Selection*, 61, citing Azara on this pest); see also on vampire bats and other horse foes of South America, Raymond M. Gilmore, "Fauna and Ethnozoology," *Handbook of South American Indians* (ed. by Julian H. Steward), Bureau of American Ethnology, *Bulletin 143* (cited hereafter as Steward, *Handbook*), VI, 365. Despite all these deterrents, "during the first quarter of the 19th century as many as 500,000 of the superfluous feral and semi-feral mares in Argentina were slaughtered annually" (Dobie, *The Mustangs*, 106, 347).

[84] John K. Townsend, *Narrative of a Journey Across the Rocky Mountains, 1833–1834*, in Thwaites, *Travels*, XXI, 283.

there were many) of known ownership, with their progeny. These were occasionally approached near enough to be identified, but they could not be run down or surrounded in the (then) soft and spongy condition of the prairie and foothill valleys, for 1902 was the "peak year" of the wet cycle of 1899–1903.

It is well to note the stringent governing conditions, both environmental and biological, which at any time required to be recognized and allowed for in the "accidental" hypothesis as a whole, even if we had no more positive knowledge to assist us. In relation to the important expedition of Coronado, however, we have something more tangible. Conjecture and argumentation, however rational and probable these may be, have been superseded by virtual certainty. A learned American scholar and specialist in Latin-American historical literature has discovered and translated the original muster-roll of Coronado's force. This was taken at Compostela, in western Mexico, February 22, 1540, prior to their departure on the famous journey. It is officially recorded that the force consisted of 286 officers and men. Of these, 222 are ranked as cavalry, and owned their own horses in varying numbers ranging from Coronado's twenty-three down to eighty-eight individuals owning one each. The total number is given as 552 horses (*caballos*) and *two* mares (*yeguas*).[85] *Caballos* need not of course necessarily signify stallions (*enteros*) any more than our own common collective term "horses" necessarily specifies sex.[86] We have seen, however, that some very competent critics consider there were literally no geldings.[87]

It may be considered reasonably certain that this overwhelming preponderance, amounting virtually to a monopoly of *caballos,* was not merely accidental. I have alluded above to a Spanish predilection for stallions as saddle beasts, a thing entirely logical in a horse-breeding people. In the earliest voyages to the Indies, it

[85] Aiton, "Muster-Roll of Coronado," 556–70. I am greatly indebted to Aiton's kindness for a reprint of this very valuable translation.

[86] Bernal Díaz writes: ."Juan de Escalante had a light bay horse with three white stockings. She [*sic*] was not very good." So, Denhardt, *Horse of the Americas,* 51. The Hakluyt Society translation, which Denhardt elsewhere pronounces the best (*Mustangs and Cow Horses* [ed. by J. Frank Dobie *et al.*], 197, 200), has Escalante's mount "a light chestnut horse with three white stockings, not much good." Compare the "mare" or "horse" (note 46 *supra*).

[87] See note 16 *supra*.

was evidently considered necessary to *ordain* that certain numbers or proportions of the horses taken from Spain should be mares. Of the first horses landing on the mainland, the sixteen animals belonging to Cortés and his followers, whose characteristics have been preserved for us by Bernal Díaz del Castillo, six were mares.[88] This high proportion, 37 per cent, may perhaps be traceable to their being—as some of them quite apparently were—old favorites of their owners. These details enjoin caution in pronouncing too definitively on the rejection of mares for riding. The possession of a mere mare did not prevent Juan Sedeño from being rated the richest man in Cortés' expedition, as we shall later see.[89]

The terrifying effect of the horses upon the Indians, to which I refer in more detail below, was noted by Columbus himself, in what was the first important military action against any tribe, in Hispaniola in 1495.[90] It is practically certain in the nature of things, whatever the actual numbers or proportion of mares may have been on this occasion, that of the two sexes considered in contrast, the stallions would affright the natives much more than would the mares. Anyone who has ever handled horses on the open range will agree that the Indians' early reaction to the strange beasts (an attitude the Spaniards would undoubtedly desire to perpetuate as long as they could; Antonio de Espejo was propagating the "man-eating" fable as late as 1582[91]) would give an additional impetus to the already existing Spanish preference for stallions as mounts.

In Coronado's time, exports from Spain, as the normal and conventional source of supply for the horses of the Spanish possessions in America, had long been discontinued. Charles V, by a royal edict in 1520, had forbidden further drains on the home reserves, which were becoming seriously threatened.[92] The later explorers, including Coronado, outfitted their expeditions from the abundant

[88] Bernal Díaz del Castillo, *True History of the Conquest of New Spain* (ed. by A. P. Maudslay), I, 86–87.

[89] *Ibid.*

[90] Denhardt, *Horse of the Americas,* 28.

[91] Herbert E. Bolton (ed.), *Spanish Exploration in the Southwest, 1542–1706,* 170, 172, 179, 185.

[92] Denhardt, *Horse of the Americas,* 40. This general prohibition had of course to be waived in the case of new colonies established directly from Spain; as with Mendoza and Cabeza de Vaca in South America, and with Pedro Menéndez' going as

island herds.[93] As early as the year 1500, beginning with Hispaniola and spreading thence to Cuba, Jamaica, Puerto Rico, Trinidad, and other suitable centers, there were royal and private *rancherías* possessing large numbers of brood mares.[94] With these reserves in the background, a military expedition of discovery into
the northern hinterlands of *Nueva España*, and with no immediate
purpose of colonization, would have no special incentive to include
any material number of mares in its cavalry force. Certainly it
would be no longer under any royal or official injunction to do so.
Actually it is not at all improbable that mares were specifically
forbidden as possibly constituting somewhat of an incumbrance to
the expedition. For it seems extremely unlikely that such an in-
finitesmal ratio as two in 554 could ever result from a free haphazard selection following individual tastes.

Bolton considers there were probably other mares beyond the
two indicated in Coronado's muster-roll.[95] The ratio of two in 554
renders it probable that a similarly exclusive policy would be
followed with respect to pack animals as (evidently) with the
caballeros' mounts. And in any case Bolton makes no mention of
Haines's crux. Even if such pack animals escaped in pairs, and
without mention, it is very unlikely that they included any stallions. For "pack animal" was a term of contempt from which *enteros*
would in all probability have been held exempt.[96] There must have
been more than the 554, if we are to accept Castañeda's postdated
estimates: ". . . 1000 horses and 500 of our cows and more than
5000 rams and ewes. . . ."[97] Bolton himself, however, rejects these
figures as an exaggeration. "Horses, mules, and stock were counted
at a certain narrow pass and there were found to be fifteen hundred animals."[98] The 554 horses make about 11 per cent of Casta-

governor to Florida in 1565 (*ibid.*, 39), although many of his horses came from
Santo Domingo (Chard, "Did the First Spanish Horses Leave Progeny?" 95).

[93] Denhardt, *Horse of the Americas*, 40, 152.

[94] *Ibid.*, 30–39; see also Johnson, "Spanish Horse in Peru," 19–21.

[95] Bolton, *Coronado*, 68, 399–400.

[96] This was evidently the case with the Portuguese, so possibly with the Spaniards also. Cunninghame Graham cites a native (Portuguese) proverb of the district
of O Sertaõ, in the Brazilian provinces of Bahia, Ceara, and Piauhy, to the effect that
"a piebald [*pedrez*] was made by God to carry packs" (*Horses of the Conquest*,
138).

[97] Castañeda, in Winship (ed.), *Journey of Coronado*, 139–40.

[98] Bolton, *Coronado*, 69.

ñeda's total of five thousand, but they would constitute nearly 35 per cent in a total of only fifteen hundred. This would make it probable that the 554 represent the total horses. Elsewhere in the same work Bolton himself once again speaks of there being "several thousand head of horses, mules, cattle, sheep, goats, and hogs."[99]

The especially significant relationship of Coronado's journey to the "accidental" hypothesis at large, and to the likelihood of that hypothesis being correct in any material or appreciable degree (in any other, later-explored region of the "wild horse" range), is fairly obvious. There were three really important early land expeditions with horses, to the terra incognita north of Mexico: those of Pánfilo de Narváez, De Soto, and Coronado. This last was by far the largest in horse numbers. It was also the only one which brought any horses back again. Of the two previous undertakings, there remained *one* horse only (accepting the statement cited above[100]), of unspecified sex, whose final fate is not historically known. Coronado's expedition supplies another such horse, whose sex is perhaps known, but whose fate is not.

There is little justification—and no necessity—for postdating the "accidental" hypothesis by the contention that while it may not have happened in Coronado's case, it could quite probably be true of somebody else later on. For in the light of that expedition's own accounts of an increasing Indian acquaintance and familiarity with horses,[101] we are approaching dangerously near to the era when the progressively lessening likelihood of such a suggestion's being true would fade into virtual impossibility. Without doubt there would be stray horses after Coronado's time, such as have been noted above. But as Haines very pertinently observes, the question under discussion is not so much whether or not there may have been survivals of stray animals, but whether or not the Indians acquired the horse in this manner.[102]

In the opinion of the same scholar, the improbability of the survival of any such early strays in Indian hands is increased by 'the tendency of Indians to eat spare animals.' [103] This latter sug-

99 *Ibid.*, 149.
100 See note 43 *supra.*
101 See the following chapter for this in detail.
102 Haines, "How Did the Indians Get Their Horses?" 114, 116.
103 *Ibid.*, 116.

gestion appears to me less convincing. We need to know more concerning the horse-eating proclivities of Indians. If (as would appear to be the case) this argument is based upon historic practice, that is too much characterized by tribal diversities to admit of reliable generalization.[104] There are other considerations also. Such a tribe as the Tlaxcaltecos of Mexico, who thought the horses were deer which allowed men (or magicians) to mount them, might conceivably eat such creatures. But it seems—to us at least—unthinkable that their fellow Mexicans, the Tabasqueños, who called the horses *tequanes*, signifying "monsters," would dare to do so.[105]

Furthermore, and very particularly in the light of Arthur S. Aiton's researches concerning Coronado, which would rule out the foregoing possibility within the limits of the march to Quivira, we find ourselves confronted with a strange contradiction. Quite probably the only natives who, in cold blood and not inflamed by battle lusts and hatreds, would dare to approach this unfamiliar creature near enough to have much chance of killing it, would be men who had already learned by contact or hearsay that the monster was not so terrible as it seemed, but was instead a very desirable friend and servant. In such circumstances, the case seems logically to suggest (or require) that some tribe or band should have been found by a relatively early Spanish expedition to be in possession of at least a few horses, considerably sooner than the known Spanish contacts with that territory could account for the fact. During the first three quarters of the sixteenth century such expeditions northward from Mexico were apparently not so numerous that many could have acquainted distant territories with the horse without their fellow Spaniards at large learning something of this from the Indian residents in such localities within a few months or years. Thornton Chard could discover nothing of this kind in the territory northeastward from Mexico during the years 1549–1565.[106] It seems incredible that to be *met* by strange Indians possessing horses would not arouse excited comment such as would inevitably find its repercussion in some official or historical document. I have found no allusion to such a thing any-

[104] See Chapter XIV.
[105] Denhardt, *Horse of the Americas,* 67.
[106] "Did the First Spanish Horses Leave Progeny?" 95.

where at this early time. D. E. Worcester states: "There is nothing to suggest that there were mounted Indians in the Southwest before the seventeenth century. . . ."[107]

Later scholars present instances of mounted Indians at much earlier dates, however, although they furnish no support to any accidental origins. What is characterized as the first official handing over of horses to natives was as early as 1541. In that year the Viceroy Mendoza mounted allied Aztec chieftains on horseback to lead their tribesmen in the Mixton War in central Mexico.[108] It furthermore appears to be the case that certain tribes in Sonora about 1567 not only rode horses, but also ate them.[109] But I cannot see any parallel between these cases and Haines's suggestion. These latter Indians *stole* their horses from the Spaniards, and regularly recruited their constantly depleted stocks in this manner. It is obvious that men competent to steal horses outdoors in the open—and from a horse people—must have already acquired a familiar knowledge of the creatures and their habits. This was unlikely to be learned by those who slew strays so rapidly as to nullify any chance of offspring from them; from which in their native wilds the Indians could perhaps have acquired the knowledge which they utilized at the Spanish colonist's expense.

Denhardt notes another circumstance which bears upon this question. He writes as follows:

. . . the natives obtained their original horses, and always by far the greatest number, from the Spaniards or neighboring tribes and not from the wild herds. The Indians had mounts by the time the wild herds dotted the plains, and they always preferred domesticated animals to the *mesteños*. Mustangs [*mesteños*] were hard to catch and, once caught, harder to tame.[110]

In other words, Indian horse culture at this early stage was that of *domesticated* horsekeepers or grooms, and such knowledge can only be acquired by personal domestic intercourse with horses. Seeing that "by about 1567" these Sonora Valley tribes were riding,

[107] "The Spread of Spanish Horses," 232.
[108] Dobie, *The Mustangs*, 25.
[109] Denhardt, *Horse of the Americas*, 91.
[110] *Ibid.*, 104.

we may well doubt whether even at this early date there were many tribes remaining in the cismontane Southwest who had neither some acquaintance with the horse themselves, *nor any neighbors or allies who could inform them.*

Whatever may be thought logically of the foregoing objections to Haines's suggestion of the early horses in Indian hands being eaten almost at once, it is in my view rendered extremely doubtful by the circumstance that—so far as I am aware—neither at the time as a contemporary fact nor even later as a tradition, does any actual reference to such an occurrence, certainly not as a general practice among the Indians at large, appear to have survived. It seems incredible that some hint of such a denouement would not have filtered through to Spanish or Hispano-American ears. The argument from the identical silence concerning the larger supposition of the "stray" theory of the Indian horse is met by the virtually mathematical certainty of its fallacy. The same explanation is, in my opinion, highly probable in this present case.

The cumulative weight of these combined factors makes the conclusion as certain as anything can be which is not directly attested by reliable eyewitnesses, that the "accidental" hypothesis is altogether untenable, and that the Indians acquired the horse by "direct action" on the part of the red race, or the white race, or both.

55

III

ABORIGINAL REACTIONS

What must certainly be considered a really remarkable feature in the Plains Indian horse culture is the almost phenomenal rapidity with which they mastered their early fears and developed into one of the two or three foremost equestrian peoples of the world. Their earliest introduction to the animal struck them with sheer terror in almost every part of Spanish America.[1] It is curious to note that this does not seem to have been the case among the northeastern tribes in New France. This circumstance is the more striking when we consider that the latter never became "horse Indians" in the sense commonly applied to the term. The attitude principally discoverable among them is one of curiosity towards "the moose of France," as these Indians termed the new creature. Probably this apathy is explained by their having been familiarized for nearly half a century with the French as pedestrians like themselves, instead of encountering them *de novo* as centaurs. Apart from one horse sent out to the governor, Charles de Montmagny, in 1647, the first importation did not reach New France until July 16, 1665.[2] In addition to this, many of the tribes having dealings with the French were acquainted with the English settlements, which had been importing horses since 1629 at least.[3] This would apply par-

---

[1] See on this at large, Chittenden, *American Fur Trade*, II, 832; Wissler, *The American Indian*, 34–35, 379; Cunninghame Graham, *Conquest of the River Plate*, 105; Webb, *The Great Plains*, 52–68; and particularly, Denhardt, *Horse of the Americas*, 27–172.

[2] Reuben Gold Thwaites (ed.), *The Jesuit Relations and Allied Documents*, XV, 235; L, 81, 215, 319.

[3] Wissler, "Influence of the Horse," 7.

ticularly to the Iroquois Confederacy, whose reactions toward the horse would in all probability attract the most attention among the French observers of that time.

In the Southwest the course of events was very different. In Mexico,[4] *Nueva España*,[5] Florida,[6] and South America,[7] the horse, like the elephants of Pyrrhus against Rome,[8] almost won battles for the Spaniards—at first! Yet from the beginning there were no doubt some Indians who either did not feel or who disdained to exhibit any fear. In Pedro de Mendoza's very first encounter with the Indians of La Plata, when 330 men sallied forth and only 85 survivors returned, 25 of his troop of 30 horsemen were slain, although both sides claimed the victory.[9] Bernal Díaz mentions an Indian chief in Cortés' Honduras expedition of 1525 riding one of the horses;[10] and Oviedo (from Ranjel) recounts a similar incident in Florida in 1540.[11] William H. Prescott states that while the Peruvians in general exhibited the common dread, Atahualpa himself maintained his composure and actually had some of them put to death for betraying this weakness before the white strangers, although the Inca chronicler, Garcilaso de la Vega, denies the truth of this occurrence. Nevertheless, a critical modern scholar accepts it.[12]

[4] William H. Prescott, *History of the Conquest of Mexico*, I, 179, 260, 311; II, 181, 229, 328, etc.; Cunninghame Graham, *Horses of the Conquest*, 22, 40, 58; Acosta says: "They were at first thought to be as ferocious as bloodhounds . . ." (all citing Bernal Díaz, *Conquest of New Spain*, I, 123–24; II, 58). Compare Castañeda: ". . . animals which, it was generally believed, ate people . . ." (Winship [ed.], *Journey of Coronado*, 33).

[5] "Horses frightened the enemy most" (Castañeda, in Winship [ed.], *Journey of Coronado*, 147); see also *Purchas His Pilgrimes*, XVIII, 57. The same thing is found in all the contemporary Spanish writers (Cunninghame Graham, *Conquest of the River Plate*, 40, etc.; *Horses of the Conquest*, 105; Denhardt, *Horse of the Americas*, 57, 91). Antonio de Espejo tried to keep up the delusion as late as 1582, possibly with some success (Bolton [ed.], *Spanish Exploration in the Southwest*, 170, 172, 179, 185).

[6] Gentleman of Elvas, in Bourne (ed.), *Narratives of De Soto*, I, 104, 201; Ranjel, *ibid.*, II, 125; *Purchas His Pilgrimes*, XV, 506, 518; XVII, 493; Cunninghame Graham, *Horses of the Conquest*, 97, 103.

[7] Cunninghame Graham, *ibid.*, 146; *Conquest of the River Plate*, 119, 129, etc.; Bishop, *Odyssey of Cabeza de Vaca*, 200, 218.

[8] Theodor Mommsen, *The History of Rome*, I, 394, 398, 406.

[9] Cunninghame Graham, *Conquest of the River Plate*, 58; cf. 252. Bishop, *Odyssey of Cabeza de Vaca*, 180.

[10] Cunninghame Graham, *Horses of the Conquest*, 27.

[11] *Ibid.*, 74–75; Ranjel himself, in Bourne (ed.), *Narratives of De Soto*, II, 122.

[12] William H. Prescott, *History of the Conquest of Peru*, I, 155, 240; Cunning-

The famous black charger of Cortés, *El Morzillo*, which he was compelled to leave behind on the Honduras expedition with a splinter in its foot, was received in charge by the chief of the village with much respect, but without any mention of fear. The poor animal later died of the injury, not helped by the unacceptable offerings of fruit and chickens which were brought him by the Indians for food.[13] When Ursua's party passed through the country in 1697, they found a rude stone image of the horse being worshipped as a god by the local Indians. The cult was denounced and the image destroyed by the Franciscan monks. Perhaps by reason of familiarity with this image, some of the Maya Indians whom Ursua encountered leaped and rejoiced on seeing living horses for the first time.[14] In Paraguay also, fear speedily gave way to curiosity and confidence; and very soon the Indians were assisting to swim and ferry horses over rivers and learning their ways in general.[15]

At about the same time, in the northern regions of *Nueva España* and beyond, Coronado and his men observed various individualisms amid the general manifestations of doubt and fear.[16] In a short time this new courage found common expression in sundry ways, beyond that of merely slaying the horses in the heat of battle. We find Indians 'touching the horses' as a feature of the ceremony in making peace; another Indian, called to hold a cavalier's horse, precisely like any ordinary groom, during a love episode at Tiguex, later successfully identifying the horse; and others at Tiguex driving off loose horses ("as at a bull-fight," according to Pedro de Castañeda) and slaying them with arrows. Castañeda also relates an occurrence of an Indian at Quivira pursuing and overtaking a Spaniard or Portuguese—the afore-mentioned Do

---

hame Graham, *Horses of the Conquest,* 68–69. For Garcilaso's denial, see Denhardt, *Horse of the Americas,* 74. The modern critic in question (giving weighty reasons) is John J. Johnson, "Spanish Horse in Peru," 25.

[13] Cunninghame Graham, *Conquest of the River Plate,* 119; Bishop, *Odyssey of Cabeza de Vaca,* 200; Denhardt, *Horse of the Americas,* 70.

[14] Denhardt, *ibid.,* 67–71; Cunninghame Graham, *Horses of the Conquest,* 32–40; J. Frank Dobie, *Tales of the Mustang,* 15.

[15] Cunninghame Graham, *Conquest of the River Plate,* 211, 252, etc.; Bishop, *Odyssey of Cabeza de Vaca,* 203; some additional details in Denhardt, *Horse of the Americas,* 151–72.

[16] "Some less afraid . . ." (*Purchas His Pilgrimes,* XVIII, 57); and an Indian daring to strike a horse at first sight (Castañeda, in Winship [ed.], *Journey of Coronado,* 34).

Campo—who fled from the camp "on a mare" (presumably one of the *two*), in which the fleetness of foot in overtaking a horseman is almost eclipsed by the daring in even attempting it.[17]

It is itself a graphic index of the striking changes wrought by the horse in a period of less than three centuries, that this tribe was almost certainly one of the later typically "horse Indian" nations. The identification of Quivira has at various times given rise to much controversy. The older school of critics placed it too far to the north. "The farthest point reached by Coronado may have been somewhere near the boundary between the states of Kansas and Nebraska or perhaps farther west at some point on the south fork of the Platte river."[18] Some few years later another learned scholar placed it in "north-east Kansas beyond the Arkansas, over 100 miles northeast from the Great Bend."[19] The accomplished editor of the written memoirs of the Coronado party, George Parker Winship, was apparently the first to identify the tribe, and virtually the locality: "a village of Wichita Indians on the Arkansas River."[20]

Some thirty years after Winship's identification, it was assailed by a body of Texas critics as being too far north. Coronado "was never off Texan soil," and Quivira was on the Canadian River or a tributary.[21] There are some stubborn facts in the way of the acceptance of this supposition. After the division of the force at the Barranca Grande (considered to be Palo Duro Canyon)[22] in the spring of 1541, the Quivira party under Coronado himself, after wandering about for weeks at the mercy of their treacherous guide, the "Turk," at last pushed northward for Quivira "by the needle,"[23] for a space variously given as being from thirty to forty-two days,[24] and thus eventually reached their objective.

The Texas hypothesis involves the supposition that the Spaniards thought they were going north (in that sunny land—even

[17] All from Castañeda, *ibid.*, 40, 48–50, 114, 144.

[18] Fiske, *Discovery of America*, II, 508.

[19] Thwaites (ed.), *Jesuit Relations*, LIX, 307; LXXI, 327. See also H. W. Haynes, in Justin Winsor (ed.), *A Narrative and Critical History of America*, II, 494; Aiton, "Later Career of Coronado," 298–304.

[20] Winship (ed.), *Journey of Coronado*, x, 209.

[21] See Webb, *The Great Plains*, 95–102. Webb, himself a Texan, is wisely hesitant about accepting this.

[22] Bolton, *Coronado*, 284–85.

[23] Winship (ed.), *Journey of Coronado*, 209.

[24] *Ibid.*, 209, 217, 233.

without the needle!) when they were really following their noses in all directions in the Canadian River headwaters region. We may remember that their northward journey was in a fairly familiar latitude, much the same as from Cádiz to Valladolid. This supposed confusion necessitates their being likewise befogged (together with their Indian guides) on the much more direct return trip from Quivira, of which we have Castañeda's graphic description of the Indians' way-making in a trackless region.[25] Such men as Winship and Bandelier, whom the Texas hypothesis would indict for something like stupidity, were at no time critics to be thrust aside without weighty cause; and "local knowledge" is sometimes overbalanced by "local patriotism." The latest scholar to discuss the question in any detail is Herbert Eugene Bolton. He endorses Winship in identifying the tribe of 1541 as the Wichita, and places Quivira at Lyons, Kansas,[26] about the apex of the Great Bend of the Arkansas, between Wichita and Dodge City.

At a later era, the central Arkansas River territory was a familiar portion of the wide Comanche range. The contrast presented by that tribe, with their short legs, squat, ungainly figures, and awkward gait afoot, and their graceful mastery astride—where man and horse seemed like one sentient being—attracted the attention of many nineteenth-century travelers and plainsmen.[27] While the Comanche may have exhibited this transformation pre-eminently, there is no reason for us to confine such changes to that tribe. François Antoine Larocque says of the Crow (1805): "They practice so little walking and running, using horses and [i. e., "on"] all occasions, that they are not so swift in running as their neighbours the Big Bellys [Hidatsas] and Mandans."[28] Probably most horse Indians were much more fleet of foot before they knew the animal.[29] It is quite clear that wherever Quivira was situated, the

[25] Castañeda, *ibid.*, 75.

[26] Bolton, *Coronado*, 291; see also his discussion, 290–95, 340.

[27] See Josiah Gregg on this, *Commerce of the Prairies*, in Thwaites, *Travels*, XX, 346; Catlin, *Letters and Notes*, II, 66, 73; Marcy, *Exploration of the Red River*. 95–97.

[28] Larocque, "Journal" (ed. by Burpee), 57.

[29] Compare the Mississippi River tribes, about 1700: ". . . men generally of tall stature, very lithe, and good runners, being accustomed from their tenderest youth to hunt wild beasts in the forests" (Father Gabriel Marest, in Thwaites [ed.], *Jesuit Relations*, LXVI, 229). It is clearly revealed by the universal pre-equestrian prevalence of the "surround" on foot, both for buffalo and every species of deer.

running powers of its people in the sixteenth and nineteenth centuries respectively would constitute a dramatic index of the changes wrought by possession of the horse.

It was suggested by the late Clark Wissler that "horse-travois in the bison area probably preceded riding," and that to such a culture "the horse would merely be a new and superior dog."[30] This may quite possibly have been the case. The dog names given to the horse may even point to a useful creature whose earliest function was to supersede the dog in harness rather than to replace the hunter afoot. These dog forms are found among several tribes in the Plains area. Sir William Butler notes that the Assiniboin had more than one name for the horse; possibly dialectal forms, as their parent stock, the Sioux, had for buffalo. Butler gives "Sho-a-thinga" and "Thongatch-shonga," both signifying "great dog." He also gives the Sarcee as "Chistli"—"seven dogs";[31] and the Gros Ventre (which may indicate either the Hidatsa of the Missouri or—more probably in this case—the Atsina[32] of southern Alberta) as "It-shouma-shunga"—"red dog."[33] The Blackfoot (Siksika) have "Ponokamita" "elk dog."[34] The Cree term is "mistatim"—"big dog."[35] George Catlin gives the Sioux name as "Shonk-a-wakan"—"medicine dog."[36] Wissler mentions an unspecified tribe whose horse name is "mysterious dog";[37] and the dog root-form for "horse" is found among the Beaver (Tsattine), Biloxi, Hidatsa, Kiowa, Nez

[30] Wissler, *The American Indian*, 35; also his "Influence of the Horse," 18. Horse travois succeeded dog travois among the Saulteaux of Manitoba and Saskatchewan: Alanson Skinner, "The Culture of the Plains Cree," *American Anthropologist*, Vol. XVI (1914), 314–18. The main (forest) Ojibwa (Saulteaux) used no travois: *Ibid.*, 315.

[31] *The Great Lone Land*, 267.

[32] The Atsina were a branch of the Arapaho, and were the "Big Bellies" after whom the Belly River of southern Alberta was named (*Place-Names of Alberta* [National Geographic Board of Canada], 18), *not* those of Larocque, note 28 *supra*. See on the Atsina: Hodge, *Handbook*, I, 113; Maximilian, *Travels*, in Thwaites, *Travels*, XXIII, 70; Thwaites, *Travels*, VI, 371 (editor's note); Coues' excellent notes, *Henry-Thompson Journals*, II, 531, 718–20, 733–36; McGillivray, *Journal* (ed. by Morton), 27; Alfred L. Kroeber, "Ethnology of the Gros Ventre," *Anthropological Papers of the American Museum of Natural History*, Vol. I (1908), 142–281; Jenness, *The Sarcee Indians*, 1–3.

[33] Butler, *Great Lone Land*, 267.

[34] Grinnell, in Hodge, *Handbook*, I, 569–71.

[35] Albert Lacombe, *Dictionnaire et Grammaire de la Langue des Cris*, 37, 60, 317, 329, 558, etc.

[36] Catlin, *Letters and Notes*, II, 59.

[37] Wissler, "Influence of the Horse," 11.

Percé, Ofo, Omaha, and Oto, although in these latter I am unaware of the precise signification.[38] The adjective "mysterious"
may be said to be latent in all the forms given above; and very
possibly the dog theme would be found upon investigation to be
very widely prevalent among tribes which had made some use of
the dog for other purposes than for food or sacrifice. Where could
they better turn than to the one useful quadruped they possessed,
in order to define another whose functions, on a more powerful
and extended scale, were to be essentially similar?

At the same time, it must be pointed out that the *summer* uses
of the dog as a beast of burden have persisted to within living
memory, as we have noted in an earlier chapter.[39] Ewers emphasizes the fact that the continued use of dog transport in a tribe possessing the horse is no index whatever of even a relative degree of
poverty in horseflesh. Considering the persistence of the practice
purely as a phase of mere temperamental conservatism, the contrast with the swift adaptability (in the same Blackfoot tribe) in
the various departments of horse culture, and particularly in utilizing the horse for riding, is so apparent that the psychological
explanation seems inadequate, while the coincident economic interpretation appears logical and probable.

Viewed in the light of Wissler's hypothesis regarding the order
of procedure, the continued use of dogs would itself release a larger
proportion of their early horse assets for use in riding and hunting.
Regarded even as an abstract probability apart from the economic
urge, we may remember that it was as a saddle mount with its
quite obvious potentialities both for warfare and for the chase that
the Spaniards apparently first—and beyond question most dra-
matically—revealed the horse to the Indians.

We have seen that in South America less than half a century
was required to evolve the Gaucho as the world has known him:

---

[38] For the Beaver, (Rev.) A. C. Garrioch (1875), MS.: "Vocabulary of
Beaver-Cree-English." I owe this to the kindness of my friend, Mrs. Robert Holmes,
of the same diocese of Athabaska, 1902 *et seq.* For the Biloxi-Ofo, J. Owen Dorsey
and John R. Swanton, *Dictionary of the Biloxi and Ofo Languages,* Bureau of American Ethnology, *Bulletin 41.* Hidatsa-Omaha-Oto, Maximilian's vocabularies of Indian languages (*Travels,* in Thwaites, *Travels,* XXIV, 210–300). Kiowa, John P.
Harrington, *Dictionary of the Kiowa Language,* Bureau of American Ethnology,
Bulletin 84. Nez Percé, Alexander Ross, *Fur Hunters of the Far West,* I, 317–23.

[39] See Chapter I *supra.*

a creature who did nothing except on horseback.[40] We have also seen that among the Northern Assiniboin at a fairly early "horse date," and then actually in the transitional stage in which the horse was not universally or solely used, Wissler's suggestion was not the prevailing order of things. Their horses were principally reserved for hunting purposes.[41] It is true that the Blackfoot and the Sioux were utilizing the horse both as a pack and a draft animal at periods, respectively, over fifty and thirty years earlier. They were nearer, however, to southern and western sources of supply, and probably possessed more; so we perhaps cannot consider this hypothesis as more than a conjecture, possibly true among certain tribes. The evidence appears to indicate an analogous individualism and lack of uniformity to the adoption of the horse in portions of the Old World.[42]

There is one particular phase of Indian horse culture in which a noticeable degree of uniformity is revealed. This is the adoption of certain Spanish usages or customary techniques. These, whether universal among Indians or not, have certainly been noted among widely-divided tribes in many regions of the horse–Indian habitat. While sundry details of Spanish horsemanship have been observed since fairly early (horse) times,[43] the outstanding phenomenon is

[40] For the Gaucho, see Cunninghame Graham's description, *Conquest of the River Plate*, 294; Cunninghame Graham also, in Dobie (*et al.*), *Mustangs and Cow Horses*, 187–96; Denhardt, *Horse of the Americas*, 19, 35, 83, 170, 245, etc.

[41] See Chapter I *supra*.

[42] A learned classical scholar notes that in what appears to be an early epoch for the horse as a domesticated animal in ancient Greece, its uses varied. In the Homeric poems, horses were driven more than ridden. In war, after horses became commoner, leaders rode to the scene and dismounted ("dragoon-wise") to fight. Riding was used more in Thessaly—the home of the Centaurs—than in Attica or Peloponnesus; and from its first (conjectural) appearance, riding was commoner in Assyria, Asia Minor, Central Europe, and in Italy, than in Greece. John Linton Myres, *Who Were the Greeks?* 102–105, 318, 325, 506–507, 602. A recent article indicates a very slow progression from mounted infantry tactics to cavalry proper (many centuries B.C.) in Near Eastern lands that later furnished the classic cavalry of ancient history (D. H. Gordon, "Swords, Rapiers, and Horse Riders," *Antiquity*, Vol. XXVII (1953), 67–78). Left to themselves, that might have been the Indians' history. See also Max Hilzheimer, "Evolution of the Domestic Horse," *Antiquity*, Vol. IX (1935), 133–39. Dobie cites a number of important works on the origins of the horse (*The Mustangs*, 3–20).

[43] See Wissler on the Indian adoption of Spanish horse usages, "Influence of the Horse," 7–8; "Material Culture of the North American Indians," 494–95. Much has been said by Charles Dickens' critics concerning the influence of *Don Quixote* as a model for *Pickwick Papers*. Possibly Spanish influences are traceable in Mr.

the Spanish practice of mounting from the right-hand side, an inheritance from the Moorish Arabs.[44]

In addition to the Plains tribes proper, this custom has also been noted in regions widely separated from the Plains, and among entirely unrelated peoples. These include the Choctaw of the Gulf States, and the Iroquois of the Great Lakes;[45] and in addition, the Blackfoot of Alberta.[46] The tribal or customary range of the latter extended southward to the upper Missouri River country; but in the latter part of the eighteenth century they were apparently in fairly direct contact with Spanish or Hispano-American influences on the frontiers of *Nueva España* itself, through their southern horse-raiding forays. The fact that these predatory expeditions were notorious in 1789 raises a fair presumption that they were then of some degree of long standing.[47] This could very readily account for the right-side mounting habit among the Blackfoot Confederacy.

Wissler, in one of his earlier papers, seems rather vague and contradictory on this question. He writes thus: "The Indian did not learn the mount from the Spaniard. It is fairly clear that if men are left to their own devices they will mount from the right side, unless left-handed."[48] Colonel Richard I. Dodge thought similarly.[49] I cannot concur in this conclusion. An "instinctive" way of approaching an animal they had never seen before seems paradoxical. Can anyone conceive of the Indians being left to their own devices or daring to leave themselves so with this portentous creature, while in plain view there were the Spaniards so evidently familiar with it—and mounting from the right-hand side! Furthermore, most of our Anglo-American people are right-handed also.

Winkle's "horse culture": " 'Blowed if the gen'l'man warn't a-gettin' up on the wrong side!' whispered a grinning postboy to the inexpressibly gratified waiter." (*Pickwick Papers,* Chap V.).
   44 See Cunninghame Graham, in Dobie (ed.), *Mustangs and Cow Horses,* 196.
   45 For these tribes, James Adair, *History of the North American Indians,* cited by Wissler, "Influence of the Horse," 7–8, 18.
   46 See Coues (ed.), *Henry-Thompson Journals,* II, 526; also Kidd, "Blackfoot Ethnography," 133; an admirable study of Siksika life and thought, with a rich bibliography. I am greatly indebted to my friend Mr. Kidd for the loan of his MS. to a (then) total stranger.
   47 These are discussed in detail in the following chapter.
   48 Clark Wissler, "The Riding Gear of the North American Indians," *Anthropological Papers of the American Museum of Natural History,* Vol. XVII (1915), 35.
   49 (Col.) Richard I. Dodge, *Our Wild Indians,* 338.

Who or what changed us over from the "instinctive" side to the left hand? And following in the same essay, Wissler describes the North and the South American horse-culture complex as having a common origin in the Spanish colonies; having "one distinct structural pattern . . . which can be traced to the Old World."[50]

A later student writes as follows, in my view more convincingly: "All of the available evidence indicates that the horses, the style of riding, the saddles, the armor, and some of the weapons used by the mounted Indians of the Southwest, were of Spanish origin or design. . . ."[51]

There are occasional allusions to early Spanish penetration farther northward, such as might assist to establish early contacts. Hubert Howe Bancroft mentions a tradition of Spaniards in (modern) Wyoming, before 1650, which he considers to be without foundation, as they "had not then passed the Arkansas River."[52] There was an (unsuccessful) expedition under Villasur against the Pawnee on the Platte in 1720;[53] perhaps the same force which was somewhere near the Forks (North Platte, Nebraska) in 1721.[54] Denhardt is probably correct in making the Spanish "pause" or halt at the Plains frontier a deliberate policy, for prudential reasons. He writes as follows:

Once mounted, the Indian with his quiver of arrows was superior to the Spaniard with his single-shot arquebus. That the Spanish fear of mounted Indians was well founded was later beautifully illustrated on the Great Plains. The great Spanish Empire was stopped short when it reached the Plains area where the natives had horses. The European nations were not even able to protect settlements within reach of the Plains Indians, much less subdue the natives themselves. The savages held the Great Plains until repeating rifles and revolvers were introduced.[55]

The present writer would prefer to say that "the savages held the Great Plains" until they were left economically helpless by the

[50] Wissler, "Riding Gear," 37–38.
[51] Worcester, "The Spread of Spanish Horses," 232.
[52] *History of Nevada, Colorado, and Wyoming*, 672.
[53] Wissler, "Influence of the Horse," 2.
[54] La Vérendrye, *Journals* (ed. by Burpee), 417. See on these questions, Alfred Barnaby Thomas, *After Coronado* (1696–1727), a richly informative work.
[55] Denhardt, *Horse of the Americas*, 103.

extermination of their mainstay, the buffalo. With that emendation, Denhardt's pronouncement is unexceptionable. Cabeza de Vaca proved disastrously wrong as a prophet. He wrote: "Horses are what the Indians dread most, and by means of which they will be overcome."[56] It did not occur to him that the horse was actually to enlarge the superiority which the rapid bow already gave to the Indian over the clumsy firearm. More than two centuries later, when the firearm had been vastly improved, and was being used by experts themselves vastly superior to the ordinary Spanish soldier (judging by some Spanish accounts),[57] the Indian was still "top dog." Bernard De Voto discusses very informatively the operations of rapid firing and recharging in the muzzle-loading days. In conclusion he writes: "It took about thirty seconds . . . to load a gun. . . . In that time an Indian could shoot eight or ten aimed arrows."[58] An earlier scholar would make the operation even longer, in the heyday of the Plains economy. Walter Prescott Webb says that the loading of the rifle of that era was "a meticulous and time-consuming task. The powder had to be measured and poured, the ball had to be rammed down the barrel with a long rod, the tube must be 'primed,' and the cap or flint had to be adjusted. All this took about a minute. . . . The Indian could in that time ride three hundred yards and discharge twenty arrows."[59]

Denhardt writes as follows concerning (modern) Florida:

Admiral Pedro Menéndez de Avilés in settling Florida carried with his colony 100 horses and mares, 200 sheep, 400 lambs, and 400 pigs. He established ranches and towns almost simultaneously. Menéndez, with his usual forethought, when organizing his expedition at Cádiz, selected 117 stockmen and farmers among his colonists. Many of the necessary horses he shipped direct from Cádiz, but as it was impossible to obtain sufficient numbers there, the King furnished the remainder from the royal ranches of Hispaniola [and Santo Domingo];[60] and these horses were taken to Florida in 1565. By 1650, this district in the south-eastern part of the present United States had seventy-two missions,

56 Bandelier (ed.), *Journey of Cabeza de Vaca*, 122.
57 See Chapter X *infra*.
58 De Voto, *Across the Wide Missouri*, 143, 430–31.
59 Webb, *The Great Plains*, 168–69.
60 Chard, "Did the First Spanish Horses Leave Progeny?" 95.

eight large towns, and two royal haciendas extending north into present-day Georgia. . . .[61]

The development of the colony did not exhibit the unbroken prosperity that the foregoing summary might suggest. The earlier history of the Menéndez settlement is one of disaster. The first generations of horses were eaten by the famine-stricken people (1566–1573). They were reduced to similar straits recurrently down to about 1601. But they progressed rapidly after 1612, and by 1650 had reached the conditions mentioned.[62] From this important center, horses came into the possession both of the Indians and the English.[63] In the light of the foregoing evidence it seems probable that the Iroquois are to be included among the Indian tribes who obtained their horses from this source; or in any event, most likely their *first* horses. For it seems unthinkable that they would adopt one foreign (i. e., non-Spanish) practice in mounting their new possession, and then exchange it for another (Spanish) one.

None the less, in respect to the date mentioned above (1650), other evidence appears to be of a somewhat conflicting character. Wissler states that in the (modern) Southern states no horses were found among the Indians, 1650–74, but that "traders and explorers used horses, and often left them with the Indians for safe-keeping."[64] It is quite conceivable that trading intercourse with the Iroquois might be carried on through the seaboard territories on the eastern side of the Alleghenies. If this were actually the case, that the mountain barrier interposed an interval of a quarter of a century or more in the advent of the horse among the tribes dwelling respectively on either side, it would cast further doubt on the extremely dubious argument for the supposed "network of trails" which covered the continent, to which reference has been made.

Be this as it may, in Virginia, about 1669, wild horses, originally imported by the "cavalier element" (presumably from England), were a pest.[65] In 1671, Jean Talon, the great Intendant of New France, who did so much for the colony and had imported

---

[61] Denhardt, *Horse of the Americas,* 39–40.
[62] Chard, "Did the First Spanish Horses Leave Progeny?" 95–96.
[63] Denhardt, *Horse of the Americas,* 40.
[64] Wissler, "Influence of the Horse," 8.
[65] *Ibid.,* 7.

horses in considerable numbers (together with other live stock) since the coming of the first horse consignment with its two stallions in 1665, pronounced that further importations into New France were needless, "since they could purchase more from the English colonies, if necessary."[66] Whether the English colonies were those of New England or of the "cavalier element" in Virginia or Maryland is not clear. The needlessness of further importation seems fairly evident, however. A prominent Canadian historian writes as follows:

The large number of horses in [early] Canada was an indication of the character of agriculture and of the use of roads [which were very bad]. The first census showing the number of horses is that of 1681, when there were said to be 94 (36 of which were in Quebec). From then on the figures show a rapid increase: 156 in 1685; 580 in 1695; 5,270 in 1720; and 13,488 in 1765. The last figure represents a proportion of about one horse to every five persons. The government became alarmed lest the increase of horses should interfere with the raising of cattle and issued an ordinance in 1709 restricting each farmer to two horses and a colt. In the following year Vaudreuil [the Governor] wrote to his minister that there were so many horses in Canada that the young men were losing the art of walking, with or without snowshoes. To remedy this, he says, it will be necessary to kill some of the horses; and to avoid loss they can be salted and sold to the savages 'en guise de boeuf.'[67]

Some rough idea of a year's increase may be drawn from the fact that the total rose from 5,270 in 1720 to 5,605 in 1721.[68] This very low ratio of virtually 6.5 per cent scarcely agrees with the official apprehensions of ten years before. It rather suggests an economy in which the use rather than the breeding of horses gave the prevailing tone. I have unfortunately been unable to discover much information concerning dissemination among the neighboring Indian tribes by theft or raiding, analogous to similar agencies in the Southwest. A recent historian of the central trans-Alleghenean area north of the Ohio River speaks of horse stealing by the

[66] Richard M. Saunders, "The First Introduction of European Plants and Animals into Canada," *Canadian Historical Review*, Vol. XVI (1935), 403; Morden H. Long, *A History of the Canadian People*, I, 137.

[67] Glazebrook, *History of Transportation in Canada*, 106.

[68] Long, *History of the Canadian People*, I, 236.

Indians, about 1778 and 1810.[69] Very probably it would be much the same as elsewhere, if numbers permitted.

With the coming of the eighteenth century, the horse had apparently acquired a firm foothold in the Southeast. Le Page du Pratz (1719) and others speak of horses being "numerous" in the South, and seemingly "different from the European horse." This, in Wissler's opinion, suggests a resemblance to Indian horses, and perhaps indicates a cross hailing from Hispano-Indian, trans-Mississippian sources.[70] This hypothesis appears to assume that the Indian horses of the Plains country along the Spanish frontiers had already assumed or developed the characteristically weedy, decadent appearance which has come to be associated with the very term "Indian pony"; and so strongly, moreover, that they could transmit its points in recognizable form to a further cross-bred type. Without any reference whatever to the biological doctrine of the noninheritance of acquired characteristics—which appears to be somewhat less strenuously asserted than formerly—I doubt whether our present knowledge would warrant such an assumption. We do not know whether the somewhat vague term "European horse" specifically recognized and included the Andalusian or the semi-Arab "breed of Córdoba" in the European category. This is doubtful unless our observer was both exceptionally well informed and very precise in his terms. American-bred horses even containing Spanish ancestry could conceivably look quite unlike the (Northern) European horse, without any admixture of deterioration arising from Indian cross-breeding (?) or any sort of mismanagement.

The Iroquois are stated to have been breeding horses for themselves "prior to 1736";[71] although a later scholar considers that horses were rare among them even in the eighteenth century.[72] Their close economic and political connections with the English colonies at this time render it not improbable that they had for some time previously drawn their horse supplies in part at least

[69] Walter Havighurst, *The Land of Promise*, 116, 132.

[70] Wissler, "Influence of the Horse," 7–8, 18.

[71] Grinnell, in Hodge, *Handbook*, I, 569–71.

[72] William N. Fenton, "Problems Arising from the Historic North-Eastern Position of the Iroquois," *Essays in Historical Anthropology in North America* (cited hereafter as *Swanton Memorial Volume*), 230.

from the various English (or Anglo-American) sources, without apparently altering their riding customs, however. And among this varied interplay of forces, there may also have been—perhaps at a later period—an admixture of Western Hispano-Indian stocks. For William Bartram, the botanical traveler, mentions as a familiar tradition of his own time and region (Georgia–Florida, etc., 1773), "nations of Indians who had emigrated [sic] from the west, beyond the Mississippi River." The same writer speaks also of the Hispano-Indian "Siminole" and "Chactaw" horses.[73] A modern student, Thornton Chard, states that the Spanish horse persisted in the Seminole and Chickasaw horses, but does not associate them with any derivation from the post-Menéndez mission stocks in Florida. He considers them to be of a later time (1740–1786), and drawn from sources west of the Mississippi.[74]

In the same broad era, the Cherokee are also singled out for mention as being good horsemen.[75] This may point to a longer acquaintance than that of the region at large. Other fragmentary evidence indicates that the northeastward spread of the Spanish horse influence had a wider range than is commonly associated with it. A contemporary historian, writing of pack horses in the trans-Allegheny area about 1800, has them from "Pennsylvania herds crossed with Spanish [Indian?] pintos from the Southwest," but mentions no distinctive name.[76]

A philological investigation of the horse terminology of the Southeast in general might possibly throw some light upon the chronology and direction (or directions) of any influx of Spanish or Hispano-Indian horses into the region, assuming such to have taken place. It is of course well known that down to the present time the riding terminology of the entire Western territory of the North American continent, far beyond the Spanish-*speaking* range, is dominated by Spanish practice. We have "cinch" (*cincha*—girth), "hackamore" (*háquima* or *jáquima*), "lariat" and "lasso" (*reata de lazar*, or *la reata*—the rope, whence our term "roping," and occasionally "lassooing." I have never yet heard the last term

[73] *The Travels of William Bartram* (ed. by Mark Van Doren), 185, 186.
[74] Chard, "Did the First Spanish Horses Leave Progeny?" 99, 105.
[75] Wissler, citing James Adair (1775), "Influence of the Horse," 7.
[76] Havighurst, *Land of Promise*, 70.

used as noun or verb on the range itself from any true Westerner in the Northern Plains area). There are also "latigo" (*el látigo*—the straps that "cinch 'em up tight"), the popular "rodeo" (*rodear* —to round up), and "cavvy yard" (*caballada*—herd of horses). To these may be added the picturesque—but highly practical—"chaps" (*chaparreras, chaparajos, chaparejos*).[77] I myself fifty years ago heard the word "buck*ayro*" (commonly "buckaroo" in print) from the lips of a northern friend whose mother tongue was Cree. This could be nothing else except the Spanish *vaquero* (b=v), and used in that precise sense of "cowman," which is itself the standard northern term. While one speaks of "the boys" collectively, no northern Westerner speaks of a "cow*boy*." With respect to the Indian adoption of these various appurtenances, a very competent student of a typical Northern Indian horse tribe presents an excellent description, with accurate drawings of native methods both of making and fastening bridles, girths, picket ropes, etc.[78] It would be of high value if such usages, together with their approximate dating, could be recovered from the Indian languages of the Southeast.[79]

In so far as it is possible or safe to generalize, it would seem that the wider adoption of the horse after its first appearance occupied a broadly similar period of time in the territories on either side of the Mississippi; perhaps in some degree accelerated in the West by the greater numbers of the buffalo in a more suitable "horse country."

[77] Dobie (ed.), *Mustangs and Cow Horses*, 272; Paul I. Wellman, *The Trampling Herd*, 32; Denhardt, *Horse of the Americas*, 122–27, 237–39.

[78] Wilson, "Dog and Horse in Hidatsa Culture," 184–89.

[79] Henri de Tonty noted in 1680 that "the Cadodaquis possess about thirty horses, which they call *cavalis*". (Cox [ed.], *Journeys of La Salle*, I, 47–50, 55, 60; cf. Father Douay, *ibid.*, II, 249, 255). The Osage term for horse, "ka-wa," is stated by a competent Indian scholar to be a corruption of the Spanish *caballo* (Francis La Flesche, *A Dictionary of the Osage Language*, Bureau of American Ethnology, *Bulletin* 109, 82, 279). Dorsey and Swanton state that the Biloxi name for the domestic cow, "wak," "waka," or "wax," is from the Spanish *vaca* (*Biloxi Dictionary*). The Choctaw term for domestic cows is the same, "wak," or "wak tek" (Cyrus Byington, *A Dictionary of the Choctaw Language*, Bureau of American Ethnology, *Bulletin 46*). The Natchez stem, "wash" or "was," means dog, horse, bison, or cow (John R. Swanton, "Ethnological Position of the Natchez Indians," *American Anthropologist*, Vol. IX (1907), 513–28).

IV

THE SOUTHERN PLAINS

Such chronological evidence as I have been able to collect is provokingly fragmentary and disjointed. In this particular phase it should of course be remembered that any recorded dates merely mark an era when some tribe is *known* to have possessed the animal; in some instances at what seem absurdly late periods. Wissler rightly emphasizes the fact that there is no reason why some of these tribes or bands may not have had horses long before. For example, he remarks that even such Northern tribes as the Crow and the Blackfoot "may have had horses for one hundred and fifty years before their mention in 1742 and 1751."[1] Quite obviously many of these eras simply record when the first white narrator visited the tribe.

Denhardt observes with reference to the essay of Francis Haines, cited in these pages,[2] that Haines brought out the fact that Wissler "placed horses with the Indians a trifle too early."[3] The earliest hypothetical date in Wissler's paper is where he considers that many tribes should have had horses before 1600.[4] This opinion is endorsed by Walter Prescott Webb, a high authority on Plains history, whose competence is freely acknowledged by Denhardt himself.[5] Presumably the passage upon which Denhardt bases this judgment is that wherein Haines cites the case of Juan

[1] Wissler, "Influence of the Horse," 10.
[2] Haines, "How Did the Indians Get Their Horses?" 112–17, 429–37.
[3] Denhardt, *Horse of the Americas*, 103, 276–77.
[4] Wissler, "Influence of the Horse," 2.
[5] Webb, *The Great Plains*, 115–17; Denhardt, *Horse of the Americas*, 277.

de Oñate's finding no horses in New Mexico in 1600.[6] Gaspar Pérez de Villagrá describes the "deadly fear" of the Indians at Ácoma, followed no great while later by horses being slain by them.[7] Denhardt has overlooked his own reference to Francisco de Ibarra in the Sonora Valley about 1567. In that account we find the tribes—or some of them—in that territory not merely acquainted with the horse, but practiced horsemen at that date.[8] So that in point of fact the very earliest definite dating for Indians as riders that I have encountered in my own inquiries (and seemingly quite authentic) down to the time of Denhardt's publication (1947) is furnished by himself. J. Frank Dobie supplies a far earlier date, however. In the Mixton War of 1541 in Mexico, Mendoza, the viceroy, put allied Aztec chieftains on horseback to lead their men.[9] Taken together with an official ordinance forbidding the natives to ride, this seems like a crowning piece of folly. It was a conclusive demonstration that the mastery of the terrible creature was no occult mystery revealed only to the white strangers.

Wissler considered that among the first tribes to have horses would probably be the Ute, Apache, Comanche, Kiowa, and Caddo (of Texas): an opinion which is weightily but not unanimously endorsed.[10] This would seem to be almost inevitable, following from the merely geographical factors alone. It is thought, as I have mentioned above, that many tribes should have had the horse before 1600.[11] Among these Wissler would include the Kiowa and the Pawnee.[12] A later important authority on the Southwest, Rupert Norval Richardson, discussing the coming of the horse to the Comanche, thinks differently. He notes that the Comanche were "said to have been first seen in New Mexico in 1705." They attacked Taos in 1716. Richardson considers the tribe was not "driven into" the south at all, but advanced thither to obtain more horses. Hence,

---

[6] Haines, "How Did the Indians Get Their Horses?" 116.

[7] Villagrá, *History of New Mexico*, (ed. by Hodge), 172–73, 231.

[8] Denhardt, *Horse of the Americas*, 87–92; see Chapter II *supra*.

[9] Dobie, *The Mustangs*, 25.

[10] Wissler, "Influence of the Horse," 2; *The American Indian*, 30–37; Webb, *The Great Plains*, 115–17, citing Herbert E. Bolton, *Texas in the Eighteenth Century*, which I have not seen.

[11] See previous citations of Wissler and Webb.

[12] Wissler, "Influence of the Horse," 10; see note 32 *infra*.

they had horses before the Kiowa, Cheyenne, or Sioux.[13] While this suggestion is doubtless correct with respect to the last two, in respect to the Kiowa it is in my view highly speculative and beyond proof.

Webb states that the Apache, lying nearer to the Spanish frontiers than the Pawnee at least, but on the other hand more in mountain territory, were apparently still unacquainted with horses in 1593, when the party under Antonio Gutiérrez de Humaña and Francisco de Leyva Bonilla was destroyed.[14] This reference seems inconclusive. This disaster occurred "in the distant north": possibly as far north as the country of the Wichitas on the Arkansas,[15] or even on the Platte,[16] and the Apache were not implicated in the affair. The guide Josephe (or Josepho), who was the only survivor, fell into the hands of the Apache on his way home, but later escaped. He makes no mention of horses among them at this time. D. E. Worcester writes: "It is impossible to determine exactly when the Apaches began using horses otherwise than for food, though very likely it was between 1620 and 1630; possibly earlier, but certainly not later."[17] At a much later date the Apache comprised sixteen divisions, probably of long standing.[18] Some of these might have had horses and others not, at a specified early date.

By the middle of the seventeenth century the Apache appear definitely as a typical horse people. An older historian writes thus:

By 1650 there are reports of horses being used by Indians in conflict with Spaniards. Apaches and Teguas joined in an attempt to overcome the colonists, and horses were stolen to be used in the revolt. The attempt failed and the horses were recovered. The Spaniards believed that they had been delivered by the Christian Indians of Sandia and Alameda.[19]

[13] Richardson, The Comanche Barrier, 19, 24–28, 55, etc.; cf. note 50 infra.
[14] Webb, The Great Plains, 121.
[15] Villagrá, History of New Mexico, (ed. by Hodge), 153.
[16] Bolton (ed.), Spanish Exploration in the Southwest, 200–201, 209, 224, 258–60, and map.
[17] Worcester, "The Spread of Spanish Horses," 226.
[18] Coues (ed.), Expeditions of Pike, II, 748. For a later classification, see John P. Harrington, "Athapaskawan Origins, Divisions, and Migrations," Swanton Memorial Volume, 503–32. Dobie gives Apache as meaning "enemy" in some Pueblo tongue; the name is said to have been applied by the Spanish to Navajo and other hostiles (The Mustangs, 37). This complicates identification.
[19] W. W. H. Davis, The Spanish Conquest of New Mexico (1869), 282.

The earliest definite date given for the Apache in this capacity is 1659, when they made a raid in the upper Río Grande country.[20] In 1672 New Mexico was totally sacked. "Though these forays were attributed mainly to the Apaches, tribes from Texas and the Plains participated in them."[21] We also find 1684 mentioned, and 'plenty after 1687.'[22] There must have been plenty indeed a few years later. For it is stated that "100,000" horses were stolen in 1694 by the Apache and their allies in Sonora and Sinaloa, Mexico.[23] It is probably these depredations to which Padre Eusebio Francisco Kino, the eminent Spanish missionary, has reference:

It was said that in the interior there were horses stolen from the province of Sonora, and since I know the contrary to be a fact, and that not these Pimas [evidently his own protégés] but the Hocomes, Apaches, and Janos, who were committing these injuries, stealing horses from this province and its frontiers. . . . In no place did we find the least trace of horses stolen from this province of Sonora.[24]

The "100,000" are, I believe, our earliest example of prodigious numbers. They will not be the last. In this very era, Fray Nicholas de Hurtado wrote from El Paso (1682): ". . . during the present month of January there have been stolen two hundred animals."[25] Not much of a contribution toward 100,000!

A careful scholar has preserved some interesting sidelights on the conditions of the time. Father Massanet wrote in 1689:

The Apaches . . . have always had wars with the Spaniards, for although truces have been made they have endured little. In the end they conquer all the tribes, yet it is said they are not brave because they fight with armoured horses.

[20] Francis V. Scholes, "Troublous Times in New Mexico," *New Mexico Historical Review*, Vol. XII (1937), 137–74; cited by Haines, "How Did the Indians Get Their Horses?" 117. The Apache had horses "in considerable numbers" by 1660 (George E. Hyde, "The Mystery of the Arikaras," *North Dakota History*, Vol. XVIII [1951], 190).

[21] Worcester, "The Spread of Spanish Horses," 227–28.

[22] Webb, *The Great Plains*, 115–17.

[23] Hubert Howe Bancroft, *History of the North Mexican States and Texas, 1531–1889*, I, 255.

[24] Bolton (ed.), *Spanish Exploration in the Southwest*, 447–52, 458, 462.

[25] Worcester, "The Spread of Spanish Horses," 228.

Writing from *Nueva Viscaya*, 1680, apropos of forays by the Apache, Cibola, and other nomadic tribes, it was said:

. . . they are voracious when they steal some cattle and horses (which is what they most eagerly desire), since they secure in this way two ends, first their maintenance, for their greatest treat is this kind of food, and second, as a result of the [Spanish] inhabitants being forced to go on foot, they are able without resistance to obtain possession of the province.

Their technique is described by José Francisco Marin, relating to the Indians of Parral (1693):

Their first care is to strike down the horses. This, with the great skill that attends them in the use of such arms, they easily accomplish. . . . If they perceive they cannot make the attack without danger to themselves they keep quiet—all of them as is their custom, being painted and varnished the same color as the earth and generally covered with *sacatón* [grass]—and permit the travellers to pass. . . .

In their robberies of horses they use the same methods. They keep watch on ranches and pastures, and upon the slightest carelessness they drive off the animals, not more than three or four being employed in such robberies. . . . Their principal food consists of horses and mules. . . .

The "law of diminishing returns" (Cerro Gordo, July, 1693):

. . . the ancient enemies, who under the name of Tobosos [?] have invaded these kingdoms 'for many years, are now driven by necessity itself and their own bad disposition to increase the ravages for, having consumed the thousands of horses and cattle that roamed through these lands, they have now no recourse except to seize those raised by the Spaniards on their estates, committing frequent outrages that they did not formerly commit so often.[26]

The Pawnee are believed by Grinnell to have had horses early in the eighteenth century.[27] The Pawnee have a story that the first horse they ever saw came into their village and permitted itself

[26] *Ibid.*, 228, 239–42.
[27] Grinnell, in Hodge, *Handbook*, I, 569–71. For the first horse: Wissler, "Influence of the Horse," 10.

to be handled. If we accept the horse, who answers for the Pawnee? It was *their* first time, as well as the horse's. It seems incredible that as late as 1600 no prior word of the horse could have reached the Pawnee. It is even more incredible that without such preliminary knowledge they would dare to handle this first horse, or even think of handling it, any more than they would handle a wolf or a grizzly bear! A later scholar considers they were "mounted," which possibly signifies equipped in force, about 1700.[28] But both Wissler and Harrison C. Dale speak of Pawnee raids into the Spanish territory in the early seventeenth century;[29] and Alice Fletcher mentions Pawnee horse raids in the early years of the century.[30] Wissler also notes a post being established in Kansas about 1704 to check Pawnee horse-stealing forays.[31] Possibly as a feature of the same policing, or perhaps as reprisals, an expedition under Villasur was sent against the Pawnee in 1720, which met with no success. He was defeated by a combined force of Oto and Skidi (Wolf Pawnee or Pawnee Loup), the latter of whom are said to have obtained horses only in 1715.[32]

Du Tisné, a French officer, found a related tribe, the Toucara (Wichita) mounted a few years after 1717, "and saddles and bridles similar to those of the Spaniards."[33] Worcester, in citing this, does not say whether the identification at that early date as the Wichita is based upon anything weightier than the geographical proximity, or whether it is that of his authority, Pierre Margry, or his own. Geographical proximity apparently meant little in itself. In 1724, De Bourgmont found the "Canzas" on the lower Missouri moving camp with their belongings loaded on the womens' backs and on

28 Webb, *The Great Plains*, 57.
29 Wissler, "Influence of the Horse," 10; Harrison C. Dale (ed.), *The Ashley-Smith Explorations, and the Discovery of a Central Route to the Pacific, 1822–1829*, 122.
30 Hodge, *Handbook*, II, 214.
31 Wissler, "Influence of the Horse," 2, 5–6.
32 *Ibid.* For the Oto and Skidi: Hyde, "Mystery of the Arikaras," 206–207. An informed and critical scholar writes that Pedro Martínez (1720) "is undoubtedly correct in his statement that the horse had not reached the Pawnee by 1720." (Thomas, *After Coronado*, 277, n. 144.) But according to Thomas himself, this assumption appears to rest upon nothing more than an inference by Martínez (cf. *ibid.*, 14, n. 30, 171–73); which may or may not have been correct, apart from that particular band of Pawnee, then about at North Platte, Nebraska.
33 D. E. Worcester, "Spanish Horses among the Plains Tribes," *The Pacific Historical Review*, Vol. XIV (1945), 409.

dog travois. Farther to the southwest he met the Padouca (Comanche?) both riding and packing goods on horses.[34]

In 1719, Du Tisné counted three hundred horses at two Pawnee villages in modern Oklahoma. He procured from them two horses and a mule bearing a Spanish brand.[35] Haines, however, cites Du Tisné at the same date as stating horses among the Pawnee to be "scarce at that time, highly valued and not for sale."[36] "Scarce" is of course a purely relative term. We do not know the numbers of the Pawnee in this era, nor their normal strength in horseflesh. A century later the Grand Pawnee, Republican Pawnee, and Skidi combined mustered some two thousand warriors.[37] In such conditions three hundred horses could still constitute scarcity. In 1806, they appear to have been well equipped. Zebulon M. Pike writes thus concerning their horse economy:

With respect to raising horses, the Pawnees are far superior to the Osage, having vast quantities of excellent horses which they are daily increasing, by their attention to their brood mares, which they never make use of; and in addition they frequently purchase from the Spaniards.[38]

J. Frank Dobie considers that the Pawnee "probably had better horses than any other tribe on the eastern flanks of the Great Plains,"[39] which, if correct, in itself necessitates very considerable numbers. We do not know what were Pike's numerical standards of "vast quantities," but even without his direct statement, the exemption of their brood mares from work clearly necessitated plenty of others to take their place. And whether the quality or the quantity of the Pawnee stock was the lure, the most recent commentator states that the "chief reliance" of the Cheyenne for recruiting their own horse strength was on raiding from other tribes such as the Pawnee, the Comanche, and the Kiowa.[40] Evidently the Pawnee

---

[34] Dobie, *The Mustangs*, 39.
[35] Wissler, "Influence of the Horse," 2, 5–6.
[36] Francis Haines, "The Northward Spread of Horses among the Plains Indians," *American Anthropologist*, Vol. XL (1938), 433.
[37] See Roe, *North American Buffalo*, App. G, 743–44.
[38] Coues (ed.), *Expeditions of Pike*, II, 533.
[39] Dobie, *The Mustangs*, 57–58.
[40] Jablow, *The Cheyenne*, 16.

were worth the trouble; and as the nearest tribe to the Cheyenne, they probably suffered heavily enough. This was only poetic justice; they did plenty of raiding themselves.

The Utes (or Eutaws—from whom is derived the later name of Utah), together with the division called Pah-Utes, i.e., Paiutes, apparently possessed the horse about 1700; and very possibly, as Wissler considers likely enough, as early as 1600.[41]

Wissler has the Kiowa possessing horses by 1682, on the authority of La Salle, who visited them in that year.[42] Here again, while this is the earliest apparently direct verification, Wissler's own conjectural date of about 1600 is probably quite sound. The Kiowa are one of those tribes which were incessantly raiding and being raided during a period of more than two centuries. Their resources in horseflesh would almost seem to have produced a state of mind, if we may judge from their profuseness at the Great Peace of 1840 between the Kiowa, Comanche, and Prairie Apache on the one side, and the Cheyenne and Arapaho on the other; and this at a time when the horse resources of some of the supposedly wealthiest Northern tribes are being seriously questioned by modern criticism, as we shall later see. When the peace was finally concluded, the Kiowa gave horses wholesale to the Cheyenne: "All the other Kiowas gave many horses, but Sa tank' [the chief] gave the most; they say that he gave away two hundred and fifty horses. Some unimportant men and women received four, five, or six horses, but the chiefs received the most. The Cheyennes did not have enough ropes to lead back their horses; they were obliged to drive them across in bunches."[43]

It may be noted, furthermore, that the foregoing are not to be taken as a common tribal stock. J. Frank Dobie says respecting this: "It is to be borne in mind that no horses were tribally owned. They were all owned by individual tribesmen, and some individuals, it seems, maintained a special line of breeding horses."[44]

[41] Dale (ed.), *Ashley-Smith Explorations*, 151; Wissler, "Influence of the Horse," 2.

[42] Wissler, *ibid.*, 2, 6; Webb, *The Great Plains*, 57; Worcester, "The Spread of Spanish Horses," 228.

[43] Jablow, *The Cheyenne*, 74–76 (quoting Grinnell, *The Fighting Cheyennes*).

[44] J. Frank Dobie, "Indian Horses and Horsemanship," *Southwest Review*, Vol. XXXV (Autumn, 1950), 274; *The Mustangs*, 43.

While this appears to have been pretty universally true *de jure*, there were no doubt modifications *de facto*. We have seen above a common (family) ownership of dogs, which could very logically be adapted to the horse; and Mandelbaum states that while some one individual *owned* horse or gun among the Cree, these might be used by his relatives.[45]

Jacob Fowler in 1821 described the Kiowa (together with the Comanche) as having great numbers of very fine horses, which Fowler considered equal to any he had ever known. The great village on the Arkansas River, comprising over seven hundred lodges of Kiowa, Comanche, Snake, Arapaho, and Cheyenne, contained a total of twenty thousand horses, of which from four hundred to five hundred were stolen after Fowler's arrival.[46] This of course only averages about one horse each for the estimated human population; but for pasturage reasons alone it is unlikely that many extra horses would have been brought along. It is quite clear, however, that in the period culminating about 1850 the Kiowa were among the wealthier tribes in respect to horses.[47]

The Southwestern horsemen par excellence, both in numbers and in horsemanship, were beyond doubt the Comanche. Dobie says: "The dominance of the Comanches as horse people is unquestioned. Their horses varied widely in quality, but probably no more widely than the Spanish supply from which they constantly drew."[48] To "ride like a Comanche" became a Western proverb.[49] We have noted their first (reputed) appearance in New Mexico in 1705. We must assume them to be horsemen at that time. What seems to be the first positive identification of the Comanche as horsemen is not until 1714, when La Harpe visited them.[50] But

[45] Mandelbaum, "The Plains Cree," 204–205.
[46] Elliott Coues (ed.), *The Journal of Jacob Fowler*, 59–61.
[47] Jablow, *The Cheyenne*, 59–60, 67–68, 73, 76, 79, 80.
[48] Dobie, "Indian Horses and Horsemanship," 273; *The Mustangs*, 60, 63–72.
[49] Wellman, *The Trampling Herd*, 41.
[50] Wissler, "Influence of the Horse," 6; Webb, *The Great Plains*, 57. Wissler (p. 2) couples the Comanche, Kiowa, and Tonkawa together as acquiring the horse in the period 1600–1682. The last are described by J. W. Powell as *colluvies gentium*, a fusion of tribes. See Coues (ed.), *Expeditions of Pike*, II, 705; Wissler, *The American Indian*, 237; Bishop, *Odyssey of Cabeza de Vaca*, 94. The Comanche were estimated, about 1690, at some 1,600 souls (James Mooney, "The Aboriginal Population of America North of Mexico" [ed. by John R. Swanton], *Smithsonian Miscellaneous Collections*, Vol. LXXX, No. 7, p. 13).

to doubt that they had been daring and skilful horsemen considerably before that date would entail the rejection both of overwhelming probabilities and of actual knowledge concerning the swift adaptability of the Indian in this precise field of horsemanship, as recorded of the earliest natives to encounter the animal. Wissler reminds us: "In every case, however, we must assume an earlier date for its [the horse's] introduction. There is no good reason why the Pawnees should not have had horses in 1650 or even in 1630."[51] Even without this, it is sufficiently clear that the Comanche country at large was perfectly familiar with the horse long before 1714.

In Pike's day, "the Tetaus, whom the Spanish term Camanches," were still carrying their horse raids into Mexico, as they had long done, and continued to do for another half-century. Pike tells us that on one occasion they swept away as many as two thousand head of horses from a single village at one fell swoop. This place was Ojo Caliente, in the Río Grande region.[52] General Thomas James was told by the Comanche in 1823 that they possessed sixteen thousand horses.[53] In Gregg's time (1831–1840), the Comanche raids on Mexico still maintained their evil fame.[54] In 1852, Marcy found the tribe still dependent upon theft and trade.[55] As a contemporary scholar expresses the situation:

The expanding Spanish empire stopped short when it reached the Great Plains. . . . The Spaniards were not even able to protect their settlements founded within reach of the Comanches, must less to subdue the Indians themselves. . . . The savages not only held the South Plains but made life and property unsafe in communities hundreds of miles south and west of the Rio Grande.

. . . the Comanches rather than the Spaniards had come to be the aggressors. Their raids extended farther and farther into the North Mexican settlements, and were far more destructive than when they were first begun.[56]

Down to as late as 1850 the Comanche still ranged as far south

[51] Wissler, "Influence of the Horse," 6; cf. note 32 *supra*.
[52] Coues (ed.), *Expeditions of Pike*, II, 537, 600.
[53] Dobie, *The Mustangs*, 71.
[54] Gregg, *Commerce of the Prairies*, in Thwaites, *Travels*, XX, 347; cf. Thwaites, *Travels*, XXVIII, 150, editor's note.
[55] Marcy, *Exploration of the Red River*, 106.
[56] Richardson, *The Comanche Barrier*, 75.

as Durango (Mexico). The raids into both Mexico and Texas, which had been notorious as early as 1780 and were probably not new at that date, persisted down to the eve of the Civil War. With such a ready scapegoat at hand, one is not surprised to note that in the nineteenth century, "Indian" horse stealing was sometimes the work of lawless white men.[57]

An old plainsman says the Comanche "thought the Great Spirit had created horses especially for them."[58] To judge from observers' enthusiastic comments on Comanche horsemanship, one might think the tribe had been created especially for horses! Catlin, who had seen the Northern horse tribes, thought the Comanche the best of all. He had heard of their wonderful horses and was eager to see them. On his arrival at the Comanche camp he rode out to see a herd of "at least 3000 horses and mules" ranging on the plain. Like so many Indian horses, to Catlin they were apparently better than their looks. "Although there were some tolerable nags among this medley group of all colors and shapes, [they were] generally small, of the wild breed, tough and serviceable. . . ."[59] Ferdinand Roemer, the German scientist, visiting a Comanche camp in 1847, thought their horses "unsightly and small." Dobie remarks that he no doubt took heavy German horses as his ideal.[60] In the famous race described by Colonel Dodge at Fort Chadbourne, the officers' Kentucky mare was beaten by a "miserable sheep of a pony"; on which his contemptuous Comanche jockey rode backwards, beckoning his American rival with "hideous grimaces" to come on a little faster![61]

Our foregoing suggestions respecting Comanche horse chronology find logical if not factual confirmation in the fact that horses were actually found much earlier than 1714 in much less typically horse tribes. The Iowa, who seem to

[57] *Ibid.*, 49, 67–75, 190, 193–205, 243, 250. I recall an old boyhood favorite dealing with this precise region (Mayne Reid, *The White Chief*), in which the heroine was abducted by the local Spanish officers, disguised as Indians.

[58] James K. Greer, in Dobie (ed.), *Mustangs and Cow Horses*, 331.

[59] Catlin, *Letters and Notes*, II, 57–60. Denhardt considers the Kiowa and the Comanche were 'probably the best Indian horsemen' (*Horse of the Americas*, 102).

[60] Dobie, "Indian Horses and Horsemanship," 274; *The Mustangs*, 72.

[61] Dodge, *Our Wild Indians*, 341–42.

have been in 1682 very much where Wissler's map places them, in the western portion of that state and far back from the Mississippi River, are described by Wissler as having been first visited by Father Zenobius (Membre) in 1676; while the earliest mention of horses among them is in 1724.[62] Yet the Missouri (tribe of) Indians, whom Wissler places in that state and on the Missouri River virtually at the Mississippi confluence near St. Louis, were visited by Henri de Tonty in 1682, and are credited with having horses at that time. Tonty wrote: "There are even villages which use horses to go to war and to carry the carcasses of the cattle [buffalo] which they kill."[63] Tonty refers also in 1682 to the Caddo (Cadadoguis, Cadodaquis, or Caddodachos), who were neighbors and kindred of the Natchez (Naouadichés, Nacogdoches, or Natchitoches), and apparently living near Natchez, Mississippi. He says: "The Cadodaquis possess about thirty horses, which they call *cavalis.*" He adds with reference to the other tribe (Natchez?):

I told the chief I wanted four horses for my return, and having given him seven hatchets and a string of large glass beads, they gave me the next day four Spanish horses, two of which were marked on the haunch with an 'R' and a crown above it, and another with an 'N'. Horses are very common among them. There is not a cabin which has not four or five. As this nation is sometimes at war with the Spaniards, they take advantage of a war to carry off their horses.[64]

Where these southern horses came from admits of little doubt, even had there been any others than the Spaniards as a possible source of supply in that territory. We have noted the Indian use of the term *cavalis.* Furthermore, M. Jean Cavelier, the brother of La Salle, mentions their party's meeting with horsed Indians who spoke Spanish (February 16, 1687): ". . . we left this great village [of the Caddo] for the smaller one of the same nation, twenty

[62] Wissler, "Influence of the Horse," 6; and the map, in his *The American Indian.* I cannot understand this "1676." Should it not be 1682? Nor can I find anything to support Father Membre's being supposed so far west from the "Riviére Colbert" (Mississippi) in that latitude, about 41° N.

[63] Wissler, "Influence of the Horse," 2, 6; Webb, *The Great Plains,* 57; Worcester, "The Spread of Spanish Horses," 229.

[64] Tonty, in Cox (ed.), *Journeys of La Salle,* I, 47–50, 55, 60; also Father Douay, *ibid.,* II, 249, 255; cf. Worcester, "The Spread of Spanish Horses," 229. On these identifications, see Appendix A *infra.*

leagues off. Thirty well-mounted young warriors took us by as well-beaten a road as that from Paris to Orleans." The Spanish-speaking Indians had horses to sell,[65] and "cheaply," says Father Douay;[66] which may or may not (after Tonty's experience) be considered an indication of plenty. In an earlier chapter we have noted other details of Spanish horse-usages among Indians. William Bartram's remarks, to which attention has been drawn,[67] may perhaps indicate, through the medium of the trans-Mississippi eastward-bound migration which he mentions, an even more rapid dissemination of those practices than might otherwise have been the case.

Another reference to the year 1724 opens up a question of some importance. It tends in my opinion to emphasize the need for caution in assuming that a specific date in a given general locality can safely be regarded as definite evidence of a progressive or connected advance of the horse northward from the Río Grande territory toward the Missouri River country. M. de Bourgmont, a French officer from New Orleans, is cited as having found a few in a Comanche village on the Missouri, at the mouth of the Kansas River, in 1724,[68] according to Richardson.[69] This is the site of the present-day Kansas City. "A few" at this point in 1724 cannot be accepted as definite evidence either of numerical ratios or of the geography of the horse advance. For we have much more specific testimony—certainly in Wissler's opinion, which seems sound—concerning its presence and utilization some considerable distance farther northward and eastward over forty years earlier, in 1682.

Father Zenobius Membre writes (1682) as follows: "The Indians assured us that inland, towards the west, there are animals on which men ride and which carry very heavy loads; they described them as horses, and showed us two feet, which were actually hoofs of horses."[70]

These people are identified by Wissler as the Metontonta (Oto).[71] Father Membre apparently neither specifies his inform-

[65] Cavelier, in Cox (ed.), *Journeys of La Salle*, I, 290–92, 298.
[66] Douay, *ibid.*, I, 240.
[67] See Chapter III *supra*.
[68] Haines, "The Northward Spread of Horses," 433.
[69] Richardson, *The Comanche Barrier*, 26.
[70] Membre, in Cox (ed.), *Journeys of La Salle*, I, 154.
[71] Wissler, "Influence of the Horse," 2.

ants nor the particular tribe (if any) to which they refer. The passage itself occurs in a mere general description of the country along the Colbert and Seignelay Rivers (Mississippi and Illinois). The party were on their return journey up the Mississippi, 1682; and Wissler's map[72] locates the Oto very much as in Lewis and Clark's time, in the southeastern corner of Nebraska, near the Missouri River. Wissler himself observes: ". . . very few of the Plains tribes are known to have permanently shifted their homes during the period 1680–1860. We must therefore accept their positions as we find them at the opening of the historical period."[73] This view seems to be well borne out by the incidental evidence at large.

Reviewing the various evidence, it seems quite clear that this encounter of 1724 reveals a local condition which chanced to exist in that vicinity at that particular time, and which is valueless as precise chronological-geographical evidence at large. It is in my opinion a parallel case to some of those erratic absences of the buffalo from commonly favored haunts, which misled various observers into pronouncing them "extinct" in this or that locality at absurdly early dates.[74]

A similar caution seems to be required with respect to certain dates relating to Texas. Considering its relative proximity to *Nueva España*, the history of the actual introduction of the horse into Texas is curiously obscure. There is at least one case of genuine "abandonment" in this general region of the Southern Plains area. The *Journal* of Diego Perez de Luxán, who was a member of Antonio de Espejo's expedition of 1582–83, states that in 1581, the year previous to their own party, a sorrel horse was left behind by Francisco Chamuscado with the Caguate, "who talked to it as if it were a person."[75] Here again, however, there are the usual cruxes, and as insurmountable as ever. We are not told whether the Spaniards recovered this animal or not, nor even whether it was a mare or a stallion. As we have noted, the chances of surviving progeny

[72] End-paper map, in his *The American Indian*.

[73] Wissler, "Influence of the Horse," 13.

[74] See Roe, *North American Buffalo*, 182, 188, 265, 356, 386, 394, 586, 864, etc.

[75] George P. Hammond and Agapito Rey (eds.), *The Expedition into New Mexico Made by Antonio de Espejo, as Revealed in the Journal of Diego Perez de Luxán*, 67. The Caguates are identified with, or were a band of, the Otomoacos or Amotomanco, dwelling along the Río Grande, about 31° N, 105° W (*ibid.*, 31, 33).

85

from one pregnant mare are almost hopeless; and whether this were so or not, we have no mention of any later allusion from any chronicler to any such consequences arising from this case. Even had such been the case, coming as it did at an era forty years later than the first advance of mounted Spaniards into neighboring regions (very much over Hernando de Alvarado's trail of 1541, thinks Bolton[76]), and being of a character such as might occur at any time, it is doubtful whether it could have been correctly termed the "origin" of the Indian horses of Texas in any accurate sense. Whether as a result of this horse's arousing a desire for further acquaintance, or whether some intertribal information of the "bush telegraph" order had trickled through to them, we are not informed, but the Otomoacos are mentioned by Luxán as attacking their horses at midnight, in December, 1582.[77] No mention is made of any actual losses, however, on this occasion.

The dates concerning the occupation of Texas by the Spaniards, and the first expeditions into the territory, are somewhat contradictory. Denhardt writes as follows:

In 1625 Nueva León was given to Martínez de Závala, who capably managed this frontier for two-score years. One of the best known of Závala's lieutenants was Alonzo de León, who was also one of the first men responsible for taking horses and cattle into Texas.

In 1665, one of the first recorded expeditions to cross the Río Grande was led by Azcué from Monterrey. . . . The Janamberes Indians revolted, attacked the settlements in 1675, and forced the Spaniards to withdraw hurriedly. . . . In this raid the Indians got . . . large numbers of horses. . . . The natives successfully drove away some two hundred broken horses.

In 1687 Alonzo de León made his first expedition into Texas. When we keep in mind the first two paragraphs, it is not surprising that he found mounted natives. On his first venture he took almost five hundred horses and descended the Río Grande to the Gulf. He made two more trips in the next two years. . . . On each trip he took between five hundred and one thousand horses and mules. In 1689, León speaks of encountering mounted Indians on his trip to Texas.[78]

[76] Bolton (ed.), *Spanish Exploration in the Southwest*, 166.
[77] Luxán, *Journal* (ed. by Hammond and Rey), 55.
[78] Denhardt. *Horse of the Americas*, 98–99.

Denhardt, who cites a rich bibliography, particularly in contemporary and (later) critical Spanish material, has consulted sources which I have been unable to see. Yet his chronology seems peculiar, in the light of other evidence. In an expedition of that character León might quite easily represent (or even suppose) himself to have been the first to see mounted Indians in that territory. He might also suppose himself to have been the first to *take* Spanish horses across the Río Grande into Texas. It seems extraordinary that a principal lieutenant of a governor who held office 1625–65 could have made his first trip into that (or an adjacent) territory only in 1687. But in view of the fact that in 1675 the Texas Indians "successfully drove away some two hundred broken horses," it certainly is not surprising that León found horsed Indians there in 1687.

The problem is further complicated by the assertion of Haines that there were no horses in Texas in 1675, and that the first specific mention of them among the Indians of Texas is from the Mendoza-López expedition of 1683–84.[79] In so far as specific mention is concerned, this appears to be correct. Spanish horses had been in Texas, however, long before this. An expedition under Diego del Castillo visited the territory in 1650, and another expedition was apparently there in 1654.[80] We have also noted the party under Azcué in 1665.[81] In none of these cases is there any definite allusion to their horses having been driven off by the Indians, but judging from the rather common experience of later explorers, it seems extremely probable.[82]

The Mendoza expedition of 1683–84, to which reference has been made, records experiences of horse depredations which might themselves furnish a good beginning for the stocking of Texas, were it not that on this very trip they were *met* by mounted In-

[79] Haines, "How did the Indians Get Their Horses?" 117 (citing Bolton [ed.], *Spanish Exploration in the Southwest*, 330).

[80] Bolton, *ibid.*, 314. Bolton remarks re Mendoza's journey of 1683 that no expedition is mentioned since 1654 (*ibid.*, 337).

[81] See the citation from Denhardt, note 78 *supra*.

[82] There is some strange critical confusion here. Haines cites the same work of Bolton (as we have seen), wherein the very relation he quotes contains the evidence presented above, which refutes his statement. Denhardt likewise, with Haines's essay at hand, which he cites (and also commends: *Horse of the Americas*, 277), makes no comment on Haines's assertion, re 1675, were it only for immediate rejection.

dians. They journeyed to the country of the Tejas (or Texas), fifteen or twenty days eastward of the La Junta region, which is the
junction of the Concho River (of Mexico) with the Río Grande,
and apparently (in Bolton's opinion) reached the Tejas about the
Río Colorado of Texas, near its junction with the main Concho
River. The Tejas are described as being in 1684 "a settled people
. . . [who] raised grain in such abundance that they even fed it
to their horses."[83] The adoption of this practice, and on something
like a major scale, seems to indicate horse ownership of relatively
lengthy standing. If these Tejas be the same as Castañeda's "Teyas,"
the latter are classed by a contemporary critic as Lipanan Apache.[84]

From other Apaches, possibly more unsettled roving bands,
they received various unwelcome attentions on their journey. They
"lost" some horses on December 26, 1683, in the Pecos River country, and apparently after reaching the Tejas more horses were
driven off by the Apaches, January 18–25; more were lost, January
29, and in February (1684), there were more thefts by the Apaches,
both from their own party and from the Jumanos.[85] In Alonzo de
León's *Itinerary* of the 1689–90 expedition, there are plentiful allusions to the likelihood of the Apache's stampeding their horses, but
there is no mention of them as the actual cause when stampedes
occurred. On April 9, 1689, a stampede was noted in which "one
hundred and two got away." These were found at various points
next day, but whether *in toto* or otherwise is not specified. On
April 17, 1689, over one hundred horses stampeded. Of these, sixty-
four or more were recovered the next day, but thirty-six were still
missing.[86]

One conclusion seems reasonably certain among these various
contradictions, apparent or real. It may be taken for granted that
many of these "first mentions" merely record when the earliest (or
thought to be the earliest) European *narrator* visited a tribe which
may have had horses for a considerable time already. Further, the
omission of any reference to the horse in any region in these (locally) early eras must be regarded as an omission in the particular
document in question, and nothing more. Any conclusions we

[83] Bolton (ed.), *Spanish Exploration in the Southwest*, 314–15, 324, 330–37.
[84] See Appendix A *infra*.
[85] Bolton (ed.), *Spanish Exploration in the Southwest*, 324, 331–35.
[86] *Ibid.*, 393, 396.

choose to draw from it, however reasonable in themselves, are conjectural. In the case of these late seventeenth-century testimonies,
an amply sufficient time had elapsed since Spanish horses are
known—or at least asserted—to have been run off by Indians of
these southern territories, for the progeny, either by contratribal
raiding or intertribal trading or by genuine strays from their stocks,
to have reached Texas, or even more distant regions. It may furthermore, I think, be reasonably urged that this stealthy approach
to the horses, rather than mere panic flight, logically implies some
degree of foreknowledge of these creatures, and of their probable
(or proven) value in the Indian economy. Denhardt mentions the
fact that on early maps Texas is marked as "Wild Horse Desert."[87]
J. Frank Dobie gives this region as being between the Río Grande
and the Nueces River; and the maps as dating 1834, 1846, etc.[88]
Neither scholar makes any comment concerning the probable age
of the name. The language of this place name makes it fairly certain that the name is not older than the nineteenth century. Had it
dated from earlier times, it would most probably have been *Llano
de los Caballos Cimarrones*, or the like, which would most likely
have been recorded, if not retained.

The Southern Plains country as a material source of supply
for more northerly tribes had assumed a somewhat different character by the nineteenth century. As a modern commentator points
out, the premier horse people of the Southwest, the Comanche, had
spread themselves across the logical route to the Spanish settlements, the eastern flank of the Rockies. Any tribe farther north
wishing to raid the Spanish herds had now to find or fight their
way past the Comanche barrier. While it was no doubt more difficult in a given instance to steal horses from the Comanche than
from the Spaniards, an incessant policy of raids along a wide fron-
tal range, together with an enormous saving of time and mileage
from the Arkansas or Cimarron River southward to Mexico, combined to make raids on the Comanche very attractive and popular.
The Comanche recouped themselves for their losses by those tremendous onslaughts on the Spanish *rancherías* to which allusion
has been made earlier in this chapter. It was largely the difficulties
arising from this situation that led to the consummation of the

87 Denhardt, *Horse of the Americas*, 101.
88 Dobie, *The Mustangs*, 106, 215, 330.

Great Peace of 1840 between the Comanche, Kiowa, and Prairie Apache on the one hand and the Cheyenne and Arapaho on the other. Much of the purpose of this pact, and certainly much of its prime effect, was to convert raiding very largely into trading; on the northern side of the Comanche barrier at least. Whether by raiding or trading, it may be considered fairly certain that most of the Spanish brands seen in the northern areas from time to time had passed through Comanche hands, with occasional exceptions.[89] The Pawnee are a case in point of the adoption of this mercantile economy, in part at least. Raiding had changed very materially into trading in Pike's day (1807).[90]

We have notices of Northern tribes penetrating considerably to the south. In some instances it seems to have been rather taken for granted by distant northern observers that their southern objective must necessarily have been Mexico, while in other cases we have more reliable evidence. David Thompson mentions an encounter between Piegans and Spaniards about 1787, at approximately "32 north latitude"; near where the Río Grande enters Mexico, resulting in much spoil in Spanish horses and saddles.[91] In reference to the same era, Alexander Mackenzie writes as follows:

The Picaneaux [Piegans], Black-Feet, and Bloods . . . are the people who deal in horses, and take [capture] them upon the war-parties toward Mexico from which it is evident that the country to the South-East of them consists of plains, as these animals could not well be conducted through an hilly and wooded country, intersected by wastes.[92]

Maximilian describes the Sioux (1833):

Many of the Sioux are rich, and have twenty or more horses, which they obtained originally from the Spaniards on the Mississippi, and the frontier of New Mexico on the Oregon, but which are now found in great numbers among the several Indian nations.

They trade . . . with the Spaniards of Santa Fé, as appears from

[89] Jablow, *The Cheyenne*, 67–77, etc.

[90] Coues (ed.), *Expeditions of Pike*, II, 533–36. Stephen H. Long's party, a dozen years after Pike, noted Pawnee horses with Spanish brands, and their large numbers: 'six-thousand or eight-thousand' (James, *Account of the Expedition under Long*, in Thwaites, *Travels*, XV, 207–208, 215).

[91] Thompson, *Narrative* (ed. by Tyrrell), 370, 371.

[92] Mackenzie, *General History of the Fur Trade*, prefixed to his *Voyages from Montreal in 1789 and 1793*, lxviii–lxix.

the Spanish blankets, crosses, etc., which they wear. There is probably no reason to doubt that they take most of these things in war, for the rifles, compasses, etc., which we found in their possession, were marked with the names of the owners.[93]

In addition to the movements mentioned above, there were also the "Flatheads" (?) along the Colorado River in 1810 (where they doubtless obtained the Spanish saddles that attracted Gabriel Franchère's notice[94]), as also the—then undivided—Cheyenne in 1811,[95] and likewise the Shoshone in 1825.[96] There were Atsina and Blackfoot below the Arkansas River in 1826;[97] and Sioux, Gros Ventre (which may signify at that date either Atsina or Hidatsa), and Blackfoot on the Cimarron River in 1829–1831.[98] Whether these various expeditions to such distant points at that era were for purposes of raiding or trading I am unaware.[99]

Wissler mentions a curious circumstance, which may throw some light on these long-continued forays, long after the tribes might reasonably have been expected to be self-supporting in horse matters. The afore-mentioned Padouca-Comanche stated in 1724 that they had not yet been able to raise any colts.[100] Wissler himself says: "Horse raiding was broken up with great difficulty [by whom?] and it was many years before the Indians made any headway with the increase of their own herds."[101] Yet surely the Indian

[93] Maximilian, *Travels*, in Thwaites, *Travels*, XXII, 310; XXIII, 96. Whether this is anything beyond contemporary local opinion is impossible to say.

[94] Gabriel Franchère, *A Voyage to the Northwest Coast of America, 1811–1814*, in Thwaites, *Travels*, VI, 341–42.

[95] Washington Irving, *Astoria*, in *Complete Works*, VIII, 205, 206, 262. The Cheyenne divided into Northern and Southern about 1820 (Jablow, *The Cheyenne*, 60).

[96] James O. Pattie, *Personal Narrative, 1824–1830*, in Thwaites, *Travels*, XVIII, 138. They were still within the 'Shoshonean range,' according to Hubert Howe Bancroft, *Native Races of the Pacific States*, I, 460–70; III, 670–79; cf. Wissler, "Influence of the Horse," 23; *The American Indian*, 224, 409.

[97] Jablow, *The Cheyenne*, 62.

[98] Gregg, *Commerce of the Prairies*, in Thwaites, *Travels*, XIX, 221–39.

[99] See, on Plains Indian trade relations, Jablow, *The Cheyenne*, 27–77.

[100] Wissler, "Influence of the Horse," 21.

[101] *Ibid.*, 21, 22. It is not clear whether Wissler here refers to action by the United States Government, or earlier by the Spanish authorities. Pike notes the efforts of the Spanish government in Mexico, about 1807, to turn the roving and marauding tribes toward agriculture (Coues [ed.], *Expeditions of Pike*, II, 785). After the fruitless (U. S.) expeditions of 1832–33, Leavenworth and Dodge in 1835 finally established contact with the Comanche and paved the way for further treaties (Jablow, *The Cheyenne*, 71).

herds must have increased to some considerable extent. For we have seen that by 1773 (which actually means some number of years before) the Indian horse was already a recognizable and named type of its own.[102] "Many tribes," says Wissler, "had special medicine formulae for increasing the number of their colts. . . . we have . . . the existence of a more or less distinct type, which suggests a certain amount of breeding. There were, however, wild herds in parts of the area with which this so-called Indian type of horse may be associated."[103]

It may be suggested that for some considerable time at least after a tribe's acquisition of the animal, the "social" conditions of Indian contratribal life, in accordance with "the good old rule, the simple plan, that they may take who have the power and they may keep who can," with its frequent raids and incessant warfare, would scarcely conduce toward the successful breeding of a semi-alien species in a sort of captivity. It is worth noting that the same "unsuccessful" Comanche were not considered so by other tribes. "The Comanche were the great horse Indians of early days. The Pawnee say that in former times other tribes named them horse Indians."[104] Curiously enough also, the same Pawnee who thus in a sense acknowledged their own inferiority in this field, themselves revealed at a relatively early date a considerable skill in caring for the adult stock they actually possessed.[105] Consequently, one is almost driven to ascribe the failure as breeders not so much to ignorance per se, but rather to extraneous unfavorable influences, not at first to be overcome easily.

[102] See Chapter III *supra.*
[103] Wissler, "Influence of the Horse," 21, 22.
[104] *Ibid.,* 15.
[105] See Chapter XIII *infra.*

V

IN THE NORTHERN AREA

In the Northern Plains area the acquisition of the horse was naturally later than in the Southern Plains, as a whole. Wissler assumes horses among the Arikara and the Plains Cree (a somewhat strange juxtaposition!) by 1738; and among the Assiniboin (which of their numerous divisions?), Crow, Mandan, Snake (i.e., Shoshone proper), and Teton Sioux by 1742.[1] The Yanktonais (Sioux) had horses in the 1770's, but we are not informed how long before.[2] Walter Prescott Webb completes his list with ". . . the most northern tribe, the Sarsi [or Sarcee], by 1784. How much earlier these Indians rode horses we do not know; but we can say that the dispersion of horses which began in 1541 was completed over the Plains area by 1784."[3] Wissler's general summary of the tribes of the northern region may appropriately be quoted here:

> The sons of La Vérendrye made a journey to the Rocky Mountains from the Mandan in 1742-43. They encountered horse Indians, also mules and asses, and on their return to Canada mention the horses of their Assiniboine companions. On this journey to the Rocky Mountains they seem to have passed down west of the Black Hills and to have reached the mountains in Wyoming or Colorado, and on their return

[1] Wissler, "Influence of the Horse," 5-6; Webb, *The Great Plains*, 57; 'Some time prior to 1742,' so W. D. Strong, "From History to Prehistory in the Northern Great Plains," *Swanton Memorial Volume*, 358. Curiously enough, a century later the Arikara are described as having 'many horses,' and the Cree 'only a few' (Maximilian, *Travels*, in Thwaites, *Travels*, XXIII, 14, 387).

[2] Narrative of Peter Pond, in Gates (ed.), *Five Fur Traders*, 58.

[3] Webb, *The Great Plains*, 57.

93

to have struck the Missouri in Nebraska or South Dakota. They were in fear of the Snake Indians. So far we have not been able to identify the tribal names of these explorers, but Beaux Hommes seem likely to be Crow, and Gens de l'Arc to be Cheyenne. Their "Le Grand Chef" was evidently the chief of the Pawnee, and the Chevaux, the Comanche. They fell in with the Prairie Sioux on the return trip. On one point they are definite: that horses were in use all along their route after they left the Mandan country.[4]

I cite another scholar who has also given much attention to this question. Lawrence J. Burpee writes as follows:

When La Vérendrye visited the Assiniboine and the Mandans in 1738–39, neither of these tribes had horses, although the latter told him of tribes more to the south who travelled on horseback. In 1741, however, the explorer's son brought two horses from the Missouri to Fort La Reine on the Assiniboine [River],[5] probably obtained from some of the southern tribes who visited the Mandans. The Assiniboine had acquired horses before 1776, when Alexander Henry visited them, but apparently still moved camp with dogs and hunted afoot. The Sioux also hunted on foot in 1766 when Jonathan Carver visited their country. He mentions some western tribes who at that time had 'great plenty of horses, always attacking their enemies on horseback.'[6]

Such general surveys, while approximately correct enough, may in points of detail require some suspension of judgment or perhaps positive revision in the light of other incidental evidence. Where so much is inevitably conjectural, some of Wissler's tribal identifications seem to rest upon insecure foundations. For example, when a hypothetical route has been adopted (for the journey of 1742–43) we have no means whatever of knowing that any nomadic (i.e., buffalo) tribe encountered in a certain order on this expedition were actually on their own territorial grounds when met. In fact,

4 Wissler, "Influence of the Horse," 2–3, 15. Antony Henday, among the Blackfoot, 1754–55, saw 'four asses' ("Journal" [ed. by Burpee], 339).

5 Near Portage la Prairie, fifty-five miles west of Winnipeg, Manitoba. The fort was burned in 1752, and the ancient site was overgrown with wood in 1933. It was so in 1793 (Gates [ed.], Five Fur Traders, 110).

6 La Vérendrye, Journals (ed. by Burpee), 108; cf. 387. The Alexander Henry mentioned is "the elder." The allusion is to Henry's Travels and Adventures in Canada and the Indian Territories between the Years 1760 and 1776, 289, 299.

the entire conception of "territorial grounds" among the nomads of the Plains rests very much upon the claims of the stronger, and upon a supposition of regular buffalo movement which history does not substantiate. This renders identifications based upon later historic tribal habitats or similar geographical data highly problematical, as Wissler himself seemed inclined to suspect in later years.[7] Similarly, one feels rather dubious about basing precise events and localities upon Jonathan Carver's authority, although inherently these may not be improbable, and he has more recently found a very capable defender.[8] Then again, it is not certain who those tribes were who the Mandan had heard possessed horses, nor whether they were Southern tribes at all. The passage runs thus: "The Pananas and Pananis had horses like the whites. . . ." The meaning of this is not, however, in my opinion altogether clear.[9]

The general difficulty of reaching accurate conclusions in these geographical-chronological problems is well illustrated by a passage from the *Journal* of Jacques Répentigny Legardeur de Saint-Pierre (1701–1755). In his account of his journey "to the Rocky Mountains" in 1750–52, he describes some nation of "traders" in the far interior. These are clearly some other than the English, even if his own words did not make the fact self-evident. For at Hudson Bay the English were then still in the stage of supine unadventurous contentment;[10] and the southerly pioneers beyond the Alleghenies had not yet even reached the Mississippi. Saint-Pierre writes thus:

[7] Correspondence to the author, February 26, 1940.

[8] For many years most critics found Carver indigestible, including Burpee himself. In an earlier work he classed Carver as 'equally entertaining and untrustworthy' with La Hontan and Father Hennepin (Lawrence J. Burpee, *The Search for the Western Sea*, 205, 285–301). More recently, Carver's authenticity is considered to have been established by later research, including his journals, found in the British Museum (Gates [ed.], *Five Fur Traders*, 58–59, note). Even this, as Jablow points out (*The Cheyenne*, 7) will scarcely commend the acceptance of his having "perfectly acquired" the Dakota language in a sojourn of five months! La Hontan's accuracy is also defended by a very competent scholar, the late Louise Phelps Kellogg (Gates [ed.], *Five Fur Traders*, 33).

[9] "La Vérendrye's Journal of 1738" (ed. by D. Brymmer), *Report of Canadian Archives*, 1889, 13; La Vérendrye, *Journals* (ed. by Burpee), 312, 335, 366. See Appendix A *infra*.

[10] This attitude has probably been overemphasized. See Richard Glover, "The Difficulties of the Hudson's Bay Company's Penetration of the West," *Canadian Historical Review*, Vol. XXIX (1948), 240–55.

. . . the road they take to go to them is directly toward where the sun sets in the month of June, which I have estimated to be West-North-West. . . . The English are not ignorant of it, and I have myself seen the horses and saddles which the Indians obtain there. But it is impossible to penetrate to that settlement just now, seeing that the journey can only be made by land and carrying provisions, and that there can be no avoiding an infinity of Nations more savage than can be imagined, from whom there is everything to fear.[11]

Saint-Pierre does not state the precise situation of the datum point from whence he calculated his "West-North-West." Speaking broadly, this point would presumably lie between the French posts of Fort Rouge (Winnipeg, Manitoba) and Fort Maurepas at the mouth of the Winnipeg River, these lying between 50° and 50° 40′ N; or between Fort Bourbon on Cedar Lake (lower Saskatchewan River) and Fort à la Corne near the Forks of the two Saskatchewans. The latter two are both about 53° 30′ N, but the river bears considerably to the northward between the two points.[12]

The first of these respective data would bring him to some region along the Bow (South Saskatchewan) River, near Calgary, Alberta; in the vicinity of which—'in sight of the Rocky Mountains' —he or his associate or subordinate, Niverville, was long supposed to have founded the famous but elusive Fort la Jonquière.[13] The same general compass bearing from the lower Saskatchewan points mentioned would land him somewhere along the central or upper Athabaska River, about the point where the Rockies may first be seen; say, about the confluence of the McLeod River, near Whitecourt, Alberta.[14] Who else could be anywhere in the far interior at that date, excepting possibly the Spanish, it seems hopeless to conjecture.[15] In any event, in the first of these two localities, he

[11] "The Journal of Legardeur de Saint-Pierre" (ed. by D. Brymmer), *Report of Canadian Archives, 1886, clxiii.*

[12] See Coues's excellent notes, *Henry-Thompson Journals,* II, 447–600.

[13] George Bryce, *The Remarkable History of the Hudson's Bay Company,* 89–90; C. M. MacInnes, *In the Shadow of the Rockies* (History of Southern Alberta), 23–29, and authorities there cited. "Near Calgary," as everybody has heard, but nobody could ever find a trace of it.

[14] A straight line from Wainwright, Alberta, to Edmonton, on the Canadian National main line, continued onward, will practically touch Whitecourt.

[15] On Spanish advances northward, see Chapter III. Saint-Pierre's "English" are of course the people of the Hudson's Bay Company; and his remarks suggest

should surely have seen Spaniards for himself if any were there, since his party 'came within sight' of the Rockies. Surely, too, a French officer in that day of French and Spanish *rapprochements*— even though, like Saint-Pierre, he were a marine officer—should have recognized Spanish saddlery, had this been such. His *certainty* of needing to carry provisions *by land* on such a journey (with the two Saskatchewans available) might conceivably be based upon or colored by La Vérendrye's nearly starving to death on his return winter journey across Dakota in January, 1739—an occurrence which would doubtless be familiar knowledge among the French frontier fur posts.[16] These discrepant circumstances taken together with the impossible jumble of directions, leave Saint-Pierre's carelessness, essential ignorance, or deliberate misrepresentation of the geography of the country as practically the only tangible conclusion which emerges from all this welter of confusion.

I am driven strongly to the last of these explanations by the fact that the actual situation of Fort la Jonquière is now known. So far from being within sight of the Rocky Mountains, it was below the Saskatchewan Forks, practically on the site of the somewhat later Fort à la Corne,[17] and considerably over four hundred miles by either branch from the points where the Rockies can first be seen. These points, moreover, are located on the high prairie "bench lands," and bring the mountains into sight much sooner than any viewpoint from the canyon-like river valleys which the voyagers traveled. Actually, this identification leaves the Rocky Mountain "viewpoint" a greater crux than ever. One could conceive of Saint-Pierre's starting from his Fort la Jonquière as a base, and pushing forward up either branch until he really came within sight of the mountains. But in each case this would involve a round trip by water of over a thousand miles, and such exploits take time. In December, 1753, Saint-Pierre was the "one-eyed com-

that the French may have heard something of the advance, which resulted in their sending out Antony Henday and others. See Glover, "The Difficulties of the Hudson's Bay Company's Penetration of the West," 240–55.

16 La Vérendrye, "Journal" (ed. by Brymmer), 13; La Vérendrye, *Journals* (ed. by Burpee), 352–59.

17 See J. B. Tyrrell (ed.), *The Journals of Samuel Hearne and Phillip Turnor*, 23; Glazebrook, *History of Transportation in Canada*, 20 (map); also Arthur S. Morton's encyclopedic *A History of the Canadian West to 1870–71*, 236–38.

mander" at Fort Le Boeuf, in the Ohio territory, where young George Washington, a rising diplomat in his twenty-second year, treated with him in that month. Saint-Pierre at this time was deputy for the same "Joncair" after whom his fort had been named.[18]

Presumably with this expedition of 1750 in prospect, Governor La Jonquière had written to the French colonial minister that Saint-Pierre was "the officer in the colony who possesses the most information regarding those countries." Lawrence Burpee writes concerning this: "As a matter of fact Saint-Pierre had never been in any portion of the western country covered by the explorations of La Vérendrye, and must have known infinitely less about the region and its inhabitants than the sons of La Vérendrye."[19] The apparently quite gratuitous touch about the sight of the Rocky Mountains suggests that Saint-Pierre did not propose to lose his high reputation with the French authorities. There is a locality where the Rockies may be seen some two hundred miles away, as the present writer can testify,[20] but I doubt whether Saint-Pierre would have found this region, which is not on either branch of the Saskatchewan. We probably do no injustice in concluding that Saint-Pierre's explorations did not extend very far beyond his post below the Forks of the Saskatchewan.

As a mere matter of historical emendation and nothing more, this question would scarcely be relevant to the present essay. Actually, it is one of immense importance, both in regard to time and place. For it extends our knowledge of a definite dating for Indian horses to a point some four hundred miles farther northeastward, and a third of a century earlier, than the suggested limits indicated at the commencement of our chapter. There can be little doubt that an eminent authority on the Plains horse, and another high authority on the Blackfoot, are correct in applying Saint-Pierre's pronouncements to that tribe, and in accepting Henday's testi-

[18] Hulbert, *Historic Highways*, III, 104–17. He was slain at the battle of Lake George, 1755 (Francis Parkman, *A Half-Century of Conflict*, II, 39).

[19] La Vérendrye, *Journals* (ed. by Burpee), 30, and cf. 265; also Burpee's *Search for the Western Sea*, 271–81.

[20] Northeast of the Red Deer Canyon they were visible from my old home (1897–1909), and scarcely anywhere else for forty miles southward, as the view was blocked by hills and woods. These peaks were in the Rocky Mountain House country, and toward the North Saskatchewan headwaters.

mony of 1754–55 as confirming them.[21] This virtually localizes the horse as being not merely known, but as a creature of familiar use and mastery in its farthest Northern (early Indian) Plains range by the middle of the eighteenth century.

Burpee mentions a tradition among the Northern Cheyenne of the Missouri country that 'they were the first tribe of this region to have horses,' and thinks it possible that they may have been the *Gens des Chevaux* of La Vérendrye (1738).[22] Neither proposition is entirely free from doubt. In so far as the *Gens des Chevaux* are concerned, there are two or three hot favorites for that distinction, in the opinion of their respective backers.[23] And if the conclusions of the most recent student of this problem are correct, the Cheyenne were a long way from being the first in the field.

George E. Hyde awards the premier place to the Arikara. He states that "the trade with the Gatakas or Padoucas for horses was being carried on by the Arikaras as early as 1680, and this trade was kept up until the end of the eighteenth century." He identifies the Padouca with the (modern) Apache, "who were called Padoucas by the French."[24] Hyde cites no contemporary authority for this assertion, and it is difficult to see how he could. As the statement stands, it raises some problems and possibly helps to settle others. The Vérendryes, father and sons, were the first Europeans to our knowledge to penetrate into this area at large. If Wissler's foregoing summary of the sons' route of 1742–43 is even broadly authentic, their return trip must have brought them through or very near the Arikara country. It seems extraordinary that they could have heard nothing of a trade of this character which had then been going on for over sixty years. For obviously a commerce of such long standing would be something more than the mere discovery of horses among some tribe that had just re-

---

[21] Wissler, "Influence of the Horse," 4; Kidd, "Blackfoot Ethnography," 131.

[22] La Vérendrye, *Journals* (ed. by Burpee), 407; cf. Grinnell, *The Fighting Cheyennes*, 34.

[23] See Appendix A *infra*.

[24] Hyde, "Mystery of the Arikaras," 190, 217; but cf. John Bradbury, *Travels in the Interior of North America*, in Thwaites, *Travels*, V, 176.

cently acquired the animal. On the other hand, Hyde's conclusion would account for the utterly apathetic, unemotional way in which the Mandan told the elder Vérendrye of those "Southern tribes" who had horses. Apparently the thing had ceased to be a nine days' wonder fifty or sixty years before. And there we have to leave it. Definite conclusions are impossible.

An anthropologist who has made a special study of the Cheyenne thinks they may have been La Vérendrye's *Gens de l'Arc*.[25] That name is itself a problem, since it is difficult to comprehend how the bow could *differentiate* any Indian tribe in a land where all were archers. Its present relevance lies in the fact that by the clearest implication the Cheyenne were *not* (in Grinnell's opinion) the *Gens des Chevaux*. They reached the Missouri at some date about the end of the seventeenth century (within a few years), from the northeast, where the Cheyenne (or Sheyenne) River of North Dakota, which joins the Red River near Moorhead, Minnesota, very probably perpetuates their earlier habitat. They formerly lived in earth lodges, "packed their property on dogs and on their own backs, and hunted the buffalo on foot."[26] In an earlier publication, the same scholar dates the Cheyenne at large as having horses about 1780.[27] Later research reaches a conclusion not materially different by striking an average between the earliest and latest suggested dates, and placing the era about 1770. The more recent critic in question would possibly prefer the earlier period, for he elsewhere speaks of the tribe as becoming fully equestrian, 1750–1800.[28]

In 1806 the Cheyenne were looked upon as being particularly skilful horsemen.[29] This opinion was doubtless that of competent judges, but whether that of Henry and his associates or a common

[25] Grinnell, *Fighting Cheyennes*, 4; also Wissler, "Influence of the Horse," 3.
[26] Grinnell, *The Fighting Cheyennes*, 4. The Sheyenne River is not to be confused with the Big Cheyenne of South Dakota. See Thwaites' notes, *Travels*, XXII, 333; XXVII, 161. We have noted (Chapter I *supra*) Frémont's meeting Cheyenne and Sioux with dog travois in 1844. This illustrates the gradual nature of the change; perhaps also the inherent worthlessness of positive chronological pronouncement on the subject.
[27] Grinnell, in Hodge, *Handbook*, I, 569–71.
[28] Strong, "From History to Prehistory in the Northern Great Plains," 370–73, 376; for "1750–1800," *ibid.*, 359.
[29] The younger Alexander Henry in Coues (ed.), *Henry-Thompson Journals*, I, 393.

contemporary belief among white and/or red folk at large, we are not informed. Judging from the detailed mastery shown by the Blackfoot after a probably much shorter acquaintance (as we shall later see), the Cheyenne, while doubtless expert, were very likely no more so than other tribes whom the critics had not seen. According to a tribal legend, it was from the Western Cheyenne that the Hidatsa obtained their first horses. This might very roughly date them at some time after 1770. The Hidatsa themselves described the horse travois as being to them (subconsciously, we may say) a recent innovation, compared with the antiquity of the dog travois.[30]

I have met with no historical reference to the three original constituent tribes of the Blackfoot Confederacy (Blackfoot [Siksika], Blood [Kainah], and Piegan) which authentically antedates their loose and somewhat ill-defined political fusion under that title. It seems improbable, however, that such a coalescence could itself have occurred, had there not already been a broad similarity in economic and social outlook; and we shall doubtless not be far astray in applying their horse chronology after about 1700 more or less generally to all the tribes in question. At the present day the Confederacy also includes the Sarcee, and at some period it embraced the Gros Ventre (Atsina?) in addition.[31]

A Montana scholar of repute (now deceased) states that the Blackfoot "had possessed horses as far back as their traditions extended."[32] A contemporary Canadian anthropologist, who has made a special study of the Blackfoot, considers Blackfoot traditions very

[30] Wilson, "Horse and Dog in Hidatsa Culture," 142, 219.

[31] Kidd, "Blackfoot Ethnography," 141. Jenness remarks: "they did not even use a common term to denote the whole three tribes" (*The Indians of Canada*, 319). John McLean says the Confederacy described themselves by two names: "Sâketûpiks"—"the people of the plains"; and "Netsepoye"—"the people that speak the same language" (*The Indians of Canada*, 130, 254). Maximilian found no common name in use, Missouri River, 1833 (*Travels* in Thwaites, *Travels*, XXIII, 95–122, 197). For the neighboring Atsina, who later retreated or returned to United States territory, see Chapter III *supra*.

[32] James H. Bradley, "Characteristics, Habits, and Customs of the Blackfeet Indians," *Contributions to the Historical Society of Montana*, Vol. III (1900); cited by Ewers, "Were the Blackfoot Rich in Horses?" 603.

frequently unsatisfactory;[33] and a detailed examination of several traditions (of much lesser antiquity than the foregoing) strongly disposes the present writer to agree concerning Indian traditions in general.[34] Burpee thinks the Blackfoot obtained horses about 1700; and a tradition exists among the Blackfoot that the Crow were the first to introduce them.[35] The Confederacy also have another tradition about their first horse, or possibly something better than mere tradition. For this was told to David Thompson in 1787–88 by an old "Nahathaway" (Cree) of "at least 75 to 80 years of age," apparently dwelling among the Piegans. This episode referred to an era somewhere about 1730, when the informant would be a young man in the twenties. I quote Thompson's own account of the old man's recital:

> . . . we pitched away . . . on the frontier of the Snake Indian country . . . and we were anxious to see a horse of which we had heard so much. . . . Our enemies the Snake Indians and their allies had Misstutim [Big Dogs, that is, horses] on which they rode, swift as the Deer. . . . At last, as the leaves were falling we heard that one was killed by an arrow shot into his belly, but the Snake Indian that rode him, got away; numbers of us went to see him, and we all admired him, he put us in mind of a Stag that had lost his horns; and we did not know what name to give him. But as he was a slave to Man, like the Dog, which carried our things; he was named the Big Dog.[36]

It is not certain whether even such a circumstantial recital as this can implicitly be accepted as it stands. Among nonwriting peoples, "historical" events tend to become traditionary in much less

[33] Kidd, "Blackfoot Ethnography," 10. Compare the following scholars: "Tribal traditions on origins usually have little validity" (Dobie, *The Mustangs,* 39). Tribal traditions unreliable, the same one being frequently found in different tribes; so, Kroeber, "Ethnology of the Gros Ventre," 146; Wissler, "Material Culture of the Blackfoot," 15–19; Lowie, "The Assiniboin," 7. Hyde notes the very hazy ideas among the Arikara of anything beyond their own father's times ("Mystery of the Arikaras," 211–14). See below in the present chapter (notes 108, 132) on contradictory traditional Sioux "winter counts" and calendar records.

[34] Frank Gilbert Roe, "The Extermination of the Buffalo in Western Canada," *Canadian Historical Review,* Vol. XV (1934), 1–23; also Roe, *North American Buffalo,* 187–89, 241–42, 276–77, 480, etc.

[35] Henday, "Journal" (ed. by Burpee), 318, note; MacInnes, *In the Shadow of the Rockies,* 174. For the Crow tradition, Kidd, "Blackfoot Ethnography," 61.

[36] Thompson, *Narrative* (ed. by Tyrrell), 330, 334.

than half a century; and probably much depends upon the reader's previous attitude toward Indian traditional accounts in general. I do not consider that such a relation as this one told to Thompson can be used at all satisfactorily for such precise calculations as those of Francis Haines. D. E. Worcester also accepts this story as authenticated fact.[37] It is pure assumption to suggest (as Haines does) that Thompson's ancient informant was older by some twenty years or so than he imagined himself to be. The general propensity in very aged people is more commonly the precise reverse: to imagine themselves older than they are. With all our familiar checks and safeguards of an organized calendar and uniformalized dates, senile memories play some strange tricks among our own peoples.[38]

David Thompson has not informed us by what means he (or his informant himself) arrived at the estimate of age. If this were attained by the very common form observed among nonliterate peoples, of assurances from younger adults of the tribe that 'So-and-so was a grown man when we were boys,' the crux still remains. In what way did these younger men compute their own years? Generations do not divide rigidly into cycles of so many years' duration. The previous generation could be almost any number from ten to fifty years older.

And this leaves untouched the major difficulty of all, which is by no means easy of explanation. The farther back we attempt by any process of calculation to push this episode, the more improbable becomes the use of the Cree term "mistatim." We gather clearly from the recital that the Cree had accompanied the Blackfoot (or Piegan) war party. They could scarcely have reached 'the frontier of the Snake country' with a war party of their own, since they would have had to cross the Blackfoot country to do so. Why

[37] Haines, "How did the Indians Get Their Horses?" 116; Worcester, "Spanish Horses among the Plains Tribes," 410.

[38] In 1934, I noted a reference to an old lady then living, born 1836, who was "a girl friend of the great John Wesley, and often accompanied him on his journeys" (*Edmonton Journal*, March 9, 1934). John Wesley *died in 1791*. In 1948, I myself met an old gentleman then eighty years old (born 1867–68), a man of culture and a publisher of international repute, who told me he had *borne a personal share* in the acceptance of R. D. Blackmore's *Lorna Doone* for publication, after many rejections. *Lorna Doone* was published in 1869–70. Among the old plainsmen, anachronisms of this character are legion, in which an occurrence may even be substantially true, but the personages are hopelessly impossible.

would not the official (Blackfoot) leaders of the expedition do the naming?

The Blackfoot horse name, "ponokamita" ("elk-dog"), is no sort of true etymon embodying either any real description of the animal, or historical clue—such as "the moose of France"—to the source of their acquaintance with it. It is an allusive or analogical term; precisely the kind of name that might spring almost instinctively to the lips at first sight, perhaps later to be coupled with some interpretative designation. It is difficult to imagine a people possessing language at all having to *wait,* or needing to have recourse to some alien speech, for a primitive *nomen* of this character. There is no true analogy here with the use of a loan-word name borrowed from another tongue (as with the Takulli, or "Carriers," and the buffalo) to describe *some animal they had not seen for themselves.*[39] Actually, in this very account as given to or by Thompson, we find the description which is (in part) embodied in the classical Blackfoot term suggesting itself almost instantly at first sight. Why not then express it in Blackfoot immediately? Are we to imagine the Blackfoot gaping at the creature tongue-tied, while the hated Cree found them a name! And all this at a time when we have no other reason to suppose that the Cree had evolved the name (or perhaps even heard of the creature) for themselves; while the Blackfoot are believed by some good critics to have possessed the horse for a generation or more. Judging by their wide-flung prevalence, it seems more probable that the dog and deer horse-names spread over the continent as "advance agents," ahead of the animal itself.[40] This account reads like an example of folk etymology.[41]

Moreover, having adopted a Cree loan-word name, why should it not have persisted to the present day? Names are stubborn things, as the universal history of names cries aloud to us,[42] and as

[39] Father A. G. Morice writes: "The buffalo was never indigenous to the Carrier country, and the Stuart Lake Indians call it by a Cree word. The Sekanais have a native name of their own for the buffalo, which circumstance confirms Mackenzie's account of its being originally found west of the Rockies" (*History of the Northern Interior of British Columbia,* 38).

[40] See Roe, *North American Buffalo,* App. A, "Buffalo Synonymy."

[41] For a specimen, see *ibid.,* App. K.

[42] The Roman historian, Ammianus Marcellinus, wrote thus about A.D. 350: "Since the name of Augusta has been bestowed upon the principal city of the

no intelligent resident of this continent can be unaware; and there appears to be no evidence of any struggle for survival between the two rival forms. Yet the Cree "mistatim" is so clearly and closely of the same analogical type as the Blackfoot name as to give the prior foreign term a very strong chance of equality in survival, or even of supremacy as having been the original one.

The literal acceptance of this account would virtually compel us to conclude that the Blackfoot derived their first *knowledge*—not necessarily personal acquaintance—of the horse from the Cree. Yet the whole current of our knowledge of the horse advance suggests, perhaps demands, that it was very possibly either through the Blackfoot or on their frontier of the Cree territory that the Cree obtained their own first horses. Both Haines and Denhardt apparently agree that the Indians who acquired horses from other tribes for the first time "acquired" them usually or preferably by theft,[43] though not of course exclusively so in future transactions. If their supposition is correct, there is nothing in the inveterate enmity between Cree and Blackfoot[44] which pins the Cree down to any necessity of obtaining their first horses exclusively—or at all—from the Assiniboin. Wherever the Assiniboin had penetrated to by 1754, it by no means follows that in 1738—not to say 1710—they were so far west of Red River as to be the only possible tribe available to the Cree as a source of horse supply, even by the Plains route. There is no reason for considering the tradition as told to Thompson to be deliberately false; people in simple societies do not invent such legends out of nothing. But it cannot be considered as a sound basis for precise chronological calculations.

Walter Prescott Webb does not mention the Blackfoot proper

Britons, the barbarous native appellation of *Lundain* will no doubt speedily fall into disuse and be heard no more." Compare the many Old Testament instances of the two names of places surviving in common use together; paralleled in many old street names in English towns even yet.

[43] Haines, "Northward Spread of Horses," 436; Denhardt, *Horse of the Americas*, 87, 91, 99, 104, etc.

[44] On the Blackfoot detestation of all things Cree, see Kidd, "Blackfoot Ethnography," 104. Jenness notes that while among the later Sarcee, perhaps also among the Blackfoot proper (Siksika), there was a measure of intercourse, even occasional intermarriage with the Cree, in the earlier times there was almost unrelenting hostility (Jenness, *The Sarcee Indians*, 3-7, 9, 73-75, etc.). On Cree hatred of the Blackfoot, De Smet, *Letters and Sketches*, in Thwaites, *Travels*, XXIV, 235; Mandelbaum, "Plains Cree," 166.

(Siksika) in his observations upon the northern advance of the horse, and it is regrettable that he did not cite some source for its appearance among the Sarcee ('the most northern tribe') by 1784.[45] For aside from any hypothesis respecting Legardeur de Saint-Pierre, it is a well-known episode in the history of northwestern exploration that Antony Henday (the hitherto familiar "Hendry,"[46] the first "Englishman" [meaning an emissary of the "English company"—the Hudson's Bay Company] to encounter horse Indians in western Canada) described the friends and neighboring allies of the Sarcee, the Blackfoot, as possessing horses in 1754, and 'well supplied.'[47] For this declaration he was denounced and discredited as a mere liar for nearly twenty years, until vindicated by the testimony of Matthew Cocking, 1772–73.[48] The "Archithinue" (Blackfoot) were not even the first horse Indians whom Henday met. For while apparently still in the Assiniboin country,[49] he encountered at least two bands of "Asinepoets" (Assiniboin) who had pack horses, of which he purchased one.[50]

It is a curious fact that while in 1754 no report had (obviously) reached Hudson Bay of horse Indians in the Canadian West (as the reception accorded to Henday conclusively indicates); yet the general tone of Henday's journal certainly suggests that to the interior tribes in 1754 the horse, if not exactly commonplace, was evidently no incredible wonder to be recounted with bated breath! He must have been informed of its advent on the Northern Plains by the Assiniboin, if not before them, for he is in hope of seeing "the Archithinue Indians, [and] hunting the buffalo on horseback," more than five weeks before seeing his first Assiniboin horses (Au-

[45] See note 3 *supra*.

[46] See Henday, "Journal" (ed. by Burpee), 320.

[47] So, Wissler, "Influence of the Horse," 10. There is no precise statement of numbers. "seven tents . . . the men all mounted," is the most definite (Henday, "Journal" [ed. by Burpee], 335). Occasional mention of "two" or "several" wild horses (*ibid.*, 329, 335) may be thought to imply plenty, but they may only have been strays escaped from their hobbles. Hobbling was practiced by both tribes (*ibid.*, 334, 338). On hobbling, with methods of fastening (drawings), see Wilson, "Horse and Dog in Hidatsa Culture," 189–91.

[48] See Burpee's note, Henday, "Journal," 320. For Cocking, see his "Journal" (ed. by Burpee), 89–121.

[49] For its general limits, as defined by Henry, 1808, see Coues (ed.), *Henry-Thompson Journals*, II, 516.

[50] Henday, "Journal" (ed. by Burpee), 334, 335.

gust 13 to September 20), and seven weeks before actually encountering the "Archithinue," in October.[51]

He relates his various horse experiences (including the natives' "smoking dryed horse-dung," which his editor not unnaturally doubts,[52]) in an entirely matter-of-fact, almost casual manner; certainly not that of one anticipating a storm of criticism and obloquy. Matthew Cocking is much more suggestive of such an attitude, quite naturally so by reason of the chastisement meted out to Henday; and even he writes as though the thing was familiar to everybody except the "stay-at-homes" at Hudson Bay. Matthew Cocking observes on the very eve of his meeting with the Archithinue-Blackfoot:

I shall be sorry if I do not see the Equestrian Natives who are certainly a brave people, and far superior to any tribes that visit our Forts: they have dealings with no Europeans, but live in a state of nature to the S.W. Westerly: they draw toward the N.E. in March to meet our Natives who traffick with them.[53]

We have an example of these movements a very few years later. We find mention of eighteen men (besides women) of the "Pegogemew" (apparently Piegan) coming to the Hudson's Bay Company post at Hudson House, some distance above the Saskatchewan Forks and the modern city of Prince Albert, November 26, 1779, with sixteen horses. In April, 1782, one "Indian" and his family arrived there with four horses, "loaded with beat meat." Possibly the devastating smallpox epidemic of 1781 had left the survivors somewhat richer in horseflesh.[54]

We have already seen that in 1795 both Blackfoot and Blood were quite evidently characterized as horse Indians whom only some exceptional occurrence "dismounted" for the moment.[55] Daniel Williams Harmon also states that about 1800 'all the Plains

---

[51] *Ibid.*, 328–35.

[52] *Ibid.*, 339, with Burpee's note. I have (like Burpee) met with no similar allusion respecting any other tribe or region.

[53] Cocking, "Journal" (ed by Burpee), 110.

[54] *Cumberland and Hudson House Journals, 1775–1782* (Second Series), 77–78, 285.

[55] McGillivray, *Journal* (ed. by Morton), 69 (see Chapter I *supra*).

Indians' were riders.[56] Among these Plains riders, Alexander Mackenzie writes as early as about 1789, clearly implying that the Blackfoot Confederacy were the northern horsemen above all others.[57] About 1800 also, David Thompson describes the "Fall" Indians (whom his editor, Tyrrell, considers to be the Atsina) as being in the opinion of the Crees (!!) "good cavalry."[58] These various particulars make Grinnell's dating of 1800 for the appearance of the horse among the Blackfoot (Siksika) extremely surprising in such a student, and of course quite unacceptable.[59]

Perhaps even more astonishing is the statement of Cyrus Thomas, usually so well informed. He speaks of horses first coming into the possession of the Piegan, about 1804–1806. He instances, apparently as confirmation of this, a certain chief, "Many Horses," born about 1800.[60] Alexander Henry the younger, however, refers to 'vast numbers' among the Blackfoot (1809); some men having forty or fifty each. He then goes on to speak of the Piegan's having 'far greater numbers'; one man owning three hundred![61] It was an old warrior-associate of the Piegan, moreover, who gave David Thompson the information we have already discussed; the main features of which I consider to be in no way necessarily invalidated by scepticism concerning the origin of *names*.

Entirely apart from direct evidence of the foregoing character, certain social horse-customs among the tribes of the Blackfoot Confederacy point in my opinion to a fairly long acquaintance with the horse, relatively speaking. This name "Many Horses" I consider to be an instance. In my judgment the bestowal of any such horse name is very strong presumptive evidence of an acquaintance with (not merely knowledge of) the horse for a sufficiently long time that its nature and characteristics have become a rooted feature

[56] Harmon, *Journal*, 291.   [57] See Chapter IV *supra*.

[58] Thompson, *Narrative* (ed. by Tyrrell), 327.

[59] Grinnell, in Hodge, *Handbook*, I, 569–71; cf. Mooney, *ibid.*, II, 570–72. See also Burpee's remarks, Henday, "Journal," 316–18.

[60] Cyrus Thomas, in *Handbook of Canadian Indians*, 273. This man would presumably be the "Many Horses" who was killed in battle with the Crow in 1866 (Ewers, "Were the Blackfoot Rich in Horses?" 604). Jenness notes a Sarcee chief, "Many Horses," 1877 (*The Sarcee Indians*, 8, 10, 73). It will scarcely be suggested that this man dated Sarcee horses.

[61] Coues (ed.), *Henry-Thompson Journals*, II, 526.

in the mental imagery of the people. Such an assimilation I believe to be a process requiring time.

The apparent implication that the name "Many Horses" is to be taken as testimony to numbers owned in the period 1800–1806 either by the bearer of the name, or his family, or the tribe, is, I believe, an even graver misconception on Cyrus Thomas' part. This is one of those symbolic names of which Indian nomenclature contains so many; they are in fact its basic foundation. The symbolism here—whether of achievement, promise, or wishful thinking; the latter is the least likely of the three—is that of *"One equal to many horses"*; the application, beyond doubt, being in relation to strength, prowess, and endurance in war and hunting. The classical example of this symbolical horse-name type is the famous "Young Man Afraid Of His Horse," the misinterpretation of which has furnished a subject for the measureless laughter of many fools. The true interpretation is, of course, "Young Man (i.e., one whom years could not enfeeble, or 'eternal youth') whose very horses bring terror to his enemies!" The imagery and its idiomatic expression are alike essentially identical with that of the Hebrew prophet at the passing of his master: "My father, my father, the chariot of Israel and the horsemen thereof!"[62] We shall later note other social symbolisms derived from the horse, and in these very tribes.

Grinnell's opinion that the earlier horses of the Blackfoot Confederacy were obtained from the Snake (or Shoshone: a supposition which appears to be latent in Thompson's relation already discussed) and from the Kutenai seems reasonably reliable;[63] without prejudice to the tribal tradition concerning the Crow, which has been mentioned.[64] The Kutenai source of Blackfoot horses finds some support in the fact that tribal intercourse through the Kootenay and other passes for purposes both of war and peace was manifestly of long standing.[65]

---

[62] The Hebrew prophet Elisha (II Kings 2:2). The same symbolism is clearly present in the Sarcee horse-name "Chistli"—"seven dogs." Nobody outside Bedlam would suggest that the horse was named "Chistli" because he owned seven dogs!

[63] Grinnell, in Hodge, *Handbook*, I, 569–71; cf. Thompson, *Narrative* (ed. by Tyrrell), 328–34, 342, 367, 377.

[64] See note 35 *supra*.

[65] See on this, Patrick Gass, *Journal of the Lewis and Clark Expedition* (ed. by

Wissler ranks the Snake as the chief distributors over a wide range. Of their earlier relations with the Spaniards very little is known. "Their range seems to have been from eastern Colorado to the headwaters of the Missouri and westward. It is probable that in 1600 the Comanche were also a part of this group."[66] Wissler notes among the Blackfoot "definite . . . traditions that horses were acquired from other tribes [the Snake and the Flathead]."[67] If we only knew exactly what is a "definite tradition"? It may be nothing more than the insistence of certain informants. Other informants might insist upon other traditions, as that recorded by Kidd, above. Such contradictions are only too familiar in anthropological investigations.

Reference has been made to the general horse chronology of the Sarcee as being probably, from the era of their association with the Blackfoot, similar to that of the Confederacy at large. Where Webb defines the Sarcee as having horses by 1784, Wissler speaks of "first mention" by Edward Umfreville *in* 1784, which is a different thing. The Sarcee shared the Blackfoot hostility to the Cree,[68] but whether this was the cause or the effect of their joining the Confederacy remains problematical. They were not always included among the Confederacy by writers, and there may have been separations. They even fought at times,[69] and Henday's observations may have reference to some such interlude. He says of the "Archithinue" (Blackfoot) whom he met: "They have other Natives, Horsemen as well as Foot, who are their Enemies; they are also called the Archithinue Indians; & by what I can learn talk the same language, and hath the same customs."[70] But they had

J. K. Hosmer), 150, 254. Thompson, *Narrative* (ed. by Tyrrell), 328–34, 389, 417, 419, 424, 529, 559. Coues (ed.), *Henry-Thompson Journals* (1811), II, 707–13, 819. Franchère, *Voyage to the Northwest Coast* (1812), in Thwaites, *Travels*, VI, 339–41. Alexander Ross, *Adventures of the First Settlers on the Oregon or Columbia River, 1810–1813*, in Thwaites, *Travels*, VII, 215. Townsend, *Narrative* (1833), in Thwaites, *Travels*, XXI, 232. For the Kootenay Trail, McClintock, *Old North Trail*, 2, 9, 40, etc. The foregoing do not include the passes north of 49° N, since probably no horses were *introduced* through the Canadian passes. Bancroft ranks the Kutenai as the farthest north (mountain) tribe of horse Indians (*Native Races*, I, 292, 460).
[66] Wissler, "Influence of the Horse," 23; Haines, "Northward Spread of Horses," 436.
[67] Wissler, "Influence of the Horse," 13, 24.
[68] See note 44 *supra*.
[69] Jenness, *The Sarcee Indians*, 2–3.
[70] Henday, "Journal" (ed. by Burpee), 339.

Flying Hoofs
CHARLES M. RUSSELL

"A band upon being threatened formed a circle, colts in the center. Running away meant exposure of the hindmost to the enemy. They did not run. Safety lay not only in numbers but in standing."
—J. Frank Dobie, *The Mustangs.*

Comanche Indian Breaking Down the Wild Horse

GEORGE CATLIN

Courtesy Smithsonian Institution

Capture of Wild Horses by Indians

ALFRED JACOB MILLER

Courtesy Walters Art Gallery

The Oasis

FLETCHER G. RANSOM

"He is in the saddle from boyhood to old age, and his favorite horse is his constant companion . . . he prizes him more highly than anything else in his possession."
—Randolph B. Marcy, *Thirty Years of Army Life on the Border.*

Courtesy Woolaroc Museum

The Buffalo Hunt
CHARLES WIMAR

"Each hunter rode upon the buffalo from the rear, coming in close on its right side and shooting at the soft spot between the protruding hip bone and the last rib. As soon as he heard the twang of the bow string, a good buffalo-running horse swerved away from its victim in order to be well out of harm's way when the wounded beast turned and charged."
Ernest Wallace and E. Adamson Hoebel, *The Comanches.*

Camp Providers

ALFRED JACOB MILLER

With the aid of two or three of the hunters the Buffalo is raised from his fallen position and placed in a sitting posture, in order to take that most superlative *morceaux,* the 'Hump Rib.' "

Alfred Jacob Miller, *The West of Alfred Jacob Miller.*

Indian Hunter's Return
CHARLES M. RUSSELL

". . . many a dusky face peered from the huts looking for signs of a good hunting day, which the thick carpet of snow and the rising wind sighing and singing over the treetops already promised."
                              —George Frederick Ruxton, *Ruxton of the Rockies.*

The Unwritten History
ELLING WILLIAM GOLLINGS

"The horse fitted in perfectly with the Plains Indian's scheme of life, with his penchant for war, and with his care for his own safety. The Indian made war for the purpose of destroying his enemy and preserving himself. Of the two, the latter was by far the more important consideration."—Walter Prescott Webb, *The Great Plains.*

The Blackfeet
ALFRED JACOB MILLER

Courtesy Public Archives of Canada

Stampede by Blackfeet
ALFRED JACOB MILLER

Courtesy Public Archives of Canada

horses in 1754; and intermittent peace and war among them proves nothing.

We have another rather loose criterion, which may yet be of some little service in our dating. Wissler (writing in 1910) considered the use of pottery vessels not definitely proved in the case of the Assiniboin, Gros Ventre (Atsina?), Sarcee, Blackfoot, Crow, Arapaho, Kiowa, Comanche, and Cheyenne.[71] Later knowledge removes the Sarcee and the Blackfoot from this list.

According to statements made to Jenness by the Sarcee, they discarded the use of clay cooking-pots about the same time that they obtained horses.[72] Matthew Cocking found their allies the Blackfoot—which may signify the Siksika proper or the Confederacy at large—using clay cooking-pots in 1772–73.[73] This is another case where any dating can only be of a very vague, indeterminate character. Nearly twenty years before, Henday found the same Blackfoot in a pretty highly advanced stage of horse culture; and if Wissler's view of their horse chronology is sound, this may be pushed back at least three, and perhaps very many more years. However favorably tribal opinion in general might regard the alternative method, whatever it was (for contacts with European traders were too recent and too sporadic for iron cooking-vessels to supersede clay ones in the Blackfoot country at that early date), there are always some in such primitive societies—as in our own— whose conservatisms resist and postpone such changes long after the innovator has adopted them. Such conservatives, moreover, are frequently the first to attract a stranger's attention, and even more readily if only a few remain. Even apart from imperfect or contradictory recollection or tradition, this leaves an indeterminate spread of some forty or fifty years or even more, during which the Sarcee's allies had possessed horses, and yet may not even have begun to discard their clay cooking-utensils. It seems not improbable that the Sarcee may have had the horse from the same era with their confederates or very shortly after. The dating of both must, however, remain conjectural.

[71] Wissler, "Material Culture of the Blackfoot Indians," 45.
[72] Jenness, *The Sarcee Indians*, 14.
[73] Cocking, "Journal" (ed. by Burpee), 109, 111.

The date of 1738 for the Plains Cree[74] appears rather early in the light of Henday's horse experiences and of other datings. The horse is thought by Burpee to have spread eastward from the more northerly (United States) Rockies to the southern territory of the Assiniboin, and so to Red River.[75] Geographically, this would be equivalent to following down the Missouri as far as the Mandan villages at least. But we have seen that in 1741, the son of La Vérendrye brought two horses from the Missouri to Fort La Reine, on the edge of the Plains Cree country,[76] and this was evidently considered a noteworthy event. Then again, Henday encountered few horses—apparently not enough to serve as more than pack animals—until he reached the edge of the Blackfoot country. Yet he himself had been traveling near the fringe of the Plains Cree territory for a considerable distance.[77] Matthew Cocking had a very similar experience even later, in 1772; and in his case his language, as quoted above, makes it fairly clear that he had no expectation of meeting any "Equestrian Natives" short of the Blackfoot country, nor did he.[78] Furthermore, in the interval between Henday and Cocking, Thomas Curry and James Finlay had pushed up the Saskatchewan River to some point between Pasquita (The Pas) and the Forks (1767),[79] where Plains as well as Wood Cree might very conceivably resort. It seems incredible that in a space of more than thirty years no

[74] Wissler, "Influence of the Horse," 6; Webb, *The Great Plains,* 57. The latter offers no additional evidence. Wissler's only evidence is that "in contact with the Assiniboine were the Plains Cree and the Plains Ojibwa" (Saulteaux); and that "in 1772, Cocking met Cree far to the west, but fails to state that they had horses, though their possession is implied" (ibid., 4). Wissler notes also (p. 4): "La Vérendrye (1738) makes a curious remark concerning an Indian near Red River: 'as he had his vehicle [*voiture*] with him. . . .' This may signify horses, but we cannot be sure." *Voiture* is used by the younger Henry, (1811)—and by many others—for a "cariole" drawn by three dogs (Coues [ed.], *Henry-Thompson Journals,* II, 677).

[75] Henday, "Journal" (ed. by Burpee), 334, note.
[76] See note 4 *supra.*
[77] See Burpee's map, in Henday, "Journal."
[78] See note 53 *supra.*
[79] See Henday, "Journal" (ed. by Burpee), 314; Coues's notes, *Henry-Thompson Journals,* II, 447–500; Glover, "The Difficulties of the Hudson's Bay Company's Penetration of the West," 240–55; *Cumberland and Hudson House Journals.*

word of this great acquisition had filtered through to any of these men. The notices of the fur traders' own horses at the posts along the central Saskatchewan between Cumberland House and the Forks during the years 1775–1782 are of ones and twos only, with two or three allusions already instanced to those of visiting Indians. There is no reference in our authority to even one wild horse being seen at any time.[80]

Harmon apparently regarded the Cree as rather slow and apathetic in taking to the horse.[81] This is endorsed by Mandelbaum, who adds: "The Blackfoot were better supplied with horses than were the Cree, who often attempted to replenish their stock from the plentiful Blackfoot bands. . . . The Crow were the hardest to steal horses from. They would give chase four days and four nights to get them back." This, and the giving away of captured horses to relatives and friends—who, however, would reciprocate and thus restore the balance—hardly seems to argue indifference, and possibly not poverty.[82] The younger Henry counters Harmon by even more direct evidence. He says that the Crees "immediately exchanged any gun they were able to get for the horses of the Assiniboines."[83]

As with the Assiniboin, there were many bands of Cree, and observed characteristics in one band might not necessarily be applicable to all. When the elder Alexander Henry stated in 1776 that the Cree "had horses like the Ossinipoille" (Assiniboin),[84] we neither know to what band or region he was referring, or whether he was alluding to numbers. This is apparently the earliest notice we have of actual possession by the Cree, though in 1772, Cocking "met Cree far to the west, but fails to state that they had horses, though their possession is implied."[85] This last statement may be a matter of opinion. The Beaver Hills Cree (who, as we have noted already, probably dwelt near Edmonton) are stated by Mandelbaum to have been generally considered the wealthiest in horseflesh.[86]

[80] Ibid., passim.   [81] Harmon, Journal, 34, 40, 73.
[82] Mandelbaum, "The Plains Cree," 182, 184, 303.
[83] Coues (ed.), Henry-Thompson Journals, II, 513.
[84] Henry, Travels and Adventures, 289, 299.
[85] Wissler, "Influence of the Horse," 4.
[86] Mandelbaum, "The Plains Cree," 167.

The date of 1742 seems late for the Snake,[87] when we find the same date suggested for the Assiniboin and the Teton Sioux. In 1800 or thereabout, the western frontier of the Assiniboin was practically on a line from Fort Vermilion on the North Saskatchewan River (about 110° W) southeastward to the Mandan villages on the Missouri (Bismarck, North Dakota), as we learn from the younger Henry.[88] In 1804, the Teton are given as occupying the territory along the Missouri between the mouth of White River and the North and South Dakota state boundary line,[89] and they were probably farther east sixty years previously.[90] We shall take the Assiniboin first in our examination.

If the Plains Cree had horses in 1738, there would be nothing extraordinary in the Assiniboin's having them in 1742. For the latter were nearer to the southern and western sources of supply. But they were Assiniboin in whose company both Henday and Cocking were traveling in 1754 and 1772 respectively, when they met the mounted Blackfoot. In Henday's case, both the "Assinepoets" proper and their kindred the "Eagle Indians," had manifestly so few horses that—despite the stimulating example of the Blackfoot— they only used them for packing purposes. Since these people dwelt on the very frontiers of the Blackfoot territory and were clearly on friendly terms with them, it is quite conceivable that those Assiniboin may have obtained their few horses from the Blackfoot.[91] It

[87] Wissler, "Influence of the Horse," 6; Webb, *The Great Plains,* 57.

[88] Coues (ed.), *Henry-Thompson Journals,* II, 516.

[89] Map, in Lewis and Clark, *Journals of the Expedition of 1804–1806* (ed. by Nicholas Biddle).

[90] The Sioux are described as being 'driven out on to the plains' by the Chippewa. James Mooney and Cyrus Thomas, in Hodge, *Handbook,* I, 277–81; also Thomas and Swanton, *ibid.,* II, 577–79. They were "immigrating from the Sauteux country," about 1790: so, Peter Grant, in L. R. Masson, *Les Bourgeois de la Compagnie du Nord-Ouest,* II, 346 (Chippewa=Ojibwa; Sauteux=Saulteaux). The Sioux and Assiniboin trend was steadily westward from their first appearance in authenticated history.

[91] Henday, "Journal" (ed. by Burpee), 331–51, *passim.* Perhaps they got horses with a white buffalo skin, the very earliest historical notice of which is in this precise territory at this time, and which the Assiniboin did not value (Coues [ed.], *Henry-Thompson Journals,* I, 159), while the Confederacy evidently did (*ibid.,* II, 646; Henday, "Journal" [ed. by Burpee], 337; Kidd, "Blackfoot Ethnography," 188; but see also Appendix A). The younger Henry remarks of the Hidatsa and their buffalo runners: "The only thing that will induce them to part with a horse of this kind

seems curious that this widespread (Assiniboin) folk had apparently heard nothing of a phenomenal development of twenty or thirty years' standing among their own people.

Edward Umfreville, apparently about 1785, saw what must surely have been either Assiniboin or Plains Cree horses 'marked Roman capitals,' which may have been Spanish brands.[92] John Macdonell (or McDonnell) found horses similarly marked among the Assiniboin in 1793.[93] Harmon described both Assiniboin and Cree as being 'well furnished with horses' about 1800;[94] and the younger Henry says the Assiniboin were inveterate horse thieves—"you are sure of your horse only when you are on his back."[95] Larocque writes very similarly (October 14, 1805): "We watched our horses all that night for fear of Assiniboines."[96] Sixty years later they bore an identical reputation, and gloried in it.[97] Where the animals were not driven off in bands—as in the Mexican raids, and in one instance recorded by the younger Henry at Fort Vermilion in 1809–10[98]—the inference seems reasonable that the skill of an individualist horse thief, like the woodcraft of an English poacher, would need some appreciable period of time for its acquirement. But the Assiniboin were sinned against as well as sinning. Horses were also stolen *from* them.[99] As in the case of the "Indian" raiders in nineteenth-century Texas (who were occasionally lawless white men), sometimes those horses which had (of course!) been "stolen by the Assiniboin" returned home later quite safely.[100]

is a white buffalo hide." (Coues [ed.], *Henry-Thompson Journals*, I, 353; cf. Maximilian, *Travels*, in Thwaites, *Travels*, XXIII, 289, 321, 371; XXIV, 48; Roe, *North American Buffalo*, 715-28.)

[92] Edward Umfreville, *The Present State of Hudson's Bay*, 178.

[93] "All over the plains" (John Macdonell's diary, in Gates [ed.], *Five Fur Traders*, 113). "Spanish brands," 1719, 1819; see Chapter III *supra*.

[94] Harmon, *Journal*, 40; cf. Mooney, in *Handbook of Canadian Indians*, 427. The Cree had "only a few horses," 1833; so, Maximilian, *Travels*, in Thwaites, *Travels*, XXIII, 14, 387.

[95] Coues (ed.), *Henry-Thompson Journals*, I, 295 ("Saulteurs and Red River Indians not so bad; anything safe with them except rum"). On the Assiniboin ("Stone Indians") as "most noted thieves," see also Thompson, *Narrative* (ed. by Tyrrell), 367; Maximilian, *Travels*, in Thwaites, *Travels*, XXII, 391; XXIII, 204–205; XXIV, 64–65, 81. Their kindred, the Sioux, were little better. See note 116 *infra*.

[96] Larocque, "Journal" (ed. by Burpee), 52.

[97] Cowie, *Company of Adventurers*, 230, 237, 347, 483.

[98] Coues (ed.), *Henry-Thompson Journals*, II, 575.

[99] Diary of Archibald N. McLeod, in Gates (ed.), *Five Fur Traders*, 179–80.

[100] *Ibid.*, 130.

Among the various loose generalizations, 'well furnished with horses' etc., I have found only one instance in this region giving any actual ratios. The younger Henry mentions a march of what, from their trailing order, were apparently Assiniboin, moving westward from Red River toward the Hair Hills (Pembina Mountain, southern Manitoba), in May, 1804: "They formed a string in the plains over a mile long—65 men and women, 10 horses, and 60 dogs."[101] Even here, however, we have no means of forming a reliable judgment whether they were a rich band or a poor one, in respect of horses. The drinking and gambling affrays which Henry relates—an appalling catalogue—could change such economic status in a night!

Two leading critics note that at a later time—apparently about 1830–1840—the Assiniboin "were said to have few horses."[102] Is not this probably to be taken as a purely comparative expression—relative to the greater numbers of certain other tribes? Very possibly such observers as Maximilian or Father De Smet were thinking of the Crow or the Flathead.[103] As early as 1776, the elder Henry (who knew nothing of the transmontane tribes) speaks of the horses "which the Osinipoilles possess in numbers."[104] In any event, if the Assiniboin actually had but few at that time, this is not necessarily evidence for chronological distribution, but points more probably to temperamental influences, such as those indicated by David Thompson.[105]

There are similar perplexing details in connection with the horse chronology of the Sioux. A recent student thinks "the Sioux probably acquired horses about the same time as the Blackfeet; the Mandans may have acquired them earlier."[106] With reference to the Blackfoot at least, the evidence scarcely appears to support that conclusion. No record of Sioux horses has thus far been found prior to the eighteenth century. Wissler noted that there is no mention of horses among them from any of the following: Radisson,

101 Coues (ed.), *Henry-Thompson Journals*, I, 244.
102 Kroeber, "Ethnology of the Gros Ventre," 147; Lowie, "The Assiniboin," 15.
103 See Maximilian, *Travels*, in Thwaites, *Travels*, XXII, 391; Hiram M. Chittenden and A. T. Richardson (eds.), *The Life, Letters, and Labors of Father Pierre-Jean De Smet, 1801–1873*, III, 1027.
104 Henry, *Travels and Adventures*, 289, 299.
105 See Chapter XIII *infra*.
106 Worcester, "Spanish Horses Among the Plains Tribes," 412.

1662 (Santee); Nicolas Perrot, Illinois country, 1665–1699; Duluth, Hennepin, La Salle, 1680; Le Sieur, 1700 (Plains Dakota.)[107] Later research has added virtually nothing to that conclusion. A contemporary scholar quotes a certain 'Sioux Winter Count' ("corresponding to 1700"), "When-the-Sioux-first-saw-the-Horse" (capturing a wild one!)[108] The critical reader must reconcile as best he can the reference given below (note 132) where this exploit is *first* recorded by the Sioux in 1812–13. It tends to indicate an isolation and mutual ignorance among scattered bands of the same nations, and once again enjoins caution in making generalizations.

Worcester mentions the Caddo's "frequently taking herds of horses to the Illinois" about 1717.[109] Whether this meant the tribe or the region (commonly "the Illinois," 1730–1810) is not clear. The Caddo may have started out for some distant objective in that general direction which they thought to be the Illinois (River?), or they might have been turned aside from some cause without reaching it. Whatever is the explanation, they never seem to have reached either the people or the country at that date. The Jesuit missionaries were working among the Mississippi River tribes during those years, and we should almost certainly have heard of it from them.

Wissler appears by an inadvertence to have antedated the testimony of an eyewitness some thirty years, in citing Peter Pond as an authority for the years 1740–1745. Pond was *born* in 1740, and reached the Mississippi in 1770.[110] Jonathan Carver found a few horses at Prairie du Chien, on the upper Mississippi, in 1766.[111] The Sioux division (or divisions) which Carver visited were still afoot at that time, but certain "western tribes" had horses then.[112] If these "western tribes" were those afore-mentioned Teton (of 1742), surely Carver's informants, their kindred, should have known of their identity after nearly a quarter of a century.

[107] Wissler, "Influence of the Horse," 6.

[108] Hartley B. Alexander, "The Horse in American Indian Culture," *So Live The Works of Men* (*Edgar Lee Hewett Anniversary Volume*), 65–74.

[109] Worcester, "Spanish Horses Among the Plains Tribes," 409.

[110] See Innis, *Fur Trade in Canada*, 195–206; also his *Peter Pond*, introduction, *et passim;* narrative of Peter Pond, in Gates (ed.), *Five Fur Traders;* Thompson, *Narrative* (ed. by Tyrrell), 171, note (Pond *born* January 18, 1740).

[111] Jablow, *The Cheyenne*, 9.

[112] See notes 5–8 *supra*.

If Carver followed the apparently usual route of those days (for British travelers), down the Ohio[113] and up the Mississippi to the Sioux country, he must almost inevitably have had to pass through or near to the lands of the Sauk. In 1804 these were on the Mississippi, below Rock River,[114] but it appears to have been the case that formerly they dwelt farther up the river,[115] being not improbably driven from thence by the powerful Sioux, who about 1800 were at the height of their aggressive arrogance.[116] Yet the aforesaid Peter Pond, the fur trader, noted in 1770 that the Sauk "go to St. Fee [Santa Fé] and bring with them Spanish horses."[117] Farther up the river, the Sioux were also found in 1774 to have horses; and at that time the Yanktonais (Sioux) had already had them at least four years, since 1770.[118]

Pond's description at that date is quaint and interesting. If the custom which he mentions was peculiar (in the north) to the Sioux alone—which is possible, for I have found no other allusion to it in that area, though J. Frank Dobie states that this was an (early) Comanche and widespread southern practice[119]—it would tend to suggest a somewhat lengthier acquaintance and possession, since modifications of such a character seldom present themselves at the beginning of things. Its familiarity among the Comanche tends also to confirm Jablow's views, noted above, on Spanish horses reaching the Northern tribes (among whom the Ponca are specifically mentioned by another scholar as obtaining their first horses from the Comanche,[120]) largely or principally through the Comanche as middlemen. Pond writes thus concerning the Sioux:

[113] This was the route of Capt. Harry Gordon, also 1766. See his journal in Newton D. Mereness (ed.), *Travels in the American Colonies, 1690–1783*, 465ff.

[114] Map, Lewis and Clark, *Journals* (ed. by Biddle). It is near Davenport, Iowa; Rock Island is at or near the confluence.

[115] Much as given in Wissler's map (*The American Indian*), about La Crosse or the Black River, Wisconsin.

[116] Lewis and Clark, *Journals* (ed. by Biddle), I, 135; Coues (ed.), *Henry-Thompson Journals*, I, 430–35; Larocque, "Journal" (ed. by Burpee). For Sioux and Assiniboin agressions against Arikara, Crow, Hidatsa, Mandan, and others, see Maximilian, *Travels*, in Thwaites, *Travels*, XXII, 341, 353; XXIII, 147, 228–33, 301, 317, 353, 383, 394; XXIV, 47, 54 (1795–1832). See also Jablow, *The Cheyenne*, 3–8, 51–58, 65, 79.

[117] Innis, *Peter Pond*, 37.

[118] *Ibid.*, 58; Gates (ed.), *Five Fur Traders*, 58.

[119] Dobie, "Indian Horses and Horsemanship," 268; *The Mustangs*, 50.

[120] Hoebel, "The Political Associations and Law-Ways of the Comanche Indians," 16.

They have a Grate Number of Horses and Dogs which carres there Bageag when they Move from Plase to Plase. . . . Thay Run down the Buffelow with thare Horses and Kill as Much Meat as thay Please. In Order to have thare Horseis Long Winded they slit thair Noses up to the Grissel of thare head which Make them Breath Verey freely. I have Sean them Run with those of Natrall Nostrals and Cum in Apearantley Not the Least Out of Breath.[121]

Much as the Iroquois did in the eastern areas, the Sioux apparently dominated the public consciousness in their territorial sphere; even in respect of their horses. The younger Henry mentions meeting an Indian, about 1800, who thought Henry's mounted party must be Sioux, 'since no others had horses.'[122] Other Indian tribes of the more central region, obtaining horses in the era 1750–1800, may perhaps have secured them from eastern sources, and scarcely concern us here.[123]

In 1805, Zebulon M. Pike noted 'innumerable herds of horses among the Yanctongs and Titongs';[124] and about the same time the Sauk and Fox (the well-known "Sac and Fox") were required in the provisions of a treaty "to return all stolen horses."[125] This rather implies fairly large numbers.

As a question of historical probabilities, this mention of the Spanish horses from Santa Fé (whether they passed through Comanche hands or not), together with the 'Roman capitals' of Umfreville, and Macdonell's 'Spanish brands' on northern horses, and the southern raids of the Blackfoot Confederacy, about 1787–89,

---

[121] Quoted by Wissler, "Influence of the Horse," 5. Re 1740 instead of 1770, the repetition shows them to be inadvertences and not technical misprints.

[122] Coues (ed.), *Henry-Thompson Journals*, I, 130. This of course cannot be considered chronological evidence.

[123] The Wyandot are said to have first secured horses at Braddock's defeat, 1755. There were some horses around Detroit, 1775 (Wissler, "Influence of the Horse," 8). A recent historian mentions horse stealing by Indians in the Ohio territory, 1778, 1810 (Havighurst, *Land of Promise*, 116, 132). Horses were rare among the Iroquois even in the eighteenth century (W. N. Fenton, in *Swanton Memorial Volume*, 230).

[124] Coues (ed.), *Expeditions of Pike*, I, 344–45. Thompson's observation, 1796, that the Sioux "now had horses instead of canoes" seems merely commonplace at that date. Haines ("Northward Spread of Horses," 434) considers it to indicate that "they had made the change in comparatively recent times, or it would not have been worth the emphasis he gave it." This is to infer an emphasis and a meaning which Thompson's language scarcely warrants.

[125] Wissler, "Influence of the Horse," 8.

raises questions of some importance. These phenomena point apparently to a quicker and surer source of supply than either trafficking with other tribes nearer at hand to the Spanish fountainhead, or breeding for themselves.[126] Thus the whole question of a possible western (i.e., transmontane) major origin for the horses of the Missouri tribes and those of the Canadian plains is thrown into the melting pot once again.[127] It seems a fair inference that if branded horses were found among such a tribe as the Arikara,[128] who dwelt very much in the current of the transmontane-Missouri River traffic, then neither that nor the Northern Plains route could claim any overwhelming predominance.

Another curious circumstance possibly tends to indicate a fairly early date for the horse toward the northeast. John Long, the Northwest Company's trader in the Nipigon country north of Lake Superior (1768–1782), mentions an Ojibwa—who should have been a Forest Ojibwa (Chippewa) in that region—bearing the name of "Ogashy" ("the horse."[129]). Considering that in so many cases the Indian tribal horse names were *names* only, adapted from the dog or deer,[130] and not true etymons, it would be of interest to learn the derivation of this word "Ogashy." It might even have been a loan word from some distant or different linguistic stock possessing horses, and bestowed in the symbolical, "nickname" sense. For although a considerable degree of resemblance has persisted between the (parental) Ojibwa and the Cree language, this word bears no resemblance to the Cree "mistatim."[131]

Perhaps one of the most connected records—scanty enough even then—concerning any Indian tribe is contained in a certain

---

[126] "A few of the northern tribes came to understand breeding." (Dobie, "Indian Horses and Horsemanship," 270; *The Mustangs*, 52–55.)

[127] See Jablow, *The Cheyenne*, 13–17.

[128] Bradbury, *Travels*, in Thwaites, *Travels*, V, 176.

[129] John Long, *Voyages and Travels, 1768–1782*, in Thwaites, *Travels*, II, 142.

[130] "Horse" in the Creek or "Muscogulge" tongue (Southeastern area) signifies "big deer" (Bartram, *Travels*, 185). In the Shawnee, "Mĭshāwā"="elk" (Grinnell, in Hodge, *Handbook*, I, 569–71). In such areas the deer might very naturally suggest themselves. The classical Blackfoot term "ponokamita" embraced both elk and dog. Alanson Skinner notes that while the Plains Ojibwa had travois—dog and horse successively—the main (forest) Ojibwa had none ("The Culture of the Plains Cree," 314–18). David Thompson says the "Oojibaways" east of Red River had no horses, 1798 (*Narrative* [ed. by Tyrrell], 246).

[131] See Roe, *North American Buffalo*, App. A.

"Sioux calendar," printed by Colonel Richard Irving Dodge, and covering the years 1799–1870. I quote the entries relating to horses:

1802–1803:   The Sioux stole a lot of horses that had shoes on— the first they had ever seen (shoes or horses?)

1803–1804:   The Sioux stole some 'woolly horses' from the Crows.

1812–1813:   The Sioux first captured wild horses.[132]

1824–1825:   'Swan,' chief of the 'Two Kettle' tribe of Sioux, had all his horses killed.

1825–1826:   High water in the Missouri River. . . . many horses lost.

1841–1842:   Sioux . . . stole thirty spotted ponies.

1849–1850:   Crow Indians stole eight hundred horses from the Brulé Sioux.

1868–1869:   Texas cattle first brought into the Sioux country.[133]

To just what extent this "calendar" may be accepted must be left to more competent judges than myself. Two possibly favorable circumstances may be noted. There is no hint of vainglorying about the Sioux' being the first to have horses, or the like. This rather tends by implication to agree with the Cheyenne tradition of Sioux horse-origins, in the western Cheyenne habitat toward the Black Hills, at least:

They declared that the first Sioux who came were very poor and had no horses, which the Cheyennes had already obtained. . . . that when the Sioux came, carrying their possessions on dog travois, the Cheyenne took pity on them and occasionally gave them a horse; that this generosity resulted in the coming of more and more Sioux to receive like presents.[134]

Secondly, the general chronology of the calendar may find some

[132] This reference, coupled with the evident mastery of the arts of horse-capture among the "Kootanae" and other transmontane tribes, about 1800 (Thompson, *Narrative* [ed. by Tyrrell], 377–78, 401), may perhaps serve as a rough chronological index of the Sioux horse-experience; perhaps only of a relationship in which pupils no doubt frequently excelled their teachers. But cf. note 108 *supra*.

[133] Dodge, *Our Wild Indians*, 400–404. It seems clear that this calendar can refer only to some particular division of the Sioux. See Thomas and Swanton, in Hodge, *Handbook*, II, 577; see also Cyrus Thomas, *ibid.*, I, 189.

[134] Grinnell, *The Fighting Cheyennes*, 34.

support in the dating of 'the first Texas cattle,' which appears to be fairly borne out by independent research.[135] A recent commentator cites other "winter counts" affecting the horses among the Teton Dakota, in the period 1826–81.[136] These will require careful consideration later from a totally different angle. Their dates render them irrelevant to any discussion concerning horse *origins* among the Sioux.

Our invaluable observer, the younger Henry, again furnishes us with the only even approximate estimate of the early ratios of men and horses that I have discovered respecting the Sioux. He describes an inroad of a Sioux war party along Red River in 1808. They acted with an insolent bravado which disdained any concealment of their numbers or resources; and from their trail they were supposed to consist of "but few horses to upwards of a hundred men."[137]

[135] Bancroft states that the first Mexican cattle were taken to the Platte, 1866 (*History of Nevada, California, and Wyoming*, 544). The first to Montana, 1866; an established trade by 1867. Wyoming uncertain, but about 1868 (so, Grace R. Hebard and E. A. Brininstool, *The Bozeman Trail*, I, 229; E. S. Osgood, *The Day of the Cattleman*, 21, 31–32, 42–46). Some other details also, with dates, in Bancroft, *North Mexican States*, II, 559–63; Webb, *The Great Plains*, 216, 260 (citing much material); and two admirable later works, Merrill G. Burlingame, *The Montana Frontier*, 272–74; Paul I. Wellman, *The Trampling Herd*.

[136] John C. Ewers, "Were the Blackfoot Rich in Horses?" 605–606; see also Dobie, *Tales of the Mustang*, 18.

[137] Coues (ed.), *Henry-Thompson Journals*, I, 435.

VI

FOOTHILLS AND MOUNTAINS

In view of the conventional application to Plains tribes, par excellence, of such terms as "characteristic" or "typical" horse Indians, it is curious to note that among those who were apparently the earliest to possess horses in really large quantities—which perhaps implies, among the earliest to possess them at all—were some of the more northerly tribes living to the westward of the first (main) range of the Rocky Mountains.[1] As we have seen, competent inquirers have even thought that it was first of all from some of these transmontane tribes that certain ultra horse-and-buffalo peoples of the Northern Plains region obtained their horses.[2]

The Astorians in 1811 (or their chronicler, Washington Irving) described the Crow as being "the grand intermediaries in such transactions between the transmontane and the plains tribes."[3] Father De Smet, some thirty years later, endorses this verdict *in esse*, though in much less ornate language:

The horses of the Crows are principally of the maroon race of the prairies. They have also many horses which they have stolen from the Sioux, the Sheyennes, and other Indians of the southwest, which they had in their turn stolen from the Spaniards of Mexico. The Crows are considered the most indefatigable marauders of the desert; they traverse

[1] Haines, "Northward Spread of Horses," 435, 436. Bancroft ranks the Kutenai as the farthest north (mountain) tribe of horse Indians (*Native Races*, I, 292, 460). This is endorsed by a scholarly Canadian anthropologist, who has the horse 'confined to that tribe' for a long period (Alice Ravenhill, *The Native Tribes of British Columbia*, 28).

[2] Haines, "Northward Spread of Horses," 436; see note 15 *infra*.

[3] Irving, *Astoria*, 208, 221, 430.

123

the mountains in all directions, bearing to one side what they have taken at the other. The name of Atsharoke, or Crow [Absaroka, Upsaroka, Upsahroku], has been given to them on account of their robberies.[4]

There is a certain amount of conflicting evidence concerning the Crow characteristics, as indicated above. Charles Larpenteur, whose intercourse with them was contemporaneous with that of De Smet, is much more liberal or apologetic in their defense, and certainly implies that their evil manners, even if authentic, were of recent date. He says:

The Crows did not drink then, and for many years remained sober; it was not until a few years ago, when they were driven out of their country by the Sioux, and became a part of the tribe on the Missouri, that they took to drinking with the Assiniboines. As they did not drink, their trade was all in substantial goods, which kept them always well dressed, and extremely rich in horses.[5]

Larocque, who is our earliest witness of all, also gives them a rather good character, which may of course have been (not unnaturally) colored by their hospitality toward him. He writes thus (1805):

[The Crows] have no other tame animals but Dogs and horses few of the former but many of the latter whom they use on all occasions, for war and for hunting, they have them in trade from the flat head Indians in great numbers and very cheap. They sell part to the Big Bellys and Mandans at double the price they purchase them and carry on a continual trade in that manner. . . .

They say that no equal number of other Indians can beat them on horseback, but that on foot they are not capable to cope with those nations who have no horses. They pass for brave and courageous among their neighbours. They seldom go to war or to steal horses, but defend themselves when attacked. . . . They have never had any traders with them, they get their battle Guns, ammunitions etc from the Mandans and Big Bellys in exchange for horses.[6]

[4] De Smet, *Letters and Sketches*, in Thwaites, *Travels*, XXVII, 180; and see the Sioux calendar, 1849–50 (Chapter V *supra*).

[5] Charles Larpenteur, *Forty Years a Fur Trader on the Upper Missouri* (ed. by Elliott Coues), I, 45.

[6] Larocque, "Journal" (ed. by Burpee), 64–65.

Notwithstanding these favorable testimonies, the general weight of evidence seems to support De Smet's characterization. J. Frank Dobie writes as follows:

The Comanches were the great horse Indians, but—in proportion to their numbers, which were much less than those of the Comanches— the Crows on the Yellowstone were not far behind them. . . . Jim Beckwourth, who in the thirties became chieftain over the Crows and who later supplied material for an autobiography, was one of the West's most remarkable liars. His figures cannot be relied upon; nevertheless he reveals the horse-hunger of the Plains Indians. According to his account, a band of Crows, headed by himself, raided down on a great Comanche camp south of the Arkansas River and cut out 5000 horses from a prairie filled with them. When, driving their booty before them, they got back to the Yellowstone, they found that another party of Crows had stolen 2700 horses from the Kootenays. Just before this some other Crow braves had taken 800 head away from the Cheyennes. Soon in the unrelenting struggle for horses Beckwourth's people lost 3000 head to the Blackfeet, then retaliated with a raid that netted them 7000 Blackfeet horses.[7]

It is recorded that as late as 1871, in the very latest era of the "contratribal" age, the Crow stole virtually all the horses of the Sioux, and that year was designated by the Sioux in their "winter count," or calendar, as "Chasing-Horses-in-Camp."[8] The apologist's argument might contend that these exploits exemplified the degeneracy of their later years. Larpenteur himself quotes an old French mountaineer in some sudden rencontre: "They are Crows —there is no danger for our lives, but they are great thieves."[9] Such reputations do not commonly grow out of nothing, and we find this one attached to the Crow in the very earliest era of Western exploration, and in regions hundreds of miles apart. Whether justly or unjustly, they were at least known to and reported by Robert Stuart, the eastbound Astorian leader in 1812, as 'expert horse thieves.'[10] Jacob Fowler, on his Santa Fé expedition of 1821–22,

[7] Dobie, *Tales of the Mustang*, 17–18. The authenticity of these "thousands" will be discussed in Chapter XV.

[8] Dobie, *ibid.*, 18.

[9] Larpenteur, *Forty Years a Fur Trader* (ed. by Coues), I, 44.

[10] Philip Ashton Rollins (ed.), *The Discovery of the Oregon Trail* (Robert Stuart's Narratives), 130–32, 134–35, 150.

states that from four hundred to five hundred horses were stolen from the great camp on the Arkansas River after his arrival.[11] These are not specifically said to have been stolen by the Crows, but it seems very probable, for Fowler mentions meeting a party of thirteen Crows with two hundred stolen horses; and later the same band tried to steal Fowler's own horses.[12] Whether by raiding or trading, the Crow were stated by Maximilian to have more horses about 1833 than any tribe on the Missouri River—'nine thousand or ten thousand of them,'[13] and the estimate is accepted by the foremost modern commentator on the tribe.[14]

Whether as thieves in the first degree, traders, or distributors, the Crows, in the opinion of an important inquirer, were only one of many Northwestern tribes who were themselves indebted to the Shoshone for their acquaintance with the horse. Francis Haines writes: "Cayuse, Walla-Walla, Yakima, Palouse, Nez Percé, Flathead, Blackfoot, Crow, and many other tribes, were furnished from the Shoshone of Southern Idaho long before horses were common among the Sioux and the north-eastern Assiniboines."[15]

Haines considers there were two main routes of supply and "advance" northward from the Southwestern Spanish horse territories. These routes were, respectively: (1) the Plains; (2) west of the Continental Divide. He thinks the Flathead horses came from the south and southeast, and that the Snake in Idaho (aforesaid Shoshone?) had horses 1690–1700.[16] The probability of the Crow's being transmontane raiders is not lessened by the fact that other tribes definitely were. David Thompson writes as follows, about 1787:

The Peeagan [Piegan] Indians, and their tribes of Blood and Blackfeet, being next to the Mountains often send out parties under a young Chief to steal Horses from their enemies on the south and west sides

11 Fowler, *Journal* (ed. by Coues), 60–61.
12 *Ibid.,* 73, 92.
13 Maximilian, *Travels,* in Thwaites, *Travels,* XXII, 351–52.
14 Robert H. Lowie, *The Crow Indians, xiv.*
15 Haines, "Northward Spread of Horses," 436; Lowie, *The Crow Indians, xv.* Dobie mentions a Crow tradition, which he considers authentic, of the Crow's getting their first horses from the Pawnee (*The Mustangs,* 39).
16 Haines, "Northward Spread of Horses," 435, 436; Francis D. Haines, "Nez Percé and Shoshoni Influence on Northwest History," *Greater America* (Bolton Anniversary Volume), 379, 391.

of the Mountains, known as the Snake, the Saleesh, and the Kootanae Indians.[17]

Possibly from these operations arose the definite tradition that horses were "acquired" from those tribes, as Wissler euphemistically puts it. More than one of the Astorians, in addition to later observers, commented upon the abundance of horses among the Flathead,[18] Nez Percé,[19] Snake (Shoshoni),[20] "Cathlasco,"[21] and "Wallah-Wallahs."[22] Among the "Sciatogas" about 1811, they were even more plentiful—and cheaper—than among the Snake;[23] and the Sciatoga territory along the "upper Columbia"[24] and its tributaries was noted for its plenty.[25] The circumstance of the large herds owned by the Cayuse Indians gave rise to the common Western name of "cayuse" for an Indian or native pony.[26] The immense numbers gave the name to "Horse Prairie"[27] or "Horse Plains,"[28] in the Coeur d'Alene country, where, as everybody said, 'horses in droves were always to be found.' A recent scholar quotes an ancient informant of the Blackfoot Confederacy whose memories reached back to the eighteen sixties, and whose comparisons are thought

[17] Thompson, *Narrative* (ed. by Tyrrell), 367.

[18] Franchère (1811), *Voyage to the Northwest Coast*, in Thwaites, *Travels*, VI, 339–41; Alexander Ross (1820), *Adventures of the First Settlers on the Oregon or Columbia River*, in Thwaites, *Travels*, VII, 215; John B. Wyeth, *Oregon, 1832*, in Thwaites, *Travels*, XXI, 87.

[19] Alexander Ross, *Adventures of the First Settlers on the Oregon or Columbia River*, in Thwaites, *Travels*, VII, 215. Coues (ed.), *Henry-Thompson Journals*, ii, 712. See also Dobie, "Indian Horses and Horsemanship," 272.

[20] Irving, *Astoria*, 274, 282–85; Bancroft, *Native Races*, I, 273; 'more than any other tribe,' Dobie considers ("Indian Horses and Horsemanship," 272); Maximilian says, 1833, and presumably quoting contemporary opinion, that they had not as many as the Blackfoot (*Travels*, in Thwaites, *Travels*, XXIV, 295). See also note 23 *infra*.

[21] Irving, *Astoria*, 309, 316, 327.

[22] *Ibid.* See also Townsend (1833), *Narrative*, in Thwaites, *Travels*, XXI, 283. For some years horseflesh was the staple diet at Fort Walla Walla (Hudson's Bay Company). Between 1821 and 1824 they consumed seven hundred head (Morton, *History of the Canadian West*, 718).

[23] Townsend, *Narrative*, in Thwaites, *Travels*, XXI, 282–85. See note 15 *supra*; the first six of those tribes are "Sciatogas" (Shahaptians); so, Hodge, *Handbook*, II, 520, 1135.

[24] "Upper" in United States territory, actually "central." See Bancroft, *Native Races*, I, 292, 460; Coues (ed.), *Henry-Thompson Journals*, II, 818.

[25] Irving, *Astoria*, 261–62, 274.

[26] Thwaites, *Travels*, VII, 137, editor's note.

[27] Chittenden and Richardson (eds.), *Life of De Smet*, III, 972.

[28] *Ibid.*, III, 995; Thompson, *Narrative* (ed. by Tyrrell), 541, editor's note.

to be reasonably valid for the thirties: "Flatheads had more horses than the Crows, Crows more than the Piegans, Piegans more than Bloods, and North Blackfeet. The Gros Ventres [Atsina?], Crees and Assiniboines had still smaller numbers."[29]

The attempt to date the horse in these territories is met by the usual contradictions and paradoxes, which are inevitable in traditional testimony from nonliterate peoples. We have seen that the suggestion of 1742 for the Snake is probably too late in itself, in the face of other evidence fully as reliable. It seems entirely too late for their supposed—and quite possible—Blackfoot disciples to have so completely mastered every phase of horse culture within ten or twelve years, and perhaps much less, that by 1754 they were the most expert of horse masters in riding, hunting, draft use, stable care, and even in swimming 'broad and deep rivers.'[30] Consequently, if the Snake are to be accepted as the source of the Blackfoot horses, their own acquisition of the horse must unquestionably be pushed back a considerable time; even without adopting Haines's suggestion, which would place the experience of David Thompson's ancient Piegan or Cree informant about 1710 rather than 1730.[31] We should in any event be compelled to date the Snake horses not later, and very probably much earlier, than 1700. Wissler notes that "Blackfoot traditions indicate that in early days the Snake were frequently found hunting on the upper Missouri, but were eventually pushed back because they lacked firearms." They were also a power to be dreaded by the Pawnee in 1742. Other Blackfoot tradition has them as a powerful horse people about 1730—perhaps 1710.[32]

We have seen that two among the best informed of our earlier students of this question—one definitely in favor of that date, and the other, favoring a date perhaps a century before—are for the

[29] Ewers, "Were the Blackfoot Rich in Horses?" 603.

[30] Henday, December 8, 1754: "Men employed make Sleds of Birch for the Women and Horses." See the complete round of horse uses, October, 1754 to May, 1755 ("Journal" [ed. by Burpee], 334-51).

[31] Haines, "How Did the Indians Get Their Horses?" 116.

[32] See Chapters III and IV *supra*, where the Comanche, 'the great horse Indians of early days,' are thought by Wissler to have had horses probably from 1600 ("Influence of the Horse," 2, 6, 13, 15). Elsewhere Wissler considers that about 1600 the Comanche were probably a part of the Snake "group" (*ibid.*, 23), and Haines himself agrees with him ("Northward Spread of Horses," 436).

Blackfoot themselves.[33] A more recent scholar, Francis Haines, argues for the Flathead's (a rather vague term without more precise specification) having acquired the horse about 1710–1720, rather than their own dating of about 1600.[34] The suggestion might not in itself be thought unreasonable, but Haines does not inform us what is his (or their) basis for the earlier date. I am very hesitant about accepting a date (that is to say, a closely specified period of time) solely upon Indian authority, although on other grounds it might be inherently not improbable. We may, I think, be quite sure that the "Sioux calendar" cited above was not *dated* by the Indians themselves. The years included there, as we date them, could be computed backwards from known (i.e., contemporary) historical dates. The Flathead "dating," in so far as we can judge from the information, seems to be purely empirical.

At the same time, aside from any discussion of the *methods* of chronological computation, the Flathead dating is in my opinion more probably nearer to the truth. It is impossible to discuss the arrival of the horse among them as an isolated problem having no relationship to horse chronology as a whole; to be decided, so to speak, by a priori impressions pro or con. One might just as logically suppose that the species as a free wild creature could be physically isolated forever from this or that temperate range on this continent. Any chronology of the Flathead horse which cannot adjust itself to evidence—at least equally authentic—from other portions of the (northern) horse habitat must *ipso facto* be adjudged defective. And in this particular case the contemporary or perhaps even earlier dating is that of tribes who are supposedly indebted to the *later* ones for their horses! Haines himself writes that the "Cayuse, Walla-

[33] Henday, "Journal" (ed. by Burpee), 317–18; Wissler, "Influence of the Horse," 10 (see Chapter IV *supra*).

[34] Haines, "Northward Spread of Horses," 435. The "Flatheads" are specified as interior Salish by Harry Turney-High, in an essay which I have had no opportunity to see ("The Diffusion of the Horse to the Flatheads," *Man*, Vol. XXXV [Dec., 1935], 183–85). According to Rev. Henry Harmon Spalding, Marcus Whitman's colleague, the "Flatheads" were derisively so termed by those tribes who practiced the head-binding "wedge" formation, for *not* following their example (Archer B. and Dorothy P. Hulbert [eds.], *Marcus Whitman, Crusader*, I, 131–32). The name is thus an exact parallel to the contemptuous "Roundheads" of Cromwell's time. But there can be no doubt that "Flathead" has been used more often in popular diction to define those who *do* deform the skull. See Hodge, *Handbook*, I, 465.

Walla, Yakima, Palouse, Nez Percé, Flathead, Blackfoot, Crow, and many other tribes were furnished from the Shoshone of Southern Idaho long before horses were common among the Sioux and the north-eastern Assiniboine."[35] Yet in another place he dates the horse among the Snake (Shoshone) only in 1690–1700;[36] while yet again he himself, as we have seen, would antedate the old Cree-Piegan's 'first horse' to about 1710.[37] The period of years which these various particulars necessitate seems in my judgment altogether too short for such widespread consequences and reactions.

A further student has discussed a tradition of the "Flathead" (interior Salish) regarding the capture of their first horses in the middle years of the eighteenth century, in an essay which I regret having had no opportunity to see.[38] If this tradition commemorates the actual *capture* on the open range of their first *wild* horses, it is quite possibly authentic, and may be considered an important event in their history. We have seen that the first capture of wild horses by a tribe which had long possessed the animal was considered to be of sufficient significance to merit special notice in the "Sioux calendar."[39] This fact furnishes additional support for Denhardt's contention that the Indians preferred to steal or otherwise obtain domesticated animals for their first horses rather than the wild mustangs of the Plains. If, on the other hand, the term "capture" is merely a general synonym for "obtaining" or "acquiring" the horse, indicating a supposition on the critic's part that the Salish secured their *first* horses in this manner, one can only say that such a supposition, at that date, clashes irreconcilably with more precise evidence.

While a tradition of an event may survive in Indian minds—instances of which in recognizable form have been recorded—my own investigations have convinced me that without the assistance of some permanent record (in which case it virtually ceases to be a tradition), Indian traditions are untrustworthy in respect of *dates*, meaning specified periods of time, beyond the memory of living persons, if not for much lesser periods. One such tradition,

[35] See note 15 *supra*.
[36] See note 16 *supra*.
[37] See Chapter V *supra*.
[38] See note 34 *supra*.
[39] See Chapter V *supra*.

which, when examined under the critical microscope, proved to be completely fallacious, was only eleven years old.[40] I do not decry the Indian; rather I respect many Indian friends I have met. But he is in my judgment the acute observer of the moment rather than the reliable critical generalizer.[41] Most of us know many white men who are neither. In any case, for our present purpose the approximate date of 1750, even if established, could scarcely be considered to furnish any hitherto undiscovered information. Wissler in 1910 suggested horses among the Pend d'Oreille about 1745.

In the more southerly regions of the Pacific Coast states, immense droves of wild horses were a conspicuous feature, quite possibly from a very early date, relatively speaking. Ross Cox, the Astorian, was told by the Spaniards at San Francisco that in 1812 it was found necessary to slaughter some thirty thousand wild horses in order to conserve the grass for the buffalo.[42] The "buffalo" in this case are cattle, since the historic buffalo, *Bison americanus*, has never been known within the coastward bounds of modern California, although their presence in northeastern California, a little westward from the Nevada state line, seems to be satisfactorily attested.[43] Frémont noted the vast herds of wild horses in the San Joaquin Valley in 1843–44;[44] and the slaughterings of large numbers are historically notorious. There was, in addition, an export trade, but whether it materially affected the horse population is another matter.[45]

There is a final question which is applicable to the topic of Indian acquisition of the horse at large, independently of the for-

[40] See Roe, "Extermination of the Buffalo in Western Canada," 1–23. For some critical judgments concerning tribal traditions, see Chapter V *supra*.

[41] Since first writing this, I have found an identical judgment from a very competent authority, George Bird Grinnell (*The Fighting Cheyennes*, 270).

[42] Ross Cox, *The Columbia River*, II, 96.

[43] See Roe, *North American Buffalo*, 280–82, etc. Early California, like early Florida, covered a far larger territory than the modern state of that name. For *B. americanus* in northeastern California, see Francis A. Riddell, "The Recent Occurrence of Bison in Northeastern California," *American Antiquity*, Vol. XVIII (1952), 168–69.

[44] Frémont, *Narrative*, 270–72.

[45] Hubert Howe Bancroft, *A History of Pastoral California, 1769–1849*, 336, 346; *History of California, 1542–1890*, II, 418–20, 668, etc.; Dobie, *The Mustangs*, 41, 106, 115, 322–24. For the exports, about 1825–35, Adele Ogden, "New England Traders in Spanish Mexico and California," *Greater America*, 401, 402. True to form, the Hawaiians shared the common aboriginal terror (*ibid.*, 404).

tunes or the chronology of any one tribe, which may be conveniently discussed before dismissing this phase of our inquiry. Haines observes: "It is interesting to note that the Indian horse thieves of later years usually stole from the tribes from whom they traditionally secured their first horses."[46]

The meaning of the statement is not entirely clear. In one sense it seems almost a self-evident truth, while in another it appears open to question. If Haines means that Indians were (commonly) not restrained by any sense of gratitude from including their earliest horse benefactors among the victims of their raiding forays, there is probably little occasion for criticism. The unstable conditions of nomadic Plains life were such that the friend of today was frequently the foe of tomorrow, and vice versa. Horses in historic times were almost always a tempting prize, from whomsoever they might be seized. And precisely as a tribe's nearest neighbors would logically be the ones to introduce—perhaps merely to reveal—the horse in most instances, very similarly the same nearest neighbors would logically be the ones "ordained to lend" (to borrow Elia's phrase) when a predatory raid was being planned. We have seen the Assiniboin presented as the boon companions who introduced the Crow to the pleasures of the bottle. According to the same informant, that did not prevent either tribe from stealing the others' horses when the opportunity arose.[47]

If, however, Haines's meaning is that this habit is to be taken as a sort of inherited practice which owed its first inception to the early preference of the Indians for stealing Spanish domesticated horses rather than capturing wild ones, this is in my view rather open to question. I doubt whether any body of Indians not previously acquainted with the animal at close range *could* successfully steal horses, or whether they would dare to attempt it. We have contemporary descriptions of Indian technique in horse stealing, dating from 1693 onward, but in every case it is quite obvious that the thieves were already perfectly familiar with horses and their ways.[48]

[46] Haines, "Northward Spread of Horses," 436.
[47] Larpenteur, *Forty Years a Fur Trader* (ed. by Coues), II, 372.
[48] Haines, "Northward Spread of Horses," 436; Denhardt, *Horse of the Americas*, 87, 91, 99, 104, etc. For 1693, see Chapter IV *supra*. J. Frank Dobie has collected a number of accounts in *The Mustangs*, 73–84. Compare also Haines's remarks

Certainly the original problem for the Indians could not be dealt with on any basis of preferences; it would be one of involuntary necessity. To an uninitiated, unskilled, individual Indian, a well-broken and "domesticated" Spanish-bred horse (doubtless none too tolerant for some time of a strange-smelling race[49]) would be only a fraction less terrible at close quarters than a wild creature of the species; and in my opinion would be entirely beyond the management, *for successful theft,* of one completely ignorant of the ways of horses. We have seen that although the Spanish authorities were for long firmly opposed—as a policy—to allowing their Indian vassals to become horsemen, their individual selfishness and indifference, together with a slave master's characteristic love of his own ease, and some measure of local necessity, led to Indians being increasingly used from the earliest horse times as grooms and stable attendants whom it frequently suited an owner's personal convenience to mount on horseback.[50] It cannot be doubted that many such slave-trained experts taught their kindred to quell their needless fears of the strange monsters, much as in later days did the *Comancheros,* the half-blood traders.[51]

Without doubt, by the time the scene of such first approaches had progressively advanced to the Platte, the Missouri, or the Saskatchewan, certain phases of the problem would be somewhat less acute. The *racial* smell of the Indian would be less unfamiliar and terrifying, but the individual smell of the particular stranger-thief then engaged on the enterprise would still be an obstacle, and the success of such horse stealing by unpracticed horsemen would still be highly problematical.

It is not necessary to suppose that the broadly normal conditions of intertribal warfare in the historic Plains world were literally so incessant and unbroken that the Indians had to steal their first horses from other Indian tribes simply because it was impossible to obtain them, or some knowledge of them, in any other

on the non-adoption of immediate riding by primitive peoples (*The Appaloosa Horse,* 27).

[49] On the difficulties of smell, to an Indian horse-breaker with a wild mustang *already captured,* see Denhardt, *Horse of the Americas,* 243–48; cf. Dobie, *The Mustangs,* 112–17, etc.

[50] *Ibid.,* 25, for a viceroy of Mexico, 1541 (see Chapter II *supra*). Denhardt, *Horse of the Americas,* 33, 103–106, 121, 235, etc.

[51] *Ibid.,* 105–107.

manner. The erratic wanderings of the buffalo, which were a common cause of hostilities among the Plains tribes, were also a not infrequent cause of peace, even though it might be at times of an uneasy and short-lived character.[52] Among the nomad tribes, whose way of life was the very antithesis of regularity, we can scarcely doubt that their horse relations would be colored by such generally unpredictable impulses. From such influences, in addition to the contacts of definite friendships or alliances, I consider that the inevitably necessary processes of initiation into some degree of acquaintance with the elements of horse lore would proceed, and be fostered. The typical horse Indian of history became a being so thoroughly and utterly at one with his mount, two fractions of the same entity, that *we* never witnessed, and indeed can scarcely conceive, any other condition of affairs. But even with such a past master there had to be a beginning.

It is mortifying to have to acknowledge how little our researches really add to our definite knowledge as to when and how any one tribe actually acquired the horse. It is only when two authentic dates approach very closely, previously to which the people in question apparently had none, and after which they were utilizing the animal, that we can feel any reasonable certainty. And even such certainty is in respect of *time* alone, and conveys no sure enlightenment concerning peoples, places, or processes. Such dates of close approach as we have are few and far between. When periods of thirty or fifty years intervene, we can but conjecture and balance probabilities. And frequently our conclusions cannot be made to agree.

[52] Even such bitter foes as the Cree and the Blackfoot were sometimes compelled to make peace for this reason. See Roe, *North American Buffalo*, 649–54, etc.

VII

PROBLEMS OF COLORATION

There is one problem that may never be solved. It would be of immense interest and value, both to the historical student and to the zoologist more purely, to learn what agglomeration of European, Asiatic, or Hispano-American breeds combined to produce the wild or "Indian" pony of the North American continent, with its hang-dog appearance so little suggestive of its almost inexhaustible stamina,[1] and its inescapable "pinto" coloration.

It scarcely seems possible to doubt that this characteristic coloration must have stamped itself upon the North American wild equine race at a really early period, when Spanish was yet the universal language of the horse country. For otherwise the animal would almost inevitably have received some such English designation as "piebald," which has been used time out of mind for similarly parti-colored ponies in England, by folk who never heard of a pinto. I have somewhere heard or read of a supposed distinction between a pinto and a piebald, white upon (predominating) brown or bay, versus brown upon white, but I forget which was which or upon what authority it rested. It is really immaterial, for nobody in the West ever observes it. Catlin himself—an Easterner

[1] I have elsewhere drawn attention to the possible action of buffalo "manuring" as an age-long process, conferring a far higher nutritive content into the pasturage of the short-grass buffalo territory than a similar bulk of ordinary or tame grasses contain (*North American Buffalo*, 384, 497, 522, 831). A recent writer considers the protein content in the same pasturage as the decisive factor in the nutritive values of the "buffalo grass," and consequently in his opinion the dominating cause of the heavy concentration of buffalo in those areas (Charles W. Johnson, "Protein as a Factor in the Distribution of the American Bison," *The Geographical Review*, Vol. XLI [1951], 330–31). It seems at least possible that the extraordinary stamina of the Indian pony may be traceable in part to the same ecological factor.

—uses the term "pied,"[2] and we find "piebald" in a translation from the Spanish in the present chapter.[3] This last, however, is possibly from Cunninghame Graham, who would use the English term.[4]

As we have seen, it was not many years after the discovery of America, and indeed while Columbus (1446–1506) was yet living, that the Spaniards began to utilize the larger West Indian islands, Cuba, Haiti, Jamaica, Puerto Rico, Trinidad, etc., as horse-breeding centers for Spanish America at large. For it was found (not unnaturally, as the Inca chronicler Garcilaso de la Vega observes), that horses reared in those environments endured the climate—or climates—of Mexico better than direct importations from Spain.[5] The favorite Spanish horse was the semi-Arab "breed of Córdoba," a renowned strain in the Peninsula. "Today," says Cunninghame Graham, "the horses born from Spanish stock in Cuba have become small and weedy by interbreeding, and certainly do not appear fiery and still less fit for war."[6] Not at all an inappropriate description of the general appearance of an Indian cayuse!

The wild horses of the South American pampas were called *baguales*.[7] Unlike the wild Plains herds of the North American continent, they did not display the pinto markings. There were occasional dark browns and dark chestnuts, but the staple coloring was bay. Felix de Azara, the Spanish naturalist, wrote about 1790: "When a cream-coloured, a grey, a piebald, or any other coat is seen, it is certain that animal is not an original *bagual*, but a tame horse who has escaped."[8] Cunninghame Graham subjoins to this a footnote of his own:

[2] Catlin, *Letters and Notes*, II, 57.

[3] See note 8 *infra*.

[4] Pinto (colloquially "paint") is one of thirty-two colors enumerated by Cunninghame Graham in English and Spanish (*Horses of the Conquest*, xi–xii, 121–26). W. A. Whatley names fifty-nine color distinctions in Spanish (Dobie [ed.], *Mustangs and Cow Horses*, 13, 228–31). Some fifteen in Denhardt, *Horse of the Americas*, 231–32, *et passim*, including some not found elsewhere; one hundred and forty-five in South America (*ibid.*, 213).

[5] Denhardt, *ibid.*, 30–40, 152; see Chapter II *supra*.

[6] Cunninghame Graham, *Horses of the Conquest*, 13, 49, 72, 109, 121,–46. See Darwin on the degeneracy of the horses on the South American Pampas, and also in the Falkland Islands (*The Descent of Man*, 188). See note 31 *infra*.

[7] Cunninghame Graham, *Horses of the Conquest*, 114; also his *Conquest of the River Plate*, App. II, 288–96.

[8] Cited by Cunninghame Graham, *Horses of the Conquest*, 114.

Although the *baguales* were long extinct, in my youth in the Argentine there were many herds of wild horses to be found, descended from escaped tame animals, but not in the prodigious numbers of which Azara writes. These horses were nearly always of broken colours, though there were many bays, chestnuts, roans, and grays amongst them. If a tame horse joined them, he became as shy and difficult to catch as the wildest.[9]

Dobie, citing official records, mentions as an illustration of the truly stupendous masses of horses that in the first quarter of the nineteenth century 500,000 feral and semiferal mares were slaughtered annually in Argentina. As on the Northern continent, they stamped their memory in place names; for example, the Sierra Baguales in Patagonia.

According to Cunninghame Graham, this term *baguales* is an Araucanian word, said to be derived from *cahual*, the Indian corruption of the Spanish *caballo*, and corrupted again by the Gauchos into *bagual*. "Mustang" is not used. Cunninghame Grahame adds: " 'Mustang' is supposed by some to be a Mexican word, *mesteño*, meaning a wild horse. . . . It seems more probable that mustang comes from the word *mostrenco*, roving, rough, or wild, and hence the final 'g' that the Texans, Arizonians, and Californians have added to it." Cunninghame Graham's derivation does not, however, appear to have commended itself to North American authorities.[10]

With respect to this wild and (later) semiwild coloration, Cunninghame Graham writes elsewhere (again based upon Azara): "The *baguales*, the true feral horses of the Americas, seem to have reverted to the colour of the original wild horse of the Old World, while the semiferal horses of both Mexico and the Pampas have sported into infinite degrees, mixtures, and shades of colour in their coats."[11] Unfortunately, it is by no means certain, after the lapse of more than a century and a half, to just what extent Azara's

[9] *Ibid.*, 115; cf. also Thompson, *Narrative* (ed. by Tyrrell), 401. Azara (about 1790) says they roamed in herds of ten thousand. See also Darwin on this (*Descent of Man*, 47, 253, where he mentions "the accurate Azara").

[10] Cunninghame Graham, *Conquest of the River Plate*, 288–96; *Horses of the Conquest*, 114. Mesteño=mustang (so Gregg, *Commerce of the Prairies*, in Thwaites, *Travels*, XX 260); also Denhardt, *Horse of the Americas*, 104; G. C. Robinson, in Dobie (ed.), *Mustangs and Cow Horses*, 3; Dobie, *The Mustangs*, 93–96.

[11] Cunninghame Graham, *Horses of the Conquest*, 121.

pronouncements concerning the "original wild horse of the Old World" would command acceptance in modern scientific thought. In a much later publication (although Cunninghame Graham's essay was originally written in 1896), he notes the following most interesting phenomenon:

> Most horses, in fact almost all breeds of horses, have six lumbar vertebrae. A most careful observer, the late Edward Losson, a professor in the Agricultural College of Santa Catalina near Buenos Aires, has noted the remarkable fact that the horses of the pampas have only five. Following up his researches, he has found that the only other breed of horses in which a similar peculiarity is to be found is that of Barbary. . . . The genet, too (the progeny of the ass and horse), has the same number of vertebrae. Is it impossible that in former times the union of an African mare and a genet may have produced the race of Berber horses which were taken by the Moors to Spain, and thence to the pampas? The genet and the mule are not characterized by the same infecundity. During the last fifty years, in the south of France, many cases have been observed of the reproductiveness of the former animal.[12]

Cunninghame Graham also relates the Arab version of the origin of the famous Hâymour (Arab) breed of horses of the western Sudan as the progeny of an Arab mare and a wild ass (onager); the mare having perforce been abandoned wounded in a desert region where the wild horse had never been known.[13] A zoological friend to whom I submitted the foregoing particulars informs me that "the ass and the zebra are practically identical internally with the horse. It is said to be impossible to tell the skeletons apart. If that is correct, the number (in each) should be six lumbar vertebrae." My informant adds that he has never seen an ass's skeleton, and can find no accounts anywhere.[14] This latter circumstance furnishes confirmation for the dictum of an eminent authority of the nineteenth century.[15]

Whatever influence may or may not have been exerted upon

[12] Cunninghame Graham, in Dobie (ed.), *Mustangs and Cow Horses*, 192–93.
[13] *Ibid.*, 194.
[14] William Rowan, Professor of Zoology, University of Alberta, correspondence to the author, April 14, 1949.
[15] According to Sam Weller, nobody ever saw a dead donkey (*Pickwick Papers*, Chap. LI).

the Hispano-American "Indian" horse by the Hispano-Arabian "breed of Córdoba" or even by any obscure and less aristocratic "poor relation" of the clan, it is doubtful, to say the least, whether the Arabian ancestor can be regarded seriously as a representative of the original feral horse of the Old World. For Hilzheimer states that the horse was not known in Arabia until about the beginning of the Christian era, and that its fame there dates from the advance of Islam (after A.D. 632). It is descended in part from the "early Egyptian horse" of about 2000 B.C., or possibly earlier.[16] It is more than probable that the characteristic horse of a great charioteering, militaristic empire such as ancient Egypt would itself be a profound modification of any original feral horse, whatever the outstanding features of the ancestor may have been.

So far from the "Oriental group" originating in the East, the progression was apparently the other way, toward the East. The oldest primitive types appear to be what is termed "Przewalski's horse" (of which a specimen was found in Mongolia, about 1935),[17] and the tarpan, which is stated to be now extinct, since the last century. The first of these is of a dun color, and the second was described as "mouse grey." The former was found on the eastern side of the fortieth degree of east longitude on the steppes of central Asia; the latter on the western side. There is also a small and very ancient breed which was indigenous to Europe in prehistoric times, the Polish "Konink." This creature (in Hilzheimer's plate) certainly presents a very striking resemblance to the Indian pony in its disproportionately large, hang-dog head—no other phrase seems quite so appropriate; but of course a single individual resemblance would possess no significance whatever, even if any known ancestral relationship existed. The pose might quite easily be due to age, overwork, neglect, improper or insufficient food, or positive ill-treatment. I quote Hilzheimer's summing up, in his own words:

In this way it appears that at least the European horse, including the so-called Oriental horse and the breed of northern Africa is to be

16 Max Hilzheimer, "The Evolution of the Domestic Horse," *Antiquity*, Vol. IX (1935), 133–39.
17 *Ibid.*, 136.

derived from the European Tarpan in its various sub-divisions. The Barb is perhaps an exception; our information about its history is at present very inadequate.

At the moment there is no conclusive explanation available as to whether we must assume the existence of a separate centre of domestication and a different primitive type in the case of the horse of central and eastern Asia.[18]

The reader will probably share my own diffidence concerning the wisdom or even practicability of basing any conclusions respecting Hispano-American coloration upon "the color of the original wild horse of the Old World." It may very possibly be the case that no attempt in this direction will bring us much closer to a real knowledge of the influences or processes which have impressed such a characteristically different appearance upon the North American descendant. None the less the subject is one which cannot be entirely passed over without an effort.

This is a phase of our inquiry which my own brief résumé in the foregoing pages of the present chapter has only incidentally mentioned: the development of the Arabian-Barb-Hispano-European ancestor into the resultant "native product" of the Plains, the North American "Indian pony." My own investigation hitherto has followed the customary course of such inquiries on this subject: the discussion of *how, when,* and *where* the Indians obtained the horse. The question now is: What was it *after* they got it, and how did it come to be whatever it is? Is there an answer to all this?

It seems obvious on a little reflection that there comes a point of exhaustion, beyond which further discussion on the *ancestry* of the Plains animal can scarcely hope to produce further results of any material value from our present insufficient data.[19] As every student of the subject is aware, there was no indigenous feral spe-

[18] *Ibid.,* 139. Some interesting details about the Barb, from Cunninghame Graham, in Dobie (ed.), *Mustangs and Cow Horses,* 192–94; Denhardt, *Horse of the Americas,* 15–22; Dobie, *The Mustangs,* 3–20, who cites a large number of authorities.

[19] See Denhardt's wide bibliography, *Horse of the Americas,* 273–80.

cies of *Equus americanus* on the North American continent within historical times to furnish its contribution to any hybrid or cross. The problem of the evolution of the type may be roughly defined as one of environmental development of a virtually fixed ancestry.

The same precise condition prevailed in South America. With respect to this, it appears that Cunninghame Graham, in the quotation cited above, has erroneously confused the issue. In speaking of the now extinct *baguales* of South America, as we have seen, he instances their staple bay coloring as a reversion to the "original wild horse" coloration of the Old World. In contrast with these "true feral horses," he describes the "semiferal" horses of his own youth in the Argentine, descended from escaped tame animals, and which have sported into "infinite" shades of color, bays, chestnuts, roans, grays, and "broken colors." Thus far his testimony is unexceptionable, as coming from an eyewitness of these phenomena, while his historical citations concerning the earlier *baguales* proper are based upon the sound authority of "the accurate Azara," as Darwin describes the latter scholar.

Unfortunately, Cunninghame Graham applies these conditions of the "second generation" to the North American continent also. His words are—"the semiferal horses of both Mexico and the Pampas have sported into . . ." (as the reader may see by turning back a page or two). I have found no evidence to support such a verdict. I have thus far encountered nothing, not even evidence of opinion, which points to any disappearance of the North American counterparts of the "true feral" *baguales* of the southern continent, and of their replacement by a later generation of parti-colored "semiferal" herds, from which the polychrome Indian ponies are descended. Such a catastrophic change would very closely resemble the disappearance of the buffalo from the northern continent, and *their* supersession by range herds; the only perceptible difference being the lack of any discoverable cause for the implied transmutation in horses. It is incredible that such a change could actually have occurred, without a historical notice of some character having recorded it. In South America the revolutionary change in the horse population has brought forth an Azara, a Hudson, and a Cunninghame Graham, to name one or two. In North America the revolutionary change in the bovine population inspired many pens. This

141

supposed epoch has produced no historian; not even the humblest chronicler. I shall proceed upon the contrary assumption, to which all the evidence I have encountered points clearly: That the Indian pony of historical times and of our own day—for they are still to be seen—is preponderantly and virtually in entirety the lineal descendant in direct succession of the earliest generations of European horses on this continent.

J. Frank Dobie writes as follows:

Comparison of the modern *criollo* horses of South America with the Spanish horses common in Texas and Mexico half a century ago leads to the conclusion that a larger proportion of Arabian blood was planted in North America than to the south.[20]

With entire respect to an outstanding student of the horse both indoors and out, I cannot concur in Dobie's verdict. In my judgment his conclusion embodies two basic fallacies. The first is the too close comparison between the modern animals with their ancestry of four centuries ago and beyond. It appears to me inconsequential and indeed almost irrelevant even to attempt such close comparison between any creature of today which is itself recognized as a modified product of centuries, and another of fifty years ago; both living under differing conditions of incessant modification. Dobie quotes Thornton Chard with entire approval. Chard makes the two a virtually identical genealogical entity whose joint excellence as the "Horse of the Americas" is very largely traceable to the influences of the American environment. He writes as follows: "I feel bound to emphasize the suggestion that the excellent points of the South American Criollo and of the Mustang are due to the hardiness acquired by four hundred years of natural selection quite as much as to the inheritance of Arabian and Barb blood."[21] Earlier in his own book Dobie himself says: "The Americas and the heterogeneous mixture of men who used and abused the mixed-blood [*mestizo*] descendants of the Arabian on these continents made what the Spanish horse became."[22] It seems to

[20] Dobie, *The Mustangs*, 8.
[21] Emilio Solanet, "The Criollo Horse" (translated and edited by Thornton Chard), *The Journal of Heredity*, Vol. XXI (1930), 454; cited by Dobie, *The Mustangs*, 297.
[22] Dobie, *ibid.*, 17.

me that in speaking of "the Americas" making "what the Spanish horse became," Dobie surrenders the argument for the essential identity of the North and South American ancestry.

Unless I have seriously misinterpreted his language, the second fallacy to which I referred lies in Dobie's apparent assumption that the conjoint ancestry of the Spanish horses themselves as they reached this continent—whatever it may have been in addition to the Moorish-Arab stock—could be distinguished into separate breed types, and that these can still be defined with something like precision after more than four centuries on this continent. Whatever influence that period of time may have exerted in the two Americas, we must not forget that similar influences had been at work in the Spanish peninsula for nearly twice as long. An authoritative scholar states what I consider to be plain historical fact when he says that the Spanish horses "were a cross between the fleet and powerful animals of the Peninsula and the fine stock introduced by the Moorish invaders. More than seven centuries of breeding had produced what were considered the finest horses in Europe."[23] Dobie himself apparently agrees. He says: "The Spanish horse was a *mestizo*."[24] In face of this I find it difficult to comprehend the grounds upon which he draws his distinction.

In both North and South America the evidence in my judgment indicates clearly enough that the Spanish parent stocks taken to the two countries respectively were about as near to being identical as it is possible for any breed to be. That is to say, as a breed (or breeds) they *were* identical in the two lands. As a sum or aggregate of individuals they and their progeny had to take their chance of the varying individualisms or "sports" that reassert themselves from time to time in any partly composite family scheme. For all practical purposes they are treated by scholarly critics as being what they apparently were: the semi-Arab "breed of Córdoba," of which the "Andalusian horse" would seem to have been a purely local division, not otherwise divergent.[25] Yet in one most important

---

[23] John J. Johnson, "The Spanish Horse in Peru before 1550," *Greater America*, 19. See also an admirable summary of the Spanish horse in history, in Haines, *The Appaloosa Horse*, 24–29.

[24] Dobie, *The Mustangs*, 7.

[25] Denhardt, *Horse of the Americas*, 21, 162, 164, 179, 194, 204, 206, 273–80; Cunninghame Graham, in Dobie (ed.), *Mustangs and Cow Horses*, 191–92.

characteristic, the historical wild horses of South America (*baguales*) and those of the northern continent were or are fundamentally different. The difference is one of color. In the Northern Plains area the Indian pony is almost typically a pinto. In the southern Pampas the pinto appears to have been virtually unknown, or at the most was very uncommon, so long as the original feral strain of wild horses remained.[26] Francis Haines quotes a South American authority on the horses of Argentina, Pedro Sarciat. This scholar states that the spotted horses of the country are a modern importation from northern Europe since 1920. He deplores their present popularity as a color fad, not in the true Spanish tradition.[27]

The pinto does not appear to have been any favorite with the Spaniards; and their contempt—unlike many Spanish prejudices—was evidently shared by the Portuguese. Cunninghame Graham cites a native (i.e., Portuguese) proverb of the district of O *Sertão*, in the Brazilian states of Bahía, Ceara, and Piauhy, which breeds a distinctive horse of its own. This is to the effect that a piebald or pinto (*pedrez*) "was made by God to carry packs."[28] Both nations may very probably have taken over their dislike from the Arabs, together with the Arab horses. For the Arabs had disliked them, possibly for centuries; for which reason, most probably—among such careful breeders—a spotted Arabian horse is very rare.[29] Dobie writes thus:

One of the most preposterous pieces of American folklore is that

[26] Pintos were rare in Uruguay, almost unknown in Argentina; Denhardt, *Horse of the Americas*, 164, 171. He mentions a paint (pinto) ridden by Aimé Tschiffely from Buenos Aires to Washington (*ibid.*, 197, 211). Cunninghame Graham (in Dobie [ed.], *Mustangs and Cow Horses*, 190) instances a piebald, but elsewhere he states that creams or piebalds are not true descendants of the Hispano-Arabian imports of the *Conquistadores*. See notes 8–9 *supra*. Cunninghame Graham also remarks (*ibid.*, 195) that the Gaucho of about 1896 liked the piebald, regardless of his Spanish ancestors' dislike of pintos. The distinction between the two (if any exists) is left very vague. See note 2 *supra*.

[27] Haines, *The Appaloosa Horse*, 36.

[28] Cunninghame Graham, *Horses of the Conquest*, 138. Maximilian noted that apart from the vegetation, a hot summer day on the Missouri recalled the *Sertão* (*Travels*, in Thwaites, *Travels*, XXIII, 38). This was evidently a region where packing was no soft snap! Cf. Denhardt, *Horse of the Americas*, 232.

[29] Cunninghame Graham, Dobie, in Dobie (ed.), *Mustangs and Cow Horses*, 195, 247; Denhardt, *Horse of the Americas*, 196; Haines, *The Appaloosa Horse*, 35–53.

Arabian horses are calico-colored. Ascribe it to Barnum. Their colors are unvaryingly solid: dark bay, chestnut, gray in various shades, nutmeg roan, white with a black skin, an occasional black, but never a *grullo* (blue) or a paint of any combination.[30]

Denhardt notes another misapprehension:

It is a common belief that the Pinto is the result of the indiscriminate breeding that took place between horses in the wild mustang bands. If spotted horses were the result of inbreeding, then the color of the Thoroughbred and other modern breeds would be kaleidoscopic. Unless at least one Pinto horse was included among the originators of the wild herds, there would have been no Pintos.[31]

We shall see that the Indians had another explanation.

It would of course have been a most extraordinary circumstance if some spotted horses had not been taken to North America, or to the Spaniards' breeding grounds, the West Indies, in the early years of Spanish domination. As a matter of historical record, there were two in the famous "first sixteen" to land on the American mainland. The sixteen in question were those that were taken to Mexico by Cortés in 1519. One of these is described as a pinto, the other as "a dark roan horse with white patches,"[32] practically, I should judge, what is classed in Spanish horse nomenclature as an *overo*.[33]

The classic description of the sixteen, from the racy pen of Bernal Díaz, reads as follows:

... the horses were divided up among the ships and loaded, mangers were erected and a store of corn and hay was put on board. I will place all the names of the mares and horses down from memory.

Captain Cortés had a dark chestnut stallion which died when we reached San Juan Ulúa.

Pedro de Alvarado and Hernándo López de Ávila had a very good

[30] Dobie, *The Mustangs*, 11.
[31] Denhardt, *Horse of the Americas*, 197.
[32] *Ibid.*, 51.
[33] The *overo* is white and mottled: e.g. the roan here mentioned. The commonly accepted pinto (*tobiano*) is white and one other distinct color. *Tobianos* were more common in North America; *overos* in South America. So, Denhardt, *ibid.*, 198. See notes 3, 26, *supra*.

sorrel mare, turning out excellent both for tilting and for racing. When we arrived in New Spain Pedro de Alvarado took his half either by purchase or by force.

Alonzo Hernández Puertocarrero had a swift grey mare which Cortés bought for him with his gold knot.

Juan Velásquez de León also had a sturdy grey mare which we called *"La Rabona"* [bob-tailed]. She was fast and well-broken.

Christóval de Olid had a dark brown horse that was quite satisfactory.

Francisco de Montejo and Alonzo de Ávila had a parched sorrel, useless for war.

Francisco de Morla had a dark brown stallion which was fast and well reined.

Juan de Escalante had a light bay horse with three white stockings. She was not very good.

Diego de Ordás had a barren grey mare, a pacer which seldom galloped.

Gonzalo Domínguez, an excellent horseman, had a dark brown horse, good, and a grand runner.

Pedro González de Trujillo had a good chestnut horse, a beautiful color, and he ran very well.

Moron, a settler of Bayamo, had a pinto with white stockings on his forefeet and he was well reined.

Baena, a settler of Trinidad, had a dark roan horse with white patches, but he turned out worthless.

Lares, a fine horseman, had a very good bay horse which was an excellent runner.

Ortiz the musician and Bartolomé García, who had gold mines, had a black horse called *"El arriero"* [muleteer or mule driver] and he was one of the best horses in the fleet.

Juan Sedeño, a settler of Havana, had a brown mare that foaled on board ship. Sedeño was the richest soldier in the fleet, having a vessel, a mare, a negro, and many provisions.[34]

Sedeño's foal, of course, brings the total to seventeen. It may be noted that while we have accounts of the deaths of horses in that

[34] *Ibid.*, 51, which I take to be Denhardt's own translation from what he terms (*ibid.*, 275) the best Spanish text of Bernal Díaz, that of Genero García, 1904. The English translation by A. P. Maudslay (tr. and ed., *Conquest of New Spain*, I, 180–81) differs from Denhardt's in some color particulars. Denhardt describes Moron's horse as "a pinto"; Maudslay translates the phrase as "a dappled horse." This may not be quite the same thing. Perhaps there was only *one* pinto.

earliest Mexican campaign, there is no mention of any further foalings, such as could possibly result in any pinto progeny's surviving, or even of the authentic survival of this foal of Sedeño's, whether it was a pinto or not, which seems unlikely from its parentage.

I use the term *authentic* for good reason. Dobie mentions a (seemingly Mexican) tradition:

> . . . the first horse to run feral on the American mainland was the brown mare's colt that had been foaled on the ship not long before Cortés landed. . . . Somewhere in the region the colt was left behind. . . . As tradition goes, said to be fortified by documents in Jalapa, soon after the Conquest, Spaniards as well as natives saw a horse running with deer on the lower slopes of Orizaba. An *hacendido* captured it and placed it with his other horses [???]. . . . Legend, adding itself to tradition, says that it is still occasionally seen in the wild lands, the sight of it bringing good luck to the glimpser. The color of it is white.[35]

This reads like a variation of the Great White Horse theme, which we shall consider in a later chapter. Possibly the colt legend grew up as an "explanation" of it.

But are we to suppose that no pintos (or animals with the pinto ancestry in them) went to South America? This is not even a case where by some incredibly exceptional working of the laws of chance, the South American horse contingents were obtained from some other, isolated area of Spain, where pintos had never been known. For the islands were utilized as a common supply depot for all parts of the Spanish possessions in the New World, and it is known that these sources were actually drawn upon for expeditions prior to the first landing of Pedro de Mendoza at the River Plate in 1536.[36] In effect, there was just one common stock of horses, upon which all departments drew at need.

This dilemma is equally problematical, whether we choose to accept Denhardt's pronouncement on inbreeding or not. I am unaware to just what extent a layman may legitimately cite the opin-

---

[35] Dobie, *The Mustangs*, 97, note.

[36] For example, Narváez in 1528 shipped his eighty horses from San Domingo: Bishop, *Odyssey of Cabeza de Vaca*, 33, 38, 43; see Denhardt, *Horse of the Americas*, 35–43, 75, 82, 151, etc.

ions of Darwin today, but they appear to conflict with that view. Discussing the question of natural modifications in horses, Darwin writes thus:

We know, also, that the horses taken to the Falkland Islands have, during successive generations, become smaller and weaker, whilst those which have run wild on the Pampas have acquired larger and coarser heads; and such changes are manifestly due, not to any one pair, but to all the individuals having been subjected to the same conditions, aided, perhaps, by the principle of reversion. The new sub-breeds in such cases are not descended from any single pair, but from many individuals which have varied in different degrees, but in the same general manner.[37]

Whatever conclusion we may adopt, one thing at least is obvious: If inbreeding is to be taken as the cause for pintos, that feature must in the nature of things have been fully as prevalent in the one continent as in the other. Why then did not the same fundamentally similar conditions produce similar results in both lands?

The ancient Hispano-Arabian dislike for the pinto was not shared by the Indians of North America. Actually he was rather their favorite. Dobie says: "The favor that paint [pinto] horses came into in Mexico and on the Plains was due to the Indian liking for gaudy colors. If his horse was not variegated in color by nature, the Plains Indian would often paint him."[38] Denhardt suggests a basic reason for their preference: ". . . the Indians preferred the grey and the pinto because they believed that the color would not only blend into the landscape but also take paint better."[39]

With entire respect for Denhardt's high competence and outstanding mastery of American horse lore, one would like some authority for this belief. As it stands it seems unconvincing. 'Blending into the landscape' would be more inapplicable than otherwise, in a horse painted in the usual pinto coloring of white upon brown or brown upon white, except perhaps in a sterile dust-blown region of lightish-colored sand; after a fall frost on the more northerly Plains; or when the buffalo grass had cured as it grew—"on the

[37] Darwin, *Descent of Man*, 188; cf. his *Origin of Species*, 345.
[38] In Dobie (ed.), *Mustangs and Cow Horses*, 247.
[39] Denhardt, *Horse of the Americas*, 101.

hoof," as the northern cowmen were wont to express it. In my own younger days in central Alberta, where the landscape was commonly dotted with bluffs and willow scrub and the heavy lush growth of the "long grass" area stayed green until much later, such light-colored animals, grays, buckskins, etc., stood out conspicuously at long distances. Yet the Indians of this territory were just as characteristically addicted to the pinto as anywhere; and if perhaps they may not have owned as many horses *positively* as the Southern Plains tribes,[40] they owned quite sufficient for conclusive demonstration of this factor.

So also, while very conceivably an Indian might turn a gray or a brown into a pinto, since he was not sufficiently "variegated in color by nature" to his owner's liking, it seems highly improbable that the man who would do this to any self-color in order to variegate it would also paint a pinto which already possessed this supreme desideratum naturally. But whatever may have been the underlying reason, both of our two very competent and authoritative commentators agree that the Plains Indians preferred pintos; and also that they *did* paint their horses.

Taking into consideration Denhardt's (probably very sound) rejection of inbreeding as the explanation of the pinto phenomenon, together with his pronouncement that "unless at least one Pinto horse was included among the originators of the wild herds, there would have been no Pintos,"[41] and coupling these positions with the Spanish dislike or lack of enthusiasm for pintos, which would logically result both in a minimum of such being deliberately selected for transmission to the Indies and in there being fewer of pinto ancestry or characteristics for the voyagers leaving Spain to choose from, even if they wished, I therefore suggest, without any reference to the ultimate purpose for which he may have desired them, that the Indian painted ponies "pinto style" *because there were not enough natural pintos to meet his wishes.*

It has been noted above that in the Southern Hemisphere the numbers of such parti-colored progeny were infinitely less, even to the degree of the negligible. So pronounced is (or was) the difference that a very reliable observer gives it as his opinion (based

[40] This will receive consideration in a later chapter.
[41] Denhardt, *Horse of the Americas*, 197.

upon the findings of an earlier investigator equally or even more competent) that the "true descendants" of the early Spanish horses —the bays, browns, chestnuts, etc.—had reverted to the coloration of the original feral horses of the Old World, and that any creams or piebalds seen among the later Pampas herds were not of the early *baguales,* but were tame horses which had escaped from the domestic environment, or the progeny of such.[42] These radical and profound differences came to pass, moreover, in descendants of the same original ancestry. What is the answer to this problem?

Biologists tell us that little-known and extremely subtle genetic forces are constantly at work—or may at any time be expected to intrude, so to say—in relation to phenomena of this character. None the less it seems peculiar (to a layman at least) that such profound and far-reaching change should operate so sweepingly in the one land and leave the other virtually unaffected. With regard to any argument that might be urged concerning change of environment as the possible dominating cause, it would seem to be the case that the early wild horse range of the northern continent bore a closer resemblance to large portions of their native Spain than did wide tracts of South America.[43] Waiving, therefore, any discussion concerning reversion of type to the feral *Equus antiquus* of the Old World (upon which the present writer is in any case incompetent to enter), and having regard solely to the color types indicated by Azara (1790) as constituting the standard coloration of the South American Hispano-Arabian horse, I consider it to be not improbable that in the color ratios exhibited by the *baguales* proper we have a very close approximation to the ratios of pintos or animals of pinto ancestry originally brought from Spain.

For some reason, during the period which elapsed between the original importations of Spanish horses and the era of the interested or scholarly observer—say roughly, the thirties of the nineteenth century, introducing such men as George Catlin, John K. Townsend, or Josiah Gregg[44]—these ratios underwent violent dis-

---

[42] See notes 8–9 *supra.*

[43] For Spain, see Richard Ford, *Gatherings from Spain,* 1–43; cf. Webb, *The Great Plains,* 85–139; Bishko, "The Peninsular Background of Latin American Cattle Ranching," 491–515 (see Chapter II *supra*).

[44] Catlin (on the Comanche horses particularly), *Letters and Notes,* II, 57–60;

turbance in the northern area. Once again, why in the north and not in the south? Furthermore, why (and again in the north exclusively) should these peculiar coloration phenomena occur in such large numbers as to manifestly preclude any possibility of *all* these having been painted by man, and in such numbers as would scarcely seem practically—even if they were mathematically—possible from the likely ratios of imported pintos in the available time?

There is an ancient story in the Book of Genesis which is fashionable in some (perhaps most) scientific circles to relegate quite contemptuously to folklore. More often, perhaps, it is not even discussed; it is merely dismissed. Yet it is along such lines that a historian must approach the whole conception of *extraneous* formative prenatal influences, which were deemed of sufficient significance to occupy a place in the intellectual outlook of the Greeks. In these modern days of Biblical ignorance, the story will bear to be repeated:

And Jacob took him rods of green poplar, and of the hazel and chesnut tree; and pilled white strakes in them, and made the white appear which was in the rods. And he set the rods which he had pilled before the flocks in the gutters in the watering troughs when the flocks came to drink, that they should conceive when they came to drink. And the flocks conceived before the rods, and brought forth cattle ringstraked, speckled, and spotted. And Jacob did separate the lambs, and set the faces of the flocks toward the ringstraked, and all the brown in the flock of Laban; and he put his own flock by themselves, and put them not unto Laban's cattle. And it came to pass, whenever the stronger cattle did conceive, that Jacob laid the rods before the eyes of the cattle in the gutters, that they might conceive among the rods. But when the cattle were feeble he put them not in; so the feebler were Laban's and the stronger Jacob's.[45]

One thing is undeniably certain in the foregoing record. It was

Townsend, *Narrative*, and Wyeth, *Oregon, 1832*, both in Thwaites, *Travels*, XXI, 87, 177, 283; Gregg, *Commerce of the Prairies*, in Thwaites, *Travels*, XX, 260–62.

[45] Genesis 30:37–43; cf. Genesis 31:8–12. Denhardt (*Horse of the Americas*, 196) and Haines (*The Appaloosa Horse*, 42) allude to this.

neither written *by* nor *for* a generation which held such consequences to be impossible. It might in our own day be convenient to ascribe the very general belief in what everyday folk term "birthmarks" to the influence of three centuries of Bible reading, although I very strongly suspect that Sir James Frazer's great anthropological treasure house, *The Golden Bough,* would ascribe a much older origin than that. But the task of those of us who repudiate the belief as being baseless is to explain its origin in those earlier times. Even if the simple pastoral peoples were given to the invention of elaborate biological theories, it is difficult to understand how such as this one could long survive after a few optimistic Jacobs had caused them to be weighed in the balance and found wanting, as of course (*pace* the mocking scoffer) they inevitably must have been. There is no parallel between this belief and some merely verbal tradition, or the myth of the "hoop snake," for example, which invariably bears reference to some distant, inaccessible, or unidentifiable scene and hearsay "authority" at second or seventh hand, and the verification of which has no relation to any incentive of gain. I acknowledge that I should have been much more hesitant in adducing this particular factor, even in the most baldly objective sense, were it not for a very vivid personal experience of my own, which occurred many years ago. Having taken the trouble to put them into writing long ago while they were still fresh, I am in a position to give the particulars at first hand; and since the episode has to do with the subject and also with the species we are here discussing, it seems to deserve a place in our presentation.[46]

It is worth noting, however, in relation to our direct topic, that more than one very important Northern horse tribe believed in birthmarks, and explained them along similar lines with our own people. The tribes in question are the Sarcee and the Nez Percé. What renders this particularly interesting among the Sarcee is the probability that this belief would be shared by their southern Athapascan kindred, the Apache; and the Apache were among the earlier Indians to obtain horses. The Sarcee have retained many of their native tribal differences very tenaciously, despite their long residence among the Blackfoot, and a recent commentator notices

[46] See Appendix B *infra.*

a similar parallel tenacity among northern and southern members of the same Athapascan stock.[47]

The Nez Percé occupy a rather different position, and may almost be said to be in a category by themselves. They may in a sense be considered as the "importers," and certainly the conservators and guardians of the famous Appaloosa horse of North America. As its history is given by the supreme authority on this breed, Francis Haines,[48] a number of spotted horses from a certain stud that was established in Chihuahua about the time of Charles II of England (1660–1685) found their way northward by the usual processes of stealing, ranging, raiding and trading to the Nez Percé country in the Columbia Basin. It would seem to have first attracted the attention of a pinto-loving people as a more splendidly and constantly marked super-pinto. As its characteristic qualities became recognized, the Nez Percé "adopted" it as their tribal horse; and their commanding capacity as horse breeders—in which they are recognized as easily first among the North American tribes[49]—brought the type to the undisputed position it now occupies.

Concerning its origin, Haines writes as follows:

There is a widespread belief in the United States that the Appaloosa is really a spotted Moroccan barb or a Libyan leopard horse. Since such horses are unknown in North Africa, it would seem that both are the products of fertile imaginations, but, like other mythical figures, they will keep cropping up for many years.[50]

Haines has very skillfully summarized a mass of evidence tending to support his conclusions that the ancestors of the Appaloosa reach back in a very similar (and readily identifiable) form and coloring to a great antiquity across an enormous Eurasiatic territory, stretching from far eastern China to the Adriatic. His final conclusion regarding their advent on the North American conti-

[47] On the persistent Sarcee conservatism, see Jenness, *The Sarcee Indians*, 31, 38, 40, 83–86. More recently, John J. Honigmann, "Parallels in the Development of Shamanism among the Northern and Southern Athapaskans," *American Anthropologist*, Vol. LI (1949), 512–14.

[48] Haines, *The Appaloosa Horse*, 23–24.

[49] This is treated in more detail in Chapter XIII *infra*.

[50] Haines, *The Appaloosa Horse*, 36.

nent is that they were shipped from the Spanish Netherlands to Mexico, and were never in North Africa or Spain.[51]

In most recognized breeds, pedigrees stand second to the characteristic markings of the type; certainly for breeding purposes. As all animal breeders are well aware, such points, and the prepotent ability to stamp them on his progeny, are what constitute a worth-while breeding sire. The markings of the Appaloosa are not quite so narrowly defined as on the Berkshire pig, whose otherwise orthodox coloration would be spurned if he lacked the six white hairs in the black expanse of the spinal area. In a fairly wide variation of detail, however, in respect of color markings, the presence of contrasting spots on loins and hips—more commonly dark on a light ground, but also the precise reverse—seem to be regarded as the most definitive characteristic of the Appaloosa, if we may judge from the efforts put forth to produce or preserve them.

In relation to the question of prenatal influence, the following account, entitled "How to Secure Spotted Colts," is of interest:

At the mouth of the Palouse River, in the heart of the horse country, lives Sam Fisher, a Nez Percé nearing the century mark. For nearly seventy years he bred and raised spotted horses, until, at eighty-eight, an accidental fall with his horse injured his ribs and he was forced to quit riding the range.

In his breeding program, Fisher found that even the best parent stock did not produce spotted horses every time. The Appaloosa strain had become diluted with the passing centuries, and this dilution showed in an occasional solid color colt. To insure that all his colts would have spots, and those spots well placed, Sam Fisher used a powerful medicine known to some of the Nez Percé horsemen.

In broad outline, this medicine consisted of marking the pregnant mare with a special kind of paint, mixed by a secret formula and applied at the critical moment, while certain magic words were said. The breeder dipped his thumb and fingers in the paint, then placed his thumb on the mare's hip bone with the fingers outspread. This was done three times, at appropriate intervals. The colt thus produced was expected to show the five-finger mark spots on the hip, in addition to other spots. To this day, a foal so marked is considered to be of superior stock.

This method of attempting to spot the offspring by prenatal influ-

[51] Correspondence to the author, January 24, 1953 (correcting his general conclusions, *The Appaloosa Horse*, 36).

ence is strongly reminiscent of Jacob's ruse to secure more spotted animals in Laban's flocks, or of folk lore among many groups to account for the so-called birth marks on children. How much of this Sam Fisher believed is difficult to determine. He did say that the medicine worked better when spotted horses were used for the breeding stock.[52]

We may unhesitatingly accept Haines's account—that of a critical scholar—of what Sam Fisher *said*. Assuming (as I consider we may) that he meant what he said, and that his statements of *fact* are admissible (since Haines accepts them), this does not explain one vital crux. The essence of the birthmark concept is that the distinctive physical or mental characteristic which it is desired to produce is placed before the view or contemplation of the female at the time of conception; the belief being that this feature can thereby be reproduced in her offspring. The implied additional "favorable circumstance" of a *spotted* mare constitutes no facilitating influence whatever for the reproduction of the *five-finger markings!* If they are true, what produced them?

The modern critic who rejects this concept as mere folklore ignores its acceptance among the Greeks in their attitude toward prenatal influence on their wives. With all our modern super-mechanization of life, we have added surprisingly little to the Greek legacy of thought. A biological friend of my own, himself a heretic (so he tells me) concerning certain scientific orthodoxies, would discuss the question no further than to say, "Nothing to it." I have known more than one competent medical man who quite evidently believed in birthmarks and imposed a "protective" regimen upon pregnant patients, but did not dare to say so openly. There is no prejudice among mankind more firmly rooted, more widely prevalent, more sedulously cultivated, or more completely inaccessible to reason than the bland fundamental assumption that the scientist is *ipso facto* incapable of prejudice.

It will probably be agreed by all schools of thought that while hard and callous treatment from many—perhaps even most—Indian owners, in addition to the necessarily severe conditions largely consequent upon Indian life on the Plains, could very conceivably contribute to, or perhaps directly cause without need of further auxiliary agencies, the downtrodden, neglected appearance al-

[52] *Ibid.,* 42.

155

ready mentioned, it seems unthinkable that it could make any difference in color. Moreover, the distribution of the Indian pinto was practically universal throughout the Plains area; and we have no ground whatever for any assumption that, aside from the inevitable hardships almost inseparable from a nomad society, *all* Indians were guilty either of callous indifference or of positive illtreatment.[53] Such a postulate would hark us back to those halcyon days of sweeping uncritical denunciation when "all the Indians" did this or that, cheerfully convicted *in absentia* of anything which might be proved—or predicated—against any one of them!

It has been seen that in this very matter of horse usages there were tribal, and doubtless individually temperamental diversities. This was a factor which impinged upon almost every angle of Indian life; sometimes, one might think, for no other reason than the very sake of being different.[54] The question of kindness among Indians toward their horses will be considered in a later chapter. Meanwhile it may be said that if the charge of cruelty were universally proved against *all* the Indian tribes of the Northern Plains are, and *could* influence coloration, I know of no reason why similar causes should not influence coloration in South America. For I have found no evidence to indicate that the South American tribes as a whole were pronouncedly any more humane toward their mounts than were the Northern ones. Actually they were much the same, as W. H. Hudson leads us to think.[55]

There is one important feature in the respective horse cultures of the two continents which appears to have been different at all times. We have seen that whatever may have been the underlying purpose in painting their horses, unexceptionable authorities concur in the *fact* that the Northern Plains Indians did so over a wide, almost general area.[56] While the natives of the South American

[53] See Chapter XIII *infra*.

[54] See Chapter I *supra* on diversities in camping usages. One might add to those: trails, tipis, moccasins, bows, rituals, buffalo practices, etc. Re one nation alone, two learned scholars observe that it is impossible to make statements concerning Sioux customs that would be true of all (Thomas and Swanton, in Hodge, *Handbook*, II, 578).

[55] See Dobie, *The Mustangs*, 90–91.

[56] I note two tribes, named respectively "Pintados" (Mexico, 1539) and "Pintos" (Texas, 1757): Hodge, *Handbook*, II, 256, 257. In the absence of further information, probably these names may be taken to refer to their painting of themselves, perhaps thought to be unique until the Spaniards penetrated farther into the land.

horse regions painted themselves in various manifestations, I have
failed to discover any evidence or even suggestion, either in history
or fiction, of their having painted their horses. Face painting was
quite widely practiced in South America; although in some tribes,
the Aymara for example, it was confined largely to the warriors.[57]
The Arucanians of Chile were among the earliest and boldest of
South American equestrian tribes;[58] yet curiously enough, "they
seem not to have practiced much face or body painting in early
times."[59] It has been suggested that painting of men or horses in
war was what we have come to term "camouflage," rather than
either vanity or the idea of terrifying the enemy. I have commented above on the frequent probability of painting making a
horse not less but more conspicuous. The two colors on railroad
signal semaphores are meant to make them plainer at a distance.
Assuming, however, that Indian horse painting was really camouflage, it becomes very difficult to explain its absence in South American tribes, whose general principles of military tactics were virtually identical with those of North America.

To summarize the foregoing suggestions briefly, it is sufficient
to say that critics who deny the possibility of a pinto development
by the workings of prenatal influences operating through the medium of artificially-painted horses should be prepared to offer some
contrary hypothesis which will be in accordance with the accepted
facts of the case. With sincere respect to a learned and careful investigator, the explanation advanced by Denhardt is not in accordance with the facts. Whether the Northern Plains area was later
stocked with the descendants of only one, or of a few, or of many
Spanish pintos, it cannot be supposed that the South American
early horse areas either received literally no pintos or horses of
pinto ancestry, or a ratio so infinitesimally small and fractional—
deriving from the same common stock in the first instance—as to
be capable of producing only the negligible pinto proportions of
the *baguales* of the South American Pampas. The theory of degeneracy through continued interbreeding, which Denhardt rejects, must of course encounter the same fatal objection.

[57] Harry Tschopik, Jr., in Steward, *Handbook*, II, 532, 548.
[58] Denhardt, *Horse of the Americas*, 155–60.
[59] John M. Cooper, in Steward, *Handbook*, II, 711.

VIII

THE WHITE STALLION

There is another possible clue to the solution of the pinto problem. This lies in the well-known Plains tradition of the magnificent stallion, the White Steed of the Prairies, with his "sleek seraglio" of splendid mares. This famous animal was long a legend of the Western Plains, if the myth (or whatever it may be) may be said to be dead even yet, for it is almost invariably dangerous to predicate the "last example" of anything. He was known, or has been called, by a multitude of names, with the white motif, implicit or specific, running through them all. The following may not even exhaust the list:

The White Steed of the Prairies	The White Steed
The White Mustang of the Prairies	The Great White Horse
The White Stallion of the Plains	The Pacing White Mustang
The White Ghost of the Prairies	The White Mustang
The Deathless Pacing White Mustang	White Lightning
The Deathless Pacing White Stallion	The Winged Steed
The Ghost of the Llano Estacado	The Prairie King
The Pacing White Stallion	The White Stallion
The Ghost Horse of the Plains	The White Sultan
The Phantom White Horse	The Phantom Mustang
The White Horse of the Prairies	The White Ghost Horse
The Phantom White Stallion	The Pacing Stallion
The White Stallion of the Prairies	The Steed of the Prairies
The Great White Stallion of the Prairies	The Great White Mustang
The Snow-white Pacer of the Canadian (River)	The White Pacer
The Pacing White Stallion of the Mustangs	The Pacing Mustang

The White Pacer of the Plains	The King of the Mustangs
The Ghost Horse of the Prairies	The Phantom Wild Horse[1]

It is not my intention to attempt a detailed account of this creature, since the task has already been performed, virtually to the point of exhaustion, by a literary craftsman with whom I cannot hope to compete.[2] In the present chapter I shall therefore give only such data as appear necessary to our present inquiry.

The legend was common both to Indians and to white plainsmen. This circumstance leads one to suspect that the Indians possessed it—or were possessed by it—first. Concerning this, Denhardt writes:

Nor was it only the white man who told stories of the White Mustang. The Indians had similar legends. They were more superstitious than their white brothers. The Kiowas felt that arrows or rifle balls could not touch the 'Phantom Mustang' and that he could run unscathed through a prairie fire. The Blackfeet believed that he was 'big medicine' and could, if he chose, breed war horses that made the rider invulnerable in battle.[3]

It seems unlikely, in my view, that such suppositions had no place in the Indian mind—to which any horse was at first a magical monster—until their adoption from the white men.[4] For according to a competent plainsman-student, the same beliefs prevailed among the Ute and the Comanche. As firearms became commoner among them, the addition of rifle balls to the immunities conferred upon, or enjoyed by, the White Mustang would be a logical accretion.

Apparently the earliest appearance of this marvelous animal in literature is due to Washington Irving. In describing 'the con-

[1] See for these, Dobie, *Tales of the Mustang*, 14, 32–33, 36–37, 44, 50, 52–55, 57–59, 62, 65; Dobie (ed.), *Mustangs and Cow Horses*, 172–79; Dobie, *The Mustangs*, 143–70, 245–51, 353; Denhardt, *Horse of the Americas*, 111; also George Wilkins Kendall's *Narrative of the Texas Santa Fé Expedition* (ed. by Milo M. Quaife), 107–10.

[2] J. Frank Dobie, in the works cited above.

[3] Denhardt, *Horse of the Americas*, 113. So also among the Ute and the Comanche, according to a competent plainsman-student (see Dobie, *Tales of the Mustang*, 55).

[4] See Chapter IV *supra* on Comanche beliefs concerning horses.

versation of the camp for the evening,' Irving says: "There were several anecdotes told of a famous grey horse that had ranged the prairies of this neighbourhood for six or seven years, setting at naught any attempt of the hunters to capture him. They say he can pace or rack (or amble) faster than the fleetest horse can run."[5]

Josiah Gregg, traveling through the same general territory in the same years (Santa Fé Trail, 1831–1840), may actually have heard of him sooner, but his work was not printed until 1845. Gregg writes thus:

The beauty of the mustang is proverbial, one in particular has been celebrated by hunters, of which marvellous stories are told. He has been represented as a medium-sized stallion of perfect symmetry, milk-white—save a pair of black ears—a natural 'pacer.' But I infer this story is somewhat mythical, from the difficulty one finds in fixing the abiding place of this equine hero. He is familiarly known by common report, all over the great prairies. The trapper celebrates him in the vicinity of the Rocky Mountains; the hunter on the Arkansas, or in the midst of the plains, while others have him pacing at the rate of half a mile a minute on the borders of Texas. It is hardly surprising that a creature of such an ubiquitary existence should never have been caught.[6]

George Wilkins Kendall, who was on the Southern Plains in 1841, just after Gregg had ceased to traverse them, heard of *Equus superbus* on the Llano Estacado, the "Staked Plain" of Texas. He gives a most interesting description of the legendary beliefs concerning its prowess:

Many stories were told in camp, by some of the older hunters, of a large white horse that had been seen in the vicinity of Cross Timbers and near the Red River. That many of these stories, like the majority of those told by gossiping campaigners, were either apocryphal or marvelously garnished, I have little doubt; but that such a horse has been seen, and that he possesses wonderful speed and great powers of endurance, there is no reason to disbelieve. As the camp stories run, he has never been known to gallop or trot, but paces faster than any horse that has been sent out after him can run; and so game and untiring is the 'White Steed of the Prairies,' for he is well known to hunters and trappers by that name, that he has tired down no less than three race

[5] *A Tour on the Prairies,* 170.

nags, sent expressly to catch him, with a Mexican rider well trained to the business of taking wild horses. The latter had nothing but a *lazo* with him. Although he changed horses whenever one was tired, he never got close enough to rope the steed, or even drive him into a regular gallop. Some hunters even go so far as to say that the white steed has been known to pace his mile in less than two minutes, and he could keep up the pace until he had tired all pursuit. Large sums have been offered for his capture, and the attempt frequently made, but he still roams his prairies in freedom, solitary and alone.[7]

Denhardt states that "most of the reports agreed that he roved solitary and alone."[8]

Much of the mass of legend that grew up around this peerless chieftain was plainly impossible in sober fact. For it was during a long course of more than half a century, from Washington Irving's time alone—and Irving's account indicates a fixed belief, evidently as deeply rooted then as anything of later times—that *the same animal* roamed the Plains from Texas or Mexico to Idaho and Manitoba. J. Frank Dobie writes:

White Horse Plains in Colorado, southward from Cheyenne, is said to have taken its name from a noted mustang stallion that roamed that region some time before 1890. 'This horse was supposed never to have broken a pace, and at this gait was able to outdistance all pursuers, though many traps were placed for him and many a horse hunter gave chase.'[9]

Another White Horse Plains, some twenty miles west of Winnipeg, Manitoba, is believed likewise to owe its name to the same ubiquitous creature of the Southern Plains.[10]

There are several variations from the common white coloration. Of these, Irving's is the earliest, and this is based evidently upon

[6] Gregg, *Commerce of the Prairies,* in Thwaites, *Travels,* XX, 260–62.
[7] Kendall, *Narrative of the Texas Santa Fé Expedition* (ed. by Quaife), 107–10. The Cross Timbers, to which Kendall refers, is a well-known forest belt, some forty miles in width, which extends from the Arkansas to the Red River across modern Oklahoma, roughly about 97° W.
[8] Denhardt, *Horse of the Americas,* 113.
[9] *Mustangs and Cow Horses,* 172; apparently citing informed local authority.
[10] Coues (ed.), *Henry-Thompson Journals,* I, 288. The earliest date I can find for this place, 1806, is from Alexander Henry himself; the name was apparently settled and well recognized at that era.

the reports of others, since Irving never saw the animal himself, or he would certainly have said so. Other testimonies, however, rest upon direct sight of a gray (or supposedly gray) animal. Captain W. S. Henry (United States Army) reported seeing the supposed prodigy in 1846 at Corpus Christi, Texas: "a handsome flea-bitten gray, with white mane and tail. . . ."[11] A certain Curly Hatcher reported the famous mustang in 1868 on the Kansas-Colorado line. The horse was stated to be "a beautiful grey," but when "recognized" in 1874 as the same one, "he was almost white now."[12] Another, an iron gray, was seen by C. M. Grady, a Texas old-timer, in 1875, and heard of later.[13] In all such cases, including the above, others denied strenuously that any instance except their own could possibly be *the* White Horse. There is yet another variant in color apart from the grays. Chief Buffalo Child Long Lance, of the Black-foot, gives it as "steel dust."[14] It was at one time a sort of cliché among the horsey fraternity in England that 'there are no white horses, only light grays.' I heard it as a boy, and it may have been far older; perhaps old enough to have had its repercussions in the "Scots Greys" (H. M. 2nd Dragoons, who ride—or rode—gray-white horses), and even to have traveled across the Atlantic and influenced color interpretation on this continent.

It seems indisputable that the various references are intended to denote the same identical creature, and not any offspring of a second or later generation. I have not encountered even a hint of such, and we have seen Denhardt's reference that 'most of the accounts have him roving solitary and alone.' There is, moreover, little doubt from the nature of the various reports which have been cited concerning him, that every locality would insist that it was *their* horse which had performed these renowned exploits; that he alone was the original and only genuine, and that all other possible "doubles" were spurious imitations.

With so much of palpable impossibility in these recitals, I am skeptical concerning the solitariness of an outstanding specimen of a gregarious and polygamous species during the peak period of life, to which its abnormal vigor and endurance clearly testify.

[11] Dobie, *Tales of the Mustang,* 44.
[12] *Ibid.,* 49.
[13] *Ibid.,* 50–51.
[14] *Ibid.,* 47.

In my view this assertion is rather suggestive of a desire to show that this super-equine was not as other horses are, but a law unto himself. The "agreement" of numerous versions of the tradition concerning the solitariness means nothing. They also agree on other sheer improbabilities. I am the more confirmed in this conclusion by the historical circumstance of an actual instance of a locally-renowned white stallion which really was captured during this very era we have reviewed. This animal would beyond doubt be regarded (and on equally just grounds with any wild white stallion) as *the* White Pacer in that neighborhood. Yet he had not merely a *manada* of mares, but one comprising about double the average number, as one might not unreasonably expect from such a lord of creation.[15] In face of these considerations, I can really see no reason for yielding to this particular detail of solitariness an almost unquestioning degree of assent, which it is impossible to extend to other details of the legend, resting upon equally sound (or unsound) authority.

This last wild mustang (he of the numerous *manada*) had all the marks of the traditional monarch. "His form was perfect; his alertness and vitality were superb. He was pure white. His tail brushed the tall mesquite grass that carpeted the earth, and his tossing mane swept to his knees. His only gait out of a walk was a pace, and it was soon found that he never, no matter how hard pressed, broke that pace."[16]

This magnificent animal, whose chosen "stamping ground" was in modern Travis County, Texas, flourished in the forties of the nineteenth century, and had become not merely mythically, but locally well known. Many plots were contrived to capture him; and at last, under conditions in which he was worn down by harassing pursuit and by excessive thirst, he was finally (when temporarily incapacitated from having drunk too eagerly after prolonged deprivation) roped and held. He refused food and water, and very shortly afterward died, unconquerable.[17]

15 Dobie (ed.), *Mustangs and Cow Horses*, 173. For other actual *manadas* seen or asserted in these cases, see Dobie, *Tales of the Mustang*, 45, 52, 61, 64, 69, 83; "fifty or sixty mares," Dobie, *The Mustangs*, 151.

16 Dobie (ed.), *Mustangs and Cow Horses*, 173; from the nephew of a contemporary of these occurrences.

17 *Ibid.*, 173-79.

What in my judgment gives this particular instance the stamp of authenticity is the fact that this animal not only "could be" but actually *was* caught. Dobie recounts another case in the experience of a Texas old-timer who settled on the Brazos River in 1839. This episode occurred shortly after his arrival there. The description of this white stallion follows more conventionally along the orthodox lines of the tradition, even to the climax that by no device whatever could the animal be entrapped or run down; and some little time later he disappeared from the locality.[18] This account derives its chief interest from certain details which appear to indicate this particular episode as the source of George Wilkins Kendall's version of the "White Steed" tradition, given above.

While there can be no reasonable doubt that in the first of these cases at least, a splendid white stallion flourished and died in this manner and at that time, not even these could have been *the* "Pacing White Stallion of the Mustangs" (etc.). According to Washington Irving, the legend was in accepted existence (or should one say "in full swing"?) some twenty years prior to this time,[19] and it continued to flourish for half a century at least after the Texas horse's death. For a report was current in 1881 that the Pacing White Stallion was along the Washita, and later on the South Canadian River in Oklahoma; while at the same time another was "supposed to be in the Snake River country" in Idaho.[20] Nearly a decade later came the afore-mentioned eponym of the White Horse Plains in Colorado, 'some time before 1900.'[21] Denhardt adduces another case of a white horse which was captured May 18, 1892, between the headwaters of the Trinity and Brazos Rivers in Texas, under conditions virtually identical with those described in the case of the captive mentioned above.[22] Such a general identity is practically inevitable with an identical species in an identical environment. At the same time one feels no surprise

[18] *Ibid.*, 172.

[19] Irving, *Tour on the Prairies*, 170. At the same time that Irving noted this, Maximilian records an Omaha chief, The White Horse (*Travels*, in Thwaites, *Travels*, XXIV, 316).

[20] Dobie, *Tales of the Mustang*, 58; Denhardt, *Horse of the Americas*, 114.

[21] Dobie (ed.), *Mustangs and Cow Horses*, 172. Almost at the same time (1889) another was captured in Arizona. See note 29 *infra*.

[22] Denhardt, *Horse of the Americas*, 114.

at this horse of 1892 "answering in many respects the description of the White Steed."[23] Finally, this deathless animal is heard of (in relation to an unspecified time) in a work published in 1902.[24]

It will not have escaped the reader's attention that the captured white stallion of the eighteen forties (somewhat like his own "reincarnation" of 1892) exhibits a rather suspicious conformity with specifications in respect to various characteristics, and above all in the style and pre-eminence of pace. It would seem as though these standardized qualities were automatically allotted to any white stallion whose local or legendary notoriety raised him into the candidate class. Charles W. Webber, an early Texan writing in 1852, who "had often heard of the White Steed," is quoted as saying: "All the white mustangs I have ever seen were natural pacers."[25] For such reasons he might possibly be caught in more than one locality; yet, as Denhardt says, "he was apparently never caught."[26] The cult being what it was, he scarcely *could* be caught. For as fast as any one specimen vanished or was rightly or wrongly thought to be caught, some distant avatar would be found to be doing business at the same old stand, while the local propagandists would unanimously insist that theirs was the true-blue Simon Pure, and not the recent victim. The problem lies not in the mere duplication but in the multiplicity of alleged white steeds, for leaders, white or otherwise, were everywhere.[27] These demonstrations were not confined to solitary champions nor even to the male sex. J. Frank Dobie says: "A white mustang was never a rarity like a white buffalo. As late as 1882 a band of thirteen white mustangs ran between the Palo Duro Canyon and the Canadian River in the Texas Panhandle —so alert that nobody ever saw them standing." Dobie also men-

23 *Ibid.*, 114.

24 Chittenden, *American Fur Trade*, II, 833 (citing no date).

25 Dobie, *Tales of the Mustang*, 41; *The Mustangs*, 168.

26 Denhardt, *Horse of the Americas*, 111.

27 John B. Wyeth (who does not mention the Great White Stallion) says "the wild horses always appeared to have a leader" (*Oregon, 1832*, in Thwaites, *Travels*, XXI, 87). John K. Townsend, a scientist, writing a few months later, says nothing of leaders (*Narrative*, in Thwaites, *Travels*, XXI, 177, 283). None the less, leaders seem well attested, as one might expect. Ferdinand Roemer, the German scientist, between the San Marcos and the Colorado River (Texas), in 1846, mentions "a magnificent white stallion" at the head of a herd of mustangs, but apparently says nothing about the "Prairie King" (Dobie, *Tales of the Mustang*, 64).

tions White Horse Springs, in Arizona, "where a never-roped mare drank alone with a succession of white colts. . . ."[28]

One instance at least, in which another of these marvelous creatures was caught, and somewhat conventionally died eleven days later, "untamable," deserves special notice as being unique for quite another reason. This animal, which for sixteen years in Arizona had been 'the unattainable lure of Arizona mustangers,' was captured in 1889 by "creasing," (shooting with a rifle so that the bullet grazes the animal's neck close to the spinal column. This causes a temporary paralysis which enables the hunter to tie the horse up before it recovers). The many accounts we have noted are virtually identical in describing a tireless pacer, which hopelessly outdistanced the fastest runners. The mustangers apparently told nobody how they approached near enough to have any hope of creasing the animal. If their success was due to sheer old age on the horse's part (after sixteen years of hunting), it is remarkable that he had not been superseded in his leadership by some younger competitor. Creasing was a manifestly difficult and apparently dubious performance,[29] and its introduction in this field rather repels than commands confidence.

From the angle of the pinto problem, the multiplicity to which I have alluded raises possibilities of some interest. The very coloring, white (or gray), is precisely the one, complementary to the prevailing bays and browns of horses in general in most countries, which is necessary to produce

---

[28] Dobie, *The Mustangs*, 169, 330.

[29] *Ibid.*, 159; cf. Dobie, *Tales of the Mustang*, 52. My earliest reference to "creasing" is 1806. It seems to have been a recognized practice then. Zebulon M. Pike says: "They came near us, giving hope of an opportunity for creasing" (which proved futile: Coues [ed.], *Expeditions of Pike*, II, 436). Three admirable observers (contemporaries) describe the business: Townsend, Gregg ("so nice an operation that many are killed in the attempt"), and Catlin, who says that creasing "always destroyed the spirit and character of the animal" (*Narratives*, and *Commerce of the Prairies*, in Thwaites, *Travels*, XXI, 87; XX, 261–62; Catlin, *Letters and Notes*, II, 57–60). G. C. Robinson, in Dobie (ed.), *Mustangs and Cow Horses*, 16, states that creasing "was generally attended with success." Two other contributors, O. W. Nolen and Frank Collinson, consider it highly problematical; almost always a failure, killing the horse (*ibid.*, 44–46, 75–76; cf. 86, 179). Dobie himself concurs in this: "the never reliable trick of creasing" (*Tales of the Mustang*, 52–53; *The Mustangs*, 83, 219–20).

the pinto polychromes; and it is also a coloring which is by no means common—as a self-color—among the cayuse population. The prominence which is given to grays noted by various observers among the wild herds raises a logical presumption of their relative infrequency. Catlin speaks of 'many iron-greys' in the Comanche country (where horses were popularly reckoned by thousands) in 1834.[30] David Thompson relates the capture of 'a fine iron-grey' in the Kootenay country, 1807, which he broke to the saddle: my earliest and northernmost reference to this precise color.[31] Maximilian (Missouri River, 1834) among all colors mentions two grays (twice), two white horses, and one more gray among the Cheyenne.[32]

David Thompson elsewhere tells a tale which might be thought strange, were it not (as I believe) true. He writes thus (December, 1797):

Mons. Jussomme's [René Jusseaume, a well-known early fur trader] Mare and my yellow Horse had both become lame of each one foot, and could proceed no further through the Plains, each of these horses had one white foot and three black feet; the white foot of each was lame in the same manner, the hair of the white foot was worn away by the hard snow, and a small hole in the flesh also above the hoof. The three black feet had not a hair worn off them. My other Horse was dark brown with four black feet. As the Horses of this country have no shoes, the colour of the hoof is much regarded; the yellow hoof with white hair is a brittle hoof and soon wears away; for this reason, as much as possible, the Natives take only black-hoofed Horses on their War expeditions. . . . Mons. Jussomme was now without a Horse and had to purchase Dogs.[33]

Fifty years and more ago the present writer owned a bright bay gelding (the one mentioned in Appendix B) that had one white-stockinged hind foot with a yellow hoof. Our horses went barefooted on soft ground, and periodically needed to have their toes trimmed, since long toes not only made them likely to stumble, but could also lame them temporarily because of the altered strain

[30] Catlin, Letters and Notes, II, 57.
[31] Narrative (ed. by Tyrrell), 378.
[32] Maximilian, Travels, in Thwaites, Travels, XXIII, 125, 145, 201.
[33] Narrative (ed. by Tyrrell), 214.

on the leg muscles, as with our changing from heeled shoes to moccasins or vice versa. This yellow hoof was excessively brittle and very difficult to cut. If such animals were largely left at home by Indian war parties, which faced a much higher risk of loss among their horses (and might not even survive to bring any back), and therefore tended somewhat to preponderate among breeding stock, this might on selective principles favor a disproportionate increase in the ratio of contributory white coloration, and thereby assist in the development of a pinto type, if the time element permitted. This last, however, would probably be the crux.

It may probably be admitted as a psychological possibility at least, that the white element in the pintos, considered as direct visible evidence of a parentage derived from the "sacred" white sire, might confer for a time some diluted degree of semi-sanctity on the partly white progeny. It might also conceivably arouse hopes of one of these producing a Great White Stallion which would be "their very own" as a tribal possession. This would tend to favor a pinto preference and a perpetuation both as individuals and as a type, however the pinto may have originated. Dobie gives an instance of this extraordinary partiality. "In 1856, a party of Crow warriors captured a paint [pinto] horse from another tribe. He was soon regarded as the most beautiful and the fleetest horse among the thousands owned by the Crows. He was the pride of the whole nation and was guarded accordingly. . . . Such a horse could not be bought, only taken." The horse was stolen by a Piegan in broad daylight, by killing his rider, and kept for years.[34]

A white horse can scarcely be classed as an albino, as certain whites and grays are almost distinct breeds. In the normal course of things or through some bypath of descent, there may quite possibly have been such a creature (or creatures) whose immediate descendants might contribute for a generation or two a few white stallions to the common stock of the North American Plains territory, before the integral white dwindled away into a thing of shreds and patches. The relative rarity of the color would make it conspicuous, and might tend to apotheosize or sanctify it, and its biological influence in the production of a partly pinto progeny whose (color) preferability in aboriginal regard was probably of long

[34] Dobie, The Mustangs, 74.

standing would assist in the same direction. For I believe it may safely be assumed from the widespread reverence for the white buffalo among the same Plains tribes—which is itself very probably only an adaptation of a pre-buffalo white cult[35]—that the *white* sanctities are far older than any knowledge of the horse. I am uncertain to just what extent we may wisely accept Indian traditions as being historic, but one which is not inherently impossible is probably as authentic as another. A well-known Western historical scholar is quoted as saying that "many years ago he asked an old Comanche Indian named Julián how there came to be so many white-spotted ponies among the horse stock belonging to his tribesmen. Old Julián answered, 'They all come from the great White Stallion of the Prairies.' "[36]

We cannot suppose that a people who (as in the case of the black hoofs mentioned by David Thompson) in fifty years or less had established purely by empirical observation something like a "law" could long remain ignorant of the visible manifestations or results of (color) crossbreeding. And we have already seen in the cases of *El Morzillo* and the Comanche that the aborigines of more than one region were under no necessity to await any prompting from Europeans to effect a deification or to adopt a belief—which is very much the same as to create a legend—concerning horses. All this is of course conjectural, but growths of this character must have a beginning somewhere. If it were possible to accomplish the utterly hopeless task of running the tradition definitely to earth, it might conceivably reveal an origin in some actual, striking occurrence.

Meanwhile, it is of interest to note, and may be thought to add some weight to the foregoing tentative suggestions, that in South America, where pintos were scarcely found or favored, there has never (so far as I can discover) been a legend of the Great White Stallion. It is my deliberate conclusion, in the light of our present historical knowledge, that whatever explanation of the pinto problem may be advanced, no satisfactory answer can be expected which is based upon purely biological premises, whether in rela-

[35] See Roe, *North American Buffalo*, App. D, "Albinism in Buffalo," 715–28, and authorities there cited.

[36] E. E. Dale, University of Oklahoma, to J. Frank Dobie, in Dobie, *Tales of the Mustang*, 55; *The Mustangs*, 163.

tion to inbreeding or to more normal descent from the original imported stock. For such biological manifestations, arising from a common parentage, must have been almost inevitably common to both continents. I believe the answer must be sought in the variable human equation.

The Northern Indians' partiality for the pinto was not shared by the white plainsmen. This anti-pinto prejudice included an Anglo-American prejudice against even white horses. On this subject J. Frank Dobie quotes a well-known United States military historian, Captain John G. Bourke, in rebuttal of the old superstition that white horses are the weakest in endurance. Bourke states that in the Sioux campaign of 1876 the white horse troop of the Fifth Cavalry outclassed any others in endurance.[37] George W. Kendall (1841) mentions a Mexican widow in the State of Durango, through whose hacienda he passed as a prisoner, and who was said to have once possessed 300,000 horses. Her herds included one thousand white horses, of which Kendall says these were all off one hacienda with "hardly a month's difference in their ages." This lady presented the regiment commanded by her son with six hundred "pure white horses, the highest compliment she could pay."[38] We are not informed whether as a Mexican she was of pure Spanish descent or had Indian blood in her veins. If the latter was the case, it would be an interesting speculation whether the white predilection was a Spanish or an aboriginal contribution. Dobie notes, however, that even among those (it would seem) who entertained the anti-white prejudice, a white or gray mare was usually preferred as bell mare for a mule train or a troop of young horses.[39]

The range prejudice against pintos was very strong. Dobie says: "Range men in America . . . have never had much use for paint horses"; and he quotes Wyatt Earp, a well-known plainsman, to this effect: "I have never known a paint horse that knew anything himself."[40]

[37] Ibid., 169.
[38] Dobie, Tales of the Mustang, 40.
[39] Ibid., 41.
[40] Dobie (ed.), Mustangs and Cow Horses, 247.

Denhardt discusses this aversion as follows:

Pintos have never been extremely popular with North American horsemen. Perhaps one of the main reasons is that with one exception, and that exception does not occur in North America, practically every recognized breed refuses to allow spotted horses in the studbooks. Regardless of the popularity of the Pinto horse with children, circuses, Indians, and certain Westerners, there is an old belief that a Pinto horse is of no account. However, almost every Westerner can tell of one paint horse that was an exception to this rule. To say that a Pinto horse, because of his color, is worthless, is like saying that a two-toned automobile is worthless. . . . It may be true that little attention has been paid to the breeding of Pintos, and that many are therefore, inferior; but that would not be the fault of the color. There are other colors, for example bays and sorrels, on equally worthless horses.[41]

It is obvious that "Western plainsmen" and "studbooks" do not refer to the same class of pinto; we are moving in different worlds.[42] I should be disposed to reverse the explanation which Denhardt advances. Instead of disliking pintos because they are not in studbooks, I rather suspect they are not in studbooks because they are disliked. In whatever degree this aversion may have grown out of the Western anti-pinto prejudice, I suggest that the explanation may very probably be discoverable in the mutual hatreds of the anti-Indian era in the West. The plainsmen regarded the pinto with contempt because the Indian liked it.

[41] Denhardt, *Horse of the Americas*, 196.
[42] The handsome pair in Denhardt (*ibid.*, 198), *tobiano* and *overo* respectively, certainly do not suggest anything in common with Indian ponies except colors!

171

PART II
THE INFLUENCE OF THE HORSE

IX

HORSES AND BUFFALO INDIANS

A considerable amount has been written at various times about the "profound changes"—economic, social, temperamental—which were effected in the Indian world by the coming of the horse into their lives.[1] As an historical generalization this may be considered indisputable. In so far as the typical horse Indian is concerned, the change is very graphically summarized by a learned authority:

Without the horse the Indian was a half-starved skulker in the timber, creeping up on foot towards the unwary deer or building a brush corral with infinite labor to surround a herd of antelope, and seldom venturing more than a few days' journey from home. With the horse he was transformed into the daring buffalo hunter, able to procure in a single day enough food to supply his family for a year, leaving him free to sweep the plains with his war parties along a range of a thousand miles.[2]

When we turn from the brilliant word picture, however, to the more prosaic task of attempting to evaluate the process in detail, it is not entirely clear just what forms these changes took. We may review some of the earlier summaries, although none of them, with the exception of Hubert Howe Bancroft (1883), are very far

[1] See Thwaites, *Travels*, XXVII, 180, editor's note; citing A. F. Bandelier on this, whose essay I regret having had no opportunity to see. This is of course Wissler's actual subject in the paper frequently cited here: "The Influence of the Horse in the Development of Plains Culture."

[2] James Mooney, "Calendar History of the Kiowa Indians," *Seventeenth Annual Report of the Bureau of American Ethnology* (1898), Part I, 161; cited by Dobie, *Tales of the Mustangs*, 17.

back in point of time. Bancroft writes as follows concerning the horse Indians:

It is by no means certain that the possession of the horse has bettered their condition. Indeed, by facilitating the capture of buffalo, previously taken perhaps by stratagem, by introducing a medium by which at least the wealthy may always purchase supplies, as well as by rendering practicable long migrations for food or trade, the horse may have contributed somewhat to their present spirit of improvidence.[3]

It may be noted that both Bancroft and James Mooney treat the improved facilities for buffalo hunting conferred by the horse almost automatically in terms of *quantity*. We shall note later that contemporary scholarship prefers to interpret them, with respect to one important buffalo tribe at least, in terms of quality. Apart from this, Bancroft's pronouncement may be considered legitimate philosophical speculation, in which the potential consequences may at least be recognized as being logically possible results from the causes here indicated. Certain other similar dicta seem less convincing. Two very discriminating Canadian scholars write as follows:

"The horse made nomads of many tribes which there is abundant evidence to show were formerly almost sedentary in character."[4] "The ease with which they could now run down the herds of buffalo on horseback led many woodland tribes to move out on the prairies." The latter of the two is also apparently of the opinion that the advent of the horses may have inaugurated wars *de novo* among the Plains horse tribes.[5]

I do not think these propositions could be at all satisfactorily established. I have found little evidence of wholesale migrations in the directions indicated *since* the known introduction of the horse to such tribes, or even since they were likely to have heard of the animal; and fewer still of such movements appear to have been voluntary. We have seen above in the case of the Chippewa and the Sioux, that what might there perhaps be termed "emigrating" is classed by learned authorities as, in the case of the Sioux,

[3] Bancroft, *Native Races*, I, 282.
[4] Norman Fergus Black, *A History of Saskatchewan and the Old Northwest*, 94.
[5] Jenness, *Indians of Canada*, 129, 256, 308–11, 316.

being "driven out" by superior foes, *who did not follow them out on to the Plains.*[6] J. Frank Dobie writes that the horse "transplanted the Comanches from north of the Platte to the land of 'Ever Summer' next to the horse supply," and the Cheyenne "from farmbound camps to a boundlessness limited only by . . . ."[7] The chronology of these movements is somewhat obscure, however. In the case of the Cheyenne migration from the Sheyenne River of North Dakota to the Big Cheyenne country southwestward, we find ourselves confronted by a somewhat perplexing crux. This migration occurred, in the opinion of competent scholars, at some time during the last quarter of the seventeenth century, when we have no ground for supposing them to have yet acquired the horse.[8] We have seen that an archaeological authority of the first rank considered permanent changes of habitation—or we may say, in the case of nomads, changes of habitual range—to have been negligible among the Plains tribes, during the period 1680–1860.[9]

If the short journeys and circumscribed life of the pre-equestrian Plains society were what our authorities pronounce them to have been, we may wonder whether the Cheyenne could even have heard of the horse at such a time. To assume their knowledge or possible possession of the animal apparently requires us to accept Hyde's chronology for the northern territory. That gives the Arikara as the first Northern Plains equestrians, having horses from the Apache by 1680.[10] This may possibly have been the case, but it conflicts materially with the generally accepted chronology for the Arikara and the region.[11]

Another contemporary student includes the Sioux and the Blackfoot in these transplanting movements. These were "induced by the acquisition of the horse to forsake the forest regions of the Northwest, and to move on to the Plains."[12] We have noted certain considerations which render this doubtful in the case of the Sioux. The Blackfoot were apparently induced much more insistently by

---

[6] See Chapter V *supra.*
[7] Dobie, "Indian Horses and Horsemanship," 265.
[8] See Chapter V *supra.* For dating in detail, see Chapter XII *infra.*
[9] Clark Wissler (see Chapter IV *supra*).
[10] Hyde, "Mystery of the Arikaras," 205, 217.
[11] See Chapter V *supra.*
[12] Worcester, "Spanish Horses among the Plains Tribes," 417.

the Cree's driving them onward;[13] a relationship which is probably reflected in the contemptuous Cree designation of "Slaves."[14] An authoritative student of the tribe suggests the existence of a Plains culture about 1492.[15]

Our earliest witnesses in both the North and South, the Jesuit missionaries Allouez and Marquette, together with Father Hennepin, on the one hand,[16] and on the other, Cabeza de Vaca and Coronado's party,[17] found tribal enmities prevailing among horseless "buffalo Indians" of the Prairie Plains, much the same as they prevailed among horseless Eastern woodland tribes.

The nomadic life likewise cannot in any sense be considered a new, post-equestrian culture. Dobie puts the case exactly when he says: "The Spanish horse made hunting tribes into nomads of Arabian mobility."[18] In other words, it *widened* their range, much as Mooney expressed it, which is a very different thing from making them nomads *de novo*. I consider the fundamental test of the nomad to be the movable dwelling. This feature is (or was) a prime characteristic of the nomadic tribes, of which, says Wissler, "the Blackfoot, Crow, Teton, Kiowa, Arapaho, Cheyenne, and Comanche may be taken as types. These are the great horse and buffalo Indians as we know them."[19]

At the same time, it is well known that the nomadic impulse was clearly recognized in the aborigines by the first Europeans in the South and Southwest, both in Plains peoples pure and simple, and also in partly agriculturist tribes. Both Coronado's followers

[13] Hodge, *Handbook*, II, 570.

[14] This term was so rooted in popular use at Edmonton that even Rundle the missionary uses it, between whom and the Blackfoot there existed mutual respect and esteem. He and De Smet were the only men who dared to traverse the Blackfoot country alone (1840–48).

[15] Kidd, "Blackfoot Ethnography," 10–16.

[16] See Thwaites (ed.), *Jesuit Relations*, LIX, 157; Father Louis Hennepin, *A New Discovery of a Vast Country in America* (ed. by Thwaites), II, 627; Father Membre, in Cox (ed.), *Journeys of La Salle*, I, 141; Francis Parkman, *La Salle and the Discovery of the Great West*, 194.

[17] Bandelier (ed.), *Journey of Cabeza de Vaca*, 119–21; Castañeda, in Winship (ed.), *Journey of Coronado*, 111, 210, 215. See also Bartram, *Travels*, 314 (Southeast, 1773). Those Mandan of 1738, who feared the Pananas and Pananis, evidently had no horses then, if their foes had; yet the enmity seems to have been already—and perhaps for long—a normal condition.

[18] Dobie, "Indian Horses and Horsemanship," 265.

[19] Wissler, "Influence of the Horse," 16.

and those of De Soto likened the former to the Arabs,[20] the super-nomads of all history; and the latter, semi-agricultural folk, stand as one of the type representatives of the "temporary migration" impulse in Indian life.[21] Wissler very pertinently asks: "Why should the Plains people have had the dog travois if they did not go on long journeys by land?"[22] We may add with equal pertinence: And why should they have had the movable dwelling which was thus transported?

Rupert Norval Richardson considers that "journeys were short-er in the era before the horse, lodge poles were lighter, if they were transported at all, and the tepees smaller and flimsier." He also states that bows were made shorter after the coming of the horse. He cites no contemporary authority for these statements, and it is not easy to see how he could, for he himself notes that Comanche tradition is negligible.[23] I shall not dispute these statements, which appear reasonable and probable enough in themselves. But we do well to remember that probability (in our eyes) is not necessarily historical fact. Alanson Skinner cites actual lodge-pole practice among a permanently and completely horseless people in the north-eastern forest lands of Canada. These carried "twenty-five, thirty, or forty lodge-poles usually, according to size."[24]

Whatever the opinion may be regarding the growth or develop-ment of new traits, we cannot doubt that the horse immensely extended the practicability and range of those which already char-acterized these tribes. In Wissler's opinion, "As an intensifier of original Plains traits, the horse presents its strongest claim."[25]

[20] Castañeda, in Winship (ed.), *Journey of Coronado*, 65; Gentleman of Elvas, in Bourne (ed.), *Narratives of De Soto*, I, 180.

[21] The Blackfoot, Teton, etc. as "typical buffalo tribes"; Pawnee, Osage, and others, as semi-agricultural. The Northern tribes of the Illinois country (prairie rather than plains) might also be included in the latter class (Wissler, "Influence of the Horse," 14). Fathers Dablon and Allouez say of the Northern tribes in 1671: "[Buffalo,] by their abundance, furnish adequate provision for whole Villages, which therefore are not obliged to scatter by families during their hunting season, as is the case with Savages elsewhere" (Thwaites [ed.], *Jesuit Relations*, LV, 195–97). See also Catlin's description of the "Great Comanchee Village," about 1834 (*Letters and Notes*, II, 70).

[22] Wissler, "Influence of the Horse," 14.

[23] Richardson, *The Comanche Barrier*, 25–27.

[24] Skinner, "Notes on the Eastern Cree and Northern Saulteaux," 12.

[25] Wissler, "Influence of the Horse," 18; "Material Culture of the North Amer-ican Indians," 484–86.

A later commentator endorses this:

> If the horse did not create traits in the Indian, but only intensified those he already had, its effect was no less upon him than the effect of the automobile and other material acquisitions have had upon his conquerors. As far back as history can scrutinize, man's intellectual and spiritual potentialities have not changed.[26]

With unfeigned respect for a master in any of his chosen fields, I do not believe the process was as gradual and slow as Wissler apparently considered. I have noted his opinion that the use of the horse travois preceded riding in the bison area at large, and have indicated certain a priori objections which militate strongly against that supposition.[27] The actual evidence we possess appears to me to be directly contrary to his view. We have seen that tribes in Sonora were apparently skilled riders as early as 1567.[28] This item of evidence, however, did not appear until long after the date of Wissler's essay, if, indeed, it appeared in his lifetime. But we have testimony of much earlier dates of publication.

The only historical evidence which I can find Wissler adducing in support of his suggestion was drawn from one of the northernmost horse-using tribes, the "Eagle Indians" of Antony Henday, 1754. Henday writes: "They are a tribe of the Asinipoet Nation [i.e., Assiniboin; these were the Eagle Hill Assiniboin]; and like them use the Horses for carrying the Baggage and not to ride on."[29] Wissler comments: "This restricted use of the horse is very significant."[30]

Yet there is nothing in this reference—any more than with the Assiniboin as a whole—which implies the possession of other horses upon which they did not care or dare to ride. Their geographical situation renders it virtually certain, whatever date we may adopt, that they would be among the very latest in the West to obtain

---

[26] Dobie, "Indian Horses and Horsemanship," 265.
[27] See Chapter III *supra.*
[28] See Chapter II *supra.*
[29] Henday, "Journal" (ed. by Burpee), 331–32, 351. Their name was from their home territory in the Eagle Hills, south of the confluence of the Battle and North Saskatchewan Rivers at Battleford, Saskatchewan (Coues [ed.], *Henry-Thompson Journals,* II, 523).
[30] Wissler, "Influence of the Horse," 4.

horses. Wissler's own (provisional) date for the Assiniboin—which presumably signifies the main tribe, anywhere from two hundred to four hundred miles farther southward—is not earlier than 1742.[31] It seems probable that these "Eagle" Assiniboin were at this time dependent upon the neighboring Blackfoot for their horses. A generation after Henday's time, the Assiniboin bore a poor reputation as horse masters;[32] and whether owing to lack of horses or lack of skill and experience, or to temperamental reasons, it would probably be no better at the earlier period. It may quite conceivably have been nothing more than sheer poverty (in horses) which caused this "restricted use" in 1754–55.

On the other hand, we have a considerable amount of unequivocal testimony to the very early adoption of riding, apart from the rather recently published reference to 1567. These examples scarcely appear to leave sufficient time for any probationary period restricted to draft purposes, either in cases where some additional form of land transport is mentioned, or where it is not. And in almost all these instances, the riding usage is mentioned by the very earliest witnesses we possess for those tribes. For our present purpose, it is immaterial whether the Indians of Henri de Tonty in 1682 were Oto or Cadadoquis-Natchez. Tonty says:

. . . the savages who have horses use them both for war and for hunting. They make pointed saddles, wooden stirrups, and body-coverings of several skins, one over the other as a protection from arrows. They also arm the breast of their horses with the same material, a proof that they are not very far from the Spaniards.[33]

Tonty also noted (among the Missouri tribe, it is thought): "There are even villages which use horses to go to war and to carry the carcasses of the cattle [buffalo] which they kill."[34] Shortly afterward in the Southwest, Father Massanet wrote concerning the Apache: "It is said that the Apaches are not brave because they fight with armoured horses."[35]

[31] Ibid., 6; Webb, The Great Plains, 57. See Chapter V supra.
[32] For detailed evidence on this subject, see Chapter XIII infra.
[33] Tonty, in Cox (ed.), Journeys of La Salle, I, 55.
[34] Worcester, "The Spread of Spanish Horses," 228.
[35] Ibid., 230.

Similarly, those horse hoofs which were shown to Father Membre in the same decade were the "feet" of certain animals far inland, "on which men ride and which carry very heavy loads."[36] David Thompson's ancient informant (of about 1730 or possibly 1710) described their enemies, the Snake Indians and allied tribes, as possessing creatures "on which they ride, swift as the deer."[37] Wissler dates the Yanktonais as having an abundance of horses in 1740–45, on the testimony of Peter Pond. It has been shown that this is some thirty years too soon, but whenever it was, they were "running down the buffalo on horseback," by all the available evidence, very soon after obtaining horses.[38] Those tribes, apparently the Yanktonais' kindred, the Sioux, whom Jonathan Carver had seen or heard of shortly before, "always attacked their enemies on horseback."[39] Farther to the west, the tribes whom the Mandan described to La Vérendrye "traveled on horseback." This was in 1738. The tribes in question are thought to have been the Arikara. If they actually got their own first horses only in that year, as most critics think, they must have been riding almost immediately.[40]

Whoever Legardeur de Saint-Pierre's Indians of 1751 may have been, Blackfoot or otherwise, he had "seen their horses *and saddles*."[41] And in 1754, whenever or from whom the Blackfoot actually obtained their first horses, such a phenomenon was so utterly unthinkable at Hudson Bay, and the general horse history of the Western regions—necessarily involving Blackfoot possession as an equally logical possibility with any other tribe—was so completely unknown, that the statements of a professed eyewitness who was known to have been in the territory were dismissed with contempt. Yet at this early date the Blackfoot had quite evidently attained that complete mastery of the horse which is associated with the tribe (and the Plains horse Indians generally) at the height of their power.

Concerning this, Antony Henday's *Journal* (1754–55) furnishes

[36] Membre, in Cox (ed.), *Journeys of La Salle*, I, 154.
[37] Thompson, *Narrative* (ed. by Tyrrell), 330, 334.
[38] Wissler, "Influence of the Horse," 3, 6; Innis, *Peter Pond*, 58; Gates (ed.), *Five Fur Traders*, 58.
[39] La Vérendrye, *Journals* (ed. by Burpee), 108, 387 (see Chapter V *supra*).
[40] Wissler, "Influence of the Horse," 5–6; Webb, *The Great Plains*, 57.
[41] See discussion in Chapter V *supra*.

a wealth of detail. Henday mentions their hunting buffalo on horseback, and riding as the common practice. In addition to these, he notes mounted scouting, use as draft animals with birch sleds in winter, winter horse care, swimming, 'broad and deep rivers,' their 'good horses,' and 'the best horsemen he ever saw.'[42] Blackfoot informants told a contemporary anthropologist that in the old days all the Blackfoot were expected to be good horsemen and swimmers.[43] Maximilian mentions that at Fort McKenzie, upper Missouri River, 1833, at a welcoming festal celebration, there were Blackfoot "frequently riding two on one horse, although there were great numbers of horses about."[44] Could this possibly be a commemorative "ancient survival" of a time when horses were few? If so, it might indicate that the Blackfoot were riding before there were enough horses to go round; or, in other words, almost at once. Wissler also gives an illustration of a decorated Blackfoot tipi depicting two men on one horse and a riderless saddle horse led behind,[45] which very possibly bears some similar symbolic interpretation.

Similar or analogous festival practices are found among the allied Sarcee. A feature of their Sun Dance festival was that, in addition to the girls' mounting behind their sweethearts, "two young braves occasionally bestrode the same horse." The ritual of the "Birds," a secret society, forbade members to ride any horse during the celebration period. If the tribe moved camp, even if it became necessary to hunt buffalo for food, they must still remain afoot.[46] This seems clearly a commemorative festival, even if borrowed in part from the Blackfoot, which the tenacious conservatism of the Sarcee renders somewhat improbable.[47]

Though perhaps not precisely a general opinion (since it necessarily combats the "escape" theory), the view appears to be held by many Southwestern archaeologists that, so far from the process being a gradual, tentative, step-at-a-time affair, the Spaniards deliberately familiarized their Indian vassals with the care and con-

[42] Henday, "Journal" (ed. by Burpee), 334–51.
[43] Kidd, "Blackfoot Ethnography," 37–38.
[44] Maximilian, *Travels*, in Thwaites, *Travels*, XXIII, 87.
[45] Wissler, "Social Life of the Blackfoot Indians," 39.
[46] Jenness, *The Sarcee Indians*, 46, 51–52.
[47] See Chapter VII *supra*.

trol of horses.[48] For twenty-four years after the conquest of Mexico, a royal edict which prohibited Indians from riding horses was enforced—or should we say was not formally abrogated? But "the necessity of forming alliances and of training native allies forced suspension of the rule."[49] The case already instanced, of Viceroy Mendoza's mounting allied Aztec chiefs in the Mixton War of 1541, is presumably the earliest of these concessions to stern necessity.[50] Worcester gives a much later date, but may possibly be referring to a wider extension of the royal sanction, rather than to its original promulgation. He writes: "In 1621, the *encomenderos* of New Mexico were authorized to use Indians as herdsmen and teamsters. Thus, at an early stage of the settling of New Mexico, converts were allowed to use horses, in contrast to the usual Spanish custom of prohibiting Indians from riding."[51] There need be little doubt that such suspensions or enactments were little more than a recognition *de jure* of what had long been an inescapable situation *de facto*. The Spanish authorities made an interim attempt to cover their retreat by permitting riding but prohibiting saddles.[52] The native Mexicans soon surmounted this feeble obstacle. Denhardt gives a delightful story of this episode:

When the renowned *talabatero* or saddle maker, Alonso Martínez, arrived in Mexico City in the early days, he hung the age-old sign of his profession, a *fuste*, or saddletree, in front of his shop. One night it disappeared. Within twenty-four hours it was back. The natives, recognizing it, took it to use as a model. From this original copy (at least according to the story) all future Mexican saddles were constructed. And, if this is true, from this same hurriedly imitated tree arose the modern stock saddle.[53]

Two illuminative passages, from Denhardt once again, reveal what was doubtless a common situation:

Close on the trail of the exploring *conquistadores* came the padres, establishing missions . . . gardens were planted and cattle and horses

---

[48] W. P. Bliss, University of New Mexico (1937), to the author.
[49] Dobie, *Tales of the Mustang*, 15.
[50] Dobie, *The Mustangs*, 25.
[51] Worcester, "The Spread of Spanish Horses," 225.
[52] Denhardt, *Horses of the Americas*, 235.
[53] *Ibid.*, 235–36.

brought in. A difficulty arose at once. Who were to be the *vaqueros?* Since there were not enough Spaniards to be cowboys, the only course was for the padres to teach the natives. Thus in the missions we have the first and primary source through which natives learned horsemanship and obtained mounts. . . . As the missions grew, so did the number of native *vaqueros* increase. Some would rebel from time to time and run off to their tribes with stolen horses and cattle. With these as teachers, the rest of the tribe required little time to become equestrian, and soon they were slipping down to the missions to steal more horses. Th civil government foresaw the dangers in the revolts of Indian *vaqueros* and the stealing of the mission animals and so forbade the padres to have natives as *vaqueros.* However, the fathers had no choice, since food was essential for their *rancherías* and there were no white men available for the work.

The Spanish conquerors did not want the Indians to have horses because they felt that they would lose their principal weapon as well as gain formidable enemies. Despite the severe regulations issued to enforce their wishes in this respect, many natives obtained mounts and became expert horsemen. How this occurred is well illustrated by the example of Fray Pedro Barrientos, who, soon after helping pass a law which was to prevent natives from riding, went to his estate to watch his native *vaqueros* give a show of horsemanship with commendable agility. It was in just such ways that the Indians became accustomed to the use of Spanish saddlery, and hence were not satisfied without them.[54]

The extent to which such ecclesiastical agencies might operate is shown by a letter written by the Governor of New Mexico in 1639. The missions owned so many horses and cattle that it was said they should be divided among the settlers. Of horses they had "as many as twenty, thirty, forty apiece—for there are many soldiers so poor that through inability to buy horses and arms they are incapable of serving his Majesty. In this way a great deal of trouble would be saved the Indians, for they are occupied in guarding the cattle and horses. . . . The worst thing is . . . that the religious [the monastic clergy] hold most of the armor for the horses, leather jackets, swords, arquebuses, and pistols."[55]

While the Spaniards might regret the necessity, it is difficult

[54] *Ibid.,* 104, 105, 235.
[55] Worcester, "The Spread of Spanish Horses," 226-27.

to understand how discerning men among them could fail to realize the inevitable consequences of using Indians as grooms and *vaqueros*. Even a mere Indian stableboy would soon learn to mount, and ultimately to steal, the animals he tended. The attitude of the Spaniards may not have been deliberate in the sense of any approved formal enactment, but in the selfish or heedless individualism which endorses a policy, while at the same time evading its personal responsibilities or inconveniences, the term seems appropriate enough.

A second source from which the Indians obtained horses was the half-breed trader, called by many names but generally referred to as a *Comanchero*. These often illicit traders would gather together a few horses and go far back on the Indian frontier to trade with the natives. Many of them could speak the native tongue, and if their customers did not know how to use a horse, the traders would take time to teach them. Again and again the Spanish colonial administration passed laws forbidding trade in horses with the Indians, but the laws did not stop the commerce.

Thus the Indians learned to ride and handle horses both at the missions and through renegade traders. Rapidly the Indian became an expert horseman, and while he did not handle his horse with the brusque impetuosity of the Spaniard, probably since he commonly had no saddle, nevertheless, in certain respects he was more clever. His ingeniousness may be explained by two principal factors: first, a saddle was lacking; and second, the hands were seldom used to guide a trained horse. The fighting native needed both hands to shoot his bow and arrow, and as a result he became a marvelous rider. Actions such as dropping on the far side of a galloping horse and shooting under the neck at the enemy, mounting and dismounting at a dead run, and picking up a fallen comrade without stopping the horse were all common feats. When it is considered that the Indians accomplished these feats without any saddle to support them and without holding the reins, guiding the horse entirely with the knees, the extraordinary skill of the Indian riders can be appreciated.[56]

Denhardt's conclusion is indisputable: "Actually the Spaniards never had a chance to keep horses from the natives."[57]

[56] Denhardt, *Horse of the Americas,* 105–106.
[57] *Ibid.,* 104.

Certainly the circumstances mentioned above, of the Comanche's having been unable to rear any colts as late as 1724,[58] could hardly be cited as any proof of a long protracted horse ignorance on the part of the Indian, who had been foolishly or contemptuously left to find out for himself as best he could, for at an early date the Comanche seem to have been acclaimed the horse Indians above all others by the acid test of "the judgment of their peers."[59] The Sarcee and the Nez Percé could devote themselves to horse breeding after what was probably a much shorter acquaintance;[60] and the *visible* phenomena of mammalian reproduction would soon reveal themselves to a sharp-eyed race with wild and domesticated animals all about them.[61]

While the tribal reactions adduced in this chapter, of early Indian reaction to the horse in his most characteristic capacity as a mount—which is our instinctive connotation when we speak of *horse* Indians—are few in number, they are drawn from the extreme north to the extreme south of the Plains area. The evident rapidity in the adoption of the riding practice which they universally reveal may in my judgment be fairly accepted as being broadly indicative of those tribes at large of whom no specific testimony has been found.

The intertribal, military, economic, and psychological influence of the horse upon Plains Indian life are subjects of too great importance and also of too much detail to be treated in a preliminary survey, and will be separately dealt with in the chapters which follow.

[58] Wissler, "Influence of the Horse," 21.

[59] *Ibid.*, 15.

[60] Thompson, *Narrative* (ed. by Tyrrell), 367 (see Chapter V *supra*).

[61] The Cree (and doubtless other tribes) have terms for every form of variation in the buffalo catena, including even the (hermaphroditic)"buffalo ox" (Lacombe, *Dictionnaire*, 326). I am surprised at Maximilian's blindly accepting the foolish yarn about these creatures having been castrated by the Indians as calves (*Travels*, in Thwaites, *Travels*, XXIII, 175). There is neither eyewitness nor even alleged witness at secondhand. The same class of informants invariably deny in the Indian the patient foresight which the long wait for the return in the form of "more tender beef" inevitably involved. Finally, how could the temporarily disabled calf, unable to follow the herd, and with the smell of blood about it, escape the wolves? On the last, see Frémont (a calf "devoured almost before it was dead"), *Narrative*, 21; cf. on wolves, Roe, *North American Buffalo*, 61–64, 155–57.

X

THE HORSE AND NOMADIC LIFE

The foregoing chapters have dealt, in so far as our ascertained data would admit, with the problems of when, where, and above all, *how* the Indians obtained the horse, and with the various attendant circumstances which characterized such an epochal event in their history. Our later discussion, from the present chapter onward, may be termed a psychological inquiry, certainly at least in some very important aspects. We have not only to inquire— What did they do with it, once they had it? We must also ask ourselves—What did the horse do to them? The preceding chapter suggested in brief outline what may be classed as the broad contemporary conclusions on the question of the impact of the horse upon the Plains tribes at the time when the present writer's discussion was first printed (1939), together with expressions of critical opinion from later commentators. As the reader will have noted, the appeal of the various criticisms cited above was mainly to historical evidence. Since that time, however, the subject has been approached from another and hitherto largely unconsidered angle. An important study by an outstanding American archaeologist (actually earlier in point of date, but not then known to the present writer) discusses the subject from the standpoint of archaeological evidence.[1] The purpose of the present and the following chapters is to co-ordinate the earlier and later generalizations (particularly in the light of historical evidence not previously considered) and to review the general conclusions.

[1] W. D. Strong, "The Plains Culture in the Light of Archaeology," *American Anthropologist*, Vol. XXXV (1933), 271-87.

At no time, it would seem, has there been any general disposition among scholars to underrate the influence of the historic horse upon the Plains Indians of the North American continent. The *visible* changes recorded concerning the Indians in the years which have ensued since the earliest European narrators first encountered them in their ancient—if not always original—habitat have been of so dramatic a character as to leave little room for doubt regarding their source.

The horse Indian was one and not the least—among the select class of the three or four truly equestrian races of the human family. It seems correct to say further that he is the only one among them of whom recorded history has any really authentic knowledge prior to his equestrian state. The same recorded history has not merely chronicled the Plains Indians as horseless creatures. It has also given us fairly definite, even if they are not precise, indications of the relatively short time within which the Indians passed from sheer terrified amazement at the mere sight of these unknown monsters to a mastery which has never been surpassed in the history of equestrian races. I use such language advisedly, for none of the great horsemen of the Old World—Tartar, Parthian, nor Arab—apparently made use of the horse as did the Plains Indians. None of these peoples procured their staple everyday subsistence in as direct a manner as did our aborigines after this important acquisition.

It is very possibly in the light of such considerations that some scholars have ascribed even the origin of some almost or quite fundamental characteristics in the Indian mentality to so relatively recent an event in their history on this continent as the possession of the horse. The fact in itself of the universal currency of the term "horse Indians" in contrast with so many tribes who were not, and particularly in view of our knowledge of an era when none were such, implies a general recognition of striking and significant change. The very selection, so to say, of such a term, as epitomizing in a word a variety of distinctions between Plains and Forest Indians of which equestrianism present or absent is only one, points also to a kind of subconscious acknowledgment that this is the supreme criterion of difference.

Yet it is not entirely clear—it is certainly far from being self-evident—what was the exact nature of these changes. I have cited in the previous chapter certain critical dicta, which it is perhaps unnecessary to repeat verbatim. Bancroft instances possible detrimental results to the Indians from the possession of the horse. These are, briefly, the following: The horse facilitated the capture of buffalo on a larger scale (Bancroft's meaning apparently is that the horse thereby hastened the final extermination of the buffalo herds). As a "circulating medium," the horse promoted wastefulness of procurable supplies among wealthy owners. As a more convenient means of transport, the horse suggested and fostered 'long migrations for food or trade.' Taking these (Indian) factors together, "the horse may have contributed somewhat to their [the Indians'] present spirit of improvidence."[2]

It also will be convenient in the present chapter to discuss the verdicts of certain other scholars whom I have quoted, and whose pronouncements, being brief, may be given in full. These have to do more particularly with the nomad influence. A Western (Canadian) historian writes thus: "The horse made nomads of many tribes which there is abundant evidence to show were formerly almost sedentary in character."[3] Denhardt writes similarly at a much later date: "The immense effect this animal had on the life and habits of the Indians has never been adequately told. From a poor sedentary group they became independent nomadic tribes and woe to man or beast that got in the way of the previously humble Indian."[4]

Bancroft merely reflected the almost universal attitude of his day in his remarks upon the "present spirit of improvidence" in the Indian as a thing so manifestly self-evident as to require no demonstration. It would be almost unjust to single out any one writer of that era for particular criticism at so late a day were it not that Bancroft himself has done more than almost any other single person to denounce the insidious propaganda by which interested parties in the West sought to "educate" uninformed Easterners in their own infamous anti-Indian prejudices.[5]

2 Bancroft, *Native Races*, I, 282. According to the younger Henry (speaking as a fur trader rather than a philosopher), having horses made the Indians "too indolent and independent" (Coues [ed.], *Henry-Thompson Journals*, I, 225).

3 Black, *History of Saskatchewan*, 94.

4 Denhardt, *Horse of the Americas*, 106.

In ascribing the mass extermination of the buffalo to the agency of the Indian horse (which seems clearly to be his meaning), we are in the province, not of opinion, but of historical fact. Such a conclusion will not bear critical examination. It may be considered perfectly certain that whenever the Indians of various buffalo tribes obtained horses or learned to ride them (in anything beyond an elementary sense of the term), from 1567–1600 onward, the use of the horse in buffalo hunting would follow shortly afterward. Peter Pond describes the Yanktonais' (Sioux) 'running down the buffalo on horseback' as an apparently established feature in their horse culture, at a time when the evidence indicates that they could not have had horses very long.[6] The mean of the various acquisition dates, which cover the period 1600–1740 (the earlier date being applicable to the Southern Plains where the herds were possibly larger), allows for about two centuries of buffalo mass slaughter by horsed Indians. During three-fourths of this period, say from 1680 to 1830, the Indians were more free to slay as they would; and we may bear in mind that prior to the terrible epidemics of 1781, 1837, and 1870—which do not exhaust the list— there were more of them to do it.[7] After 1830, the era of "systematic destruction" began,[8] with the much more highly organized annual drain of the (buffalo) fur trade culminating in the shocking holocausts of 1870–74 in the south,[9] and the final one of 1880–83 in the northern habitat.[10]

Modern American scholarship is worthily endeavoring to render posthumous justice to the Indian of the buffalo days.[11] The question of Indian improvidence, with its wide documentary data, cannot adequately be discussed in a paragraph. Three crucial points may be briefly indicated: (1) All Indians were not improvident,

[5] On this "educating" process, see Bancroft, *North Mexican States*, II, 104; also his *History of Oregon*, II, 404; Thwaites, *Travels*, XIV, 21, editor's note.

[6] Innis, *Peter Pond*, 58; Gates (ed.), *Five Fur Traders*, 58 (see Chapter V *supra*).

[7] See Roe, *North American Buffalo*, App. G, "Estimates of Indian Populations Subsisting Wholly or Partly upon Buffalo," 742–803.

[8] William T. Hornaday's phrase ("Extermination of the American Bison," *Smithsonian Report, 1887*, Part II, 484–86).

[9] Roe, *North American Buffalo*, 416–46.

[10] *Ibid.*, 447–66.

[11] *Ibid.*, 664–79, 804–16, etc.

even in our sense of the term.[12] (2) Had they been, why should they practice a hitherto needless frugality, merely to leave more buffalo for utterly conscienceless white butchers? (3) Indians did not judge the buffalo by our criteria of "vital statistics." They were sent by the Manito, who could give or withhold at will; hence what we term waste had no meaning to the Indian mind.[13] I have elsewhere noted the irreconcilability of the loose assertions that Indians were "too lazy to cure much buffalo meat." Huge Indian stores of buffalo meat were destroyed by United States troops in various campaigns.[14] This is a subject upon which the present writer may reasonably claim to speak with some authority. There is not a fragment of evidence that I have been able to discover to suggest that the Indians would ever have exterminated the buffalo herds.

The erratic absences that were noted at times in localities of (reputedly) never-failing plenty, which led visitors in the thirties and forties of the nineteenth century to pronounce the buffalo already extinct in this or that region, may be paralleled by similar absences in various other regions long before the horse was known there.[15] The final extermination of the great buffalo herds was due neither to the Indian nor to the Indian horse, but to the white hide hunters.

And the hide hunters were only the instruments; they were not the underlying cause. In the long-range perspective of the historical philosopher, the Indian horse might perhaps in an indirect sense be termed the "cause" of the extirpation of the buffalo. The horse placed the Indian in relation to the United States military forces in the precise position he occupied two centuries earlier in relation to the Spanish Plains frontier. As Denhardt puts it, along the Río Grande borderlands the Indian was a better man than the Spaniard.[16] The same was exactly true in the relation of the Plains Indian to the United States Army man in the mid-nineteenth century.

[12] *Ibid.*, 654–59.
[13] *Ibid.*, 642–49.
[14] "Too lazy to cure much buffalo meat" (Hornaday, "Extermination of the American Bison," 499). "The Indians formerly cured great quantities of meat for use in winter" (*ibid.*, 449). For the immense masses destroyed ('400,000 pounds in one village'), see Roe, *North American Buffalo*, 658.
[15] *Ibid.*, 495, 575–77; and cf. Chap. XX ("Irregular Migrations"), 543–600.
[16] Denhardt, *Horse of the Americas*, 103 (see Chapter III *supra*).

It was only natural that the Indian should be the better man. He was in his own country. Wherever he might turn someone in the band or war party of the moment knew every pass and ridge and gully in the neighborhood; and he had sucked in the lore of the Plains warrior and the scout with his mother's milk. As another high authority puts the case, we may grasp the essential problem:

> ... the loading [of the cap-and-ball muzzle-loader] was a meticulous and time-consuming task. The powder had to be measured and poured, the ball had to be rammed down the barrel with a long rod, the tube must be 'primed,' and the cap or flint had to be adjusted. All this took about a minute. ... The Indian could in that time ride three hundred yards and discharge twenty arrows.[17]

Richardson considers the Comanche "were no match for an equal number of white frontiersmen on the field of battle."[18] But his own account of Kit Carson's engagement at Adobe Walls on the Canadian River, November 25, 1864, against a force principally of Kiowa, with some Comanche, Apache, and Arapaho, scarcely endorses this verdict. Carson, in his report, "flattered himself that he had taught the Indians a severe lesson"; but Richardson comments that "all the accounts indicate that these Indians might well have flattered themselves that they were still a formidable factor to be reckoned with when attacked in their own villages in the heart of the plains."[19] With his formidable force of volunteers, Carson could only destroy one of the three enemy villages that were his objective.

And if such could be the case at times with the seasoned plainsmen, it was even more emphatically true of the purely military personnel. With the latter type in all probability in any era, it was never (as against the Indian) any question of the fortunes of war or of equipment between equal rivals, each a master in his own field. As long ago as 1690 Father Massanet made note of some of the soldiers sent with the De León-Massanet expedition of that year:

[17] Webb, *The Great Plains*, 168–69; see also De Voto, *Across the Wide Missouri*, 143, 430–31.
[18] Richardson, *The Comanche Barrier*, 102, 115, 237.
[19] *Ibid.*, 286.

The forty from Zacatecas were for the most part tailors, shoemakers, masons, miners—in short, none of them could catch the horses on which they were to ride that day, for when they had once let them go they could manage them no longer. Besides, we had saddles that could not be worse.[20]

Bernard De Voto speaks of "the [officers] of the United States Army who were sent West on the hopeless job of disciplining a hundred thousand Plains Indians with half-companies of incompetent cavalrymen."[21] Richardson writes similarly concerning the situation in Texas in 1866: "The United States did station troops along the frontier, but they were men unacquainted with Indian warfare and therefore ineffective—especially during the first year or two of their service."[22] To send a slum townsman, an Eastern farmer's son, or a recent immigrant against such a seasoned expert was pathetic; it was to be paralleled by the British Tommy's being sent against the Boer in South Africa. And as in the case of the Boer, it was the horse that put the Indian in first place.

As long as the United States authorities remained in the belief that the Indians could be conquered in the field, the mass slaughter of buffalo by white visitors was very strongly discountenanced, as is seen in the instance of Sir George Gore and his men in 1855–56.[23] The buffalo were going to be needed to feed the subjugated warriors and their families on their respective reservations. When at last, largely resulting from persistent (though not unanimous) representations from Western Congressmen, it was realized that as long as he had the buffalo for his own use and to exchange for arms and ammunition (which Eastern firms were quite willing to furnish in return for robes) the Indian would long remain unconquered, a change of policy occurred.[24] The railways were there to ship the buffalo butcher into buffalo land and to ship the hides out. The onus of the terrific slaughter has been thrust historically upon the hide hunter, who often did his best to deserve it, but politicians and army men made no secret of wanting the buffalo

[20] Bolton (ed.), *Spanish Exploration in the Southwest*, 369.
[21] De Voto, *Across the Wide Missouri*, 188; for a soldier's performance of these disciplinary duties, see Inman, *Old Santa Fé Trail*, 453.
[22] Richardson, *The Comanche Barrier*, 292.
[23] See Roe, *North American Buffalo*, 435, 810.
[24] *Ibid.*, App. H, "Buffalo, Indian, and Legislation," 804–16.

destroyed.[25] In this sense and in this sense only, it might be said that the Indian horse hastened the extermination of the buffalo herds. Without the horse the Indian would most probably have been finally conquered in the field; whether that would or would not have saved the buffalo is another question.

That the possession of the horse should enlarge the range of a nomad society is virtually a self-evident proposition. But it is in my opinion an essential fallacy to ascribe the *origin* of such an utterly fundamental, basic instinct as the nomad impulse—which may be defined as going further in hope of finding something better—to the possession or the lack of what was in the final analysis a mere convenience. Human ingenuity everywhere throughout the world has surmounted the obstacle of the necessary *facilities* for attaining its ends. As our familiar proverb has it, necessity is the mother of invention. The nomadic and the sedentary life constitute the two basic concepts, mutually antithetical each to the other, of primitive economic conditions of existence. Primitive peoples are forced into the one or the other by the underlying conditions which govern their food supply. An agricultural people almost inevitably become sedentary, since their crops require constant attention either to protect them from marauders or for cultivation (or intermittently at fairly definitely recognized intervals for the latter purpose). Furthermore, any animals which the agriculturist may keep for cultivating his lands or for food purposes must be regularly tended.

A hunting people, on the contrary, inevitably incline much more strongly toward the nomad way of life. I cannot but think, with reference to these classifications, that many scholars, perhaps more particularly academic students who have had no experience of actual life in the wilder lands, have rather put the cart before the horse in this matter of the nomad. They appear to have assumed as their initial premise that certain men or peoples were nomads to begin with; therefore *ipso facto* they wandered. Such a description would very well suit certain known peoples of historic

[25] Compare Col. Richard Irving Dodge, *viva voce* to Sir William Butler, 1867; and in print, 1877 (Roe, *ibid.*, 357–58, 477, 810).

eras (and the buffalo Indians themselves as history has known them are a case in point), just as the same description would apply to some in our own societies who follow callings whose very conceptions are founded upon regularity. Actually, of course, the *origins* of the nomad life offer little choice to a hunting people. If their favorite or principal food supply is derived from some wandering animal, they must either wander after it or go without. This makes them nomads.

In discussion of the changes produced or fostered in the horse by contact with the Indian, and in the Indian by contact with the horse, the vital consideration necessary in these evolutionary processes appears to have been forgotten. What would have had to be changed in order to effect an alteration of any real significance in the life of these aboriginal hunters was neither the horse nor the Indian, but the buffalo.

While it is of course true and well recognized that the buffalo, even among so-called "buffalo Indians," did not literally furnish the whole of the Indian's flesh diet,[26] the deer and other species which did contribute thereto were themselves either so relatively few as to exert no material influence against that of the buffalo, or were so erratic in their own wanderings as to impel no change in a nomad psychology of life. The buffalo, moreover, in addition to food resources proper, supplied so many more basic needs of Indian Plains life than did the deer—as the very term "buffalo Indians" tacitly recognizes—that one does no violence to truth or logic in considering the buffalo as the source of subsistence among these tribes, and its habits as the major controlling influence in their way of life. To change the animal was beyond the power of such a primitive or simple society as that of the Indians. What then was the character of the buffalo?

A vast amount of fine writing has been expended upon the regular, annual, general, seasonal, periodic,[27] systematic,[28] constant,[29] orderly,[30] or boundless[31] migrations of the buffalo; their unchang-

[26] *Ibid.*, 601–607.
[27] Nuttall, *Journal*, in Thwaites, *Travels*, XIII, 145; Long, *Voyages and Travels*, in Thwaites, *Travels*, XV, 256.
[28] Henry Youle Hind, *Report on the Assiniboine and Saskatchewan Exploring Expedition of 1858*, 106.
[29] Sir John Richardson, *The Polar Regions*, 275.

ing times; and the undeviating routes, turning neither to the right nor to the left as they traversed the continent on their mighty highways from the Río Grande to the Saskatchewan. If this were true, it would indeed go far to demonstrate the Plains Indian to be a creature who even according to my own necessitarian theory outlined above was under no compulsion to be a nomad, and who would probably never have dreamed of becoming a nomad until the horse happened along and showed him how easy and pleasant it would be!

Unfortunately for such a thesis, the concept of buffalo regularity will not bear detailed investigation. It vanishes into thin air under the critical microscope.[32] Actually the buffalo were one of the most irregular, erratic, incalculable species that ever trod the earth; most amazingly so, when their truly vast numbers are considered. To the Plains Indians, the animal furnished a preponderatingly large proportion of their daily necessities in food, together with clothing, bedding, housing, fuel, tools, weapons, amusements, personal adornments, ritualistic regalia, and "foreign" trade both before and after the coming of Europeans.[33] The Indians became perforce as nomadic as the buffalo itself; it was the only way in which they could procure such requirements in the quantity necessary to meet the basic, irreducible needs of existence.

Amid the enormous mass of available evidence in support, historical, chronological, geographical, and anthropological, one consideration alone will reveal the force of this assertion. A "regular migration" of such vast hosts, following the same great buffalo trail routes each year, crossing the rivers at the same well-known fords, and so forth in the familiar shibboleths of the orthodox, is absolutely and unanswerably irreconcilable with the frequent historical occurrence of privation and even of positive famine in the lives of the Plains tribes. This latter fact is too well known—certainly to informed critical students—to admit of denial, and is of course a part of the normal experience of most hunting peoples.[34]

[30] Seton, *Life Histories of Northern Animals*, I, 153. Applied to buffalo not specifically, but by implication: "the moose have no orderly migration."
[31] Washington Irving, *Adventures of Captain Bonneville*, 300.
[32] Roe, *North American Buffalo*, 75–84, 521–600, etc.
[33] *Ibid.*, 601–607.
[34] *Ibid.*, 659–64.

If words are to possess any meaning, such a concept of regularity involves the buffalo herds' being always available to the hunters at the same seasons and in the same places each year.[35] None could conceivably be better judges of these annually recurring experiences than the Indians themselves. Their unrivaled mastery of the lore of the game animals of their various tribal habitats is extolled without exception by observers of all eras.[36] Even more completely incompatible with such a supposed regularity is the physical and temperamental capacity for enduring starvation during long-protracted periods. From the very earliest European contacts with any Western tribes, this very practical stoicism has been amazing to persons from more regular societies who have witnessed it. Cabeza de Vaca wrote thus, about 1530: "They are very well able to endure hunger, thirst, and cold, as they who are more acquainted therewith than any other."[37]

It cannot be doubted that the development of this power in such remarkable degree must have required a long period of time. The anthropologist of our later days might urge that this was an inheritance from an earlier time when game was less plentiful or aboriginal skill in capturing it less developed; and such a critic would very probably be right. But there would still be two problems requiring answers. Anthropological science with its vast array of comparative examples was scarcely even in its infancy a century ago; and in any case the plainsmen of that era were not learned anthropologists. It was from their information in the beginning that the wide inductions of the science (relating to Indians) had to be built up. Such men could by no possibility have suspected the survival of such a latent inheritance in the Indians—as of course this must have been, once the need for its active use had vanished

[35] A very courteous review by a Canadian historical critic takes exception to my concept of regularity, contending that even "regular" migrations exhibit irregular recurrences. Then why use the term? The same critic endorses the theory of the regular migratory movement of the Western Canada herd, on the sole authority of Hind, covering one season only (1858). (1) Hind obtained his buffalo itinerary at secondhand; (2) its "regular" route was disproved in the very season of Hind's exploration; (3) firsthand testimony in rebuttal is presented from experienced residents of the territory, 1787–1883. These facts are ignored (The Beaver, Hudson's Bay Company, June, 1952, 46).

[36] Roe, North American Buffalo, 663.

[37] Purchas His Pilgrimes, XXVII, 493. For starvation at large, see Roe, North American Buffalo, 659 ff.

in the presence of the buffalo hosts—had they not witnessed it in active operation. Secondly, assuming the unfailing plenty which logically follows from the traditional concept of the buffalo migration, how came such a capacity for starving to survive at all, even in any latent form? Why had not it atrophied and vanished through sheer disuse? So far from that, the Indian may very well have been styled one of the champion fasters of the human family. Such a position could only be reached and maintained by ages of active, even if intermittent, practice.

A moment's reflection will demonstrate likewise the soundness of the contention that hunting peoples are basically what the characteristic habits of the predominating game species of their own tribal or hunting habitat force them to become. It is a well-known fact that woodland animals, which cannot so readily see their foes, are much more wary and cautious than Plains animals of the same species. This requires the hunter to be similarly more wary and cautious in approaching them, over and above the necessity for not allowing them to scent him, which is a practically universal proviso in hunting any wild creatures. It is perfectly certain that the whooping, yelling, buffalo Indian of the Plains would have starved to death if he had employed that technique on the suspicious and vigilant mountain buffalo of the Colorado foothills region,[38] the huge, aboriginal northern wood buffalo of the Canadian Northwest,[39] or the moose[40]—creatures which fled in panic at the crackling of a twig!

This conception, which finds the underlying causes of the nomadic life of the Plains tribes in forces altogether unrelated to and wholly independent of the possession of the horse and possibly present long before such an acquisition, derives abundant support from historical testimony of the first order, that of eyewitnesses. It comes from the very earliest European observers of the Indian, not merely among the later horse tribes of the Plains, but also among

[38] *Ibid.*, Chap. III.

[39] For the mongrelizing of the aboriginal northern wood buffalo by the admixture of the prairie importations from the Wainwright Buffalo Park, see *ibid.*, 33–54, 829–41, and authorities there cited.

[40] See on this, Thompson, *Narrative* (ed. by Tyrrell), 95, 197; also Sir William Butler's classic description of the tactics of moose hunting: *The Wild North Land*, 206–10.

many tribes dwelling east of the Mississippi who never became horse Indians in the Western connotation of the term.

The nomadic character of many of the more southerly tribes, both those in the Mississippi Valley region of ancient Florida (an immensely larger area than the modern state of that name)[41] and those of the buffalo range far to the west of the great river, is placed beyond question by the testimony of the earliest Spanish explorers. Cabeza de Vaca writes thus (1528–36):

> The greatest part of all this Nation drinke raine water, gathered together in certaine Trenches. For although they have Rivers there, nevertheless, because they have never any certaine and settled place of abode, they have no particular water knowne to them, or appointed place where to take it.[42]

A similar characteristic is recorded by the Gentleman of Elvas, with De Soto's expedition in Florida, 1539–43. Writing of 'the country farther on' (meaning west of the Mississippi), he says it is one "where the Indians wandered like Arabs, having no settled place of residence, living on prickly pears, the roots of plants, and game."[43]

The description of the Plains tribes as being "like Arabs"—the typical nomads of all history and well known to the Spaniards, some of whom might quite easily have served in Charles V's great expedition to Tunis in 1535[44]—is found also among the accounts of Coronado's journey during the same years as that of De Soto, 1540–42.[45]

[41] "Florida" as defined by Menendez, 1565, and the same territory as "Virginia," after 1584 (Roe, North American Buffalo, 212–14).

[42] Purchas His Pilgrimes, XVII, 480. For more modern versions, see Bandelier (ed.), Journey of Cabeza de Vaca, 97; Bishop, Odyssey of Cabeza de Vaca; Hallenbeck, Journey and Route of Cabeza de Vaca.

[43] Bourne (ed.), Narratives of De Soto, I, 180, 181.

[44] Cabeza de Vaca (whether from his own personal experience or otherwise I know not) compares the soldierly vigilance of his Indians: ". . . as if they had been trained in Italy" (Bandelier [ed.], Journey of Cabeza de Vaca, 119). Bernal Díaz (1519) speaks of his comrades as Spanish soldiers "who had been in many parts of the world" (Conquest of New Spain [ed. by Maudslay], II, 75). Some of these could easily have been in Cardinal Ximenes' earlier expedition to Oran in 1509 (Prescott, Ferdinand and Isabella, III, 314–21).

[45] Castañeda, the Traslado de Las Nuevas, the Relacion del Suceso, Coronado to Charles V, and Juan Jaramillo, in Winship (ed.), Journey of Coronado, 65, 75, 111, 195, 209, 214, 217, 230.

Similar testimony is borne by the early missionaries to the nomadic life of the tribes of New France (Canada),[46] and what they conceived to be the prime causes of the nomadic impulses are indicated:

. . . game is not always to be found in a place where people are obliged to live upon it, and where there is a permanent settlement. This is what makes nomads of the Savages, and prevents them from remaining long in one place.[47]

Contemporary evidence of the foregoing character entirely justifies such verdicts as these:

Dependence on the buffalo and the herbivorous animals associated with it compelled a meat diet, skin clothing and dwellings, a roving life, and industrial arts depending on the flesh, bones, hair, sinew, hide, and horns of these animals.[48]

The appearance and disappearance of fur-bearing animals, their retreat from one part of the country to another, influenced the movements of various tribes. This is particularly true of the movements of the buffalo.[49]

Such testimony as we have cited in the foregoing pages constitutes clear proof that among the buffalo tribes of the Great Plains the birth or development of the nomadic impulse is in no way originally traceable to the horse.

While it is true that the horse has been considered as the crucial test of the nomad by some Old World scholars, that cannot in my view be accepted as a really satisfactory criterion, even apart from

[46] Champlain describes the Indians as being sedentary at "Ochelaga" in Cartier's time, 1534 (Hakluyt, *Voyages*, VI, 89; Edward G. Bourne [ed.], *The Voyages and Explorations of Samuel de Champlain*, I, 13). The term is not again used until 1734. Father Aulneau observes: "Our Iroquois, like all the other savage tribes, with the exception of the Sioux, are sedentary" (Thwaites [ed.], *Jesuit Relations*, LXVIII, 275). For the contrary classification in abundance, see Roe, *North American Buffalo*, 612–29, and authorities there cited.

[47] Marc Lescarbot (1612), in Thwaites (ed.), *Jesuit Relations*, II, 167; Lescarbot, *A History of New France* (ed. by H. P. Biggar), III, 28.

[48] O. T. Mason, in Hodge, *Handbook*, I, 428. See also Wissler, "Material Culture of the North American Indians," 447–505; Edgar Lee Hewett, *Ancient Life in the American Southwest*, 23, 205, 251.

[49] A. F. Chamberlain, in Hodge, *Handbook*, I, 478.

the question of its *originating* influence. Although there is little or no positive evidence, in so far as I am aware, for the existence of nomad peoples in the ancient world who are definitely known to have lacked horses—or some almost equally powerful or convenient substitute such as the camel or the ass—there is abundant evidence for peoples *not* being made nomads by its possession, both in the Old World at large and in the precise area of our present investigations in the New. In relation to any hypothesis of the Indians of the North America continent being thereby transformed into nomadic folk, our historical knowledge shows that, aside from the equestrian use of the animal itself, there is nothing which has been or which very well could be considered a feature of their horse culture in their days of independence which was not practiced *in esse* prior to their acquisition of the horse—practiced with greater difficulty and general cumbrousness ("the hard way") but, broadly speaking, practiced successfully none the less.

Furthermore, the horse could be utilized periodically to transport a tribe or band and its camp furniture from what was essentially one fixed (and seasonally permanent) homesite to another at certain more or less regular seasons each year. Even this, however, would constitute no proof of the nomadic contention, for two principal reasons:

(1) Such a move would not be nomadic in any strict sense, but migratory, as a learned authority considers was the case with the Comanche prior to the coming of the horse.[50] At the very least it would be semi-migratory, as in the case of the Pawnee. That tribe were wont to leave their permanent winter villages in the Lower Platte country (Nebraska) every spring, and to wander southward to the buffalo grounds for the summer, which was commonly spent following the roving herds. I have no direct proof to offer showing this to be an ante-equestrian practice, since we have no ante-equestrian observers who can be definitely associated with the Pawnee. Parkman in 1846 described "the great trail of the Pawnees . . . to their war and hunting grounds to the southward, but throughout the summer the greater part of the inhabitants are wandering over the plains."[51] A high-ranking contemporary archaeologist writes thus concerning this area:

[50] Richardson, *The Comanche Barrier*, 24–25.

202

Bison were taken by regular summer and winter hunts in which entire villages participated for months at a time. During these excursions, which were usually to the west or southwest, the people lived in tipis and followed in every respect the manner of life practiced by the true nomadic tribes. . . .

Whether seasonal bison hunts on a communal basis were customary among the corn-growing village [Plains] peoples in prehorse days is not known.[52]

We may note, however, that certain very competent scholars have included the Pawnee among tribes who are thought to have probably obtained horses before 1600.[53] This would almost inevitably necessitate some prior acquaintance with the intervening territory between the Platte and the Río Grande. The inference seems not unreasonable that their more or less nomadic summers were in all probability considerably older as a practice than their possession or even knowledge of the horse. Even if they did not reach back to the more remote eras of the archaeologist, they most probably went quite far enough back to refute any supposition of post-equestrian origin. Waldo R. Wedel himself writes:

By comparison with the known Siouan, Shoshonean, and other tribes inhabiting the central Plains in historic times, the Pawnee probably have the strongest claim to the title of true indigenes, and there is reason to believe that they were in the area long before the first Europeans arrived. . . .

As to the probable identity of the early historic people whose village remains on the lower Loup have just been noted, there is every evidence that they were directly ancestral to the Pawnee of the nineteenth century. . . .

One is tempted to suspect that some of the ancient practices and customs were probably much like those witnessed among the bison-hunting Apaches by the earliest Spaniards to venture into the Great Plains in the sixteenth century.[54]

[51] Parkman, *The Oregon Trail*, 74, 78.
[52] Waldo R. Wedel, "Cultural Sequences in the Central Great Plains," 330, 340.
[53] Wissler, "Influence of the Horse," 2, 10; Dale (ed.), *Ashley-Smith Explorations*, 122; Webb, *The Great Plains*, 115–17; see also Denhardt, *Horse of the Americas*, 277.
[54] Wedel, "Cultural Sequences in the Central Great Plains," 301, 313–14, 332.

Another factor may finally be noted. We must presume that those opinions quoted above on the horse's "changing the Indian" in certain very important respects—so that 'from a poor sedentary group, the previously humble Indian' became independent—are meant to imply an advance in general cultural standards. Wedel, a particularly well-informed inquirer, apparently holds the precisely opposite view: "As revealed by archaeology, nineteenth century Pawnee material culture parallels that exhibited by the proto-historic villages on the lower Loup, but is generally much inferior to it. The mode of life, inferentially, must have been essentially identical."[55]

(2) By whatever name we agree to designate the Pawnee practice, such annual movements were unquestionably ante-equestrian in other portions of the western buffalo territory. Father Hennepin records a similar seasonal procedure among the Miami of the Illinois River country, about 1680. In winter, says Hennepin, "it is then their Custom to leave their Villages, and with their whole Families to go ahunting Wild Bulls, Beavers, etc."[56] They moved southward to a point on Peoria Lake famed for the winter plenty of the buffalo, and from whence onward the waters were said never to freeze.[57] At this time the horse had evidently not reached this general area, and probably did not until some three-quarters of a century or more later.[58]

The true criterion of the nomad in my judgment is the movable dwelling, as Gibbon long ago held it to be,[59] and as modern scholars

[55] Ibid., 339. For contemporary descriptions of the historic Pawnee and their villages, see Irving, Astoria, 381; Captain Bonneville, 80; Coues (ed.), Expeditions of Pike, II, 533; Coues (ed.), Henry-Thompson Journals, I, 334, 338, 348; Dale (ed.), Ashley-Smith Explorations, 119–22; James, Account of the Expedition under Long, in Thwaites, Travels, XV, 203–33; Gregg, Commerce of the Prairies, in Thwaites, Travels, XX, 91, 140, 351; Frémont, Narrative, 318; Rollins (ed.), Discovery of the Oregon Trail (Robert Stuart's Narrative).

[56] Hennepin, New Discovery (ed. by Thwaites), I, 145, 146, 153.

[57] This place was known as "Pimiteoui" ("a place where there is an abundance of fat beasts"; Hennepin, ibid., I, 154–55). Father Le Clercq mentions the place and gives the same interpretation (Cox [ed.], Journeys of La Salle, I, 100). For the "never freezing," which former residents in the vicinity deny, cf. N. S. Shaler, Nature and Man in America, 241. There may have been confusion between the lake and the (Illinois) river.

[58] See Chapter V supra.

[59] Edward Gibbon, The Decline and Fall of the Roman Empire, Chap. XXVI, on the ancient Tartars or Huns; with whom cf. Herodotus on the Scythians (Book

on this continent have agreed.[60] This is a much more reliable standard of definition than any primitive or later method of transport, for such methods could obviously be used for migratory movements like those of the Miami, semimigratory-nomadic movements like those of the Pawnee, and of course, for emigrations identical in principle to the covered wagon type of exodus in historic times. These last would be neither nomadic nor strictly migratory, being really a permanent removal to another permanent home. The regular *sole* use of the tipi alone would stamp its denizens (and in primitive times its designers also) as typical nomads. To conceive of sedentary peoples evolving a portable home would be paradox gone mad. This inevitable conclusion derives additional support from the fact that the semi-sedentary tipi dwellers such as the Pawnee and the Eastern Sioux preferred a more substantial and presumably more comfortable domicile for the winter months.[61] The sedentary Mandan preferred a permanent hut or lodge of some character throughout the year, analogous to the grass or bark or brush-covered dwellings of forest tribes in both the eastern and far western regions of the continent, or to the pueblos of the Southwest.[62]

It is quite clear from the Coronado chroniclers' descriptions of tipis—the 'tents of skins'—that in their day the technique of construction, erection, and transportation (by dogs prior to the horse) was as fixed and familiar in all its phases as the nineteenth-century observers found it to be.[63] There is not the least reason to doubt that it was ancient then. One feature alone demonstrates what may be a high antiquity, the well-known "ear flap." By means of this most beautifully ingenious device, the draft may be regulated to suit the almost incessant and ever-changing prairie winds, so that

4, Chap. 46). Gibbon also on the Arabs of Mohammed's day (Chap. L). His editor, Dean Milman, preferred the horse as the test (*History of the Jews*, I, 55).

[60] See Wissler, "Influence of the Horse," 14–16, etc.

[61] See Roe, *North American Buffalo*, 624–25, and authorities there cited.

[62] On Indian dwellings of various types, see Hodge, *Handbook*: William H. Holmes (I, 77–82); Alice C. Fletcher (I, 410, 505); Cyrus Thomas (I, 515); James Mooney (II, 758). For the Plains area (1855), some good descriptions of the lodges of many tribes in Sir Richard Burton, *The City of the Saints*, 85–86. For the Sarcee, Jenness, *The Sarcee Indians*, 12–27. Assiniboin, Blackfoot, and Hidatsa respectively, see Lowie, "The Assiniboin," 222; Wissler, "Material Culture of the Blackfoot Indians," 108–17; Wilson, "Horse and Dog in Hidatsa Culture," 243.

[63] See Wedel's remarks, note 54 *supra*.

from whatever quarter they may blow, they are still the servant and never the master of the fire within. This remarkable contrivance has been in use long enough to have developed an "improved variety," a circumstance which stamps it unmistakably as no innovation of yesterday. For our present purpose, not the least significant fact is that this improved type is found in a tribe who have never become horse Indians—as the term is more commonly understood—the northern Chipewyan.[64]

[64] On "ear flaps," see McClintock, *Old North Trail*, 233, 518; Mooney, in Hodge, *Handbook*, II, 758. A good illustration of the special pole that holds them in position, in Jenness, *The Sarcee Indians*, facing title page. For the Chipewyan pattern, Ernest Thompson Seton, *The Arctic Prairies*, 149.

INDIAN TRANSPORTATION
BY LAND

Thin →

DOG PACK
Used in both open
and wooded country.

Thick

HORSE TRAVOIS

The Travois was used
on the plains.

Note the 2 types of
carrying frames and
ends of poles.

Thick

DOG TRAVOIS

Thin →

From C. W. Jefferys, *The Picture Gallery of Canadian History*, I

"The travois was apparently more common in the open Southern Plains area, and the dog-packing in the more northern territory. . . . A striking feature is the persistence, or at least the survival, down to the very late times, of dog transport among tribes possessing an apparent abundance of horses."

Potawatomi

Unidentified

Sioux

Horses and Riding Equipment
From *The Journal of Rudolph Friederich Kurz*
(Bureau of American Ethnology *Bulletin 115*)

Courtesy Smithsonian Institution

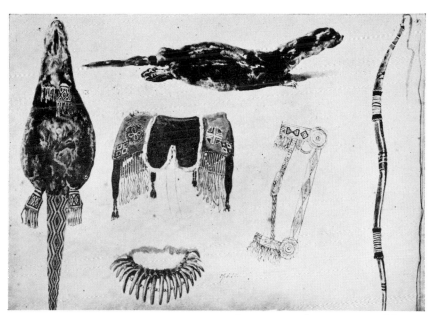

Two medicine pouches, two necklaces,
a ceremonial bow, and a saddle cloth

Saddled Blackfoot Pony
Both from *The Journal of Rudolph Friederich Kurz*
(Bureau of American Ethnology *Bulletin 115*)

Indians Escaping after the Burning of Julesburg
FREDERIC REMINGTON

Courtesy Woolaroc Museum

Return from the Hunt
CHARLES M. RUSSELL

Courtesy Woolaroc Museum

Pony with Woman's Saddle and Accessories (Cayuse)

FROM A PHOTOGRAPH BY MAJOR MOORHOUSE

Courtesy Smithsonian Institution

Indian Girl (Sioux) on Horseback

Courtesy Walters Art Gallery   ALFRED JACOB MILLER

Blackfoot Woman with Horse Travois

"There can be little doubt that the accession of the horse has exerted a very considerable influence in elevating the status of women in the horse tribes. . . . The Blackfoot woman owned her own horse and saddlery."

Sioux Tree Burial, 1868

FROM A PHOTOGRAPH ATTRIBUTED TO ALEXANDER GARDNER

". . . the men took this to a high place away from the camp and placed
it upon a scaffold set up in a tree. . . . It is in this manner that the gross
body is given back to the elements from which it came; it is left exposed
to the agents of heaven: the four winds, the rains, the wingeds of the
air, each of which—and with the Earth—absorbs a part."

—Joseph Epes Brown, *The Sacred Pipe.*

The Voice of the Great Spirit (A Crow Platform Burial)
J. H. SHARP

" 'Then they brought him home, grieving they took him to the camp, all the Crow, the entire camp cried. They laid him on a scaffold, they stuck a tipi pole into the ground and tied his sashes to it, his drum and rattle they tied to it. Above they were blowing in the breeze. Then without him they moved.' "—Robert H. Lowie, *The Crow Indians*.

XI

MIGRATIONS AND THE HORSE

Many—perhaps most—of the historic Plains tribes were not aboriginally resident from the early beginnings of Indian life on this continent in those areas of the buffalo habitat where the earlier European intruders found them. I should be quite prepared to discover the impelling cause of the migratory (or economic) impulse which actuated their removal thither, in the generally abundant and relatively easy subsistence which the buffalo furnished.

I consider, however, that chronological objections alone are fatal to the supposition that the horse influence is the decisive and significant factor in this field. With undiminished respect for the distinguished anthropologist who advances the suggestion along this line[1] (and whose findings are not lightly to be contested), I must say that he himself has furnished some important items in the body of evidence which prevents me from accepting his conclusions in their entirety. While cases existed where the "lure of the horse" is considered with some apparent reason to have been the principal motive for the migration, the larger number of the Plains tribes appear either to have moved prior to the horse era, or to have been unwilling to do so after learning of or seeing the animal, despite those attractions which had—supposedly or actually—impelled other tribes, and which should have been at least as self-evident to the people most nearly interested as they are to modern critics.

It is not necessary to attempt even the briefest résumé of the

[1] Jenness, *Indians of Canada*, 129.

207

general prehistoric movements that finally resulted in the geographical distribution of the historic tribes of this continent as history knows them. It is sufficient to say here that linguistic affinities have been generally accepted as the basis upon which tribal stocks and families are now differentiated and defined. The widespread and haphazard manner in which the various linguistic groups, Algonquian, Athapascan, Caddoan, Shoshonean, Siouan, etc., are found to be scattered over the western areas of the continent in particular, with alien stocks in close neighboring proximity and kindred groups separated by hundreds or perhaps thousands of miles, points clearly to the workings of the migratory impulse in what may have been very remote ages. We may, however, instance one or two tribes of the horse and buffalo area whose migratory history is somewhat better known, and belongs to more recent periods.

Some of the principal "immigrant" peoples into the Plains habitat were not merely earlier than any authenticated knowledge of the historic horse in their historical tribal areas; they are considered to be anterior there even to the possibility of such a thing. The same high authority to whom I referred at the opening of our present chapter, writing of the Cree as a whole (that is, both Wood and Plain Cree inclusively), says this: "Their western limits are uncertain, but in the early sixteenth century they appear to have wandered over part of the country west of Lake Winnipeg, perhaps between Red River and the Saskatchewan. . . ."[2]

The generally accepted geographical relations of the Cree to the Blackfoot point to some strong inferential conclusions. Wissler, in an early paper (1910), discusses certain Blackfoot traditions, of which some bring the Blackfoot to their historic range from somewhere beyond the Rockies to the southwest. He notes Grinnell's hypothesis that the opprobrious Cree term "Slaves" is to be assimilated with the (Northern) Slave Lakes, and apparently supports the suggesion for the Blackfoot as a far northern tribe. Wissler, in the same essay, is wisely dubious concerning Blackfoot traditions,[3] in which conclusion he finds support from a later specialist on the same tribe.[4] The "Slave" (Lake) hypothesis is unconvincing. Such

[2] *Ibid.*, 283–87.
[3] Wissler, "Material Culture of the Blackfoot Indians," 15–19.

a term could be applied in any territory to any people by a self-supposed superior. As the Blackfoot were moving or being driven westward ahead of the Cree—the latter being better armed—"Slave" in the mouths of the Cree had a logic of sorts. But it is inconceivable that the Cree would have applied it to a tribe coming from a transmontane region who have never at any historic era since reaching their recognized habitat given any indication of inferiority, such as being "driven before" the Cree; and the term was apparently never used by any tribe but the Cree. Wissler was mistaken in thinking that none but the younger Alexander Henry used the term.[5] George Simpson wrote thus, 1841:

Thus formidably equipped [with firearms] the Crees had a great advantage over their comparatively defenceless neighbours, whom they stigmatized as slaves—a name still applied, though without any offensive reference, to the Chipewyans, the Yellow Knives, the Hares, the Dogribs, the Loucheux, the Nihannies, the Dahotanies, and others on the shores of M'Kenzie's and Liard's rivers and their tributaries.[6]

Paul Kane, the artist, wrote in 1846:

The Crees have been from time immemorial at war with the Blackfeet, whom they at one time conquered and held in subjection; even now the Crees call the Blackfeet slaves, although they have gained their independence, and are a fierce and warlike tribe.[7]

Actually the term "Slaves" had become so embedded in common use in the Cree territory in the eighteen forties that even Rundle the missionary (Fort Edmonton, 1840–48)—though a warm friend and admirer of the Blackfoot, who returned the feeling—used it quite as often as anyone.[8]

---

[4] Kidd, "Blackfoot Ethnography," 10.
[5] Wissler, "Material Culture of the Blackfoot Indians," 15–19.
[6] Sir George Simpson, *Narrative of a Journey Around the World in the Years 1841 and 1842*, I, 87.
[7] Kane, *Wanderings of an Artist*, 114.
[8] "... some slave Indians consisting of Blood Indians, Sarcees, and Blackfeet ..." (Piegans not then present), Robert Terrill Rundle, "Journal" (unpublished MS. ed. by J. P. Berry and F. G. Roe), July 29, 1843. He refers to one of the many southward "Blackfoot Trails" from Edmonton as the "Slave Indian Road" (*ibid.*, Oct. 17, 1844). Such usages are common in the journal.

The Blackfoot approach to the Plains territory from the northeast appears furthermore to be supported by other Blackfoot tribal traditions. An "adopted son" of the Siksika tells us that the tribal tradition is that "ages ago their people lived far to the north of their present country, where the dark fertile soil so discolored their moccasins that they were called Siksikaua or Black Moccasins."[9]

To one who has both farmed and freighted in each of the respective areas, the utter contrast between the light clean sandy soils of the modern Blackfoot habitat and the sticky black northern loams at once puts the Blackfoot ecological geography beyond criticism. The demarcation of the two territories across Alberta runs diagonally on the map, roughly from where the Bow River leaves the mountains west of Calgary, northeastward to where the North Saskatchewan crosses the provincial boundary of Alberta and Saskatchewan, practically at old Fort Pitt. I have crossed this line at seven different points, and at many the contrast is so swift and complete—or used to be—that within three hundred or four hundred yards one has passed from scrubby forest land "high enough to lose a man on horseback" to "baldheaded plains" extending unbrokenly to Mexico. The old Calgary and Edmonton Trail crossed the line at a point fifty-five miles north of Calgary. From there onward the northern soils were impassable for the great six-yoke bull trains in the last days of the buffalo era,[10] and were mere quagmires in the wet cycle of 1899–1903. Dirt roads in the same area today are a motorist's headache in summer, for fear of a sudden thunderstorm; whereas in the southern region's gritty soil thunderstorms are harmless, and are actually welcomed as helping to pack the loose slippery sand in the hill countries. The Blackfoot tradition fixes the general direction of the trek pretty definitely. These factors make them a Plains people at an even earlier date than the Cree. An authoritative student of their polity dates their Plains culture circa 1492.[11]

Whatever may have been the cause of the original separation of the Assiniboin from the parent Sioux, the occurrence is placed

[9] McClintock, Old North Trail, 2.

[10] MacInnes, In the Shadow of the Rockies, 175. See also L. R. Jones and P. W. Bryan, North America (regional geography), 165, 172, 215, 224, 374, 495–502; and an incident, 1809, in Coues (ed.), Henry-Thompson Journals, II, 545.

[11] Kidd, "Blackfoot Ethnography," 10–16.

about 1640. At that time the tribe as a whole was dwelling in the Great Lakes region.[12] The Assiniboin and the Sioux had both reached the buffalo habitat on the Red River and on the upper Mississippi, respectively, before their acquisition of the horse.[13] The westerly progress of both divisions was apparently nothing beyond a continuance of a general direction they had already followed for long distances. I have encountered no evidence—beyond evidence of opinion—indicating any sort of precipitate advance or "leap" toward the horse country when this useful and wonderful animal became known to them. Moreover, such evidence as we possess regarding the horse chronology of the Sioux would suggest that such an advance would have been quite as probably and perhaps more logically to the south (or southwest) as westward up the Missouri or those southern tributaries in the Sioux territory between the main stream and the Platte. For one tradition has the Sioux receiving their first horses from the transplanted Cheyenne at a computed mean period about 1770.[14] There is nothing in this tradition as we have it to indicate that the Cheyenne gave horses to the poorer Sioux immediately after they got their own. This seems unlikely, but it may have occurred some years later. Such horses might conceivably have come down the Missouri route from the transmontane tribes. Yet in that year, 1770, we have a direct intimation from Peter Pond, then in the territory, that the Sioux actually had horses.

As we have seen, Pond noted that the Sauk were obtaining horses at that time from "St. Fee."[15] We have also seen Pond's description of the Sioux practice of slitting their horses' nostrils, stated to be a Comanche and southern custom, but not elsewhere observed in the north.[16] This raises a reasonable presumption that the early Sioux horses reached them by the Plains route. Yet they evidently made no serious concerted effort to move southward, such as could be termed a tribal migration. Even after making

[12] Thwaites (ed.), *Jesuit Relations*, LXVI, 341, editor's note.
[13] See Chapter V *supra*.
[14] See Chapter V *supra*.
[15] Worcester speaks of the Caddoes (?) frequently taking horses to "the Illinois" (tribe or locality?) in 1717, apparently following Pierre Margry. They can never have reached there (Worcester, "Spanish Horses among the Plains Tribes," 409.
[16] Dobie, *The Mustangs*, 50.

allowance for their numerous subdivisions, they seem in 1770 to have been very much where they were in 1679, when they captured Father Hennepin.[17] These queries respecting the Sioux are even more acutely applicable to the Assiniboin. If the Arikara actually had horses on the central Missouri by 1680,[18] it seems unlikely that the Sioux (and through them, the Assiniboin) would not have heard of them long enough before they got some of their own; similar to the Mandan sixty or more years later. Yet the Assiniboin persisted in going on—not merely westward, but northwestward. Henry Kelsey's companions above the Forks of the Saskatchewan in 1691 are thought to be Assiniboin.[19] One might almost say of the horse history of the Assiniboin at large that the horse sought them out, rather than they the horse.

What was described by a contemporary resident in the area, about 1790, as the Sioux' "emigrating" on to the prairies, at a time when some at least of the many Sioux divisions possessed horses, is classified by more modern scholars as being "driven out" by the Chippewa (Ojibwa, Saulteaux, or Sauteux).[20] It is possible, though not certain, that the Ojibwa had the horse at this time. It may be definitely stated that they knew of them,[21] and had probably heard something of their extraordinary powers. Yet in spite of this the victorious tribe did not follow the Sioux out on to the Plains. They described the situation to David Thompson thus:

> While [the Sioux] keep the Plains with their Horses we are not a match for them; for we being footmen, they could get to windward of us and fire the grass; When we marched for the Woods they would be there before us, dismount, and under cover fire on us. Until we have horses like them, we must keep to the Woods and leave the plains to them.[22]

The remote original movement of the parent Siouan stock from

[17] Hennepin, *New Discovery* (ed. by Thwaites), II, 469, 488; Parkman, *La Salle*, 263.

[18] See Chapters V, IX *supra*.

[19] See *The Kelsey Papers* (ed. by A. G. Doughty and Chester Martin), introduction.

[20] For the emigrating, 1790, Peter Grant, in Masson, *Les Bourgeois de la Compagnie du Nord-Ouest*, II, 346. For the driving out, Mooney and Thomas, in Hodge, *Handbook*, I, 277; Mooney and Swanton, *ibid.*, II, 577.

[21] See Chapter V *supra*.

[22] Thompson, *Narrative* (ed. by Tyrrell), 264.

their apparently earliest ascertainable home region in the Carolinas antedates not merely the historic horse but the historic buffalo itself.[23] One of the principal subdivisions, the Dhegiha, had already attained the Great Lakes region and was identified as the Sioux, at a time when the buffalo had not reached the Atlantic states, if indeed they had yet much more than crossed the lower Mississippi, on their original eastward penetration.[24]

The case of the Pawnee is of particular significance in this connection. In the preceding chapter we have seen Wedel's view that the Pawnee were occupants of their Central Plains habitat "long before the first Europeans arrived," and have probably the strongest claim to the title of true indigenes. We have seen that they were far from being indifferent toward the horse. They are thought to have been among the very earliest to acquire the animal, perhaps before 1600; and they were one of the first tribes to be definitely associated with the ownership of large herds of really good horses.[25]

In early post-European times the Comanche were apparently their neighbors to the north. Contemporary scholars consider that the horse "transplanted the Comanche from north of the Platte to the land of 'Ever Summer,' next to the horse supply."[26] Richardson dates this approximately at the opening of the eighteenth century, and like Dobie, classifies the movement as a voluntary "advance," conditioned almost purely by the horse. In relative (tribal) timing, Richardson places the Comanche acquisition of the animal not merely prior to the acquisition by such Central-Northern tribes as the Sioux and the Cheyenne, but even to the Kiowa, which is more contentious.[27] Other critics have it that the Comanche were "driven south" by the Sioux,[28] which conveys a very fair idea both of the general earlier locality, and of the approximate dating. In any event, the Comanche moved south; their movement was an out-

[23] See Mooney and Swanton, in Hodge, *Handbook*, II, 577; Mooney, *ibid.*, II, 855.

[24] In twenty-four descriptions of "Florida" and "Virginia" (identical after 1584) from 1540 to 1625, buffalo are either omitted or specifically denied. See Roe, *North American Buffalo*, 214–15.

[25] See Chapter IV *supra*.

[26] Dobie, "Indian Horses and Horsemanship," 265. In *The Mustangs*, 42, this is applied to the Kiowa.

[27] Richardson, *The Comanche Barrier*, 19.

[28] Mooney, in Hodge, *Handbook*, I, 327–29.

standing example of an actual migration *toward* the horse (*post hoc, ergo propter hoc?*) and one of the few cases that sustain critical scrutiny.

The Pawnee, whom we must assume (chronologically) to have been at this time better mounted than the Comanche, allowed the latter to pass through or around their country and take up a situation on the Spanish frontier, which virtually made the Pawnee's future supply of Spanish horses depend upon the alternatives of Comanche forbearance or war.[29] Whether the Pawnee acted thus from indifference or fear is irrelevant. In either case, retention of their home ground—and with it, beyond doubt, much of their way of life—pulled so strongly that the horse was unable to conquer the prior attachment. Yet certainly they were not indifferent to the advantages of the horse.

The Mandan are perhaps the most extreme example in the Plains area of that almost abject condition which Denhardt typifies—in my judgment much too sweepingly—as being terminated en bloc by the acquisition of the horse. Denhardt writes as follows:

> The immense effect this animal had on the life and habits of the Indians has never been adequately told. From a poor sedentary group they became independent nomadic tribes and woe to man or beast that got in the way of the previously humble Indian.[30]

The Mandan had all the earmarks of this conception of the pre-equestrian society. Like their neighbors, the Hidatsa, they were sedentary. This made them partly dependent upon the more or less erratic appearances of the buffalo for food, as a reinforcement to their field crops. Yet their crops—as many another dweller in North Dakota has learned since—were by no means certain; and between the two stools they not infrequently fell to the ground. We have two thumbnail sketches from contemporaneous observers. Maximilian writes as follows:

> The Indians residing in permanent villages have the advantage of the roving hunting tribes, in that they not only hunt, but derive their chief subsistence from their plantations, which afford them a degree

[29] See Jablow, *The Cheyenne*, 15, 24, 67–72.
[30] Denhardt, *Horse of the Americas*, 106.

of security against distress. It is true, these Indians sometimes suffer hunger when the buffalo herds keep at a great distance, and their crops fail; but the distress can never be so great among the Missouri [River] Indians, as in the tribes that live further northwards.[31]

George Catlin emphasizes the buffalo uncertainty:

Buffaloes, it is known, are a sort of roaming creatures, congregating occasionally in huge masses, and strolling about the country from east to west or from north to south, or just where their whims or strange fancies may lead them; and the Mandans are sometimes by this manner most unceremoniously left without anything to eat. . . .

The Minatarees [Hidatsa], as well as the Mandans, had suffered for some months past for want of meat, and had indulged in the most alarming fears that the herds of buffalo were emigrating so far off that there was great danger of their actual starvation, when it was suddenly announced through the village one morning at an early hour that a herd of buffaloes was in sight.[32]

We may note that the foregoing pictures are dated about 1832. At that time these tribes had been acquainted with the horse for very nearly a century, and had quite probably possessed it for most of that period. In Maximilian's time there were "probably above 300 horses in the two Mandan villages," and the Hidatsa had "250 or 300" more.[33] These widened their buffalo-hunting range very considerably, which furnishes some rough index to their pre-equestrian condition. Yet despite this, together with the uncertainty of their crops, the precarious trading tenure upon which they must rely for further supplies of horses, and the hostile pressure of the Sioux and other allied tribes,[34] nothing could induce these people to leave their stationary villages.

The Arikara reveal a similar attitude. Maximilian states that in 1832 they deserted their villages and adopted the nomadic life. This action was forced upon them by the failure of their crops,[35] and not by any influence of the horse. At this time they had horses

[31] Maximilian, *Travels*, in Thwaites, *Travels*, XXIII, 274.
[32] Catlin, *Letters and Notes*, I, 127, 199.
[33] Maximilian, *Travels*, in Thwaites, *Travels*, XXIII, 272; cf. 235, 237, 245, 370.
[34] See Chapter V *supra*; also Jablow, *The Cheyenne*, 3–8, 51–58, 65, 79.
[35] Maximilian, *Travels*, in Thwaites, *Travels*, XXII, 335; De Smet, *Letters and Sketches*, in Thwaites, *Travels*, XXIX, 196.

in abundance, and are thought to have had them since 1738, or possibly 1680.[36]

The Kickapoo constitute a fairly late exemplification of the same negative principle, and in their case the approximate dates are known. They got the horse about 1800–1820, while they were still on the eastern side of the Mississippi. They often crossed during that time to hunt buffalo. About 1820 they migrated permanently into Missouri, but they did not become nomads.[37]

The foregoing review has covered an enormous portion of the main Plains area, extending from the Saskatchewan to the Spanish frontier. Over this tract one tribe only, the Comanche, can be shown with reasonable probability to have migrated because of the attraction of the horse. The others either migrated for other (pre- or post-European) reasons, or did not migrate at all.

There are also two tribes of the Athapascan linguistic stock, which takes the name from its basic territory in northwestern Canada, whose migration southward is known with fair precision; certainly in respect of fact if not of chronology. The earlier migrants of the two, the Apache, trace farther back as a Southwestern tribe than any authentic historical knowledge of this continent. Members of this linguistic stock are believed by a very highly competent critic to date back perhaps to a remotely early era in (modern) Utah; and in their historic habitat in Arizona they antedate the introduction of the horse beyond any reasonable question.[38]

The second of the two, the Sarsi or Sarcee, are considered by their most authoritative student, Diamond Jenness, to have started on their southbound exodus from the lower Athabaska River country about the end of the seventeenth century.[39] The lure of the Plains buffalo—as a creature much more plentiful and far easier to hunt than their own local wood buffalo—is perfectly conceivable and in my own view very probable as the actuating cause; and

[36] See Chapter V *supra*.
[37] Hodge, *Handbook*, I, 684.
[38] For the Apache, see Hodge, *Handbook*, I, 63–68, 806; II, 337, etc.; Mooney, "Aboriginal Population of America North of Mexico," 22; Webb, *The Great Plains*, 121; Alfred L. Kroeber, *Cultural and Natural Areas in Native North America*, 34–38; Harrington, "Athapaskawan Origins, Divisions, and Migrations," 503–32. For Utah, Julian H. Steward, "Native Cultures of the Intermontane Area," *Swanton Memorial Volume*, 271, 474.
[39] Jenness, *The Sarcee Indians*, 1.

this may also, perhaps, have been true in the earlier case of the Apache. Neither the "lure" nor the knowledge of the horse seems even possible as the cause impelling the Sarcee, if we may place any reliance upon the account given by David Thompson's ancient informant, which has been discussed above, and which gives about 1730 as the probable time when the Blackfoot saw their first horse.[40]

Even if we accept the suggestion of Francis Haines, which would antedate that episode by some twenty years, or adopt the provisional dating which would place horses among the Blackfoot by 1700,[41] we cannot consider ourselves much nearer toward establishing the horse as the likely cause of the Sarcee migration southward. For their progress was very slow; not at all what might be expected with such a direct incentive impelling them forward. Almost a century and a half from the estimated era of its beginnings, their march had brought them no farther than the very fringe of the Blackfoot country as it was then. Duncan McGillivray (1794) and the younger Alexander Henry (1809) mention their tribal habitat as being 'south of the Beaver Hills,' which are east of Edmonton.[42] In 1840, the "Sarcee Hills" were along the upper Battle River, some sixty miles southwest of Edmonton, where Governor (later Sir George) Simpson met them in July, 1841.[43] Such an allocation would have been unthinkable for the Sarcee fifty years later. They were south of Calgary before 1890. There appears to be no Sarcee tradition even, not to say historical evidence, of any possession of horses among them prior to their membership in (or association with) the Blackfoot Confederacy, which may perhaps roughly date their horses about 1730–1750.

It is perhaps not irrelevant to point out, with reference to archaeological evidence affecting these questions, the wisdom of being on guard against misinterpreting the archaeologist's use of such relative terms as "earlier" or "later" phenomena of various kinds. To the archaeologist, there are probably comparatively few of his "later" classifications which do not themselves antedate the

[40] See Chapter V *supra.*
[41] See Chapter V *supra.*
[42] McGillivray, *Journal* (ed. by Morton), 27; Coues (ed.), *Henry-Thompson Journals,* II, 532, 727.
[43] Simpson, *Journey Around the World,* I, 110.

horse, sometimes very considerably. With respect to our immediate topic of the present chapter, we may recall Wissler's opinion, apparently a very sound one: "Very few of the Plains tribes are known to have permanently shifted their homes during the period 1680–1860. We must therefore accept their positions as we find them at the opening of the historical period."[44] In so far as our all-too-meager horse chronology serves as a guide, this is virtually equivalent to saying that in the larger portion at least of the territory in question, the horse constituted little or no influence in impelling leading tribes to migrate. The migrations were effected before the horse came.

[44] Wissler, "Influence of the Horse," 13.

XII

THE HORSE AND WARFARE

We have seen that the horse has been suggested as an originating cause in creating and fostering warlike propensities in the Plains tribes since its appearance among them. Without doubt, as a highly desirable asset to be secured by fair means or foul, the possession of which beyond immediate needs constituted a widely popular conception of wealth, the animal exercised considerable influence over the Indian mind. The horse added an important item to the various causes or reasons (or pretexts) of dispute which not only generated wars as we commonly use the term, but also kept alive that uneasy condition of armed truce with its constant surprises, forays, raids, and reprisals, which characterized so much of what was ostensibly "peace." But to assume—which seems to be the intended meaning—that above and beyond any mere facilitating of warlike operations or extending their geographical range, the Indian *desire* for war was a new reaction following upon the advent of the horse, and a condition which would not have arisen without the horse, is a conception for which in my opinion the historical evidence affords very little warrant. As with previous phases of our inquiry, chronology is the stumbling block.

The chronological evidence for the existence of a generally contratribal warlike society in the Indian world at large, and prior to the impact of the European on the North American continent, groups itself in two principal categories. In the first of these we may note that such enmities are to be found from the very earliest eras of European contact. In more than one instance they were of an inveterate and quite definitely crystallized character, clearly

219

older than any possibility even of knowledge, not to say influence, of the historic horse. A number of outstanding examples may be noted; and in several of these the observers recording them are among the very earliest of the white race to encounter the aborigines in that particular territory.

Cabeza de Vaca's Indians are described (and apparently in a comprehensive tribal sense) as having perfected a war technique "as if trained in continuous wars and in Italy,"[1] which evidently points to a long continuance. Coronado's expedition noted that the Querechos and the Teyas—both of them buffalo tribes—were enemies.[2] The League of the Iroquois furnishes a classic example. The rise of this powerful confederacy is commonly dated about 1570. While economic causes operating between New France and the English settlements in New England unquestionably played a significant part in perpetuating its tribal animosities with their ferocious hatreds and wartime horrors, it could scarcely be maintained that these were the originating impulse of the League.[3]

It is of course well known that Champlain, even before the Pilgrims had landed in New England, took sides with the Hurons against the Iroquois in a tribal strife which was manifestly of long standing; and the French paid dearly for his unwisdom during a century or more. Later it became axiomatic in the Indian country that the avoidance of such partisanship was the very beginning of wisdom. For it was almost fundamental in Indian thought that the friend of their enemies was their enemy likewise, if once he raised his hand against them. It was thus that the son of La Vérendrye paid with his life at the hands of the infuriated Sioux for his father's error in joining forces with the tribal foemen of the Sioux as against a common enemy of the human race.[4]

Concerning the Illinois country, about 1670, Father Marquette says: "These people are very obliging and liberal with what they have, but they are wretchedly provided with food, for they dare not go and hunt wild cattle [buffalo], on account of their enemies."[5] In the same region, 1680, Father Hennepin observes that

[1] Bandelier (ed.), *Journey of Cabeza de Vaca*, 119.

[2] So, Castañeda, in Winship (ed.), *Journey of Coronado*, 111, 210, 215.

[3] Long, *History of the Canadian People*, I, 30–36, 47–108; Hodge, *Handbook*, I, 546.

[4] See note 107 *infra*.   [5] Thwaites (ed.), *Jesuit Relations*, LIX, 157.

"the Wild Bulls are grown somewhat scarce since the Illinois have been at War with their Neighbors, for now all Parties are continually hunting of them."[6] La Salle himself is quoted as follows, in reference to the same time:

The Indians do not hunt in this region, which is debateable ground between five or six nations who are at war, and, being afraid of each other, do not venture into these parts except to surprise each other, and always with the greatest precaution and all possible secrecy.[7]

In the lower Mississippi territory, Father Zenobius Membre, with La Salle's second expedition in 1687, noted that "the people on one bank are generally enemies of those on the other."[8] All the foregoing examples, apart from the Spanish sources, refer to tribes and to regions that have never at any time been associated with horse Indians.

The second of the two phases of the evidence to which I referred above is that of the general applicability and relevance of testimony gathered from Indian nations at large to the buffalo Indians; that is to say, the equestrian tribes. This question is in my opinion to be decided quite satisfactorily in the affirmative by the factor which I have already noted: that so many of the Plains tribes are themselves immigrants of distant forest descent; sometimes of the very family stocks that revealed their warlike propensities in their earlier habitat. In fact, an outstanding specialist on the war psychology of the Indians says definitely that the Plains war system was "applicable to all of North America east of the Rocky Mountains."[9] This brings us to a consideration of the Indian war system in itself. What was it which the horse is supposed to have revolutionized or extended?

[6] Hennepin, *New Discovery* (ed. by Thwaites), II, 627. The scarcity of buffalo was more probably the *cause* of the war rather than the effect.

[7] Parkman, *La Salle,* 194.

[8] Membre, in Cox (ed.), *Journeys of La Salle,* I, 141.

[9] Marian W. Smith, "The War Complex of the Plains Indians," *Proceedings of the American Philosophical Society,* Vol. LXXVIII (1938), 439; cf. 453.

It appears to the present writer that our conceptions of Indian warfare have been colored and dominated altogether too strongly by what may be termed the classical history of war in all ages prior to our own era of mechanized warfare. We have assumed too readily that "war was war," and that all peoples possessing *in esse* the same military assets would utilize them in precisely the same manner. This reasoning has apparently been applied almost instinctively to cavalry operations, which in many eras from Carrhae to Khartoum have so frequently been the deciding factor in the field. We have taken it for granted that the coming of the horse to a warlike race not previously acquainted with the animal, coupled together with their rapid and phenomenal mastery of all forms of equestrian skill, would almost necessarily transform the Indians into cavalry fighters in our connotation of the term. Even in the true—but limited—sense in which the horse automatically extends the range of anyone possessing it, the history of the Iroquois Confederacy alone should have made us more critically cautious. They journeyed by land on foot; yet no North American people ever had a wider war range. It is not easy to comprehend just what agency short of railways could have extended this in their case. Historically, the horse certainly did not. A contemporary specialist on Iroquois history states that horses were rare among them even in the eighteenth century.[10]

Our basic conception of a war, in which from action to action and from campaign to campaign, regardless of immediate success or failure, a Hannibal, Caesar, Cromwell, Marlborough, Frederick, Washington, Napoleon, Wellington, or Grant pursues a definite objective until victory is attained or failure can no longer be denied, apparently had no place in Indian thought. Marian Smith, who has studied this subject deeply, says that (apart of course from sheer massacres which left no survivors on the losing side) the literature contains no record "of any war-party which did not return [home again] after its first fight."[11] Despite our conventional use of

[10] W. N. Fenton, "Problems Arising from the Historic North-Eastern Position of the Iroquois," 230.
[11] Smith, "War Complex of the Plains Indians," 443.

the term, Indian hostilities were not wars. They were attacks, virtually approaching massacres if they were successful, and not even battles unless the party attacked proved able to offer a stubborn resistance. Marian Smith says again with respect to any conceptions we may entertain concerning a Hundred Years' War between "inveterate enemies": "There was no state of continued blood feud existent in any Plains tribe."[12] As a corollary to this, hostilities between allied tribes were not infrequent, even in alliances as (relatively) permanent as the Blackfoot Confederacy.[13] The intermittent alternations of war and peace between the Blackfoot and the Cree, which in later days hinged largely upon the exigencies of trade and probably for ages upon the erratic wanderings of the buffalo,[14] demonstrate the essential soundness of both conclusions.

Battles, when they occurred, bore no relation to those tactical maneuverings which, in the careers of the great captains of history, testify to the military skill of the "born soldier." Primarily, they were separate engagements. Richardson, speaking of the "general policy" in the field, very prudently adds: ". . . (if we may speak of a general policy among a people where each individual warrior did about as he pleased). . . ."[15] Collectively, battles might be considered as the unpleasant consequences of a partial failure in surprising the foe. "The mortality in Plains fighting was highest when attacks took the enemy unprepared for defense. In such cases the weaker groups were often completely annihilated. The mortality of pitched battles, which were of more frequent occurrence than is generally supposed, was considerably lower."[16]

The main governing motive in these hostile activities, the one common element amid much tribal diversity, was self-aggrandizement. Whether as cause or effect of this, individualism was inevitable. Among the Hidatsa, for example, the specific training of the horses themselves made pronouncedly for individualism. The war pony was trained to dance; that is, never to be still for a moment, thus presenting a more difficult mark. He was also trained

[12] *Ibid.*, 453.
[13] Kroeber, "Ethnology of the Gros Ventre" (Atsina), 146; Wissler, "Material Culture of the Blackfoot Indians," 7; Jenness, *The Sarcee Indians*, 2–3.
[14] See Roe, *North American Buffalo*, 652–54, etc.
[15] Richardson, *The Comanche Barrier*, 209.
[16] Smith, "War Complex of the Plains Indians," 431.

to leap over the fallen enemy, which counted as a "coup" and facilitated a possibly fatal wound to the prostrate man. The boys were also trained to vault or leap from the ground to the back of a horse in full career (alone or behind a comrade), in addition to hanging over or beneath the horse's neck. These accomplishments were of high service in the rescue of an unhorsed or wounded comrade, but they were the very reverse of concerted cavalry action.[17] There was a general resemblance in the "coup" theory among many tribes; and the act of daring frequently ranked higher than sheer slaying.[18]

In leaders, self-aggrandizement was naturally conditioned by success. But success itself was not precisely definite in our terms. A "successful" enterprise such as a horse-stealing raid in which good numbers were carried off but where some of the war party were killed was not "success," and even one such outcome might, while a repetition almost certainly would, be enough to ruin the reputation of a war leader. Among the Crow, however many a war party might slay, there was no perfect victory, and certainly no celebration, if even one Crow were slain.[19] In European warfare, great fame has been won even by unlucky warriors such as old Earl Douglas, "The Tineman," who never tasted victory in a lifetime spent in the saddle, or the two Williams of Orange, whose respective reputations stemmed from an unparalleled skill in retrieving defeat. Such captains would be out of the running in an Indian tribal society, for war leadership was not the fixed prerogative of a despotic or hereditary chief who could draft followers, willingly or unwillingly, into his projected force. While no doubt there were tyrants here and there like Alexander Henry's Le Borgne[20] or Parkman's Mahto-Tatonka,[21] in very many cases war leaders were not even chiefs. The famous Cheyenne warrior, Roman Nose, was a case in point.[22] According to Mandelbaum's na-

---

[17] Wilson, "Horse and Dog in Hidatsa Culture," 150–54.

[18] Hoebel, "Political Associations and Law-Ways of the Comanche Indians," 21–23.

[19] Lowie, "Material Culture of the Crow Indians," 264. For the self-aggrandizement motive, see Lowie, The Crow Indians, 219.

[20] A well-known Hidatsa chief about 1800; frequently mentioned by Thompson, Lewis and Clark, Henry, Larocque, and in Masson, Les Bourgeois de la Compagnie du Nord-Ouest.

[21] The Sioux despot in Parkman's The Oregon Trail.

[22] So, Grinnell, The Fighting Cheyennes, 240, 271, 281.

tive informants, among the Cree a brave and even fortunate, but unthrifty warrior (that is to say, unable in consequence to make frequent gifts) "couldn't be a chief."[23] With respect to this particular phase, Marian Smith observes that "War leadership in North America seems never to have been in the hands of a particular set of permanent officials, and membership in war parties never lost its voluntary character."[24]

With the followers also there were rather stringent geographical, cultural, and perhaps tribal idiosyncrasies. What was very frequently stigmatized by white critics as mere cowardice (and applied to such tribes as the Comanche,[25] Ojibwa,[26] Osage,[27] Pawnee,[28] and Sioux[29]), such as the stealthy utilization of cover, or the retreat in the face of odds or stubborn opposition, seems actually to have been a rooted aversion to needlessly endangering the life of a tribesman. As we have noted, a Pyrrhic victory, or what the Greeks termed a "Cadmean victory" long before the days of Pyrrhus,[30] was no success in their estimation. Mere collective courage —"where no one wants to face 'em but every beggar must"—meant little. That was taken for granted. There must also be the personal coup on the individual foeman.

While the Iroquois beyond doubt terrorized the eastern areas of the continent from the very beginnings of the seventeenth century (and probably long before then), a recent scholar considers that the latter half of that century represented the culmination of wartime horrors west of the Mississippi. He writes as follows:

All the evidence that we have from French and Spanish sources and from Indian tradition indicates that the period from 1660 to 1700 in the lands west of the Mississippi was one of frightful raiding, the aggressors being those tribes that had obtained metal knives, hatchets,

[23] Mandelbaum, "The Plains Cree," 221–24.
[24] Smith, "War Complex of the Plains Indians," 438; cf. 460–61.
[25] Gregg, Commerce of the Prairies, in Thwaites, Travels, XX, 140, 347.
[26] ". . . of course, cowards . . ." (Coues [ed.], Expeditions of Pike, I, 184).
[27] Henry Marie Brackenridge (1811), Views of Louisiana, in Thwaites, Travels, VI, 80.
[28] "Worse than the Osage" (Coues [ed.], Expeditions of Pike, II, 532–33).
[29] Maximilian, Travels, in Thwaites, Travels, XXII, 306, 342.
[30] George Grote, A History of Greece, Chap. XLI.

firearms, and horses, the victims being the Indians who still had only flint weapons.[31]

Beyond doubt the horse conferred an enormous advantage on its possessors. Whatever critical examination may resolve in George E. Hyde's picture concerning points of detail (which in some respects appear to clash with other items of his own evidence[32]), in some areas at least the immediate effect of the horse would probably be to create such a world of hideousness as he suggests. This would seem to be the underlying argument of those critics who consider the horse to have been an active influence in the intensifying of war. When we carry the process onward for a generation or two and consider the *ultimate* influence of the horse from the time when more, and finally all, Plains tribes had become equestrians, we find its matured influence to be the precise opposite. So far from aggravating ferocity and bloodshed, the horse softened life and manners. This in my judgment must be considered the supreme achievement of the horse in relation to Indian warfare. I rank it so for three principal reasons. It was of much longer and, in fact, of permanent duration, for it endured down to the final days of the native culture. It prevailed over a vastly wider geographical area than the "horse territory" of circa 1700, we may be quite sure—define the latter how we may. Unlike many economic or psychological relationships to the horse which are purely an adaptation or extension of pre-equestrian, cultural, dog usages, this influence on manners had no predecessor. As we shall realize when we come to consider in detail the place of the horse in Indian warfare, both as the incentive and the instrument, it is impossible to conceive of wars upon anything like the scale of the equestrian Plains tribes having ever been waged *by means of* or *for* the dog.

[31] Hyde, "Mystery of the Arikaras," 197.

[32] At the very peak of this period, 1680, Hyde has the Arikara obtaining horses by trade with the distant Padouca (Apache?); *ibid.*, 190, 205, 217. Trading between Arizona and South Dakota seems impossible in such a world as he depicts (see Chapter V *supra*).

We cannot in my opinion grasp the essential nature of Plains Indian warfare so long as we continue to regard the horse as a mere "cavalry arm": something which enabled the Indian to reach his enemies more easily than afoot, or to attack more effectually or at a greater distance from home. The horse was all these, but it was far more. It was not only the means of war; it was also the end. In plain English, what we persist in terming "wars" were more basically and much more commonly horse raids. As J. Frank Dobie says: "White people never understood that Indians who raided their horses usually had no design on scalps." Similarly, Martin S. Garretson considers (not improbably) that many a raid on a settler's cabin in the territory east of the Mississippi was for no other purpose than to obtain hoop iron for arrowheads.[33] The scalps came into the picture when the owners, whether red or white, resisted the proceedings.

In tribe after tribe, there was no need to take scalps or even to slay the foeman to acquire merit. The honors attaching to successful thievery were almost as great, and might in certain circumstances be even greater.[34] Among the Crow, the credit acquired by stealing a picketed horse from under its owner's nose surpassed any fame that might be achieved by running off a dozen horses in what we should call "a brilliant dash." To the Crow, also, the recovery of stolen horses was much more glorious than capturing new ones.[35] "They would give chase for four days and four nights to get them back."[36] The Assiniboin attitude was essentially similar, with much caution. They were not "out for glory," apart from the glory of successful horse thievery rather than bloodthirstiness.[37] Results in captured horses were the supreme criterion of success in Blackfoot war psychology.[38] Among the Sarcee, horse

[33] Dobie, *The Mustangs*, 74–75; Martin S. Garretson, *The American Bison*, 179–80.

[34] Smith, "War Complex of the Plains Indians," 429, 430, 460.

[35] Lowie, "Material Culture of the Crow Indians," 264.

[36] See Mandelbaum, "The Plains Cree," 303.

[37] David Rodnick, "An Assiniboine Horse-Raiding Expedition" (against the Piegans, about 1869), *American Anthropologist*, Vol. XLI (1939), 611–16. See Dobie on the renowned Cheyenne horse thief who boasted that he had never killed a man (*The Mustangs*, 75).

[38] Wissler, "Material Culture of the Blackfoot Indians," 155.

stealing and war were virtually the same thing. It was equally as meritorious to steal an enemy's horse as to slay its owner.[39] The Cree did not consider the mere taking of horses in itself particularly meritorious. Danger must have been incurred in the doing of it.[40]

When we consider the equally well-organized and expert scouts assembled in defense of such property, it seems unjust, despite the element of "skulking," to stigmatize such assailants as "cowards" any more than one would an English poacher, simply because he worked by night. Horse stealing of this individual character was organized almost to the degree of a science. As I have contended in an earlier chapter, such expert skill requires time to develop. When found in any era, it may justly be adduced as good inferential evidence for a relatively lengthy prior acquaintance with the animal in question.

The foregoing data point unmistakably to the one pivotal factor that was inherent in all Indian warfare, overriding tribal diversities as nothing else apparently could, and universal throughout the continent. This was the positive passion for the secret approach and the unexpected blow. The war leader's reputation rested upon the power to make successful surprises.[41] The general history of Indian warfare at large stamps this last as the ruling feature in Marian Smith's contention for the broad identity of aboriginal warfare east of the Rocky Mountains.

Independently of anything which direct evidence may establish for the antiquity of intertribal war in the Plains area, the psychological implications of one widespread practice indicate clearly enough in my own opinion that the "technique" of Plains war tactics was a thing of long standing. This was the common Indian custom (Plains or otherwise) of conducting their actual operations in the field on foot. Marian Smith notes that Grinnell "has expressed the opinion that only with the coming of the horse did the Blackfoot begin their systematic sending forth of war parties

[39] Jenness, *The Sarcee Indians*, 33, 65; cf. Lowie, *The Crow Indians*, 216, 228; Smith, "War Complex of the Plains Indians," 430.

[40] Umfreville, *Present State of Hudson's Bay* (1790), 188; Mandelbaum, "The Plains Cree," 295-306.

[41] Hoebel, "Political Associations and Law-Ways of the Comanche Indians," 24-35; Smith, "War Complex of the Plains Indians," 429, 460.

against neighboring tribes."[42] I am extremely doubtful concerning so radical an innovation as the institution of the war party, previously unused, at so late an era. It seems fairly clear that it was on an apparently conventional war party (Piegan or the Blackfoot Confederacy) that that famous "first horse" was seen, before they had any of their own.[43] Furthermore, Wissler draws attention to the precisely contrary practice among the Blackfoot: the sending forth of war parties on foot against the Crow and the Dakota down to very late dates.[44]

There are, I believe, only one or two historical instances on record of what may strictly be termed cavalry action, even if it applies in these cases; that is to say, where the Indian force actually charged on horseback, as in the famous fight under Colonel (later General) George A. Forsyth at Beecher's Island on the Republican River (September 17–25, 1868), when the heroic Cheyenne, Roman Nose, fell at the head of his band. It is, moreover, highly probable that in this action the Indian tactics were conditioned by those of the opposing force; and that might be the case elsewhere. At the (second) battle of Adobe Walls, June 27, 1874, a large body of mounted Indians charged at the gallop—"towards a thousand," according to Billy Dixon, who was present.[45] Other accounts have seven hundred, which Richardson considers "probably an exaggeration."[46] But it is obvious that this could not be classed as a cavalry attack in any sense analogous to the sword-and-lance combats of ancient or modern cavalry, for the defenders were solidly and inexpugnably entrenched (so to say) behind stacks of buffalo hides, against which cavalry action was futile, and only one or two of them were slain.[47] Larocque says of the "Flatheads": "They generally fight on horseback & have 2 bows and 2 quivers full of arrows, with which they defend themselves and greatly annoy their enemies even in flying. They are expert horsemen."[48] Even this,

[42] Smith, *ibid.*, 432.
[43] See Chapter V *supra.*
[44] Wissler, "Influence of the Horse," 15.
[45] In Dobie, *The Mustangs*, 44–45.
[46] Richardson, *The Comanche Barrier*, 378–79. "Seven hundred" in Grinnell, *The Fighting Cheyennes*, 308–15, etc.
[47] Grinnell, *ibid.*
[48] Larocque, "Journal" (ed. by Burpee), 72. See also Grinnell, *The Fighting Cheyennes*, 240, 271, 281.

however, scarcely suggests the charge. It is much more indicative of the Comanche "feint" practice. To consider the foregoing examples as cavalry actions in our sense involves their abandonment of the fundamental individualism of Indian warfare, and the adoption of our conceptions of massed tactics. The general Indian practice of riding barebacked in battle, said by some tribes to be because a saddle impeded the "hang over" on the horse's neck,[49] reveals pretty clearly what cavalry tactics meant in their minds.

As against this, we find the converse practice in a number of tribes, stated by unexceptionable authorities. The Atsina, the Cheyenne, and the Crow generally went to war afoot.[50] We have seen that war and horse stealing were virtually indistinguishable, both in ethics and practical technique. Dobie notes that Indians habitually went afoot in the last act of the horse-stealing drama, leaving their mounts in charge after reaching the vicinity of the destined booty.[51] Richardson's concurrence in this view is clearly implied in his remark: "Unlike most other 'horse' Indians, the Comanches even went mounted when on horse-stealing expeditions."[52]

Apparently the function of the horse in Indian warfare was seldom more than that of conveying the warrior to the area (not the *scene*) of operations, where he dismounted, dragoonwise, to fight, or preferably to surprise the enemy. Such Indian forces were really, or normally, mounted infantry. In one of the very few historical notices I have encountered of an Indian force actually observed on the warpath in any other circumstances than those of battle itself, we may note what may have been a disdain or distrust of the horse in war, carried to a much farther extent. The war party in question were a band of some division of the Sioux, in 1808, when that nation was at the height of its most aggressive arrogance. The party scorned concealment or anything of the secrecy usually so dear to the Indian warrior.[53] So far from that, they exhibited themselves with a contemptuous confidence in broad daylight. This

[49] Wissler, "Material Culture of the Blackfoot Indians," 155; Wilson, "Horse and Dog in Hidatsa Culture," 153, 164, 170.

[50] Kroeber, "Ethnology of the Gros Ventre" (Atsina), 191; Grinnell, *The Fighting Cheyennes*, 43, 69; Jablow, *The Cheyenne*, 68, 83, etc.; Lowie, "Material Culture of the Crow Indians," 262; *The Crow Indians*, 222.

[51] Dobie, *The Mustangs*, 76.

[52] Richardson, *The Comanche Barrier*, 28.

[53] Parkman, *La Salle*, 194 (see note 7 *supra*).

gave our witness, the younger Alexander Henry, an excellent opportunity to observe their arrangement. From their trail they were judged to consist of "but few horses to upwards of a hundred men."[54] War parties on the Plains—like the aggressors in most wars —commonly consisted of incurable optimists who very frequently set forth afoot in the comforting conviction that they would ride back on somebody else's stolen mounts. In this instance the Sioux were proceeding toward an almost horseless territory, in any really well-stocked sense, where neither tribal foes nor white fur traders offered much likelihood of such plunder.

Among many tribes the warrior on a military expedition (or horse raid) is stated to have commonly ridden an ordinary pack pony or the like, leading the war horse, which he reserved for battle or other vital occasions.[55] Richardson says the Comanche war horse was never ridden except in battle or in important hunts.[56] The same reservation is affirmed by Gilbert Wilson's Hidatsa informants in the case of their own tribe, but only with reference to the "buffalo runners," war not being mentioned.[57] The only documentary source I have found is Henry A. Boller (1868), whose work I have myself been unable to see, and of whom I know nothing more.[58]

Against the foregoing view of the horse as a dragoon's transport asset rather than a cavalry arm in direct action, the preference for proceeding afoot might have stemmed from prudential more than from psychological reasons. It could very sensibly be urged that the use of the horse in actual attack upon hostile encampments swarming with other horses and with innumerable dogs would be fatal to any hope of secrecy, the supremely vital element in Indian warfare, and that this was the deciding factor in leaving the horses behind.[59] Grinnell notes the extreme precautions that were taken to preclude detection by sharp-scented animals. He states that war parties on horse-stealing expeditions sometimes killed and ate horses.

[54] Coues (ed.), *Henry-Thompson Journals*, I, 435.
[55] Dobie, *The Mustangs*, 47.
[56] Richardson, *The Comanche Barrier*, 28.
[57] Wilson, "Horse and Dog in Hidatsa Culture," 181, 193.
[58] Henry A. Boller, *Eight Years in the Far West, 1858–1866*, 225.
[59] See Dobie on the sense of smell (*The Mustangs*, 113–19, 236, 238–39).

When this was done the leader of the party was always careful to warn his men to wash themselves thoroughly with sand, or mud and water, before they went near the enemy's camp. Horses greatly dread the smell of horseflesh or of horse fat, and will not suffer the approach of anyone smelling of it.[60]

This is corroborated by Chief Buffalo Child Long Lance, the Blackfoot scholar, from whose tribe Grinnell, an intimate student of the Blackfoot, may have derived his information.[61] This practice would of course require to be followed whenever a horse had been slain for food; but the argument would prove too much. As I have remarked regarding other phases of horse psychology, such insight into the horse's likes and dislikes requires time. It cannot be attained by the inspiration of a moment. It seems inconceivable that the vital element of surprise in warfare, with its complicated technical minutiae of scouting and what we term "camouflage," so indispensably essential to the successful consummation of the surprise theory, could have attained its position as the fundamental key-tactic of all their military science, a position so entirely dominant as to be virtually unassailable even by such an unparalleled phenomenon as the horse, other than by the gradual processes of an extended period of time. Such a period, we may be quite certain, would be vastly longer than that which has elapsed since the first coming of the horse into Indian life.

I do not accept the exclusively economic interpretation of history as some historical students would appear to do. The economic motive alone cannot explain the fanatical stupidity of a Philip II or a Louis XIV in slaughtering or banishing large numbers of the most economically valuable of their subjects. None the less, it can no more be ignored among Indians than anywhere else. Marian Smith considers there is "no reason to believe . . . that the prevalence of horse stealing rested upon a purely economic motive." The animal possessed a considerable 'ostentation value as a feature in the emphasis on gift giving.'[62] With refer-

[60] Grinnell, in Hodge, *Handbook*, I, 570.
[61] Chief Buffalo Child Long Lance, *Long Lance*, 69.
[62] Smith, "War Complex of the Plains Indians," 433; cf. Lowie, *The Crow Indians*, 228.

ence to the horse solely, the crucial word *purely* reduces our respective positions to something very like agreement. The data presented in Jablow's important monograph (under Marian Smith's own editorship) concerning the Cheyenne and other tribes, and particularly in relation to the "Comanche barrier" mentioned above and the large numbers involved, render certain economic aspects undeniable.[63] In view of the fact that economic causes of Indian wars are recorded by competent observers in widely sundered territories, and among tribes which never became horse Indians in the true Plains connotation, it appears very probable that economic influences quite apart from the horse were a material force in the Plains area.

In that region the supreme governing influence above all was the buffalo. I consider that the buffalo would operate as a cause of war or peace (perhaps also in other phases of political action) in the direct ratio to its importance in the tribal economy as a source of subsistence. A number of historical instances will serve to illustrate the wide and varied workings of the economic urge.

William Bartram, the early scientific traveler (1773), noted among the semi-agricultural tribes of Georgia and Florida that, in addition to hunting-ground disputes, wars were also caused by the necessity for newer and richer areas for their plantations.[64]

Daniel W. Harmon, a fur trader of the Northwest Company, whose experience was acquired (1800 onward) in the northern forest territories as well as among the Saskatchewan Plains tribes, mentions among the general causes of Indian wars that "sometimes the members of one tribe have hunted on the lands of another."[65]

It would be wholly illogical, even if we possessed no direct evidence whatever, to exclude from the workings of such influences the most typical portion of all the western buffalo habitat, the Plains; some of whose tribes almost totally neglected agriculture (as well as almost every other source of livelihood apart from buffalo[66]), and none of whom could very securely rely even upon

---

[63] Jablow, *The Cheyenne*, 24, 62, 68, 70, etc.
[64] Bartram, *Travels* (ed. by Van Doren), 314.   [65] Harmon, *Journal*, 309.
[66] La Vérendrye, 1738: "We were going among people who did not know how to kill the beaver, and covered themselves only with ox-skin" ("Journal" [ed. by Brymner], 7; *Journals* [ed. by Burpee], 301). On the absence of fishing in the bison area, see Wissler, *The American Indian*, 220; cf. also Katharine Coman, *Economic Beginnings of the Far West*, II, 77.

such agriculture as they practiced.[67] For we may repeat that the buffalo, despite their prodigious numbers, and regardless of the sonorous platitudes on the "regular migration," were about as erratic and undependable a species as our earth has ever seen. As we have noted above, even the Plains tribes had learned by bitter experience what starvation meant.[68] It is not among such game species that the inquirer of today may expect to discover any exception to the laws of supply and demand in regard to human needs.

We are not, however, without direct evidence, and it exists in some abundance. Father Marquette, in the Illinois or upper Mississippi territory about 1670, writes thus: "These people . . . are wretchedly provided with food, for they dare not go and hunt wild cattle [buffalo] on account of their Enemies."[69]

Similarly, La Vérendrye found the Mandan in 1738 "afraid to go far from their villages because of their enemies, the Pananas and Pananis."[70] Seventy years later the younger Alexander Henry bears identical testimony concerning the same tribe in the same situation: "These people always hunt in large parties, as the continual danger from their numerous enemies obliges them to be very cautious in leaving their villages."[71]

On the upper Missouri plains, this factor in Indian life was well recognized. It has been recorded by Lewis and Clark,[72] the Astorians,[73] and Father De Smet,[74] in addition to plainsmen and historians since the earlier days.[75] Ross Cox (1812) writes thus concerning the retaliatory forays of the Blackfoot and the Flathead on either side of the Rockies: "The only cause assigned by the natives of whom I write, for their perpetual warfare, is their love of

---

[67] Maximilian, on the Arikara's having to abandon their Missouri River villages owing to crop failures, 1832: *Travels*, in Thwaites, *Travels*, XXII, 335; cf. De Smet, *Letters and Sketches*, in Thwaites, *Travels*, XXIX, 196.

[68] See Roe, *North American Buffalo*, 543–670.

[69] Marquette, in Thwaites (ed.), *Jesuit Relations*, LIX, 157.

[70] La Vérendrye, "Journal" (ed. by Brymner), 13, 19, 21; *Journals* (ed. by Burpee), 312, 355.

[71] Coues (ed.), *Henry-Thompson, Journals*, I, 336.

[72] Lewis and Clark, *Journals* (ed. by Biddle), I, 218, 220.

[73] Irving, *Astoria*, 231–33.

[74] Chittenden and Richardson (eds.), *Life of De Smet*, I, 360; II, 533; IV, 1375.

[75] Dodge, *Our Wild Indians*, 380; Chittenden, *American Fur Trade*, II, 854.

the buffalo."[76] Alexander Ross (1820) says of the Nez Percé and the Snake (Shoshone) people: "Their occupations are war and buffalo-hunting."[77] It is true that the tribes in that area at large were in possession of the horse at the era to which these witnesses refer; but considered in the light of the general evidence we have reviewed, it is extremely improbable that all these enmities were of only recent origin. The horse was doubtless only the passive "legatee" and perpetuator of ancient hatreds. And other buffalo-engendered tribal wars and antipathies were certainly anterior to the acquisition of the horse.

Alexander Henry the elder, who had a long experience of the tribes he mentions, says of the Chippewa (Ojibwa) and the Sioux in the period 1760–1776: "The cause of the perpetual war between these two nations, is this, that both claim, as their exclusive hunting-ground, the tract of country which lies between them."[78] A competent plainsman-scholar tells us that the long enmity between the Cheyenne and the Assiniboin is said to have originated in a quarrel about a herd of buffalo that each tribe was trying to surround. Such an occurrence must almost inevitably have taken place before either tribe acquired the horse,[79] or at some period apparently between about 1675 and 1705, the Cheyenne migrated from the neighborhood of the Sheyenne River in North Dakota to a locality farther to the southwest, where the Assiniboin were hardly likely to be encountered.[80] Buffalo are also said to have been the cause of the separation of the Hidatsa from the Crow.[81] Buffalo in historic times were repeatedly the occasion of bloody outbreaks

[76] Ross Cox, *The Columbia River*, I, 216–19; II, 133.

[77] Alexander Ross, *Adventures of the First Settlers on the Oregon or Columbia River*, in Thwaites, *Travels*, VII, 215.

[78] *Travels and Adventures*, 197.

[79] W. D. Strong, "From History to Prehistory in the Northern Great Plains," 359; Jablow, *The Cheyenne*, 9–10.

[80] Grinnell, who mentions the buffalo surround episode, has them reaching the Missouri about 1676 (*The Fighting Cheyennes*, 4–5), and considers they did not get the horse until about 1780 (in Hodge, *Handbook*, I, 569). See also Thwaites, *Travels*, XXIII, 333; XXVII, 161, editor's notes. Later scholars date their removal some time after 1700: see Wedel, "Culture Sequences in the Central Great Plains," 327; Strong, "From History to Prehistory in the Northern Great Plains," 359, 370–73, 376; Jablow, *The Cheyenne*, 9–10, etc.

[81] Maximilian, *Travels*, in Thwaites, *Travels*, XXIII, 367.

between the Northern (Canadian) Blackfoot and the Cree,[82] and may well have been a feature in the original source of their animosities, although Mandelbaum's native informants (presumably) considered the horse to have been the foremost *casus belli* between the Cree and their enemies, principally Blackfoot.[83] A critic of very high standing is rather suspicious of some of these traditions of the "original causes" of this or the other long-established conditions of tribal relations. He points out that traditions of this type are found in more than one tribe.[84] In respect of such a commonplace factor as buffalo, however, there is nothing at all farfetched in the supposition that such situations could actually arise in far more than one pair of tribes. Whether buffalo were actually the cause or not, the relatively late dating of the horse in these respective tribes renders it virtually certain that their persistent mutual hatreds are far older than their horsemanship.

Another factor of some significance may be noted in relation to the economic interpretation of Indian wars. One of the most aggressively and ferociously war-loving Indian "military states" ever known on the North American continent, the aforesaid League of the Iroquois, consisted of tribes who were aboriginally perhaps as independent of external economic forces as any people could ever hope to be. For, being agriculturists when at home (and on a relatively extensive scale),[85] in a generally favorable region, and furthermore enjoying, by reason of the terror they inspired over a wide range of country, a greater degree of immunity against attack than almost any other tribe, the Iroquois could probably have had little occasion in their career to have to fight to defend their

---

[82] For Blackfoot and Cree hostilities see, among others, Simpson, *Journey Around the World*, I, 107 ff.; Rundle, "Journal" (ed. by Berry and Roe, particularly February to August, 1841; John McDougall, *In the Days of the Red River Rebellion*, 118; *Western Trails*, 172; Cowie, *Company of Adventurers*, 239, 304, 314; (Gen.) Sam B. Steele, *Forty Years in Canada*, 56–80, 116, 137, 276; John Hawkes, *Saskatchewan and Her People*, I, 149–55; MacInnes, *In the Shadow of the Rockies*, 96–99; Sir Cecil Denny MS., 34.

[83] Mandelbaum, "The Plains Cree," 195.

[84] Kroeber, "Ethnology of the Gros Ventre," 146.

[85] See Lescarbot (1612), *History of New France*, (ed. by Biggar), III, 28; Walter Hough, in Hodge, *Handbook*, I, 466; Cyrus Thomas, in Hodge, *Handbook*, I, 790; Fiske, *Discovery of America*, I, 27–29, 292; Long, *History of the Canadian People*, I, 36, 232 ff., etc.

subsistence. Yet one may wonder whether more inveterate war-mongers ever lived.

In this connection an anthropologist of the very foremost rank advances a thought-provoking and apparently very probable suggestion. War among Indians was not in his opinion what it is—at least in theory—among the white peoples: a mere final expedient when negotiation has failed, in order to secure some definite desideratum such as the vindication of the "national honor," or the attainment of some specific territorial or economic objective, which, when achieved, automatically terminated the war, and allowed a conventionally normal condition of peace to prevail once more. To the Indian, war was rather a state of mind, from which it followed logically that victory in the field, or the attainment of some professed objective for which the war was ostensibly waged, was a mere phase or incident, in no sense constituting any reason for terminating that or any war.[86] If this reasoning is sound—and the name of Alfred L. Kroeber carries immense weight on such questions—it becomes difficult to understand how such a concept could fail to spread, from the mere impulse of self-preservation, throughout the entire Indian world with which its first or principal demonstrators or exponents came into contact.

As against this conception of Iroquois psychology, a later critic offers another suggestion in an essay which I regret having had no opportunity to see. The scholar in question considers that an underlying cause of the Iroquois war policy was the necessity of obtaining captives for adoption. This procedure, of which the well-known instance of the Tuscarora (adopted by the Iroquois circa 1722) is an outstanding illustration, is regarded by this writer as having been the rule rather than the exception.[87]

This concept seems in a quite fundamental sense to put the cart before the horse. Had there been any antecedent necessity for those terrific war expeditions of the Iroquois, which covered the northern continent from Ontario to below the Ohio Valley and from the Atlantic seaboard to the Missouri, the necessity for adopting some convenient method of keeping up their military strength

[86] Kroeber, *Cultural and Natural Areas in Native North America*, 148.

[87] George S. Snyderman, "Behind the Tree of Peace: A Sociological Analysis of Iroquois Warfare," *Pennsylvania Archaeologist*, Vol. XVIII (1948), 2–93. For the Tuscarora, see Hodge, *Handbook*, II, 842–53.

would obviously be forced upon them also. Considered historically, however, the war lust seems clearly to have antedated the need for such adoptions, and was actually their motivating cause. Neither does this hypothesis explain why other tribes would decide (or even dare) to offer what was all too commonly a hopeless resistance to the dreaded Iroquois, if adoption were the worst they had to fear. It is almost more difficult still to explain the dread itself, which was felt by tribes at enormous distances and in directions seemingly remote from danger.[88] In the original basic conception more particularly, we may note the appalling contrast between war as the Iroquois made war, and the post-equestrian condition in the Plains area, to which I have earlier drawn attention, where in countless cases since the coming of the horse the same essential passions could find vent and satisfaction without a tithe of the shedding of human blood. It must be considered extremely improbable, whatever the true interpretation of the ferocious Iroquois psychology may be, that its development would be deferred until as late an era as the coming of the European and his horse; especially with tribes *which waged war on foot.*

I have maintained the conception of Indian contratribal animosities and warfare, with their resultant deeply-rooted antipathies and hatreds as a condition reaching back probably to immemorial eras, on the basis of historical evidence. The field of social anthropology yields some curious results in confirmation. The immense profusion of Indian languages and dialects is very generally regarded by philological science as an almost self-evident implication of a more or less normal condition of passive (when it was not active) social enmity, or at least isolation.[89] In this particular province of *unwritten* languages, less open

[88] On this dread among the distant Mistassini Cree of the James Bay regions, see "Recent Publications Relating to Canada," *Canadian Historical Review,* Vol. XXX (1949), 202.

[89] About 1890 opinion varied between 400 and 1,264, the question being which were languages and which dialects; see Fiske, *Discovery of America,* I, 38, 48. Some interesting facts on Indian languages, though his conclusions require revision, in Bancroft, *Native Races,* III, 574–722. See further, Franz Boas, in Hodge, *Handbook,* I, 757; Alexander F. Chamberlain, in Hodge, *Handbook,* I, 766; "North American Indians," *Encyclopaedia Britannica.* An admirable review, summarized

to extraneous influences arising from alien users, this must almost necessarily have prevailed for long ages. The converse history of the English language tends to support this hypothesis by logical induction. We know at least that its immense receptivity to foreign terms arose from the precisely opposite social condition: world-wide travel and association with speakers of many tongues.

The etymology of many Indian tribal names reveals an unsocial attitude of mind. Their self-bestowed tribal designations fall quite frequently into the Jew-and-Gentile, Greek-and-barbarian, ourselves-and-*outsiders*, *we*-and-*they* categories, indicative of a higher order which the "foreigner" cannot attain. The Comanche, for example, term themselves "Nērm" or Nĭm'ma," signifying the (*the* ?) people."[90] ThePlain Cree tribal term is "*nehɪawak;* a term [adds Mandelbaum] which cannot be etymologized to my knowledge."[91] A scholarly missionary-philologist stated over sixty years ago that "Naheyownk" signifies "the exact people."[92] This is the same word as David Thompson's "Nahathaway." Thompson's editor, J. B. Tyrrell, himself a Cree scholar, traces the phonetic change from "nath" to "nahe" in the growth of the word.[93] Names of this type are characteristic of many lands and ages.[94]

Among those names bestowed by Indians upon other Indian tribes, friends and allies seem frequently to be distinguished by honorably descriptive names, topographical or otherwise. "Dakota," for instance, is said to signify "friendly."[95] One would need

to 1932, in Jenness, *Indians of Canada*, 17–27. Franz Boas considers attempts to reduce Indian languages to a few linguistic stocks "not very satisfactory" (Diamond Jenness [ed.], *The American Aborigines*, 367). An informative discussion on the relation of a polyglot race to the sedentary life (as advanced long ago by Black, *History of Saskatchewan*, 94), in Steward, "Native Cultures of the Intermontane Area," 476. In any event, the inveterate enmities of Cree and Blackfoot (both Algonquian) and of Sioux and Mandan *et al.* (both Siouan) overrode linguistic or any other form of kinship.

[90] Richardson, *The Comanche Barrier*, 16.

[91] Mandelbaum, "The Plains Cree," 169.

[92] (Rev.) John McLean, *Indians of Canada*, 254. Father Lacombe's monumental *Dictionnaire de la Langue des Cris* (p. x) cites "Nehiyawok," but is dubious: "*Les Cris s'appellent dans leur langue* Nehiyawok, *mot dont la signification n'est pas certaine. Cependant il paraîtrait que ça veut dire la même chose que* iyiniwok, *les vrais hommes, les êtres de première race.*"

[93] Thompson, *Narrative* (ed. by Tyrrell), 79, editor's note.

[94] A host of examples in Isaac Taylor, *Words and Places*, 55–79.

[95] Cyrus Thomas, *The Indians of North America in Historic Times*, in G. C. Lee and F. N. Thorpe (eds.), *The History of North America*, II, 325.

to know who bestowed the name; the more so when we compare
"Sioux." What we should term nicknames are very often found
to betoken contempt or active hatred.[96] "Mohawk" is said to signify "cannibal."[97] Chipewyans are *ouant Chipouanes* ("dwellers in
holes").[98] The Atsina (otherwise Fall, or "Gros Ventre—'Big Bellies'
—of the Prairie," a branch of the Arapaho, after whom Belly River,
southern Alberta, is named) are "beggars" or "spongers,"[99] also
"gut,"[100] which looks like a translation. The Sarsi or Sarcee are
given as "sa arsi" ("not good" in Siksika [Blackfoot]).[101] The famous
name "Sioux" comes from "Nadowe-is-iw," in its French form
Nadessioux, which means in Chippewa or Ojibwa "snake" or "ad-
der," that is to say, "enemy."[102] We may compare the Hidatsa description of the same tribe, which is anything but complimentary.[103]
"Apache" is a Pueblo word signifying "enemy," which was applied
by the Spaniards to the Navajo and other hostiles.[104] The Kutenai
names for certain tribes are of the same character. The Siksika are
"Sahantla" ("bad people"); the Assiniboin are "Tlutlamaeka" ("cut-
throats"); and the Cree are "Gutskiawe" ("liars.")[105] It is probable
that further investigation would yield many more very similar
examples.

Nor were these etymological characterizations mere abstract
or historical conceptions which had ceased to possess living significance, as with so many of our own English names which are
now *names* only and nothing more. In the course of a fairly wide
review of first European contacts with almost every Indian tribe
on the northern continent during three centuries or more, I have
not found an instance of any tribe according an otherwise than
friendly reception to the white strangers on their *first* meeting.
Yet such Indians, as we have seen, were quite commonly enemies

[96] A very good note by Thwaites on these principles of Indian nomenclature,
in *Jesuit Relations*, LIX, 319. See also Hodge, *Handbook,* under Abenaki, Athabaska,
Blood, Chipewyan, Kutenai, Minatari, Hidatsa, Piegan, Potawatomi, Sarsi, etc.
[97] *Ibid.,* I, 921.
[98] Thwaites (ed.), *Jesuit Relations,* LXVIII, 251, 332, editor's note.
[99] Hodge, *Handbook,* I, 113.
[100] George Bird Grinnell, *Blackfoot Lodge Tales,* 244.
[101] Hodge, *Handbook,* II, 467.
[102] *Ibid.,* II, 577. See also (Rev.) John McLean, *Canadian Savage Folk,* 103–20.
[103] Larpenteur, *Forty Years a Fur Trader* (ed. by Coues), II, 383.
[104] Dobie, *The Mustangs,* 37.
[105] Chamberlain, in Hodge, *Handbook,* I, 740.

of the tribe "on the other side of the river." I have also referred to the crowning folly of taking sides in an Indian war, since very commonly in Indian psychology the friend of their enemies was their enemy likewise.[106] This form of intervention cost the life of the younger La Vérendrye in 1736, at the hands of the Sioux, and his father was prepared to repeat the error by joining the Cree, Assiniboin, Mandan, or anyone else, to avenge his son upon the slayers, which would probably have cost many more lives.[107]

But it must be recorded to the honor of the Indians that the *guest* of their enemy was not necessarily their enemy likewise. In later eras, when relations between the red and the white races had become dubious or positively hostile—doubtless with some immediate reason on both sides—and were recognized as being such, we none the less find that such men as George Catlin and Marcus Whitman could pass back and forth among the Plains tribes unarmed and unhurt. Yet it was perfectly well known to their Indian hosts that either from necessity or from choice these men had lodged in the camps and had eaten the meat of their tribal enemies.

It was not at all an unheard-of thing for a chief to assure the visiting stranger how completely safe he might consider himself; that "no white man's blood had ever been shed in their village." At the same time the traveler is warned most earnestly to be on his guard while staying with the treacherous and bloodthirsty murderers "over the hill," or "across the river," who would pay no regard to hospitality or any other decent restraint. In due course the (very probably suspicious) pilgrim meets with an equally cordial welcome from these people so much to be dreaded, who marvel openly that he has escaped with his life from the unscrupulous red-handed miscreants he has just quitted.[108]

This (historically rather amusing) propensity has found abundant mention in the early literature. Zebulon M. Pike in 1805 described the "Yanctongs" (Sioux)—on what ground beyond hearsay we are not told—as "the most savage band of the Sioux"; but their chief proudly declared that "white blood had never been shed in

[106] See note 4 *supra.*
[107] Thwaites (ed.), *Jesuit Relations,* LXX, 251–53; La Vérendrye, *Journals* (ed. by Burpee), 174, 208–39, 262–74, 295–96, 321.
[108] See Maximilian, *Travels,* in Thwaites, *Travels,* XXIII, 387; James Mooney, in Hodge, *Handbook,* I, 571.

the village of the Yanctongs, even when rum was permitted."[109] On the same journey the Winnebago were described to Pike by the chief of a neighboring tribe as being "brave . . . but a white man should never lie down to sleep without precaution in their villages."[110] Elsewhere Pike mentions that a small camp of "Sacs" (Sauk) received him courteously, yet he states later that with the Sac "all strangers were enemies,"[111] which sounds rather like a local cliché.[112]

In the same year, 1805, we find the Hidatsa warning Larocque against the "Cayennes" and "Ricaras"—"who would probably murder him." They also gave the worst possible character to the "Rocky Mountain Indians" (Crow). Larocque himself, the very man to whom these sinister warnings were given, says this of the Crow: "Any person of any nation going to their Camp will be well treated and received, but when coming at night or seen skulking about need not expect mercy."[113] This is precisely in keeping with the Saxon "Law of Ine" (King of Wessex, 688–726), under which any man approaching through the wood without sounding his horn might lawfully be slain as a thief.[114] Yet we should not dream of portraying our Anglo-Saxon forefathers as "savages" upon any such basis. It is a bitter commentary upon later history that the friendly Apache (of all people!) warned Jacob Fowler in 1821 against the "Utaws" (Utes).[115]

There is an unconscious humor in some of these manifestations. The Comanche in 1851 refused to go to Fort Laramie for a general council of the Plains tribes with the United States government. "They said they had too many good horses and mules to risk on such a journey among such horse thieves as the Sioux and Crow."[116]

Perhaps no tribe have had more opprobrium heaped upon them on both sides of the International Boundary than the Blackfoot. Their two earliest English-speaking visitors, Antony Henday and

---

[109] Coues (ed.), *Expeditions of Pike*, I, 208.

[110] *Ibid.*, I, 340.

[111] *Ibid.*, I, 5, 20.

[112] It is quite certain they would never say this themselves, *to the man they were receiving!*

[113] Larocque, "Journal" (ed. by Burpee), 16–20, 65.

[114] J. M. Kemble, *The Saxons in England*, I, 46, 260.

[115] Fowler, *Journal* (ed. by Coues), 137.

[116] Richardson, *The Comanche Barrier*, 183.

Matthew Cocking (1754, 1772), who both wintered among them, considered them "very kind people."[117] The change in their attitude is ascribed by contemporary and later critics to the action of Meriwether Lewis in shooting a Blackfoot thief.[118] Doubt has been thrown upon this conclusion: years ago by Wissler,[119] who was aware of Henday and Cocking; and more recently by Bernard De Voto, who apparently is not, since he cites no testimony earlier than Lewis and Clark themselves. The bitterness of the Blackfoot against white men is attributed to a native ferocity, accentuated (in the opinion of Chittenden and others) by John Colter's having assisted the Crow against the Blackfoot.[120] The tradition lost nothing in the telling. John K. Townsend wrote in 1834: "The Blackfoot is a sworn and determined foe to all white men, and he has often been heard to declare that he would rather hang the scalp of a paleface to his girdle, than kill a buffalo to prevent his starving."[121] That, from a stranger in the land, may be classed as typically loose, campfire talk. Who had ever heard the Blackfoot say it?

We have no means of ascertaining definitely just what it was that changed the Blackfoot, nor even whether any change ever occurred of so far-reaching a character as is popularly believed. The action of a *leader* like Lewis, is a far more probable explanation—as it was to David Thompson, an experienced contemporary —than anything done by a starving rank-and-filer such as John Colter. Whatever it was, the legend of innate Blackfoot ferocity dissolves into myth in the crucible of historical fact. About the same time as Townsend, we find the Blackfoot advising Larpenteur not to go to the Flathead, for fear of the consequences.[122] Rundle the missionary (Fort Edmonton, 1840–48), heard of the Blackfoot

---

[117] Henday, "Journal" (ed. by Burpee), 316, 337, 351; Cocking, "Journal" (ed. by Burpee), 110–12, 116.

[118] See Thompson, *Narrative* (ed. by Tyrrell), 375; Irving, *Astoria*, 120, 130–31, 136, 164; also his *Captain Bonneville*, 58–59, 152, 276; Hebard and Brininstool, *The Bozeman Trail*, I, 30–31.

[119] Wissler, "Material Culture of the Blackfoot Indians," 11.

[120] De Voto, *Across the Wide Missouri*, 82, 139, 421, 430. De Voto has evidently bolted the legend whole, "hook, line, and sinker." He speaks of a certain episode (p. 82)—"the right way to treat Blackfeet"—in a tone not applied to any other tribe.

[121] Townsend, *Narrative*, in Thwaites, *Travels*, XXI, 214–15; cf. Brackenridge (1811), *View of Louisiana*, in Thwaites, *Travels*, VI, 28.

[122] Larpenteur, *Forty Years a Fur Trader* (ed. by Coues), II, 276.

both from the Cree and the traders. On his first trip to Rocky Mountain House (not yet thirty and four months in the country) he met a kindly welcome from a party thought to be Mountain Cree, but who proved to be the dreaded Blackfoot! On his return journey, with only a (Blackfoot) guide for company, he met the redoubtable governor, George Simpson—with a guard of twenty armed men.[123] Rundle and Father De Smet were the only men of the eighteen forties who traversed the Blackfoot country alone; no others dared. Captain John Palliser in 1857 was similarly warned against the Blackfoot by the Cree;[124] but although he does not himself say so, some of his colleagues—like many critics since—thought the Blackfoot the better of the two.[125] It may perhaps be urged that these examples are late, and may possibly apply to some milder type of Northern Blackfoot. David Thompson was traversing the Lewis and Clark country both before and after their passing. There is nothing in his accounts that indicates any special apprehension of danger from the Blackfoot.

We have noted the Hidatsa opinion of the Sioux. It was very probably the Sioux, farther down the Missouri, who furnished the following characterizations to Father De Smet in 1841: "The Arikaras and the Big Bellies [Hidatsa], who had been described to us as most dangerous, received us as friends whenever we met them on our way."[126]

Marcus Whitman (Oregon, 1835–47) has recorded this propensity among the transmontane tribes, though his editor, Archer B. Hulbert, has in my judgment completely misinterpreted it. The missionary writes thus: "The Nez Pierces [sic] do not like my stopping with the Cayous [Cayuse], and say that the Nez Pierces do not have difficulties with the white man, as the Cayous do; and that we will see the difference."[127] Hulbert, who cannot have real-

<hr />

123 Rundle, "Journal" (ed. by Berry and Roe), February 22, April 16–19, July 29, 1841; Simpson, *Journey Around the World*, I, 58–59, 107–10.

124 Palliser, *Journals*, 53, 55.

125 (Lieut.) Thomas Blakiston, "Report on the Exploration of the Kootanie and Boundary Passes of the Rocky Mountains in 1858," *Occasional Papers of the Royal Artillery Institution*, 253; Steele (1874 et seq.), *Forty Years in Canada*, 71, 80, 115; Father Scollen and Governor Laird (1877), in Alexander Morris, *Treaties with the Indians of Manitoba and the North-West Territories*, 247–49, 253–54; John Macoun (1879), *Autobiography*, 149; McClintock, *Old North Trail*.

126 De Smet, *Letters and Sketches*, in Thwaites, *Travels*, XXVII, 184.

ized the wide prevalence of these tribal innuendos, treats this as
an isolated instance of such, and (by a double fallacy) regards it
as evidence of psychological change from servility to insolence produced in the Cayuse tribe by the owning and trading of horses. He
apparently attributes Whitman's disregard of the warning (and
hence the final catastrophe) to an unwise excess of the charity that
thinketh no evil.[128] It is probable that the missionary had heard
these gloomy intimations so often in his transcontinental journeys
that they had lost their power to impress him. The supposition
that these contratribal insinuations are in any way conditional or
consequent upon changes arising from the advent of the horse is
wholly untenable, for they were encountered again and again by
the first transmontane explorer to reach the Pacific Coast in the
northern area, and in a region which was not then and which never
became horse Indian territory. I refer to Alexander Mackenzie in
the year 1793.[129]

The cumulative effect of the foregoing data has been to convince me that the conventional "bloodthirsty savage" of tradition
is a composite portrait, built up from the *Indians'* descriptions of
their own tribal enemies in particular, in which the worst of characteristics are alone emphasized. These have been interpreted literally and fused into one as being typical of all Indians, propagated
with unscrupulous avidity by men who had something to gain
thereby, and in turn accepted in good faith by others who were
in no position to judge for themselves.

Beyond reasonable doubt tribal wars prevailed from remote
ages. Taken in combination, the various considerations we have
discussed, illustrations of which could be greatly extended, render
the contrary conclusion unthinkable to me: that the originating
causes of so ingrained a propensity as war could have been in any
degree dependent upon so late an innovation in the Plains world
as the historic horse. In a passage which was not published until
long after my own first expression to the foregoing effect was al-

[127] A. B. and D. P. Hulbert (eds.), *Marcus Whitman*, I, 71, 76–77, 234; cf.
II, 1–20.

[128] *Ibid.*, I, 71. The Whitmans were murdered, 1847, by the Cayuse.

[129] Sir Alexander Mackenzie, *Voyages from Montreal . . . in 1789 and 1793,*
115, 177, 182, 184–85, 219, 215–52.

ready in the printer's hands, the most authoritative student of the Plains concept of war writes almost identically:

Both the horse and the gun loomed large among the 'indirect Caucasian influences' which rocketed the Plains area to a 'cultural intoxication' which is hardly precedented in anthropological annals. With due consideration to their cultural importance, there is, however, no conclusive evidence that they revolutionized war procedure. Apparently their effect was not radically to change the existing war complexes, but to accelerate the momentum of warfare.[130]

[130] Smith, "War Complex of the Plains Indians," 432. See also Alice C. Fletcher, in Hodge, *Handbook*, II, 914.

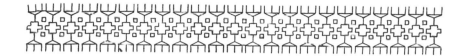

XIII

INDIANS AS HORSE MASTERS

In any attempt to ascertain something of the methods or processes by which the Indians acquired a more or less material degree of skill in caring for their horses, this question seems to divide itself naturally into two phases. The first of these is direct imitation, as in the primary article of riding itself, or as we have seen above—if the legend instanced by Denhardt may be relied upon—in the making of the first Mexican saddle.[1] The second is natural induction from observed facts, or what in everyday life we should probably call "gumption" or "savvy." We cannot doubt that the latter agency had taught them much of the lore connected with their aboriginal domesticated creature, the dog; for example, the futility of feeding their train dogs until the day's work was done, if they expected it to be done at all. The northern *voyageurs* speedily learned the wisdom of this from the Indians, and it became a credo equally among both. In this phase of our inquiry, moreover, as in every other, we must keep in mind that while we speak of "the Indians" doing this or that—since we have no other phrase—it is extremely improbable that their "horse education" followed along uniform lines with tribes any more than with individuals. In fact, we have their own implied assertion that it did not.

As we have seen to be the case with the acquisition of the horse itself, our chronological evidence in this particular department is painfully meager. The earliest notice of any special care for Indian horses that I have been able to discover is not until 1683. In that year, Juan Sabeata, a baptized Jumano, described the Texas (Tejas

[1] See Chapter IX *supra.*

or Teyas) as being "a settled people who raised grain in such abundance that they even fed it to their horses."[2] The somewhat incredulous tone of this allusion almost suggests that the Spaniards themselves had not sufficient grain for that purpose, although it may express mere astonishment at Indians doing this. In any case one must suppose that the Spaniards possibly had never heard of such a thing before, as it seems they would have done had it been practiced on the western side of the Río Grande; but this may actually have been the first instance. It has been seen above that Spanish horses were taken into Texas as early as 1650. In fact, if Denhardt's datings are correct, there seems a possibility as early as 1625.[3] We thus have no means of judging whether the grain-fed horses were a condition of rather long standing not previously known, or a much later and comparatively recent innovation. We must surely in any event conclude that the possession of horses among the Texas themselves preceded the grain feeding perhaps by a good many years.

Wissler cites a most interesting comment which indicates a rather rapid spread northward of a knowledge of winter horse care in tribes which almost certainly had no cereal crops to spare for horses. The comment refers to the Pawnee (1704), only some twenty years after Sabeata's statement, and reads as follows:

[The Pawnee] went into winter quarters in some places where water, wood, and unburnt grass in abundance for the horses were to be had. Here they remained till forage became scarce, when another place was sought. If grass could not be found in sufficient quantity, they cut cottonwood trees, and subsisted the horses on the bark and tender twigs. The return to the villages did not take place till the young grass was started in the spring.[4]

The significant feature in this recital is that at this relatively early date the Indians had already acquired a familiar mastery of what was *in esse* (or was to become) the standard native practice throughout the horse range where winter feeding was required. It would be of interest to learn whether the Indian winter practice

2 Bolton (ed.), *Spanish Exploration in the Southwest*, 315.
3 See Chapter IV *supra*.
4 Cited by Wissler, "Influence of the Horse," 20.

was a native concept, or was acquired from the Spaniards. In the English royal forests it was for centuries the standard regulation to cut branches ("deer-browse") for the deer in severe weather.[5] I have also read of such expedients, for horses, in the Continental wars of Europe.

In 1525, when Cortés' famous black charger, *El Morzillo,* had to be left behind on the Honduras expedition with a splinter in its foot, the Indian village to whose charge the animal was committed brought fruit and chickens for provender, which the horse not unnaturally refused.[6] Those days had been left far behind! It may be noted further that the Pawnee are not to be regarded as a specially adaptable tribe, far in advance of any others, for they themselves were among those—it would seem—who in early times acclaimed the Comanche as the horse Indians par excellence.[7]

Exactly half a century after the foregoing description of the Pawnee, Antony Henday found similar practices in use among the Northern Blackfoot, and these bands, as we have seen, apparently ranged as far north as the Forks of the Saskatchewan (53° N). If we take the Arkansas River as the mean of the Pawnee range about 1704, from that point (38° N) to the Forks represents fifteen parallels of latitude, or some 1,050 miles in a direct line northward: a distance which is known to have been spanned in fifty years or less by a most important cultural achievement.

Henday noted the Blackfoot women in January, 1755, "getting grass for the horses," and later observed "horses feeding on willow tops," and getting thinner. I have thus far found no notice of haymaking by Indians prior to the white era; and getting in standing grass in sufficient quantities even in the best of central Alberta winters (which are commonly the mildest in the northern latitudes) would be a toilsome and starvation task for women and horses respectively. This item of winter horse care may reasonably be considered as the culmination of an expert mastery which covered every aspect of the field. In addition to hunting buffalo on horseback and riding as the common usage, there were mounted scouting, use of horses as draft animals with 'birch sleds' in winter, swim-

[5] See on this, G. J. Turner, *Select Pleas of the Forest;* J. Charles Cox, *The Royal Forests of England.*
[6] Cunninghame Graham, *Horses of the Conquest,* 32-40.
[7] See Chapter IV *supra.*

ming 'broad and deep rivers,' together with 'good horses,' and 'the best horsemen [Henday] ever saw.'[8] A century after Henday the Blackfoot method of swimming rivers with horses was to ride in until the horse lost his footing, then slip off his back and hold on by the tail.[9] All the Blackfoot in the old days were expected to be good horsemen and swimmers.[10]

There are some few rather fragmentary notices of winter feeding practices in the intermediate territory. To be in the vicinity of cottonwoods was an important factor at that season. "The location of winter camps in the central Missouri River territory was partly determined by accessibility of cottonwoods." The Assiniboin and other tribes "turned horses loose to winter on range well supplied with cottonwood. They would not drift off. Only during the worst spells of weather were many horses hand-fed,"[11] and commonly these were selected animals only. Larocque writes thus, September 23, 1805: ". . . having been unable to find grass for our horses throughout the day we were obliged to cut down three Lairs [*liards* = cottonwoods] and let the horses feed on the bark."[12]

This diet and the general winter accommodation and treatment of the northern horses of the Missouri territory met with the severe disapproval of John Bradbury, the English naturalist who journeyed westward with the Astorians in 1811. He writes as follows:

The Arikaras do not provide any better for their horses than the other nations of the Missouri. They cut down the cottonwood (*Populus angulosa*) and the horses feed on the bark and smaller branches. I have seen instances exhibiting proofs that these poor animals have eaten branches two inches in diameter.[13]

Bradbury would without doubt apply English standards of comfort in his horsekeeping criticisms. While this was natural and inevitable, it was none the less unjust. Bradbury may have heard it said that the horses preferred it. He would very probably put that

[8] Henday, "Journal" (ed. by Burpee), 335–51.
[9] Kane, *Wanderings of an Artist*, 112.
[10] For these, as told by native informants, see Kidd, "Blackfoot Ethnography," 37–38; cf. Jenness, *The Sarcee Indians*, 19, 28.
[11] Dobie, "Indian Horses and Horsemanship," 269; *The Mustangs*, 48.
[12] Larocque, "Journal" (ed. by Burpee), 64.
[13] Bradbury, *Travels*, in Thwaites, *Travels*, V, 175.

down as a piece of idle propaganda, to be ranked in the same class with the Negroes' "preferring" slavery, as visitors were frequently told. But he could surely never have known that during the winter stay of the Lewis and Clark party at the Mandan villages some of the visitors offered bran mash to certain of the Indian horses, but the horses rejected it, preferring the cottonwood bark to which they were accustomed.[14] Cottonwood bark was actually considered more nourishing by the Indians; doubtless because they too were more accustomed to it. Gilbert Wilson's principal Hidatsa inform- ant, Wolf-chief said "it fattened the horses." His accounts of his father's winter horse-routine (in a bitter climate) suggest a con- scientious owner who regarded the life of his beast to the utmost of his power. He would cut down trees of six to seven inches in diameter which could be burnt after the bark was stripped off;[15] although anyone who knows the wood (and the winters) will sin- cerely hope they had some other fuel to mix with the cottonwood. The Hidatsa no doubt shared the common western opinion of cot- tonwood, for they would not use it for tipi or travois poles, "pre- ferring poplar."[16] This of itself must have been a case of "Hobson's choice," when spruce or pine were not to be had.

While geographical (or topographical) situations or tempera- mental predilections produced variations in detail, the Northern tribes, with the apparent exception of the Assiniboin, seem to have recognized the need for such additional winter protection as they could furnish their horses. This would probably be realized at rela- tively early dates in their horse chronology, for by the time the

[14] Lewis and Clark, *Journals* (ed. by Thwaites), I, 258–59; *ibid.* (ed. by El- liott Coues), I, 232–33.

[15] Wilson, "Horse and Dog in Hidatsa Culture," 172–80, 208.

[16] *Ibid.*, 193. It is not altogether clear whether "cottonwood" and "poplar" sig- nify the same species or not. "Cottonwood," as in Dobie (above, note 11), was the common term among the American settlers for the three familiar species of *Populus*: White poplar or aspen (*P. tremuloides*), black poplar or "Balm of Gilead" (*P. bal- samifera*), and the true cottonwood (*P. angulosa* of Bradbury: above, note 13); *P. monilifera* of John Macoun, 1882 (*Manitoba and the Great Northwest*, 316, 322); or later, *P. Sargentii Dode* (*Native Trees of Canada*, 4th ed. [1949], 100). This last species, which gave the name to Liard River (tributary of the Mackenzie), grows to a large size in the North. I have seen them three feet in diameter, tower- ing upward to a great height without a limb, and yielding an admirable wide board for interior work; whereas *P. balsamifera* was commercially worthless, though the handsomest of all while growing. Except when specifying precisely, the ordinary Canadian usage (which we unconsciously adopted) was to speak of them generally as "poplar," which is perhaps Maximilian's sense.

earliest white observers began to penetrate into the territory the tribes had evidently adopted a settled routine. Larocque writes concerning the Crow: "They are very fond of their horses and take good care of them."[17] Nearly thirty years later (1833) Maximilian tells us: "[The Crows] are said to possess more good horses than any other tribe of the Missouri, and to send them in the winter to Wind River [Wyoming], to feed on a certain shrub which soon fattens them."[18] As we shall have occasion to notice later, the Crow were in the relatively warmer western climatic belt. The Mandan dwelt in the sterner climate of Dakota. They were even more solicitous for their horses, or at any rate for their security. Maximilian observes elsewhere: "Inside of the [Mandan] winter huts is a particular compartment, where the horses are put in the evening, and fed with maize. In the daytime, they are driven into the prairie, and fed in the bushes, on the bark of poplars."[19]

The Mandan were not the only tribe who housed their horses in the winter time, in such fashion as they could. Their close neighbors, the Hidatsa, also kept their horses—or some of them—in their lodges at night, confessedly as much for security as for warmth;[20] the housing itself would facilitate warmth. The Sioux "customarily built sheds against their winter lodges to protect selected horses from severe weather and from thieves in the night. The women provided a limited supply of hay against winter and during that season brought cottonwood bark and branches to the stabled animals. Men occasionally helped at this work. Some horses chewed up branches as thick through as a man's arm."[21] The outside shed was apparently used by the Mandan and the Hidatsa as well as the Sioux, for Larocque noted at their villages (October 1, 1805) that "Outside the fort was a kind of Stable in which the[y] kept their horses." This was a disused Mandan or Hidatsa lodge.[22]

The two tribes in question, which shared several customs and held certain views in common, termed March and April "the horses' winter." This was because "when the weather is warm, the horses

---

17 Larocque, "Journal" (ed. by Burpee), 64.
18 Maximilian, *Travels,* in Thwaites, *Travels,* XXII, 352.
19 *Ibid.,* XXIII, 272; cf. 235, 245.
20 Wilson, "Horse and Dog in Hidatsa Culture," 156–61, 174.
21 Dobie, *The Mustangs,* 48.
22 Larocque, "Journal" (ed. by Burpee), 51.

are often driven to pasture in the prairie, and then violent storms of snow sometimes occur suddenly, and destroy many of these animals."[23] Any old-timer on the Northern Plains and prairies (on which the present writer spent fifty winters) can recognize the accuracy of the description at sight.

The 'occasional assistance' of the Sioux men in the women's task of bringing in cottonwoods for horse fodder apparently went somewhat further among the Hidatsa. One gathers from the accounts given to Gilbert Wilson by his Hidatsa informant that, in their family at least, the father made it his share in the work to fell the cottonwoods, both for fuel and for horse provender,[24] which the girls brought home with their dogs. He does not state specifically that this was a tribal custom, but it seems unlikely that only one man would do it, and subject himself to the ridicule of the other men. In other tribes the men of more recent generations have receded somewhat from the ancient disdain of rendering any assistance whatever to the other sex.[25] The Hidatsa, too, make mention of bringing in 'dried grass' for the horses in winter, which would seem—as with Antony Henday's Blackfoot a century before—to have been cut as they needed it in the winter.[26] Dobie's account of 'providing against winter' rather suggests *hay* in our sense; of the cutting and putting up of which in summer I have found no notice elsewhere. This may be another instance of tribal diversities.

We must suppose that any necessity for shoeing their horses would largely be a question of the type of country in which one was traveling. This is perhaps the reason why the only allusions I have found to foot protection of any character occur in the upper Missouri country, with one single exception. J. Frank Dobie states that the Comanche "sometimes hardened tender feet by burning wild rosemary—artemisia—and applying the smoke and heat to them."[27] All other references are to rawhide shoes, or "mockersons" as the Lewis and Clark scribes termed them.[28] Larocque writes of these (September 25, 1805): "We shoed our horses with

[23] Maximilian, *Travels*, in Thwaites, *Travels*, XXIII, 237, 370.
[24] Wilson, "Horse and Dog in Hidatsa Culture," 172–80.
[25] See Chapter XVI *infra*.
[26] Wilson, "Horse and Dog in Hidatsa Culture," 176–77.
[27] Dobie, "Indian Horses and Horsemanship," 269.
[28] Lewis and Clark, *Journals* (ed. by Thwaites), III, 3; (ed. by Coues), II, 559.

raw deer hide as their hoofs are worn out to the flesh with continual walking since last Spring with their feet on loose stones [, which] lames them and sometimes makes them bleed."[29] We have noted above the unhappy condition of the horses of David Thompson and Réne Jusseaume.[30] We must conclude that either they had not heard of the rawhide expedient (which seems improbable), or that literally they had seen no buffalo or deer from which to contrive horseshoes. It would not have been the first time that Thompson had traveled enormous distances without seeing buffalo, in the very heart of the range.[31]

The Comanche (and Sioux) method of achieving long-windedness has been noticed.[32] Dobie says that "another method . . . probably equally effective, was to blow the pulverized root or leaves of certain plants up a horse's nostrils. The blowers were specialists —horse doctors—and their medicine was applied only in ceremonial manner."[33] Maximilian noted that the Mandan and Hidatsa had remedies for horse complaints, apparently of a less occult and (to us) more acceptable character.[34] Kroeber found similar specifics among the Atsina,[35] and they are also recorded in other tribes. The Cree apparently bore a special reputation among the western Canadian tribes, both for horses and for human ailments.[36]

Breeding seems to have become very largely a matter of individual (tribal) capacity or practice; or perhaps even inclination. J. Frank Dobie, who has a wide knowledge of horse lore in more than one connotation, says that "Good horses were more plentiful among the northern [United States] tribes than they were among the southern, though they were from the same base." He attributes this to the more bracing northern climate and possibly resultant pasturage. The great Indian defect as breeders was not, in Dobie's opinion, poor stallions as much as nonselection of mares. He ob-

[29] Larocque, "Journal" (ed. by Burpee), 49; Alexander Ross, *Fur Hunters of the Far West*, II, 124.

[30] See Chapter VIII *supra*.

[31] See Roe, *North American Buffalo*, 577, 585–86, etc.

[32] See Chapter V *supra*.

[33] Dobie, "Indian Horses and Horsemanship," 268; *The Mustangs*, 84.

[34] Maximilian, *Travels*, in Thwaites, *Travels*, XXIII, 360.

[35] Kroeber, "Ethnology of the Gros Ventre," 226; for other tribes, see Grinnell, in Hodge, *Handbook*, I, 571.

[36] Jenness, *The Sarcee Indians*, 73–75; Mandelbaum, "The Plains Cree," 253–58.

serves that a few of the Northern tribes came to understand breeding.[37] Like so many other Indian phenomena, this varied among tribes. The Sarcee were seemingly good horse breeders;[38] the Cree made no attempt to control breeding.[39] The outstanding horse breeders among the Northern tribes were indisputably the Nez Percé. The foremost authority on this tribe is Francis Haines. The famous Appaloosa horse of the Nez Percé is classed by Haines as "a direct result of care in breeding," and not to be confused with the pinto. I take Haines's argument to be that as a breed the Appaloosa was developed in the Orient, and reached the Spanish Netherlands from the Near East by the ordinary channels of Mediterranean sea-traffic. It was brought direct from the Netherlands to Mexico, and was never in North Africa or Spain.[40] If I have interpreted Haines correctly, its preservation as a type has been due not as much to any necessity for breeding up, as of care in not breeding *down*.

With reference to this question, Dobie takes (if I conceive him rightly) what seems a somewhat narrowly restricted attitude. He writes thus in reference to Indian horse breeding:

The Arabs have through the centuries controlled breeding only by keeping their stallions secured. The only selective breeding of consequence among the North American Indians was west of the Rocky Mountains—a mighty fence shutting out the ceaselessly shifting and raiding tribes of the Plains and the increasing numbers of wild horses.[41]

This rather contradicts his own apparent conclusions on the Nez Percé's being poor breeders, which are also the conclusions of Lewis and Clark. It may have been that the explorers only saw "another pinto" in the prized Appaloosa, and discounted their own-

[37] Dobie, "Indian Horses and Horsemanship," 270; *The Mustangs*, 53–58, 139.

[38] Thompson, *Narrative* (ed. by Tyrrell), 367.

[39] Mandelbaum, "The Plains Cree," 196.

[40] Francis D. Haines, "Nez Percé and Shoshoni Influence on Northwest History," *Greater America*, 379–93; also his collaborated work, *The Appaloosa Horse*, 9–53. His final conclusion re North Africa and Spain is an amendment; in correspondence to the present writer, January 24, 1953.

[41] Dobie, "Indian Horses and Horsemanship," 273. On the Nez Percé, cf. *ibid.*, 271; also Lewis and Clark themselves (*Journals* [ed. by Thwaites], IV, 76–77; [ed. by Coues], III, 840). Yet in spite of this, the explorers refer again and again to 'excellent horses' in more than one tribe (*ibid.* [ed. by Thwaites], II, 329, 339, IV, 325; [ed. by Coues], II, 489; III, 840, 977–78).

ers' paeans proportionately.[42] With respect also to a lack of selectiveness among the Plains tribes, we have furthermore seen that David Thompson, circa 1797, indicates what was apparently a fixed preference of some long standing among certain Plains tribes for black-hoofed horses on their war parties.[43] This would certainly require a period, perhaps of years, of observation and discussion to reach a definite conclusion, and to crystallize it into settled custom, with a logical tendency toward elimination of typically unsuitable stallions. I imagine a breeder's intuitive judgment would soon suggest this last procedure.

Gilbert Wilson has recorded one detail of Hidatsa horse management that indicates an understanding which is borne out by horse experience at large. In my judgment such an understanding also indicates the essential capacity of a successful horse breeder, whatever course personal inclination might dictate. They left the mare alone when expecting her to foal. One foal was *said* to have been borne in a Hidatsa earth lodge, but no such occurrence was known to Wolf-chief, Wilson's principal informant.[44] Among countless associates during many years who had lived all their lives among horses, I have met only one man, an old neighboring farmer of thoroughly reliable character, who had ever witnessed the delivery of a foal. He was an old freighter, and the occurrence took place unavoidably, on the trail, near the Missouri River in western Iowa.

We have seen that the Comanche, about 1724, confessed that they had not yet been able to raise any colts; meaning, presumably, to any really material or satisfactory extent. The wide acclaim of other tribes to Comanche pre-eminence may of course have referred purely to their equestrian skill. But the period is rather early and the environmental conditions were not specially favorable to breeding requirements.[45] It may be noted, however, that with the exception of one single possible reference—which is also of the same year, 1724[46]—amid all the interchanges in raiding and

---

[42] See Dobie's remarks, *The Mustangs*, 56.
[43] See Chapter VIII *supra*.
[44] Wilson, "Horse and Dog in Hidatsa Culture," 145.
[45] See Chapter IV *supra*.
[46] Bourgmont noted the Comanche's "trading three robes for a horse"; unless this means trading a horse for three robes? (Worcester, "Spanish Horses among the Plains Tribes," 410.)

trading between the Comanche and the more northerly tribes, I have found no mention of horses being taken *to* the Comanche. So perhaps we may fairly assume, in the case of such past masters, that the Comanche did eventually contribute their share toward the development of an Indian type of horse.

The historical circumstance that the raiding-and-trading Plains economy continued to prevail in the northern area virtually until the extinction of the native culture suggests two possible explanations: (1) Breeding was positively unsuccessful or distasteful. (2) Conditions of life and warfare, etc., or of temperamental phenomena, were so unfavorable that a fairly high positive degree of success in breeding was relatively insufficient to supply the demand. In the case of one very widely spread Northern tribe, one or the other of these explanations seems inescapable. David Thompson writes thus of the Assiniboin, circa 1800: "The Sussees [Sarcee] content themselves with rearing horses, but the Stone Indians [now commonly "Stoney"] are always in want of horses, which appears to be occasioned by hard usage."[47]

This characterization finds support from a number of incidental items of evidence. We have seen that while certain other tribes sheltered their horses and cut cottonwood boughs or other fodder for them, the Assiniboin were content to merely turn them loose in a cottonwood area to take their chance.[48] Among the numerous references to different tribes as particularly expert horse Indians, for example, the Comanche or the Kiowa in the south, and the Blackfoot, Cheyenne, Crow, or Hidatsa in the north, we find just one such allusion to the Assiniboin. They are described by Harmon (who is endorsed by Mandelbaum) as 'better than the Cree.'[49] Whether this is praise or damning with faint praise is not indicated. In an economy where almost all Indians were horse thieves if opportunity offered or could be made, the Assiniboin enjoyed (literally, as we have seen) an unapproachable "bad eminence" over half the area.[50] Taken in conjunction, these factors may per-

[47] Thompson, *Narrative* (ed. by Tyrrell), 367.

[48] See note 11 *supra.*

[49] Harmon, *Journal,* 40; Mandelbaum, "The Plains Cree," 194–95.

[50] See Chapter V *supra.* It is Maximilian who notes their "not having many horses" about 1833 (*Travels,* in Thwaites, *Travels,* XXII, 391). While commending the Crow and the Hidatsa as particularly skillful horsemen (*ibid.,* XXIII, 354, 360), he has no such praise for the Assiniboin.

haps explain their "not having many horses" about 1833, though it is also said that the Assiniboin ate many. It is one of the curiosities of tribal idiosyncrasy that after all this apparent callousness or inhumanity, while other tribes are recorded as carrying water in buffalo-paunch containers or the like for their children on long journeys, the Assiniboin are the only tribe who are stated to have done this for their dogs.[51]

The castrating operation, like Indian therapeutic or ceremonial surgery at large, was apparently very much of a ritual in most tribes, though there were some exceptions. The Flatheads followed the Spanish technique, as very possibly other tribes also may have done, through the influence of dispersion. After watching its effect upon several stallions in 1806, Meriwether Lewis considered the Flathead surgery superior to both American and English practice.[52] Although most of the mounts among the Northern tribes were *enteros*[53] (which Duncan McGillivray in 1794 thought to be the explanation of the famous "buffalo runners"), the fact that the Indians could apparently practice the gelding operation upon adult animals with success is of immense interest. It would be a very valuable study in Indian psycho-anthropology to ascertain precisely how the knowledge and the art disseminated itself across a continent. It was believed by Gilbert Wilson's Hidatsa informant to be a European operation. The Flathead use of the Spanish technique tends to support the supposition, as also does the further fact that it was not applied to dogs by the Hidatsa until after its use on horses, which probably familiarized the procedure in their minds.[54]

Castration, among the Hidatsa at least, was not an operation everyone could perform: it was done only by reputed experts.[55] This is in conformity with white practice. While the majority of the farmers castrated their own cattle and pigs, few castrated their colts; and fewer still would allow any self-proclaimed adept among

[51] Wilson, "Horse and Dog in Hidatsa Culture," 196–99.
[52] Lewis and Clark, *Journals* (ed. by Thwaites), V, 36–40; (ed. by Coues), III, 1012.
[53] Dobie, *The Mustangs*, 54–55. Dobie makes it a (universal) "native opinion" that stallions were superior. See note 56 *infra*.
[54] Wilson, "Horse and Dog in Hidatsa Culture," 146.
[55] *Ibid.*, 146–49.

their neighbors to exercise himself at their expense. Curiously enough, while Duncan McGillivray found the explanation of the pro eminence of the "buffalo runners" in their being stallions (as we ourselves would very probably have done), the Hidatsa reason for castrating their horses was "because they did not tire so easily" in soft and swampy ground![56] In this field, the Cree furnish another example of the endless tribal diversity. The castration operation was no ritual in their practice.[57] If this implies a corollary that the operation among the Cree *was* a job anybody could perform, perhaps we need search no further for reasons for their being considered poor horse masters.

It would in my judgment be futile, and in fact essentially unreasonable, to expect much "humane'" consideration to be shown by the Indians toward their mounts *while they were in actual use.* The Indian's horse was not a wealthy man's luxury to be gently ambled for an hour in the park, and then handed over to a solicitous groom for a restorative routine that was almost a ritual in itself. The Indian world being what it was, it was only too frequently inevitable among the Plains tribes, both for procuring food and for the preservation of life itself, that their horses had to be forced to the maximum effort, regardless of any other consideration, where anything less than the "all out" would have been suicidal. Then even Wolf-chief whipped his horse![58] All we can fairly do is to judge their attitude toward their horses in less strenuous relationships.

The first horse Indians encountered by Lewis and Clark were the Mandan. These are characterized as "invariably severe riders." They would sometimes be chasing buffalo and bringing in the meat on their horses for days at a time. During such periods the horses were seldom "suffered to taste food; yet this valuable anamall [*sic*] under all those disadvantages is seldom seen meager or unfit for service."[59] We have a curious sidelight on this aspect of the Mandan from an entry in Larocque's *Journal* (near the Mandan villages,

[56] *Ibid.*, 147.
[57] Mandelbaum, "The Plains Cree," 196.
[58] See note 86 *infra.*
[59] Lewis and Clark, *Journals* (ed. by Thwaites), I, 258–59; (ed. by Coues), I, 232–33. They write similarly of the Chopunnish (Nez Percé): "These indians are cruell horse masters" (*ibid.*, [ed. by Thwaites], IV, 342).

August 21, 1805): "There is plenty of ash here. There were very few persons in the camp that were not employed in making themselves horse whip handles with that wood; it was with that design they came here, as that wood is seldom found elsewhere."[60] Such severity may perhaps help to explain (as with the afore-mentioned Assiniboin) why the Mandan market for Crow horses continued to be fairly brisk.[61] Yet we have seen that the Mandan when "off duty" could show consideration for their beasts, even if it were only that of ultimate self-interest. These facts concerning the Mandan incidentally furnish an additional commentary upon those tribes which the possession of the horse did *not* turn into nomads.[62]

It is of course well known that very often the Indian horses needed no spurring. This was particularly true of the buffalo runners. After a day's hot chase, a Sioux warrior "would not water his horse until next morning, giving him all night in which to cool off."[63] This was also a Hidatsa practice,[64] and may have been common to other tribes. This is clearly a case of intuitive induction, or of judicious imitation confirmed by experience, for their prior acquaintance with the dog could teach them nothing concerning an animal of a totally different nature, and which was their first domesticated creature under personal control.

It is not always easy to mark the exact line which differentiates the care born of mere self-interest from positive kindness. Our own rather cynical proverb that "honesty is the best policy" implies what is probably true enough: that more of us shun dishonesty from fear of the consequences than from pure native integrity. That the Plains children should make friends of the horses they had grown up with, and had ridden from the days when they had to be tied on, need surprise nobody. It would be a great occasion for the small Indian boy when he was advanced to the dignity of a day herder to the horses of the village. Sioux boys, says J. Frank Dobie, "went into the water with their horses and there stroked

60 Larocque, "Journal" (ed. by Burpee), 38.
61 Jablow, *The Cheyenne*, 38, 60, etc.
62 See Chapter X *supra*. Despite this, they practically anticipated the cliché of the Western cowman: "If it can't be done o' hossback it's too much like work!" Re trapping (1805), see Charles Mackenzie, in Masson, *Les Bourgeois de la Compagnie du Nord-Ouest*, I, 331.
63 Dobie, "Indian Horses and Horsemanship," 267.
64 Wilson, "Horse and Dog in Hidatsa Culture," 181.

the wildish colts, unable to get away, gentling them as they grew up. Men and boys alike delighted in swimming on horseback."[65] This was also the standard horse-training technique among the Hidatsa, in their case in the Missouri River.[66] Apropos of this, during World War I a "reclamation camp" was established in England for "untamable" army horses, instead of destroying them. This activity was handled entirely by young women, daughters of wealthy country gentlemen, and familiar with horses from childhood. Their technique was identically the same as that of the Indian: they rode the animals into deep water, which before long rendered them docile. It was said at the time there was not a single failure.

To an Indian boy, a favorite horse was even something more than a pet. A boy herder would say to his charges: "You are my gods. I take good care of you." Both horses and dogs were pets and "gods" to the Hidatsa;[67] and quite evidently to the Assiniboin, for Lowie was told of a supernatural revelation from a horse to a "shaman," or medicine man.[68] Probably this attitude was far more widespread than our present evidence shows.

We cannot doubt that the callousness that runs the gamut from indifference to positive cruelty was all too prevalent. It is probable that Indian saddles were frequently fearful and wonderful affairs. We may take leave to doubt the exactitude of that copy of a Spanish saddle which the Indians, according to the legend related by Denhardt, made *in one night*.[69] Even if we grant both the authenticity and the accuracy, we are not much better off. J. Frank Dobie writes thus: "Indian saddles were either skin pads stuffed with hair or poorly-fitted and poorly-padded wooden frames imitative of Spanish saddles, which were themselves notoriously cruel on horse backs."[70] We have an admirable description of a Hidatsa saddle which appears to differ essentially from Dobie's type: this was a slung seat of hide, suspended hammock-fashion between pommel and cantle. This would certainly cushion

[65] Dobie, *The Mustangs*, 48.
[66] Wilson, "Horse and Dog in Hidatsa Culture," 151–56.
[67] *Ibid.*, 142, 178, 198.
[68] Lowie, "The Assiniboin," 44.
[69] See Chapter IX *supra*.
[70] Dobie, *The Mustangs*, 51.

the rider very considerably, and perhaps to some extent (it was considered) the horse also.[71] It seems probable that with both Spaniards and Indians the basic idea was ease to the rider much more than adjustment to the horse. An incidental reference from a Spanish commander (Juan Dominguez de Mendoza, 1684) tends to confirm this supposition. After describing the complete uselessness of his forty "soldiers" as cavalrymen, Mendoza concludes: "Besides, we had saddles that could not be worse."[72]

Indians in general, thinks Dobie, were, like Mexican *vaqueros*, completely insensate. Dobie writes:

North and south alike, the backs of Indian horses were generally sore. The Indian might tie a rag over the sore as a defense against the voracity of magpies or daub it with mud to ward off blowflies. A traveler among the Snake Indians about 1800 saw their horses upon being saddled 'bite and tear raw flesh until the blood flows, and then kick and roll for some time, whilst their whole bodies quiver and appear in great agony.' Yet the next day the owners would saddle and ride them with 'indifferent composure.' The wounds, Captain Meriwether Lewis observed, seldom became too 'horrid' to deter a rider. A setfast on his back accounted for the pitching of many a Texas bronco of the old days.[73] The current idea was that a sore does not hurt after it has 'got warmed up.' . . . William R. Leigh once saw a Navajo pony gasping for breath on account of a tightly knotted rope about its neck that had been wet by rain and then had shrunk. 'A bunch of Navajos were looking on, laughing.' When the white man pulled his knife and cut the rope off, he was 'regarded as a killjoy.'[74]

[71] Wilson, "Horse and Dog in Hidatsa Culture," 182–94.

[72] Bolton (ed.), *Spanish Exploration in the Southwest*, 369.

[73] At Calgary, Alberta, September 28, 1901, when the Duke of York (later King George V) and party were there, a certain brown mare won her rider a purse of $100 for riding her past the grandstand "without touching leather." The rider was the foreman at the Chipman Ranch. This animal (supposedly "an outlaw straight off the range") was in service at the ranch *on the hay rake*, and was habitually ridden in from the job bareback when the day's work was over. As long as no saddle ever touched her, this could be done by anybody. I myself worked at the Chipman Ranch the following year, 1902, and am conversant with the facts. Readers of *Uncle Tom's Cabin* may remember the beechnut under Haley's saddle (Chap. VI). A favorite trick to make a horse "pitch" for show purposes was carbolic acid under the saddle blanket. Any old Westerner is well aware that one of two things happens to a bronco. Either it dies of rage and despair, untamable (which sometimes occurs), or, as a result of constant handling—not to say shipping around the country by train or truck to the rodeos—it becomes philosophical if not gentle; rodeo boosters and their "suckers" to the contrary notwithstanding. See Dobie, *The Mustangs*, 277, 302.

However broadly true this may have been, none the less there seem to have been exceptions. Larocque's description of the Crow horse economy, which indicates a much closer approximation to our own ideas, deserves to be presented in his own words:

Their saddles are so made as to prevent falling either backwards or forward, the hind part reaching as high as between the shoulders and the fore part of the breast. The women's saddles are especially so. Those of the men are not quite so high, and many use saddles such as the Canadians make in the North West Country.

They are excellent riders, being trained to it from their infancy. In war or hunting if they mean to exert their horses to the utmost they ride without a saddle. In their wheelings and evolutions they often are not seen, having only a leg on the horse back and clasping the horse with their arms around his neck, on the side opposite to where the enemy is. Most of their horses can be guided to any place without bridle, only by leaning to one side or the other they turn immediately to the side on which you lean, and will not bear [?[75]] turning until you resume a direct posture. They are very fond of their horses and take good care of them; as soon as a horse has a sore back he is not used until he is healed, no price will induce a man to part with a favorite horse on whom he places confidence for security either in attack or flight.[76]

If any Indian tribe practiced kindness toward their horses, it would be illogical to suppose that this was the case in one tribe only. While tribal diversities are almost infinite, there are yet some tribal resemblances in certain of the foregoing details. So much has been said about the famous Comanche trick of riding under the horse's neck that many fail to realize that it was practiced by many (perhaps most) tribes; it was also practiced in South America

[74] Dobie, *ibid.*, 51–52; "Indian Horses and Horsemanship," 269.

[75] This expression is rather vague. It may mean the horse "will forbear turning," or "will not endure to turn in one direction while the rider leans in the other." Both meanings would suit a cowhorse.

[76] Larocque, "Journal" (ed. by Burpee), 64–65. For saddles among the Blackfoot, Cree, Hidatsa, Shoshone, etc., see Wissler, "Material Culture of the Blackfoot," 92–94; "Riding Gear of the North American Indians," 1–38; Mandelbaum, "The Plains Cree," 196; Wilson, "Horse and Dog in Hidatsa Culture," 182–94; Lewis and Clark, *Journals* (ed. by Thwaites), III, 30–32; (ed. by Coues), II, 562. For "Spanish" saddles, Cadodaquis, 1682, see Chapter IX *supra*; Flathead, 1812, Franchère, *Voyage to the Northwest Coast*, in Thwaites, *Travels*, VI, 340–41. See also Harmon, *Journal*, 291; Coues (ed.), *Henry-Thompson Journals*, II, 526.

by the Gauchos.[77] In addition to the reason given by Larocque for the Crow's riding bareback "whenever the horse was to be urged to the utmost" (doubtless to relieve the strain of a tight girth on the horse's wind), saddles were discarded in war because they interfered with the "hang over." This was the reason specified in more than one tribe.[78]

We have definite testimony concerning a positive and active spirit of kindness existing in the two principal farthest northern and farthest southern horse tribes, respectively. Chief Buffalo Child Long Lance gives a most vivid description of Blackfoot horse-breaking procedure. Even if he did not specifically mention this as "the method of our warriors," the context would indicate a tribal, rather than a merely individual technique. He writes thus:

> It is a strange fact that a wild horse, of either the ranch or the open ranges, will not react to quiet kindliness at first. He must first be treated gruffly—but not harshly—and then when he is on a touching acquaintance with man, kindness is the quickest way to win his affections.[79]

The skeptics need not necessarily accept the Crow's refusal to sell as any evidence per se of real affection, unless they prefer to do so. This could no doubt be explained as purely self-interest, precisely as the (frequent) burial of a deceased Crow's favorite horse together with his master could easily be explained as a provision for the needs of the spirit world.[80] The outstanding modern authority on the Comanche says their superior horses were well cared for.[81] Gregg goes further (1831–1840): "Like [the Arabs] they dote upon their steeds; one had as well undertake to purchase a Comanche's child as his favorite riding-horse."[82] But another Comanche example renders inference superfluous. Randolph B. Marcy offered a handsome price to the Comanche chief, Sanaco,

[77] Darwin, *Voyage of the Beagle*, 75–76, 103, etc.

[78] Lewis and Clark, *Journals* (ed. by Thwaites), II, 329, 351; III, 48; IV, 27, 322, 342-44; V, 27; (ed. by Coues), II, 500; III, 967, 977–78. Wissler, "Material Culture of the Blackfoot," 155; Wilson, "Horse and Dog in Hidatsa Culture," 153, 164, 170. For the Crow "hang over," see a picture in *The West of Alfred Jacob Miller* (ed. by Ross), Plate 134.

[79] See his *Long Lance*, 202–206.

[80] Lowie, *The Crow Indians*, 267.

[81] Richardson, *The Comanche Barrier*, 28.

[82] Gregg, *Commerce of the Prairies*, in Thwaites, *Travels*, XX, 346.

for his buffalo-and-war horse. The owner, after explaining that he could not think of parting with an animal so needful to the welfare of his people, added, "Moreover, I love him very much."[83] Sanaco was no "tame Indian," who might have learned kindness from other men.[84] It is in my opinion psychologically very improbable that any tribe could *create a legend* of an actually never-existent horse named "Never-Whipped," which had all his life been treated "with the kindness and respect due to a relative,"[85] if such qualities had no place whatever in the treatment of their own animals. Wolf-chief, the Hidatsa, told Gilbert Wilson that he never whipped his horse except when pursued.[86]

We have had occasion to note in other connections the Indians' unapproachable command of every phase and form of horsemanship. It passes understanding how these marvels of equestrian skill, master demonstrations of conjoint and co-ordinated effort of man and beast unquestionably demanding long and assiduous mutual training, could ever have been effected without some bond of sympathy between the two. There is no parallel here between the accomplishments of an animal living in more than partial freedom, which it could regain *in toto* almost at will, and the inane performances of the hapless victims of fear and the lash which languish in our circuses.

Nor were such achievements exclusively those which might be termed *active* "tricks," however purposeful and dignified. There was also a power of passive obedience and response. J. Frank Dobie writes:

According to the biographer of Geronimo of the Apaches . . . he rode 'a blaze-faced, white-stockinged dun horse,' trained in a way that must have been exceptional. In close fights a warrior sometimes had to leave his horse and escape on foot. 'My horse,' Geronimo said, 'was trained to come at call, and as soon as I reached a safe place, if not too closely pursued, I would call him to me.'[87]

[83] Marcy, *Exploration of the Red River*, 96–97.
[84] Richardson, *The Comanche Barrier*, 28, 220.
[85] Dobie, *The Mustangs*, 46.
[86] Wilson, "Horse and Dog in Hidatsa Culture," 163.
[87] Dobie, "Indian Horses and Horsemanship," 267. As a boy in England I often saw the huge railway dray horses left standing while the drayman and his boy (who were generally very proud of their friend) were checking their "collections"

As a former horse owner and breeder, and a student of long standing, I shall require some strong evidence to convince me that kindness had no place in Geronimo's training methods. Nor shall I believe that he was the only such Indian.

---

at the different warehouses to be called for later; often reappearing on the street a block or more from where the horse had been left. They would come up the street in response to the driver's whistle. In breaking in the same intelligent creatures for railway use, where they place ("spot") trucks in narrow warehouse tracks where no engine could operate, the common technique is to allow a barely moving truck to touch them on the rump from behind. The shunters say the horse is never caught again.

XIV

ECONOMIC AND SOCIAL ASSETS

Even if we had no definite historical information to enlighten us, it would, I believe, be an almost instinctive assumption that the tribes it is agreed to designate "horse Indians" would not confine their utilization of the animal to mere pleasure or even to primary practical uses as a hunter or draft beast. The horse became a fairly fixed and recognized medium of exchange, not only between tribes, but in various economic, social, or "legalistic" phases between individual members of the same community.

The fairly definite and—*in esse*—almost "codified" character of many of these units of exchange leads one to think they are of relatively lengthy persistence in the Indian world, dating very probably since almost the very possession of the horse itself. For once the stage had been reached where the individual ownership and control of these great creatures was seen to be a possibility, with its corollaries of potential trafficking and exchange, it would seem —to us at least—that further reflection concerning the superiority of the new circulating medium would be needless. The evident speed with which the Indians mastered the earliest and most difficult art, that of riding,[1] and adapted it to its most fundamental purposes of war and the buffalo hunt may reasonably be taken as a rough index of the more or less general facility with which they utilized the horse in other fields. Nowhere, however, have I been able to discover any sort of "table of exchange" which could give a clear idea

[1] Considered in the light of the (American) evidence, I think Haines rather overemphasizes the contrary proposition: the *necessarily* protracted slowness of such an advance (*The Appaloosa Horse*, 27).

of the ratios of value between the horse and its only conceivable (animal) predecessor as a market commodity, the dog. While a people can make a "circulating medium" of any convenient article that may strike their fancy, the dog, whether considered as wealth or merely as the symbol of wealth, would be a most inconvenient one, for it could neither be carried on its owner's person, nor even be trusted to remain at his disposal.

Almost the only definite estimates of horse values I have found are in the Southwest, about 1820. Edwin James, of Stephen H. Long's expedition, records that among the Kaskaias or "Bad Hearts" (whom he thought to be Comanche, but who are identified as Kiowa-Apache or possibly Wichita), who had no tipi poles in their country, one horse was exchanged for five lodgepoles.[2] This practically meant two horses for every tipi, for although they used far less than the more prodigal tribes farther north, who had their own nearer sources of supply, they needed from eight to ten poles for each dwelling.[3] A contemporary student of the Blackfoot polity states that for a painted (i.e., decorated) tipi for Blackfoot newlyweds the recognized price was four dogs.[4] I presume this must be considered equivalent to saying that it was not worth one horse; certainly not on the Sarcee horse equation of "seven dogs."[5] In both these cases we lack the key to the comparative values. In general, one is left with the impression that very few regular tariffs existed. The transaction was governed largely by the necessities or eagerness of the parties, or other purely evanescent impulses of the moment.

It has been a very common experience of the earliest European traders among primitive peoples that until the aborigines learned the value of their own commodities, articles worth a high price in the trader's home market could often be obtained for a mere song. This does not seem to have been prominently the case among the Plains tribes, even at early dates. We have seen that Henri de Tonty in 1682 gave (or had to give) "seven hatchets and a string of

[2] James, Account of the Expedition under Long, in Thwaites, Travels, XV, 211; XVI, 117. Identified as Kiowa-Apache, in Hodge, Handbook, I, 701; II, 1031, 1070; as perhaps Wichita: Richardson, The Comanche Barrier, 49.
[3] Some figures in Roe, North American Buffalo, 874–76.
[4] Kidd, "Blackfoot Ethnography," 55; cf. 50–52, 151.
[5] See Chapter III supra.

large glass beads" for four Spanish horses. Tonty describes horses as being "very common" in this tribe (Natchez ?).[6] This implies prices which the Indians themselves considered reasonably average, particularly since the horses had (most probably) been stolen from the Spaniards.

In 1805 Larocque found that the arts of the middleman were well understood among the Mandan and Hidatsa. They were "anxious to sell horses, but twice as dear as the Rocky Mountain Indians [Crow] who have so many horses," and from whom were being obtained the animals which the Mandan wished to sell to Larocque. The trader bought one horse from them, or from the Crow; for this he paid "a gun 200 balls, one flanel Robe, one shirt, one half axe, one battle do, 2 Wampoon hair pipes, 2 axes, one Wampoon shell, 40 B. Blue Beads, 2 Mass Barley Corn do and one fm W. S. Red Stroud." On the following day Larocque writes: "I purchased a saddle [and bridle?] for the horse I purchased yesterday for which I paid 40 shots Powder Being short of Balls."[7] Concerning beads, he later mentions "those blue Glass beads they have from the Spaniards, and on which they set such value that a horse is given for 100 grains." If such prices represent the much cheaper Crow horses, the Mandan tariffs must have been appalling. Yet Larocque obtained another (saddle) horse from the Mandan for thirty pounds of ammunition.[8]

It is of interest to note the progressive inflation of prices as the market worked eastward from the transmontane tribes down the Missouri. Larocque says of the Crow horses: "They have them in trade from the flat head Indians in great numbers and very cheap. They sell part to the Big Bellys [Hidatsa] and Mandans at double the price they purchase them and carry on a continual trade in that manner."[9] Elsewhere he describes the Flatheads as having "a great number of horses which they sell for a trifle, and give many for nothing." Whether a horse for seventy or eighty elks' teeth ranks as a trifle or not I am unable to say.[10] Twenty or thirty years later, however, the Mandan wanted one hundred or one hundred and

[6] See Chapter IV *supra*.

[7] Larocque, "Journal" (ed. by Burpee), 19, 36, 57, 64. The query in brackets is Burpee's. "Strouds" were a coarse cloth or blanketing originally made for the Indian trade at Stroud, England.

[8] *Ibid.*, 45, 19.   [9] *Ibid.*, 64.   [10] *Ibid.*, 71.

fifty elks' teeth (which were prized as ornaments) in exchange for a horse.[11]

At the very time that Larocque characterized the Flathead as being generous or indifferent, the Lewis and Clark party were buying horses either from the Flathead or the Shoshone. For ten or twelve horses, they paid for each animal with "an axe, a knife, a handkerchief, and a little paint," while for a mule—much more esteemed by the Indians—the price was "2 knives, a shirt, 2 hand-kerchieves, and a pair of leggings."[12] It may have been that the explorers' extremity was the Indians' opportunity; but if such prices were doubled by the Crow and doubled again by the Mandan, by the time the Mandan villages were left behind, one's "kingdom for a horse" would not appear to be an altogether incredible trans-action. We cannot wonder that the Mandan were very strongly opposed to Larocque or other traders going up the Missouri. They saw clearly that this foreshadowed the beginning of the end. Charles Mackenzie, the Northwest Company fur trader, writes at this time:

> They [the Mandan] asserted that if the white people would extend their dealings to the Rocky Mountains, the Mandanes would thereby become great sufferers, as they would not only lose all the benefit which they had hitherto derived from their intercourse with these distant tribes, but that in measure as these tribes obtained arms, they would become independent and insolent in the extreme.[13]

Of the Rocky Mountain tribes, the Crow were among the most important customers of the Mandan. Larocque says of the former: "They have never had any traders with them, they get their battle Guns, ammunitions etc from the Mandanes and Big Bellys in ex-change for horses."[14] As a part of their schemings to prevent the elimination of the middleman, the Mandan and Hidatsa uttered

[11] Maximilian, *Travels*, in Thwaites, *Travels*, XXIII, 289, 321–23, 371.

[12] Lewis and Clark, *Journals* (ed. by Thwaites), III, 28; (ed. by Coues), II, 547.

[13] Masson, *Les Bourgeois de la Compagnie du Nord-Ouest*, I, 331. See also Bradbury, 1811, on the Sioux' blockading the Missouri to prevent Hunt's party of Astorians from trading with the "Ricaras, Mandans and Minaterees" (Hidatsa), *Travels*, in Thwaites, *Travels*, V, 103.

[14] Larocque, "Journal" (ed. by Burpee), 66.

their portentous jeremiads regarding the murderous intentions of the Crow toward the white intruders, to which the reader's attention has been drawn.[15] The clear economic incentive here illustrates the basic fallacy of treating slanders of this character as authentic native analyses of Indian temperament and normal behavior. We have also seen that whatever its true interpretation may be, it was in no sense an originally post-equestrian manifestation. No doubt the traders themselves saw through this. Charles Mackenzie mentions the Cheyenne's wishing to trade (1806); but the Hidatsa "would not hear of my going there with goods, but concealed their real motives under pretense of my personal safety."[16]

The place of the horse in the marriage customs of many Plains tribes is well known. Among the Blackfoot, Blood, and Piegan, from one to twenty horses (or one gun) was the common price for a wife,[17] while the Sarcee had no specific number.[18] Maximilian, writing about 1833, stated that any number of horses from two to ten was customary among the Mandan and Hidatsa.[19] Washington Matthews, a specialist on the latter tribe, demurs to the naked "purchase" concept. He considers the horses were more as evidence of the good position and standing of the suitor.[20] This appears to have been very much the case in other tribes also. Kroeber states that with the Atsina, gifts of horses for wives were more of "honor" than of purchase.[21] The same was also the case among the Comanche, with whom horses held high value as "prestige tokens"[22]—a fact which seems somewhat surprising in a tribe which has always had such numbers. It may be a survival from early horse times, when their fewness made them prized.

By a natural correlation, the horse frequently played a significant part in marital disagreements. Larocque remarks that in cases of unfaithfulness "the most common revenge taken by the enraged

[15] See Chapter XII *supra*. Also cf. my remarks on the probable repetition of this attitude producing indifference in the Whitmans. For data on this restraint of trade, see Jablow, *The Cheyenne*, 30–44.
[16] Masson, *Les Bourgeois de la Compagnie du Nord-Ouest*, I, 375.
[17] (Rev.) John McLean, *Indians of Canada*, 26, 39–40, 80.
[18] Jenness, *The Sarcee Indians*, 23, 37.
[19] Maximilian, *Travels*, in Thwaites, *Travels*, XXIII, 280.
[20] Thwaites, *ibid.*, editor's note.
[21] Kroeber, "Ethnology of the Gros Ventre," 180.
[22] Richardson, *The Comanche Barrier*, 32; Hoebel, "Political Associations and Law-Ways of the Comanche Indians," 15, 21.

husband is Killing or taking the horses of the wifs galant, besides unmercifully beating her." In his daily jottings he remarks elsewhere (August 19, 1805): "Horses have been Killed and women wounded since I am with them on the score of jealousy."[23] Among the Cree, the gift of a horse from an adulterer generally satisfied the aggrieved husband.[24] One or two horses were exacted from a Sarcee alienator of a wife's affections,[25] and among the Blackfoot this was generally the penalty for seduction.[26] We might have expected severer punishment for the male offender, for the Blackfoot are one of two tribes who are said never to have lent their women to visitors in their camps;[27] the other are the Comanche.[28] The evidence is not entirely clear in either case. In many tribes the common punishment for an adulterous wife was to cut her nose off, or to the bone. Maximilian at Fort McKenzie in 1833 says that scores of the Blackfoot squaws had their noses cut off. This of itself would prove nothing against the men, but he adds specifically that "they are very ready to give up [these women] to the Whites."[29] The evidence against the Comanche men is less incriminating. As in the Northern tribes, the gift of a horse from an adulterer generally smoothed matters over, and some cut noses were seen among the women,[30] but this does not prove that the Comanche ever *lent* their women to strangers. Here again, however, the acceptance of a horse in such relations tends to suggest, among a tribe that had so many, that adultery was a relatively minor offence. In reference to killing horses, it is of interest to note that among the Assiniboin "Killing the Horses" (ceremonially, but not actually unless the offender proved impenitent) was the penalty for disobedience to the buffalo-hunt regulations.[31] This may be noticed in its relation to the frequent claptrap about Indian wastefulness.

[23] Larocque, "Journal" (ed. by Burpee), 58, 38.

[24] Mandelbaum, "The Plains Cree," 246.

[25] Jenness, *The Sarcee Indians,* 22.

[26] Thompson, *Narrative* (ed. by Tyrrell), 353; Maximilian, *Travels,* in Thwaites, *Travels,* XXIII, 117; Kidd, "Blackfoot Ethnography," 50–52, 151. See also Grinnell, in Hodge, *Handbook,* I, 571.

[27] MacInnes, *In the Shadow of the Rockies,* 20, citing Gen. Sam Steele.

[28] Gregg, *Commerce of the Prairies,* in Thwaites, *Travels,* XX, 344.

[29] Maximilian, *Travels,* in Thwaites, *Travels,* XXIII, 110.

[30] Richardson, *The Comanche Barrier,* 32, 228.

[31] Lowie, "The Assiniboin," 35–36, 96.

Whatever was the exact function of the horse in what may be termed honorable marriage negotiations, as between families in the same tribe, the horse was definitely a frequent price in slave-dealing transactions, whether the captives were later promoted to matrimonial rank or not. This traces back to relatively early horse times. As early as 1680 "Fray Alonso de Posadas reported that he had seen Apaches trading captive Indian women of the Quivira nation [Wichita ?] for horses with the Indians of the Pecos pueblos."[32] Seventy years later the tables were turned. Richardson mentions an intertribal trade about 1750, "in which the Comanche exchanged Apache slaves and horses and mules for French weapons and Wichita agricultural products. The center of this trade was the Wichita village on Red River."[33] There is evidence of such traffic in the northern area, even among tribes whose women and girls were nominally free. Plains Ojibwa exchanged their women for Plain Cree horses.[34] A note of the younger Alexander Henry gives us an idea of dates. He writes (October 24, 1803): "Livernois . . . exchanged his mare for a young wife, of about eight years of age; it is common in the North West to give a horse for a woman."[35]

The significance of the horse in tribal funeral rites appears to have been influenced very considerably by temperamental and possibly by economic considerations. There was also the potent factor of the convenience and dignity of the warrior in the spirit world. These could only be served as they had been served in the present one, by his horses. Grinnell considers that in earlier times dogs probably performed the spirit functions of the horses that were later slain when a Blackfoot warrior died,[36] very much as the white buffalo sacrifice of the Illinois tribe is thought to have superseded the white dog ritual that prevailed before the buffalo had become known to them.[37] Grinnell's view may possibly explain the large numbers of dogs formerly owned by individuals in such tribes as the Crow, which did not eat dogs. Lowie says of them: "In pre-equestrian days, I heard a wealthy man was one who owned many

---

[32] Worcester, "The Spread of Spanish Horses," 228.
[33] Richardson, *The Comanche Barrier*, 59.
[34] Mandelbaum, "The Plains Cree," 164.
[35] Coues (ed.), *Henry-Thompson Journals*, I, 228.
[36] Hodge, *Handbook*, I, 571.
[37] *Ibid.*, II, 403, 939–44.

dogs. One Crow of old was said to have owned as many as a hundred."[38]

The numbers of horses slain on the occasion of a warrior's death seem to have varied quite as much from tribal usage as from the wealth or accepted importance of the deceased owner. Among the Crow, the dead man's favorite horse "was often killed";[39] which implies a parsimonious attitude. The Arikara were apparently even worse. Maximilian says that "Sometimes 'a good horse' was slain on the graves of eminent men."[40] There were "often several" slain in earlier times, among the Sarcee, and a slain warrior's horse was frequently kept by the dead man's father.[41] Sometimes as many as twenty were sacrificed when a Blackfoot warrior died,[42] and Maximilian states that ten or fifteen were not uncommon for a chief. He mentions one Blackfoot chief at whose death one hundred and fifty were slain.[43] Among the Atsina, parents might give away all their horses, mourning for an only child.[44] In 1844 a Comanche chief killed his horses, destroyed his lodges, and moved his band elsewhere, from grief at the loss of his son.[45] The Comanche were Shoshonean; the Chopunnish (Nez Percé), who were associated with the Northern Shoshone in the intermontane area, were observed by the Lewis and Clark party to have the bones of many dead horses "lying about their sepulchres."[46] The Assiniboin ritual varied. Lewis and Clark speak of the Assiniboin, Mandan, and Hidatsa sacrificing the favorite horses and dogs of a deceased owner.[47] A contemporary inquirer, more than a century later, states that Assiniboin horses were turned loose at an unmarried owner's death, and the best of them when a married man died.[48]

In earlier times at least, the tribe apparently did not practice

[38] Lowie, *The Crow Indians*, 91, 228.
[39] *Ibid.*, 67.
[40] Maximilian, *Travels*, in Thwaites, *Travels*, XXIII, 394.
[41] Jenness, *The Sarcee Indians*, 30, 39, 65.
[42] Grinnell, in Hodge, *Handbook*, I, 571; Kidd, "Blackfoot Ethnography," 60–63.
[43] Maximilian, *Travels*, in Thwaites, *Travels*, XXIII, 121, 132.
[44] Kroeber, "Ethnology of the Gros Ventre," 181.
[45] Richardson, *The Comanche Barrier*, 121–22.
[46] Lewis and Clark, *Journals* (ed. by Thwaites), IV, 371; (ed. by Coues), III, 1018.
[47] *Ibid.*, (ed. by Thwaites), I, 323.
[48] Lowie, "The Assiniboin," 42.

inhumation, for Maximilian noted a dead Assiniboin, wrapped in a robe, "on a tree" with his saddle and stirrups hanging near him.[49] Those inveterate thieves must have expected others to regard *their* feelings! Very probably the Assiniboin ritual may be considered broadly true of the Sioux also. The dedication-burial of saddlery has been found in other tribes as well: a present-day investigator has recorded the presence of horse gear in Arikara burial sites.[50]

The use of the horse for food varied considerably among tribes, and a parallel study of tribal custom in this particular, together with the same tribes' ritualistic usages, might throw an instructive light upon these erratic partialities. Denhardt notes the practice in Sonora as early as 1567.[51] An even earlier instance is recorded in Coronado's expedition of 1540, but this can hardly be cited as a practice. Some of the Indians ate an old worn-out horse, which they cooked alive, singeing and half-roasting it.[52] This need not imply the origin of any such practice among the tribes, any more than would the Lewis and Clark party's (in similar extremities) eating dogs.[53] Considered as a deliberate and persisting custom, it seems probable that the earlier dog-eaters became the horse-eaters. Such a name as the Shoshonean "Shirrydika" ("dog-eaters")[54] must surely imply other tribes—Shoshonean or otherwise—who were not. Aside from such inferential evidence, Dobie cites a Shoshonean legend concerning Black Devil, a notable man-eating black stallion, in which the Shoshone ate every mare they could catch before the black stallion tore it to pieces.[55] Yet we find the Comanche (themselves Shoshonean) terming the Arapaho "Dog Eaters" as a term of reproach and contempt.[56]

These horse-eating proclivities were far from being uniform, even among the Shoshone themselves. John K. Townsend records the disgust of a Snake chief who instantly detected horseflesh

---

[49] Maximilian, *Travels,* in Thwaites, *Travels,* XXIII, 32, 36; cf. XXII, 310.

[50] Strong, "From History to Prehistory in the Northern Great Plains," 367.

[51] Denhardt, *Horse of the Americas,* 91, 104.

[52] See Bolton, *Coronado,* 196, 345.

[53] *Journals* (ed. by Thwaites), IV, 317–23, 333–35, 340–42, 356–58; (ed. by Coues), III, 962–66, 969, 972, 984–86.

[54] See Alexander Ross, *Fur Hunters of the Far West,* I, 249; Coues (ed.), *Henry-Thompson Journals,* II, 818; Hodge, *Handbook,* I, 130, 743, etc.

[55] Dobie, *Tales of the Mustang,* 72; *The Mustangs,* 171–78.

[56] Hugh Lenox Scott, "Early History and Names of the Arapaho," 551.

(which he surely must have eaten at some time) in a hodgepodge of many sorts.[57] The chief horse-eaters, according to J. Frank Dobie, were the Apache; the Sioux, Blackfoot, Cheyenne, and other Northern tribes seldom ate horseflesh except in emergency.[58] Dobie has omitted any reference to the Comanche. Horses were "eaten and relished by them," and in fact were the principal food of some of the Comanche bands.[59] The Crow would eat neither dogs nor horses; the former have, however, been introduced in recent festival uses.[60] The Mandan "would eat anything but the horse."[61] On the other hand, Catlin says that 'vast numbers' were eaten by the Indians when buffalo were scarce.[62] The chronic shortage of horses among the Assiniboin, to which reference has been made,[63] may perhaps have been partly due to the fact that they ate many horses, as well as dogs (1833).[64] Lowie, eighty years later, gives what may be an illustration of the change in manners upon which I commented at the outset of this essay.[65] He writes (1909) that his Stoney (Assiniboin) interpreter did not "like to dream of anything he eats; he likes to dream of horses."[66] The Sioux ate dogs—probably horses also—like their kindred, the Assiniboin.[67] We have seen above that the "Beaver (Hills?) Cree" were driven to eat their horses and dogs in 1781,[68] but I have found no further allusion to them doing so; and taken together with Dobie's general conclusion and the asserted scarcity of horses among them, we may conclude this was not a common Cree practice. I am unaware if the esteem of the Flathead for mules was the gourmet's appreciation of a dainty dish,[69] but the Chiricahua Apache were said to prefer mule meat before any other.[70]

[57] Townsend, *Narrative*, in Thwaites, *Travels*, XXI, 252.
[58] *The Mustangs*, 26, 54.
[59] Hoebel, "Political Associations and Law-Ways of the Comanche Indians," 14–15; Richardson, *The Comanche Barrier*, 27.
[60] Maximilian, *Travels*, in Thwaites, *Travels*, XXII, 352; Lowie, *The Crow Indians*, 91, 228.
[61] Maximilian, *Travels*, in Thwaites, *Travels*, XXIII, 297.
[62] Catlin, *Letters and Notes*, II, 59.
[63] See Chapter XIII *supra*.
[64] Maximilian, *Travels*, in Thwaites, *Travels*, XXII, 391.
[65] See the Introduction *supra*.
[66] Lowie, "The Assiniboin," 47.
[67] Maximilian, *Travels*, in Thwaites, *Travels*, XXII, 310.
[68] See Chapter I *supra*.   [69] See note 12 *supra*.
[70] Grinnell, in Hodge, *Handbook*, I, 570.

For basic reasons similar, no doubt, to those of the Indians, the Lewis and Clark expedition were only too glad to have horseflesh to eat at times; not to mention dogs when horses failed.[71] For some years horseflesh was the staple diet at the Hudson's Bay Company's post of Fort Walla Walla (Washington). Between the years 1821 and 1824 the post consumed seven hundred head.[72] Some twenty years later, Narcissa Prentiss Whitman, the great pioneer missionary's wife, testifies to similar problems and a similar solution: ". . . we have killed and eaten ten wild horses bought of the Indians. I do not prefer it to other meat, but can eat it very well."[73] Dobie cites testimony from other (white) consumers, both from necessity and choice, who rated it far more highly—"better eating than beef."[74]

Much of our incidental information concerning various details of horse exchange values comes from Maximilian, writing circa 1833. With regard to the Mandan-Hidatsa villages at least, one is led to suspect that since the monopoly of trade with the upper Missouri territory had ceased, a change had come over the scene. During the intervening thirty years (or since Larocque's time) the numbers suggest that the Mandan had been compelled to breed their own horses. With a people who had acquired a knowledge of horse remedies[75] and probably of other lore—this could in thirty years or less return them far more horses than their numbers of earlier trading days, such as might permit or encourage them to be less exacting. Also, perhaps the white traders had acquainted them with new wants which they had become eager to meet almost (relatively) regardless of cost. Whatever may be the reason, while in some transactions the older, seemingly exorbitant values appear to persist, in other cases a horse would be given for a mere trifle. Maximilian tells us that "ten or fifteen dollars, sometimes even a horse, would be given by the Mandan for a 'silk (buffalo) robe,' a horse for 100 or 150 elks' teeth, or for an ornamental Mandan 'bow-lance,' and sometimes for one or two mere trifles.' "[76] The contrast

[71] *Journals* (ed. by Thwaites), III, 66, 69; IV, 363, 368; V, 68, 71; (ed. by Coues), III, 962–66, 969, 972, 984–88.
[72] Morton, *History of the Canadian West*, 718.
[73] A. B. and D. P. Hulbert (eds.), *Marcus Whitman*, II, 38, 148.
[74] Dobie, *The Mustangs*, 54.
[75] See Chapter XIII *supra*.
[76] Maximilian, *Travels*, in Thwaites, *Travels*, XXIII, 289, 297, 321–23, 360, 371.

with the older times (and incidentally perhaps the then high price of a horse) is revealed in an allusion by Lewis and Clark, with reference to the so-called "Calumet" or bald eagle: "Two tails of this bird is esteemed by Mandans, Minnetares, Ricaras, etc., in the full value of a good horse, or Gun and accoutrements." Among the Osage and "Kanzas," "where this bird is more rare"—and where horses were possibly cheaper—the same were worth two horses.[77]

Similar incidental values, no doubt governed largely by the immediate circumstances of the case, prevailed in other tribes. About 1810 a horse or a gun would be given by the Piegan for a sinew-backed bow.[78] On the Missouri River, 1811, John Bradbury noted that a horse and a blanket were the price of an "Osage orange" bow.[79] Both of those were very highly prized weapons. Among the Crow, a gift of ten arrows was considered equal to a horse.[80] In a tribe where horses have always been plentiful, this rates the arrows rather cheaply, and suggests that in the Crow social scale the craftsman—as in European societies—ranked far below the cavalier. The Sarcee would give six, eight, or ten horses for a 'medicine pipe bundle,' and very similarly for other valuables.[81] With them also, a horse was a common payment to a medicine man for the selection of a name for a child;[82] and similarly among the Atsina and the Assiniboin, "doctors [i.e., shamans] were paid a horse or more for their services."[83] It may be thought to add weight to my foregoing suggestion concerning the Mandan, or it may be pure coincidence, but the Sarcee at least had been breeding horses since the beginning of the nineteenth century.[84] In this very field, however, the inescapable tribal diversity asserts itself once again. At the precise time that Maximilian tells us that the Arikara had "many horses,"[85] the same authority mentions that they offered white captors three horses in exchange for three Arikara prisoners. The offer was re-

[77] Lewis and Clark, *Journals* (ed. by Thwaites), IV, 159.
[78] Coues (ed.), *Henry-Thompson Journals*, II, 713–14.
[79] Bradbury, *Travels*, in Thwaites, *Travels*, V, 170.
[80] Lowie, "Material Culture of the Crow Indians," 230.
[81] Jenness, *The Sarcee Indians*, 78–88.
[82] *Ibid.*, 18.
[83] Kroeber, "Ethnology of the Gros Ventre," 223; Lowie, "The Assiniboin," 31, 43.
[84] See Chapter XIII *supra*.
[85] Maximilian, *Travels*, in Thwaites, *Travels*, XXIII, 14, 387.

fused, and was not increased. The Arikara rode away, singing the death song; and the prisoners were burnt.[86] We have noted the Comanche in earlier horse times "trading" (asking ?) three robes for a horse.[87] At some unspecified era in the nineteenth century a case is recorded of the Comanches, who were seldom short of horses then, accepting seven each for three white female captives.[88] The Arikara could not have rated their tribesmen highly;[89] a direct antithesis to the common war cult of the Plains tribes.

What may perhaps be considered the summit of achievement in the economic significance of the horse is the fact of its furnishing an acceptable medium of exchange for that most highly prized of all the Plains or prairie commodities—the white buffalo skin. It seems at least possible that the (wider) *distribution* of these articles and their acquisition in consequence by Indians other than the fortunate finders may be traceable *de novo* to the horse. Alexander Henry the younger said of the Hidatsa and their adored "buffalo runners": "The only thing that will induce them to part with a horse of this kind is a white buffalo hide."[90] When we reflect how widespread was the Indians' attachment to their buffalo horses, and also that the vendor of a white buffalo hide could almost command his own price (in horses), it becomes difficult to conceive just what *could* have occupied the same place in the scale of values before the horse appeared. In so far as it is possible to equate dogs with horses, a whole troop of dogs would scarcely equal one buffalo runner, and *one* horse commonly meant little in trafficking for a white buffalo hide. To attempt to express its value in terms of the commoner articles of aboriginal intertribal trade—e.g., lodgepoles, bowstaves, copper for hair fillets, etc.—seems merely laughable. A whole village could scarcely transport the value of one hide.

Maximilian notes that his own Mandan or Hidatsa informant had given five horses for a white buffalo skin. Others gave as much

---

[86] *Ibid.*, XXIV, 104; De Voto, *Across the Wide Missouri*, 94–95.

[87] See Chapter XIII *supra*.

[88] (Rev.) John McLean, *Indians of Canada*, 217–20.

[89] Wilson P. Hunt, of the westbound Astorians, 1811, noted that the Arikara wanted more for their horses than the Cheyenne. See Rollins (ed.), *Discovery of the Oregon Trail*, 281–85; cf. Bradbury, *Travels*, in Thwaites, *Travels*, V, 130 ff.

[90] Coues (ed.), *Henry-Thompson Journals*, I, 353. At Fort Vermilion (North Saskatchewan River), 1810, Henry obtained a buffalo runner for twenty pints of rum (*ibid.*, II, 619).

as ten horses, besides a gun, a kettle, and other things; up to even fifteen horses. This was also the case with the Hidatsa, who were said to have learned this veneration from the Mandan.[91] Even the miserly Arikara gave five horses for a white skin.[92] Among the Mandan-Hidatsa at least, such prices were only for a young buffalo cow; to kill one of which was, in these tribes, a greater exploit than to slay an enemy. A horse would be given to someone else, even to skin it. Older cows, or white bulls, were of much less value.[93] Buffalo skins with white spots, were also highly esteemed.[94] Even a "silk robe" was worth a horse.[95] Their (commercial) value lay in their rarity. Hornaday supposed that the entire history of the buffalo yielded only eleven specimens of white animals, but that was an error even for his own time.[96]

Yet we must not lose sight of one important consideration. We have, in so far as I am aware, no historical notice of any extratribal trade in white buffalo skins, whether among later horse Indians or others, in the pre-equestrian era.[97] Our very earliest definite allusion, that of Antony Henday (1754), while literally post-equestrian, is perhaps not too late to belong psychologically to the older world. This reference itself, moreover, is rather vague, for Henday states that the white skin was in use as a seat or cushion by the Blackfoot chief, which does not quite suggest "worship."[98] The Blackfoot later (though some discrepant testimony exists) were apparently among the worshipping tribes,[99] and hence were *ipso*

[91] Maximilian, *Travels*, in Thwaites, *Travels*, XXIII, 322, 350.

[92] *Ibid.*, XXIII, 350, 390; Coues (ed.), *Henry-Thompson Journals*, I, 354.

[93] Maximilian, *Travels*, in Thwaites, *Travels*, XXIII, 321-23.

[94] Coues (ed.), *Henry-Thompson Journals*, I, 354; II, 646 (1806, 1810); cf. "Head of a Pied Buffalo Cow" (photo, in Garretson, *The American Bison*, 13).

[95] Maximilian, *Travels*, in Thwaites, *Travels*, XXIII, 289, 321-23, 371 (sometimes "ten or fifteen dollars"). For "silk" or "beaver" robes, see Roe, *North American Buffalo*, 64-65.

[96] See *ibid.*, App. D, "Albinism in Buffalo," 715-28.

[97] The Illinois Indians had a white buffalo ritual (Hodge, *Handbook*, II, 403, 939-44); and Catlin gives a name for white buffalo in Tuscarora, which indicates a knowledge at least (*Letters and Notes*, II, 262-66).

[98] Henday, "Journal" (ed. by Burpee), 337; cf. the cap of white buffalo skin worn by a Hidatsa chief (Maximilian, *Travels*, in Thwaites, *Travels*, XXIV, 72). It is difficult in these cases to distinguish between personal (non-reverential) use, social dignity, or ritualistic adornment.

[99] See Roe, *North American Buffalo*, 722, where several authorities are cited in support of this. Yet Catlin mentions their bringing a white skin to the Mandan in trade (*Letters and Notes*, I, 133). There was a similar cleavage of thought among

facto unlikely to be handing on white buffalo skins to other tribes. Consequently, while the foregoing suggestions regarding the *extension* of the white buffalo cult by commercial distribution since the coming of the horse seem reasonably logical and probable, none the less in the final analysis they remain conjectural.

But with this one possible exception, every other phase of the economic field points in my judgment clearly to the post-equestrian phenomena being little or nothing more than an extended application of long-existent prior conventions. A contemporary scholar, in discussing these questions, cites Wissler's—as yet unrefuted—pronouncement which "conceived the influence of the horse in terms of an intensification and diffusion of cultural traits already in existence at the time of the advent of that animal."[100] He himself endorses the view of other critics who largely reject Wissler's conclusions or amend them beyond recognition. Yet Jablow's own important and valuable monograph, the central thesis of which is the economic importance of the Indian horse (particularly in the northern area), does not place the formal period of these activities earlier than 1795.[101] This deprives the question of the immediate or early economic influence of the horse of almost all significance.

the Sioux: the Yanktonais traded theirs, while the Uncpapa observed a sacrifice (see Roe, *North American Buffalo*, 723).

[100] Jablow, *The Cheyenne*, 11. His reference is to Wissler's opinion that "It is as an intensifier of original Plains traits that the horse presents its strongest claim." (Wissler, "Influence of the Horse," 18; cf. "Material Culture of the North American Indians," 484–86.)

[101] Jablow, *The Cheyenne*.

XV

INDIAN "WEALTH IN HORSES"

Whether we regard the cultural phenomena of the Plains tribes relating to the horse as original manifestations since the advent of the animal, or as extensions and developments of long existent prior conventions, one thing at least may be taken for granted. Such a study as the present essay could not even approach completeness without some attempt to ascertain, however roughly, something of the tribal resources in horse numbers by means of which these processes were effected.

It is needless to tell the reader that our material for this purpose is very imperfect. We have neither any definite census figures covering the great horse Indian tribes at large during any one portion of the horse era, nor have we such figures for any single tribe during the era as a whole. With respect to large aggregates, our working data are practically confined to mere assertions of totals, and what seem rather loose comparisons of tribe with tribe, concerning which we frequently encounter highly contradictory statements from observers of apparently equal credibility. Having regard to these factors, to follow along lines of cautious and tentative comparison seems the only safe procedure, and we shall adopt this course in the present chapter. Fortunately, the meagerness of our original source material has in some measure been relieved by secondary studies from later commentators who have themselves been oppressed by the same lack. One secondary study in particular is of great significance, since it has to do with the precise topic indicated by our present title, and discusses this with reference to a tribe which has always been considered prominent among the great

horse tribes of the Plains, and is actually the farthest northern example of such in this major sense, the Blackfoot.[1] I cannot but feel,
however, that the author has fused into one two questions which
in my view are totally distinct, and which I shall myself treat from
that angle.

I am completely in accord with Ewers in his rejection of the
literal acceptance of precise numbers in cases of "hundreds" and
"thousands," and I consider that in discussing this question he has
rendered valuable service to Western historical criticism. The adoption of assertions of this character—commonly without hesitation—
raises questions to which we require answers; and these will be
found difficult. I myself have protested vigorously elsewhere and
in detail against the blind acceptance of sweeping assertions about
"millions" in the case of the buffalo. The "thousands" in the case of
the horse demand a similar scrutiny.

Ewers doubts the credibility of the statement made to Maximilian at Fort McKenzie (upper Missouri River) in 1833, that a
certain Blackfoot chief, Sachkomapoh, who had died prior to Maximilian's visit, had owned between four thousand and five thousand
horses.[2] I consider Ewers entirely justified in querying an assertion
of this very definite character. "Thousands" mean *thousands;* or
they do not. We are not informed whether this estimate or computation came from an Indian or a white man. If the former, by what
method did an Indian count into the thousands, and who guar-
antees his accuracy? Or how could he—or anyone else likely to be
available in the region—reduce some (presumably) aboriginal principle of computation into any such alien equation?

This crux is not to be met by learned reference to native Indian
numeral systems or definite terms for hundreds and thousands, of
which many could be brought forward.[3] We have no ground whatever for any assumption that the originating authority in this case
was necessarily (1) an accurate master of his tribal arithmetic; and
(2) that he was intellectually and temperamentally competent to
apply it correctly and recount it candidly and reliably. We have nu-

[1] Ewers, "Were the Blackfoot Rich in Horses?" 602-10.
[2] Maximilian, *Travels*, in Thwaites, *Travels*, XXIII, 121.
[3] For example, see an elaborate paper giving fifty-eight tables of linguistic
and dialectal data, by Roland B. Dixon and John R. Swanton, "Numeral Systems
of the Languages of California," *American Anthropologist*, Vol. IX (1907), 663-90.

merical systems of absolute accuracy in our own Euro-American societies. To suggest that the mere existence of these is a guarantee against error or exaggeration would be to invite a well-deserved contempt. We have some descriptions of the manner in which Indians in the north and the south respectively applied such powers of computation as they possessed. David Thompson writes (about 1800):

> The Northern Indians count numbers the same manner as we do to the numbers of a 100 which they call the great ten; and a thousand the great great ten; beyond which they do not even pretend to number; and even of this they make no use, and any things, as of birds and animals that would amount to this number, they would express it by a great many. But the Indians of the plains count only by tens, and what is above two tens, they lay small sticks on the ground to show the number of tens they have to count and in describing the herds of Bisons or Deer, they express them by a great great many; and the space they stand on; for numbers is to them an abstract idea, but space of ground to a certain extent they readily comprehend and the animals it may contain; for they do not appear to extend their faculties beyond what is visible and tangible.[4]

Richardson notes among the Comanche the superstitious or "psychic" avoidance of certain terms, particularly those which entered into the name of a dead man. This might involve the use of "enough" as a synonym for an inhibited or tabooed "ten."[5] The resultant possibilities of confusion are analogous to the well-known Biblical "forty days." This, in the earlier versions, is traceable to an erroneous caligraphic identification with a similar Hebrew word signifying "many," in which sense such passages should be understood. In the case of the Indian the danger of error in these connections is increased infinitely by the lack of a written language.

If the estimate is from some white observer, how did this man reach his total? Did he possess the requisite qualities to judge accurately and relate candidly? If by counting, how did he get the opportunity to count thousands so precisely in an unfenced, open country? If by computation or a purely conjectural estimate, who

---

4 Thompson, *Narrative* (ed. by Tyrrell), 367.
5 Richardson, *The Comanche Barrier*, 20.

was this individual, and why should we accept his figures without knowing more about him? Theodore Roosevelt wisely and repeatedly warns his readers against a too ready literal acceptance of details from the precise type of plainsmen (or their ancestors almost certainly: the trans-Alleghenian Revolutionary fighters) to which Maximilian's informant almost inevitably belonged, and above all in this very matter of numbers.[6] Even if this man were the commandant at the post, that by no means authenticates everything he might choose to say. He was often of the same essential type. Politeness, respect due to an old-timer, or prudence might close one's mouth at the moment, but later critics need not be bound by such conventions. It is the old-timer who retails the nonsense about the "hoop snake." I have had occasion elsewhere to analyze a number of typical statements of this class from similar witnesses, also in the Plains territory, in relation to loose assertions concerning buffalo numbers. I do not feel justified in regarding these definite "thousands" as signifying more than "a large number," which at times possibly contained hundreds.

When we are told that a rich Mexican widow in Durango presented her son's regiment with six hundred white horses, such numbers are not wholly beyond belief, for they commonly find their way into official records, from which this is said to be taken. They could even be counted; either directly, or in relation to the strength of the regiment. It may be true that there were, as George Wilkins Kendall stated, "over one thousand of them, all off one hacienda and hardly a month's difference in their ages." But Kendall was also told that the widow-owner "had once possessed 300,000 head of horses."[7] Whether Kendall believed this or not, we are under no obligation to do so; and I do not.

It has been noted that critical scholars consider that the Pawnee may have had the horse before 1600.[8] In 1719, Du Tisné, a French explorer, counted three hundred horses at the Pawnee villages, at which time they were said to be scarce.[9] In 1806 Zebulon M. Pike

---

[6] See Theodore Roosevelt, *The Winning of the West*, I, 259, for a specimen.

[7] George W. Kendall, *Narrative of the Texas Santa Fé Expedition* (1847 edition; which I have been unable to see), II, 110–11; cited by Dobie, *Tales of the Mustang*, 40; *The Mustangs*, 70.

[8] Wissler, "Influence of the Horse," 25–26; Haines, "Northward Spread of Horses," 433. (See Chapter IV *supra*.)

[9] See Chapter IV.

said they had "vast quantities."[10] In 1819, Edwin James specifies "six thousand or eight thousand";[11] that is, a suggested aggregate in thousands, augmented in the act of speaking by 33 per cent! Thomas James saw a band of Comanche on the Canadian River in 1823 who captured in a few hours "more than a hundred mustangs." Such a number is credible, since these could be counted, or even half their number counted and the remainder computed. But when the Comanche went on to tell James that at their home camp on the Red River they had sixteen thousand horses,[12] I must know, as in the case of Maximilian's informant, something more of their methods of computation, and of their general capability as accountants.

It might possibly be the case, as Pike tells us it was, about 1807, that the Comanche swept off two thousand horses from one village in a single raid,[13] since this may have been something of the nature of a "town herd," and the Comanches would no doubt take them all. But when we are told that as early as 1694—if dates are of any importance in these affairs—the Apache and their allies ran off 100,000 horses in Sonora and Sinaloa (Mexico),[14] mere critical hesitation scarcely defines one's feelings. I see little occasion for much hesitation of any character. The more closely one peers into such mysteries the more closely they resemble the famous instance of the "million cats in our yard." In my judgment they may fittingly keep company with Simon Kenton's buffalo-and-Indian trails in Kentucky, "a hundred yards wide";[15] Daniel Ott's "piles of buffalo hides a hundred feet high," in a prairie town in Kansas;[16] or (from a scientist!) Spencer F. Baird's "3,500,000 buffalo" slain annually by the upper Missouri tribes alone, about 1852—that is, by some twelve thousand hunters in an estimated population of less than fifty-five thousand.[17]

10 Coues (ed.), *Expeditions of Pike*, II, 533.

11 James, *Account of the Expedition under Long*, in Thwaites, *Travels*, XV, 207–208, 215. See Chapter IV *supra*.

12 Dobie, *The Mustangs*, 71–72. Thomas James bought 323; these again could be (and doubtless were) *counted*.

13 Ojo Caliente, Río Grande region: Coues (ed.), *Expeditions of Pike*, II, 537, 600.

14 Bancroft, *North Mexican States and Texas*, I, 255. See Chapter IV *supra* for contemporary comparisons and rebuttals.

15 Edna Kenton, *Simon Kenton, His Life and Period*, 63–64; cf. 304.

16 See Roe, *North American Buffalo*, 493.

17 *Ibid.*, 502.

But to make the incredibility of definitive "thousands" the basis for a reasoned insistence upon a *positive* lack of horses among the Blackfoot, beyond a virtually irreducible minimum,[18] is another affair entirely. The inherent likelihood of this condition of things, and also the detailed data by which Ewers seeks to establish his contention, require careful examination before they can be accepted. In respect of the general characteristics which mark the horse Indian in his mastery of the equestrian culture, the Blackfoot in the north were what the Comanche were in the Southwest—the acknowledged leaders. How then came the former to be acclaimed "horse poor," either by later scholars or by those contemporaries upon whom such critics must base their conclusions? Any demonstrated large-scale reduction in our conceptions of normal Blackfoot horse numbers *ipso facto* necessitates a material modification in our views concerning the significance of the horse in the Northern Plains area at large. Ewers himself appears to have fallen into the same error upon which he comments in the case of Oscar Lewis (whose monograph I have had no opportunity to see): the error of using imperfect data as a basis for too definitive conclusions.[19]

As I remark elsewhere in the present essay, the precise date at which the Blackfoot acquired the horse is unknown. But we do know that eighty years prior to Maximilian, Antony Henday (whom Ewers does not mention) wintered with the Northern Blackfoot, in 1754–55.[20] The geographical factors regarding their habitual range at this time have been reviewed above, in their connection with the identification of Fort la Jonquière.[21] The authentic site of this post has been decided by scholars who were not in the least concerned with any thesis regarding the horse. These combined factors make it virtually certain that those northerly bands would be almost inevitably the latest to obtain horses, whether the animal reached them from the south or from the west. Yet when Hen-

---

[18] Ewers, "Were the Blackfoot Rich in Horses?" 602–10.

[19] *Ibid.*, 602; re Oscar Lewis, *The Effects of White Contact upon Blackfoot Culture.*

[20] Henday, "Journal" (ed. by Burpee), 307–54.

[21] See Chapter V *supra.*

day encountered them they exhibited every indication of a typical horse Indian society. An evident mastery such as we have seen was theirs in 1754[22] cannot be attained at a single bound. Neither can it be attained, in my judgment, without a sufficient strength in horseflesh to allow of constant equestrian practice; any more than the man who has to borrow a gun or an axe is likely to become an expert in his respective art.

The value of old-timer reminiscence (white or red) is in my judgment very easily—and very frequently—overestimated. The mere fact that a man was born, or has lived for fifty years, in a country does not necessarily justify an implicit belief in everything he may say or even insist upon. Assuming the requisite qualities of the accurate chronicler, we must take the circumstances into consideration. If written from day to day, as the journal of the younger Alexander Henry was written (the final entry was made upon the very day of his tragic death),[23] the material may reasonably be relied upon. Written years afterward, reminiscent matter may—and commonly does—require some very careful checking. I do not decry the Indian; I have had several Indian friends myself. But it would be idle to claim, for "Indians," capacities which the Indian commonly does not possess. He is one of the world's acutest observers of the moment. But he is not a generalizer;[24] and still less is he the annalistic scribe. We know well enough from our own people that the mechanical art of writing (which several northwestern Plains tribes possess in high ratio[25]) and the *habit* of written record are totally different things. We have seen, moreover, that senile memory can play strange tricks even in minds whose active careers have been those of systematized record.[26] I have elsewhere shown that an Indian tradition only eleven years old proved utterly fallacious when examined at close range.[27] In an-

[22] See Henday, "Journal" (ed. by Burpee), 334–51 (see Chapter XIII *supra*).

[23] Henry was drowned on the Columbia Bar, off the present Astoria, Oregon, 1814. See Coues (ed.), *Henry-Thompson Journals*.

[24] See Grinnell, *The Fighting Cheyennes*, 270.

[25] Since the designing of James Evans' Cree Syllabary in 1841, it has been in use among the Cree, Ojibwa, Assiniboin, Blackfoot, and others, and is still the written medium in the northern fur trade.

[26] See Chapter V *supra*.

[27] Roe, "Extermination of the Buffalo in Western Canada," 1–23. (See below, note 52 ff.)

other instance, and in this very region of northern Montana, a
Blood chief, One Spot, is quoted as corroborative evidence for a
buffalo movement diametrically opposed to his own testimony,
but which nevertheless possesses historical support.[28] Since this
old-timer reminiscence is considered acceptable at face value, however, I shall myself adduce it in evidence. The witnesses in question
are Alexander Culbertson, an early agent of the American Fur
Company in the upper Missouri country (about 1833–1873); the
broadly contemporary Charles Larpenteur, of the same service;
and "elderly informants on the Blackfoot Reservation, Montana"
(1942–43).[29] The younger Alexander Henry does not belong to this
class. His journals are not reminiscence; they are current knowledge of their time. I shall cite these witnesses in their chronological
order.

Henry writes as follows: ". . . some of the Blackfeet own 40 to
60 horses. But the Piegans have by far the greatest numbers; I
heard of one man who had 300."[30] Culbertson is cited to this effect
by a much later historian: "The Blackfeet had possessed horses as
far back as their traditions extended [?] but never in considerable
numbers in early times, and even as late as 1833 they were poorly
mounted."[31] To this general period belongs also the Blood chief,
Seen From Afar (circa 1810–70): "He was the greatest chief Major
Culbertson ever saw amongst the Blackfeet—having 10 wives and
100 horses." Larpenteur writes of the period circa 1860: "It is a fine
sight to see one of these big men among the Blackfeet, who has
two or three lodges, five or six wives, twenty or thirty children, and
fifty to a hundred horses; for his trade amounts to upward of
$2.000 [sic] a year."[32] Larpenteur certainly seems to suggest a num-
ber of such magnates among the Blackfoot.

On such a man, Ewers comments thus: "Obviously Larpenteur
was writing of no ordinary man. He was describing an important
headman or chief."[33] But quite as obviously, so was Maximilian.

[28] Ibid., 8–9; Roe, North American Buffalo, 477–80.
[29] Ewers, "Were the Blackfoot Rich in Horses?" 602–603.
[30] Coues (ed.), Henry-Thompson Journals, II, 526.
[31] (Lieut.) James H. Bradley, "Characteristics, Habits, and Customs of the
Blackfeet Indians." I have not seen this; cited by Ewers, "Were the Blackfoot Rich
in Horses?" 603.
[32] Ewers, ibid., 603.
[33] Ibid., 603.

For the latter adds (what Ewers overlooks) that at Sachkomapoh's funeral 150 horses were slain.[34] There is no reason to suppose that these constituted his total possessions in horses. Such a clearly exceptional event (in numbers at least; for I have found nothing resembling it) would almost certainly have been mentioned. Another point may be noted. We have no ground for any assumption that "Sachkomapoh's" horses really belonged to the tribe of which he happened to be chief; and that 150 of these were requisitioned for his funeral ceremonies. J. Frank Dobie writes very emphatically as follows: "It is to be kept in mind that no horses were tribally owned. They were all owned by individual tribesmen."[35] I have thus far met with no testimony to the contrary. We have noted common (family) ownership of dogs,[36] but I have found no indication of its extension in any form to horses. Ewers himself quotes James Willard Schultz relative to the Piegan in the late eighteen seventies. While Schultz certainly speaks of "tribal wealth," he makes it quite clear that this term really signifies an aggregate of individual property owned in severalty. Schultz writes: "Horses were the tribal wealth, and one who owned a large herd of them held a position only to be compared to that of our multi-millionaires. There were individuals who owned from one hundred to three and four hundred."[37] This passage constitutes rather strange testimony to the Blackfoot Confederacy's poverty in horses, at least. And Ewers, as we shall note, apparently conjoins all their tribes together in discussing the "Blackfoot" horse conditions.

With respect to private ownership as a social concept, we have, in so far as I am aware, very little evidence for any general hypothesis of Indian polities north of the Aztecs (if theirs was one) where the chief, as a "Son of Heaven," could blaze in an unapproachable Oriental splendor while his "subjects" groveled in uncomplaining poverty around him. Unless such men as Maximilian's chief were merely the mountain peaks in a range of broadly general tribal sufficiency, I gravely doubt whether the prestige of personal prowess and of a "wealth," which no possessor could hope to de-

---

[34] Maximilian, *Travels*, in Thwaites, *Travels*, XXIII, 121, 132.
[35] Dobie, *The Mustangs*, 43.
[36] See Chapter I *supra*.
[37] James Willard Schultz, *My Life as an Indian*, 152; cited by Ewers, "Were the Blackfoot Rich in Horses?" 603.

fend without his tribesmens' help, would long survive an economic inequality in which one or two had enough and to spare while the *hoi polloi* perished with hunger. We have seen how little permanent authority, beyond that of the sergeant-major for the nonce, was attached even to the leadership of a war party; and war parties were an enterprise which a man could scarcely launch without considerable prior influence.[38]

The details which Ewers gives of Piegan philanthropy—in which the great man helped the poor and the poor man loved the great—are presumably derived from the ancient informants. They introduce us to a "capitalistic" state to which I have thus far encountered no parallel in Indian tribal societies. That the wealthy horse owner should refuse to lend a horse to a horseless ne'er-do-well (for hunting purposes) need perhaps occasion no surprise. But unless buffalo were plentiful—which was by no means always the case[39]—even undeserved poverty received no further concession than the "renting" of a horse, which was paid for by dividing the spoils of the hunt with its owner. "Thus the owner of many horses used them to insure a steady food supply for his household. Thus the aged and infirm . . . who owned good horses insured their [own] subsistence."[40] Unless this social polity rests upon much sounder authority than that of the ancient tribesmen who furnished the numerical details for the period of their own youth and beyond, I remain dubious.

We have noted Henry's statement that the Piegan owned far more than other members of the Confederacy. Ewers goes on to add:

Yet even among the Piegan, informants stated, a man who owned 40 or 50 horses in the time of their youth was considered well-to-do. They named less than a dozen men who could count their horses in hundreds at that time, bearing out Schultz' contention that such men were the 'multi-millionaires' of their tribe. When asked to name the Blackfoot who owned the largest number of horses ever possessed by a single individual among the three Blackfoot tribes, all informants, without hesitation, told of Many Horses (Heavy Shield), the Piegan

[38] See Chapter XII *supra*.
[39] See Roe, *North American Buffalo,* 521–600, etc.
[40] Ewers, "Were the Blackfoot Rich in Horses?" 608–609.

chief who was killed in battle with the Gros Ventre and Crow in 1866. Our informants were mere children when Many Horses died. But several of them are descendants of Many Horses, and the others had heard a great deal about him from their parents and other older Indians. Their estimates of the number of horses owned by Many Horses when his herds were at their greatest size vary from 'about 500' to 'less than 1000.' One informant, through his grandmother, had heard of Maximilian's Sachkomapoh. He had heard of him as a man who had been very rich in horses, but felt certain that he had never owned many more than Many Horses did at a later date.[41]

As traditional evidence from unlettered sources, these items require to be examined in detail. It is pure assumption that because these informants "named less than a dozen men," *ergo*, there were no others.[42] We are frequently hearing of university students who cannot name the last President preceding Franklin D. Roosevelt. *Ergo* (presumably), there are none. The unhesitating agreement respecting Many Horses' many horses means very little in my opinion. He was nearest to them, and his name was probably a household word in their childhood. He would appear almost chronologically, moreover, to have been "The Last of the Barons." A more serious crux confronts us in their numbers. We are not informed, any more than in Maximilian's instance, by what scheme of computation they determined their totals; and these totals vary by something dangerously near to 50 per cent. Another consideration is more crucial yet. I maintain my rejection of the literal thousands in Maximilian's case, but the sole feature which differentiates the respective statements is the smaller size of the Piegan totals. This hypothesis as advanced by Ewers requires us to reject testimony respecting a well-known figure in his own locality, who had apparently died but a short time previously, and to implicitly accept testimony identical *in esse,* concerning another who had been dead nearly eighty years and of whom none of the witnesses could possess anything beyond hearsay knowledge. As for our English idiom, "between five hundred and one thousand," which Ewers makes his own,[43] I very much doubt whether it could even be made in-

[41] *Ibid.,* 604.
[42] See note 71 *infra* on the omission of 1882–83, etc., from their reminiscent catalogue of hard winters.
[43] Ewers, "Were the Blackfoot Rich in Horses?" 604, 609.

telligible to a noneducated Indian. The "certainty" that Many Horses owned more horses than anybody else ever did need not detain us long. This is the mental attitude of the English rustic of the last century who was immovably certain that the village squire or the local small-town banker was the richest man in the world.

I am worse than dubious concerning statistics of Indian horse numbers based upon average numbers of horses per lodge among different tribes. I have elsewhere presented detailed evidence respecting the numbers of *men* (or souls) per lodge or hut, which robs the term "Indian average" of any meaning. Calculations based upon any such supposed uniformity are vitiated at the outset. My own tables include some of the tribes quoted by Ewers from Lieutenant James H. Bradley's calculations, which I give below:[44]

Horses per lodge	Crow	15
"　"　"	Piegan	10
"　"　"	Blackfoot and Blood	5
"　"　"	Gros Ventre	5
"　"　"	Flathead and Nez Percé	50
"　"　"	Assiniboin	2

We might perhaps anticipate some degree of uniformity between the Sioux and their kindred the Assiniboin. Pike and Long (1805, 1823) give Sioux and Assiniboin averages per lodge as being respectively 16.6 and 12.6 for the Sioux and (Long) 9.33 per lodge for the Assiniboin.[45] The Blackfoot Confederacy vary similarly. The younger Henry gives a Piegan average of two warriors per tent. At the same time, the Siksika had 160 warriors in one group of 80 tents, while in another they had 360 warriors in 120 tents—an increased ratio of 50 per cent.[46] Alexander Mackenzie in 1789 estimated 8 persons per tent for the Siksika, which is endorsed by a competent modern investigator;[47] and David Thompson, circa 1800, has 7.22 for the Sarcee.[48] Among other prairie tribes in the Lewis and Clark tables, the Gros Ventre (which in their case prob-

[44] *Ibid.,* 603.
[45] Roe, *North American Buffalo,* 745–46.
[46] *Ibid.,* 747.
[47] *Ibid.,* 747; cf. Kidd, "Blackfoot Ethnography," 26.
[48] Thompson, *Narrative* (ed. by Tyrrell), 327; cf. Jenness, *The Sarcee Indians,* 1–10; Roe, *North American Buffalo,* 747.

ably signify the Hidatsa) yield an average of 15.8 persons per tent.[49] The same explorers mention several bands of the Nez Percé ("Chopunnish") whose general average of 33.0 per house conceals a variation from 7.66 to 60.6. The Wappatoo, a transmontane confederacy of thirteen tribes or bands, do not enter into our present discussion, but to cite their general average of 52.33, resulting from 5,590 persons in 107 houses, would be completely misleading, when the individual averages of the thirteen bands range from 23.33 to 133.33 per house.[50] It is furthermore obvious on a moment's reflection that such averages (!), illustrations of which could be widely extended, might be altered beyond recognition in a day of Indian life. A slaughter of warriors, or of women and children in the warriors' absence, or a destruction of dwellings where the occupants escaped, would render calculation fantastic.[51] I am not at the moment concerned whether these discrepancies favor Ewers' immediate contention or my own. They reveal clearly that no reliance may be placed upon any hypothesis that is built upon a supposed uniformity in numbers per lodge.

The question of physical deterrents to the increase of the Blackfoot herds is one of immense interest. The principal phenomena noted by Ewers are occasional epidemic disease and losses from privation in exceptionally severe winters. By reason of fifty years' residence in north-central Alberta (1894–1944), the present writer can speak with some personal knowledge in both fields. We shall take the question of disease first.

Apart from certain visitations mentioned by Ewers, to which I shall refer later, the only historical notice known to me of epidemic disease in the early literature that has reference to animal life in the Blackfoot territory is from Hector, of the Palliser expedition. Hector wrote as follows in 1858, being then in the North Saskatchewan headwaters country, above Rocky Mountain House (about 52° N, 117° W):

[49] *Ibid.*, 746.
[50] *Ibid.*, 748.
[51] *Ibid.*, 742–43, giving historical instances, about 1800, of each type of wartime catastrophe.

Near our camp we found some old buffalo dung, and the Indians told us that not many years ago there were many of these animals along the valley of the North Saskatchewan, within the mountains. Eleven years ago, they say, there were great fires all through the mountains, and in the woods along their eastern base; and after that a disease broke out among all the animals, so that they used to find wapiti [elk], moose, and other deer, as well as buffalo, lying dead in numbers. Before that time there was abundance of game in all parts of the country; but since then there has been great scarcity of animals, and only the best hunters can make sure of killing. I have heard the same description of the sudden change that took place in the abundance of game from half-breed hunters in different parts of the country; so there is little doubt that there is some foundation for the account given by the Indians.[52]

Hector was a most cautious and trustworthy inquirer. But he was only a transient visitor, debarred inevitably from the wide accumulation of comparative data on the region and dependent sometimes upon reckless generalization from others, of which I suspect this to be an instance. Since I have given the evidence in full detail elsewhere,[53] it is sufficient to say here that both the extraordinary plenty prior to circa 1847, and the almost normal condition of scarcity after that time, are destitute of historical support. Hector himself mentions a Stoney (Assiniboin) hunter who had killed fifty-seven "moose-deer" in one recent season.[54] Fires are recorded in 1847 by Rundle the missionary, but they were in the Little Red Deer (River) foothill country farther east,[55] and the immense masses of lumber since produced from Hector's very region indicate that they could only have been local in their extent. The disease finds no further mention, historical or traditional, in an almost exhaustive examination of the local literature.

The general credibility of the disease which *followed* the fires and which attacked "all the animals," may perhaps be estimated from the following particulars, which are drawn from the present writer's own personal experience. The great epidemic of "swamp fever" (gleet) and glanders of 1901, which almost exterminated

[52] Hector, in Palliser, *Journals*, 111.

[53] See Roe, "Extermination of the Buffalo in Western Canada," 1–23.

[54] So Hector was told at Rocky Mountain House: Palliser, *Journals*, 76, 102, 107–108.

[55] Rundle, "Journal" (ed. by Berry and Roe), May 19, 1847.

the valuable imported horses of Alberta, affected the hardy, native range-bred horses comparatively little, and the horned cattle not at all. The swamp fever, whose name betrays its supposed origin at least, was fostered, if not originally occasioned, in the opinion of careful observers, by the circumstance that for five consecutive years (1899 to 1903 inclusive; its outbreak in the worst form was in the third of the cycle) almost incessant rains from spring until autumn made prairie fires an impossibility. Vegetation during those years was abnormally luxuriant and rank. Meadows were turned into swamps or something more; swamps were converted into lakes;[56] enormous areas of land were homesteaded and bought in districts which previous to 1899 had been regarded as being for all time suitable only for ranching unless irrigated;[57] and some phenomenal crops were harvested on long-abandoned fields.[58] During this period the never very uncommon midsummer experience in many parts of western Canada of cloudless mornings and overcast or wet afternoons was to be noted almost unbrokenly for weeks at a time.[59] The lower lands were like forcing-beds. The hot steamy atmosphere of the woodlands and the scrub gave forth that peculiarly fetid exhalation which is only associated with rotting vegetation. A very competent medical man, well known in the early medical history of the province,[60] called in to attend a near neighbor and old friend of my own then living among rather marshy woodlands, whose complaint brought him very near to death, stated to us that, absurd as it might seem in such a latitude and altitude (about 2,500 feet), he could call the malady by no other name than

[56] I myself learned to swim in 1901 in a former hay slough eight feet deep in water, out of which we hauled the hay in full loads in 1898. See Frank Gilbert Roe, "The Alberta Wet Cycle of 1899–1903," *Agricultural History*, Vol. XXVIII (July, 1954), 112–20.

[57] It was this wet cycle that settled southern Alberta, from 49° N to Olds, fifty miles north of Calgary. In 1898 there were four houses on the last-named stretch.

[58] In 1902 I saw fields south of Calgary raising timothy four feet in height, over which I rode in 1896–98; at which time the soil was blown out to the ploughing depth, and there was no vegetable growth whatever beyond a few scattered clumps of wild sage.

[59] For a mass of testimony on this over the entire Western Plains area, see Roe, *North American Buffalo*, 85–86.

[60] The late Dr. W. J. Simpson, then of Lacombe (Alberta), 1899 *et seq.* In 1943 I had the pleasure of again meeting Dr. Simpson, who remembered the circumstances perfectly.

malaria; and would unhesitatingly have diagnosed the case as such had he encountered it in a more southerly climatic region.[61] The foregoing statements are not guesswork. I kept a daily diary, including notes on weather (without instruments) for many years. During this wet cycle we had practically no mosquitoes, as the surface water was kept cold and fresh by the incessant rains.[62] In 1904, the first more normal season, I had grown cattle which did not know the use of a "smudge" for the flies—a thing we had not seen about the place since 1900.

Since that time I have neither seen nor heard of more than one wet season at a time; nor have I heard of any reappearance of swamp fever on the grand scale of an epidemic. It was thought at the time, and seems not unreasonable, that the purifying agency of the prairie fires had some connection with this. They were especially bad in 1904. The lush growth of the wet years embosomed scrublands and fences in sheer thickets of long dry grasses, and control was extraordinarily difficult. Among countless others, I myself lost a mile (320 rods) of rail fencing.

I have mentioned the fact that no similar scourge has been recorded since that time. By peculiar good fortune, which occurred within my own experience, it can be said with some assurance that no such excessively flooded condition had been known for at least some seventy years previously. This phenomenon is not to be confused with river floods, which in the Rocky Mountain Basin are commonly caused by suddenly melting snows. The absence of any allusion to such a wet cycle in the early literature of the region from Henday and David Thompson onward probably justifies us in pushing its likelihood backward to the pre-equestrian era. The test I have mentioned arose as follows: The roof tree for my log house was cut in 1897 from a small clump of white poplars growing

---

[61] What is sometimes termed "Rocky Mountain fever" is asserted by an old Northwest Mounted Police veteran, who assimilates it to the common "local fever" of many lands, to be "the typho-malarial scourge." He ridicules the idea put forth in early immigration literature that "there is no malaria" (John G. Donkin, *Trooper and Redskin in the Far Northwest*, 41). The foul miasmic exhalation here mentioned was noted by Lescarbot in New France, which itself could scarcely be called tropical (*History of New France* [ed. by Biggar], II, 264).

[62] In 1900 and again in 1903, two or three of us had to fence across a wide hollow nearly four feet deep in water. We stripped down to hats and shoes alone. This tells its own tale. It would have been patently impossible in ordinary "fly years" (in June!).

along the edge of the slough-lake in which I learned to swim in 1901. In 1903 the remainder of the clump were drowned and dead, as the result of three years' submersion in three or four feet of water. My roof log was twenty-four feet long and one foot in diameter at the butt. I am informed by high botanical-ecological authority on Alberta vegetation that *Populus tremuloides* of those dimensions would most probably be about seventy years of age.[63] As may be noted along the Mississippi, for example (where I observed the condition in 1942), most trees can endure submersion of their roots for about one season and no more. Had my log ever encountered three years' submersion before, it could never have reached that size. That is, there had been no such condition since about 1830. And this, as we have seen, was in the actual area of the Northern Blackfoot long before and long after 1830.

In a letter to Father De Smet from Father Hoecken, written in the spring of 1857, there is an allusion to some outbreak which was affecting men and horses alike. It reads thus:

... an epidemic disease is making terrible ravages among the Blackfeet. According to the last news, about 150 Indians had perished in one camp alone, near Fort Benton. When the malady had ceased scourging men, it fell upon the horses. Many are dead and many dying. We have lost five. Our hunters are forced to go to the chase on foot; for according to their account all the horses are sick.[64]

This may have been the same as the visitation of smallpox among the Blackfoot, which is noted by James Mooney as occurring in 1857–58.[65] In 1856 the Sarcee were decimated by scarlet fever,[66] which could very easily spread to the Blackfoot. But neither disease explains the malady's extending to the horses. This is a consequence I have never seen suggested before; and one must suspend judgment pending further information. It seems at least possible that the condition of the horses may have been traceable to the enforced neglect arising from the deaths of so many of their mas-

[63] E. H. Moss, Professor of Botany, University of Alberta.

[64] Chittenden and Richardson (eds.), *Life of De Smet*, IV, 1248.

[65] Mooney, in Hodge, *Handbook*, II, 471. Mooney notes an outbreak of measles among them in 1864.

[66] Jenness, *The Sarcee Indians*, 6.

ters. It may be noted that this was in spring, which was frequently a precarious time for Indian horses.[67] Mention is also made about 1880 of a skin disease from which a great number of the Blood and Piegan horses died, and which has been thought to be mange. "This blow . . . left large numbers of these Indians afoot at a time when the buffalo had become scarce and they could ill afford to be without good horses." I have no further information concerning this, beyond the statement that young men of the tribe "were encouraged to recoup their losses through frequent expeditions to the Crows, Assiniboines and Crees in the early eighties, at a time when intertribal horse raiding should have become an anachronism in the Territory of Montana";[68] I shall refer to this statement again before concluding the present chapter.

Concerning winters as an adverse agency, Ewers writes thus:

Winters in the Blackfoot habitat, the northwestern corner of the Great Plains, vary in severity. Some winters are relatively mild, rather free from heavy snows and extended periods of intense cold, much more pleasant than might be anticipated in that latitude and altitude. But other winters bring blizzards, deep snows, heavy ice, prolonged weeks of temperatures of thirty or more degrees below zero. Blackfoot Indian methods of winter horse care were generally adequate to pull the animals through an average winter in a lean but healthy condition. They fattened quickly on the rich spring grasses. Winter losses in normal years during the nineteenth century were probably light. They were probably somewhat heavier among the bands wintering in the present Alberta than among those wintering south of the International Boundary because the snows were generally deeper in the north. . . .

But what of those unpredictable, unusually severe winters when the snow was deep on the ground and intense cold continued for weeks on end; when the Indians looked in vain for a warm Chinook wind from the west? Our records on the number and frequency of such winters during the nineteenth century are very fragmentary. But they are suffi-

[67] See Chapter XIII *supra*.
[68] Ewers, "Were the Blackfoot Rich in Horses?" 606-607, citing James Willard Schultz for the occurrence itself.

cient to show that they did occur, and that they brought disaster to Blackfoot horse herds.[69]

Disregarding the final conclusion for the moment, pending its discussion in detail, the foregoing presents an admirable thumbnail sketch of the scene, subject to one or two minor corrections. Happily it is possible to supplement the meager data of the nineteenth century from the first half of the twentieth. "A tough winter about every four or five years" sums up the popular Alberta verdict on their frequency, and gives a rough approximation to the truth. It is improbable that any fundamental climatic change has occurred since the appearance of the horse. After careful observation I formed the conclusion many years ago that the deciding factor is the *heavy* initial snowfall in early November (sometimes October) which in every one of these instances but two throughout my experience ushered in the winter. It was not that the southwest winds did not blow, but they were unrecognizable as Chinooks. For they were almost as bad as the bitter southeast winds that cut like a knife, which were our winter's worst. Expressed in popular terms, I concluded that three to six feet of snow which covered hill and dale alike *froze* the Chinook instead of the Chinook's melting the snow! For it was commonplace in this type of winter that months passed unbrokenly without a single thaw. Consequently the snow was as dry and fine as flour, and the least breath set it drifting. This was the cause of the incessant blizzards. For a "blizzard" (in its native region on the Plains at least) is not a snow*fall*, but a snow sirocco; perhaps even more commonly occurring under an unclouded sky. The intense cold and the violence of the wind, which swirls around seemingly from all quarters and raises an impenetrable cloud of fine snow, cause one to turn this way and that for breath, until all sense of direction is often lost. When experienced residents of the Plains perceive a blizzard coming, they very commonly stretch a rope between house and barn, since the storm will often last three days and nights. Lacking such a guide, many persons have been lost and frozen to death within two hundred yards or less of their own doors.[70]

[69] Ewers, *ibid.*, 605.
[70] On the blizzard, see Webb, *The Great Plains*, 25, citing some historical

Ewers notes two such winters, in 1842 and 1876 respectively. We can make numerous additions to the list, in chronological order, from the terrific "Cochrane winter" of 1882–83 (September to May) onward.[71] These are as follows: 1886–87,[72] 1890–91,[73] 1896–97, 1897–98, 1903–1904,[74] 1906–1907,[75] 1908–1909, 1915–16, 1919–20,[76] 1924–25, 1927–28, 1932–33, 1935–36, 1942–43;[77] and two bitter winters since I left Alberta, 1946–47 and 1951–52—which, like those of 1906–1907 and 1919–20 (and doubtless others) were by no means confined to the Alberta or Blackfoot territory.

As the foregoing dates indicate, I have only once seen two of these winters follow consecutively, 1896 and 1897. In both those years snow fell for forty-eight hours unbrokenly (November 3–4) on unfrozen ground and, I believe, generally throughout north-central Alberta. In the Red Deer Canyon country, halfway between Calgary and Edmonton, the soil remained unfrozen from April, 1896 until November, 1898. It was possible to sink fence posts into the ground in the dead of winter (as many of us did), providing the earth was tamped in again at once.[78] Similarly, I have

studies; and for personal experiences and trail expedients in a dangerous region, Cowie, *Company of Adventurers*, 207, 244–48, 353, 387, etc.; also David Thompson, both Alexander Henrys, John McDougall, etc., at large.

[71] This was first described to me by Frank Oliver (Edmonton, 1876–1933), who remembered it well. For good accounts, see also Sir Cecil Denny (another contemporary), *The Law Marches West*, 157, 186; MacInnes, *In the Shadow of the Rockies*, 208. It got the name from the virtually complete extermination of the five thousand "pilgrim" stock on the Cochrane Ranch west of Calgary. Note the omission of this phenomenal winter and others from the Piegan reminiscence (note 42 *supra*).

[72] MacInnes, *In the Shadow of the Rockies*, 210, 217. For the same winter, cf. Dobie, *The Mustangs*, 90, 292.

[73] Information from Jack Urquhart, who then kept the first stopping-house south of the Lone Pine, on the Calgary and Edmonton Trail; 1890 was his first Alberta winter. I was caught at his place en route to Calgary, November 4, 1896, in the terrible initial storm of that winter.

[74] Not enough snow for sleighs before January 31, 1904, when it snowed for sixty hours, followed by two fearful months. See note 81 *infra*.

[75] Snow for seventy-two hours, November 15–18, 1906; still sleighing, very late April.

[76] Ground white, October 9, 1919 to April 21, 1920. See note 81 *infra*.

[77] Thirty-six hours of snow, November 15, 1942, but not cold. January 14, 1943, very warm to 10:00 P.M.; below zero, 11:00 P.M.; January 15, 8:00 A.M., 58° below zero.

[78] Such winters are proof *ipso facto* of uninterrupted snow. In the Red Deer Canyon district snow lay for five and a quarter months in 1896–97, five in 1897–98, over five and a half in 1906–1907, over six in 1919–20, four in 1924–25, five in 1935–36, and over five in 1942–43, with scarcely a single thaw.

only once seen two milder winters follow consecutively, 1904–1905[79] and 1905–1906; the latter was pronouncedly so.[80] The snow was insufficient for heavy loads on the main trails into town, and scanty enough in the woods. Many people never used a sleigh from the end of March, 1904, until November 15, 1906, after which wheels were impossible for more than five months. As Ewers observes quite truly, these anomalous winters are completely unpredictable. My face was frozen severely on March 29, 1904, and also on April 4 and 5, 1920.[81] On the other hand, I saw gophers, in the central Battle River country, March 1, 1926, and February 23, 1931.[82] A distinguished citizen of Alberta, Frank Oliver (Edmonton, 1876–1933), was fond of saying that "the man who foretells Alberta weather is either a newcomer or a fool."

Apparently because of the paucity of available records for the Blackfoot country itself during the nineteenth century, Ewers has drawn four out of his six chronological weather notices in support of his thesis from the (geographical and tribal) Dakota territory. He says:

A study of four Dakota winter counts reveals no less than four winters over a period of a half-century when the Teton suffered severe losses of horses—1826–27, 1852–53, 1865–66, and 1880–81. It seems probable that if we had as complete records during this period for the Blackfoot as for the Dakota, whose habitat was considerably farther south, we would find as many if not more severe winters when many of the horses were lost by the former people.[83]

Actually we have some winter counts for the Blackfoot. Wissler cites two, for 1845 and 1850 respectively. In the first year, we find an entry: "Many cattle died," but no mention of horses. The second makes no allusion whatever to any deaths or shortage of horses.

[79] I finished fall ploughing, November 22, 1904; some neighbors ploughed later. One man sowed wheat March 9, 1905. My own fall ploughing was all sown before March 31, 1905.

[80] This was the first winter I shod my horses in eleven years.

[81] See notes 74, 76 *supra*.

[82] Reported by me, *Edmonton Journal*, March 2, 1926; *Edmonton Bulletin*, February 25, 1931.

[83] Ewers, "Were the Blackfoot Rich in Horses?" 606. For the Blackfoot winter counts, see Wissler, "Social Life of the Blackfoot Indians," 45–50.

The Stagecoach Attack

CHARLES M. RUSSELL

"The Indian, the horse, and the weapon formed a perfect unit. They were adapted to each other, and, taken together, made a formidable fighting unit."—Walter Prescott Webb, *The Great Plains.*

Westward Ho!
WILLIAM R. LEIGH

"It is when mounted that the prairie warrior exhibits himself to best advantage; here he is at home, and his skill in various manoeuvres which he makes available in battle is truly astonishing."
    —Randolph B. Marcy, *Thirty Years of Army Life on the Border.*

Kiowa Braves

". . . he was generally a muscularly-proportioned, copper-colored figure; he wore his hair plaited in long queues wrapped in otter fur; he had fierce dark eyes."—Carl Coke Rister, *Border Captives.*

Blackfoot Indian Camp, 1883
FROM A PHOTOGRAPH BY MATHERS
COPYRIGHT ERNEST BROWN COLLECTION

*Courtesy Cultural Activities Branch, Department of
Economic Affairs, Government of the Province of Alberta*

Sioux Camp and Horses at Pine Ridge, South Dakota
Collected by Col. Hugh D. Gallagher, United States Indian Agent at
Pine Ridge, 1886–90.

Courtesy South Dakota State Historical Society

Cheyenne Captives at Camp Supply, Oklahoma, June, 1869
Left to right: Little Bear, Hairless Bear Comes in Sight,
Island-High Wolf II

Courtesy Muriel H. Wright

Comanches Drawing Rations at Fort Sill, 1869

Courtesy Oklahoma Historical Society

The Pass Finders (Piegan)
FROM A PHOTOGRAPH BY ROLAND W. REED

"Here is the winesap air of the high places, the clear green sky of evening fading to a dark that brings the stars within arm's length, the cottonwoods along the creek rustling in the wind."—Bernard De Voto, *Across the Wide Missouri.*

An Indian Pony of the Southern Plains

". . . a typical product of the indiscriminate coupling and winter hardships of the prairie horses—small, tough, deer-legged, big-barreled, with slanting quarters, mulish hocks, a hide fantastically flared and blotched with white, and one wicked glass eye that showed the latent devil in his heart."—Stanley Vestal, *Happy Hunting Grounds.*

Cree Indians

FROM A PHOTOGRAPH BY MATHERS

COPYRIGHT ERNEST BROWN COLLECTION

". . . they drag on to their final destiny; and the day is not far distant when the American Indian will exist only in the traditions of his pale-faced conquerors."—George Frederick Ruxton, *Life in the Far West.*

Courtesy Cultural Activities Branch, Department of
Economic Affairs, Government of the Province of Alberta

I am astonished that a learned American scholar, who has himself lived in the West, should draw a *standing* parallel between the winter climate of the Blackfoot country and the pitiless "baldheaded plains" of the Dakotas; the more so when the only reason given for the implied milder character of the latter region is the fact of its being "considerably farther south." It is also considerably farther east, which is much more to the point. We have seen in an earlier chapter that while the Sioux, Mandan, and Hidatsa had to house as well as feed their horses in the bitter Plains winters, the Crow sent theirs to the Wind River (foothills) country in western Wyoming, where they soon fattened—manifestly out of doors. Ewers' argument here is of a piece with the supposition noted above, of Alberta's having *uniformly* more severe winters because it is farther north.[84] Both comparisons are inadmissible. Our own earliest neighbors in Alberta were predominantly Western Americans, and those on the adjoining homestead were actually from the town of North Platte, Nebraska, and had lived in every state from the Missouri to the Rockies and from Kansas to Idaho. North Platte is over seven hundred miles in a direct line south from where we dwelt, yet these friends told us "we didn't know what winter meant!" I have since railroaded for two winters in Manitoba and Saskatchewan, which are part of the Great Plains area. I am in complete agreement with their verdict. One thing, however, is indisputable. If it is true that Alberta is really a colder land, then on Ewers' own premises any winter survivals of horses in Alberta should apply even more pertinently in Montana.

It is obvious on reflection that the very frequency of these tough winters—"every four or five years"—discounts them very heavily as a probable cause of really serious depletion. Critics who write thus about range horses and cold weather can surely never have watched a herd of such on a bitter winter evening, indulging in their gallopings and (literal) horseplay of every description, evidently to warm their blood. I have known regularly-stabled working horses which had been turned out to enjoy a sunny afternoon and obstinately refused to be caught, sometimes staying out all night.

From the inception of the Fort Assiniboine pack trail in 1825,

[84] See notes 74, 79, 80 *supra*.

which connected the Saskatchewan with the Athabaska water route, a large herd of pack ponies was maintained at Fort Edmonton. Their service period was, of course, from spring to fall; during the off time they were under the care of a horse guard some few miles out who varied their range as pasture conditions necessitated. Rundle frequently refers to this in his *Journal*. I have met with no allusion that fodder was provided for them, and shelter certainly was not.[85] On the Chipman Ranch in 1902, we put up 700 tons of hay—'an unusually good crop' in the owner's opinion—for 2,400 head of stock. This was in the (Canadian) Blackfoot country itself. Only breeding mothers and youngsters were fed. Where some of the smaller bands of range horses disappeared to in the longer cold snaps we never knew. It seemed fairly certain they sought refuge in the woods and scrublands, but with the easing of temperatures they would reappear. The Blackfoot condition—"lean and healthy" —did not apply. It was proverbial among us that they came out in spring rolling fat, which we ourselves were puzzled to explain. The instance cited by Ewers to prove that in even the milder winters "the Indians" normally anticipated horse losses is irrelevant on two counts. The case is that of Matthew Cocking, February, 1773. His *Journal* reads thus: "An elderly man died; also several Horses for want of food; which they say is the case at this season of the year. . . . Two more Horses died with hunger and cold."[86] The region was central Saskatchewan—a ruthless land, whose aver-

85 See on this, Sir George Simpson, *Fur Trade and Empire* (ed. by Frederick Merk), 22–29, 38, 69, 150; Alexander Ross, *Fur Hunters*, II, 205; Kane, *Wanderings of an Artist*, 363; Rundle, "Journal" (ed. by Berry and Roe), November 18–20, December 24–28, 1841; Minutes of Council, Hudson's Bay Company, 1830–43, in Edmund H. Oliver, *The Canadian North-West*, I, 640, 661; II, 694, 714, 729, 761. There are various references in Rundle, "Journal," to the Fort Edmonton horse guard (February 17, 1841, August 3, 1842, April 8, 1844, etc.); and they ran their horses loose in this way as far north as the Lesser Slave Lake post (*ibid.*, April 12, 1846). Horse Hills, seven miles below Edmonton (with a horse pound there, 1809–10), was named from the horse guard's being there at times (Coues [ed.], *Henry-Thompson Journals*, II, 581, 594; *Place-Names of Alberta*, 66). Other horse names, far enough away from any post, may perhaps commemorate Indian impoundings, and possibly indicate a greater plenty than has been thought. There are Horse Pound Creek (i.e., Medicine River), rising about 52° 30' N, 114° 30' W (*ibid.*, 85; Coues [ed.], *Henry-Thompson Journals*, II, 638), and Horse Hills about forty miles farther south (Rundle, May 20, 1847). These two were in the (then) Blackfoot country itself. About 1870 there was another Horse Hills, near Turtle River, in the Battleford country, roughly 52° 30' N, 108° W (McDougall, *Pathfinding*, 265).
86 Cocking, "Journal" (ed. by Burpee), 114 (February 16–17, 1773).

age winters would eclipse the worst in the foothill country. The Indians were clearly Assiniboin, for the Cree would never have trusted themselves in what was then the Northern Blackfoot frontier. David Thompson said thirty years later that the Assiniboin were always in want of horses, a condition which was occasioned by hard usage, and we have seen what this meant, in part.[87] It is quite probable that these tragical occurrences were the outcome of "hard usage." They furnish no argument whatever for similar implications in reference to the Montana foothill country.

There is in my judgment one basic fallacy which is implicit in Ewers' entire argument. Assuming these malign influences to have been everything that he considers was the case, have we any grounds for supposing them to have considerately postponed their activities until the worst they could do would be to check and annoy the Blackfoot, however seriously, but not to absolutely and completely strip them of their horses? We have no reason to suppose these climatic phenomena to be some meteorological innovation unknown before 1800 or so. We have seen that Kidd's native informants told him that "in the old days all the Blackfeet were expected to be good horsemen and swimmers."[88] The particulars recorded by Antony Henday in 1754 make it clearly evident that the first of these aims had even then been successfully achieved. I have insisted—and I believe with entire logic—that such proficiency was not attained overnight. But Henday also mentions winter care of their beasts. I consider it to be self-evident that the *care* of their new possessions would take longer to acquire than their mere *use*. It is true that along with the horses' "feeding on willow-tops," and the Blackfoot women's "getting grass" for them (January, 1755), Henday notes that the horses were "getting thinner"; but there is no mention of horses' deaths, either as an event or as a normal winter expectation.[89] Getting thinner need occasion little surprise; the Indians did not possess a white breeder's resources in housing and fodder. Henday wintered (broadly) in the same bitter region as Cocking. Detailed examination increases the probability of my suggestion above: that the Assiniboin indifference and neglect had

---

[87] See Chapter XIII *supra*.
[88] Kidd, "Blackfoot Ethnography," 37–38.
[89] Henday, "Journal" (ed. by Burpee), 334–51.

as much to do with the deaths of their horses as even a Saskatchewan winter.

The true crux, however, is this: During this early—and possibly lengthy—probationary period, the Blackfoot would stand in a highly accentuated danger from two distinct angles. Their aggregate horse numbers would naturally be smaller in the beginning. While they had yet to develop their knowledge both of everyday winter horse care and of such veterinary lore as they possessed in later times, their ratio of losses from these adverse agencies would inevitably be much greater. With the periodical percentage of such winters as I have instanced, together with the attendant consequences that Ewers has maintained, it is extremely probable that the Blackfoot as horse Indians would never have been heard of.

Ewers observes quite truly: "The term 'wealth in horses' is meaningless unless it can be defined. . . . To be rich in horses a man had to own a considerable number of animals over and above those required for subsistence."[90] The latter clause is the more concrete of the two; and "rich in horses" is apparently the term by which tribal or individual wealth in this field was indicated. As an index of positive numbers, it is actually meaningless. But it can bear two definitions, as applied to some particular tribe. It can signify a general status among the horse Indians at large, to which this tribe in question were no exception. Or, it could signify a wealth in horses superior to that of the neighboring horse tribes in general. It is of interest to note (whatever it might have been worth), that the term was applied to the Blackfoot in the very period when Ewers insists that they were poor. Curiously enough, it is used by Larpenteur, whom Ewers himself quotes. Larpenteur mentions a well-known Assiniboin chief, Left Hand (alias "Gauché"), about 1835–36: "At this time he had raised a party of 250 to 300, to make war on the Blackfeet, who were rich in horses."[91] (Three hundred horses were captured.) The identical phrase is used by an outstanding anthropologist to describe an always important horse tribe, the powerful Kiowa, about

90 Ewers, "Were the Blackfoot Rich in Horses?" 607.
91 Larpenteur, *Forty Years a Fur Trader* (ed. by Coues), I, 91–92.

1805,[92] and in synonymous or analogous terms it was applied to such recognized horse distributors as the Flathead,[93] the Shoshone (Snake),[94] and the Crow.[95]

Which tribes actually had the most seems to have been largely a matter of opinion, although in the Northern Plains area the changes are rung on the same three or four. On this Ewers writes as follows:

> Some of the older men remember conditions and events of the late sixties. Our oldest informant indicated that in his youth the relative number of horses in the various tribes of the northwestern plains was about the same as portrayed by Bradley's table for about 1830; *i.e.*: 'Flatheads had more horses than the Crows, Crows more than the Piegans, Piegans more than Bloods, and North Blackfeet. The Gros Ventres, Crees and Assiniboines had still smaller numbers.' He also stated, 'The Piegans have been known for a long time back as having larger numbers of horses than the Bloods or Blackfeet.' This is in agreement with both Bradley's figures and Henry's observations near the beginning of the [nineteenth] century.[96]

That may be the case with respect to Bradley and Henry, but the assertion is far from being in agreement with several statements that were made at the time in question (1832–1840) concerning these and other tribes.

Both this oldest informant and his modern commentator likewise omit certain tribes which were of great historical importance in this relationship. In the first of the two, this omission furnishes a sidelight on the apparent assumption that such reminiscent particulars can be treated as being exhaustive; against which I have protested above.[97] The tribes in question are the Cheyenne on the

---

[92] Mooney, in Hodge, *Handbook*, I, 702.

[93] Larocque (1805), "Journal" (ed. by Burpee), 57, 71. Franchère (1811), *Voyage to the Northwest Coast*, VI, 339–41; Alexander Ross (1820), *Adventures of the First Settlers on the Oregon or Columbia River*, VII, 215; Wyeth (1833) *Oregon, 1832*, XXI, 87; all in Thwaites, *Travels*. See also Whitman's letters: *Marcus Whitman* (ed. by A. B. and D. P. Hulbert, I, 130).

[94] Irving, *Astoria*, 274, 282–85; Bancroft, *Native Races*, I, 273; Dobie, "Indian Horses and Horsemanship," 270, 272; *The Mustangs*, 41, 54–55, 81.

[95] "Extremely rich in horses" (Larpenteur, *Forty Years a Fur Trader* [ed. by Coues], I, 45).

[96] Ewers, "Were the Blackfoot Rich in Horses?" 603–604.

[97] See notes 71–72 *supra* on the omission of 1882–83, 1886–87, etc., from the "hard winters."

Plains, and the transmontane Nez Percé and Shoshone (Snake). The territory of the two latter would have to be crossed or flanked before the Blackfoot confederated tribes could reach the Flathead country. The high importance of the Snake has been emphasized by two competent and recent critics, Francis Haines and J. Frank Dobie, whom I quote in chronological order:

"Cayuse, Walla-Walla, Yakima, Palouse, Nez Percé, Flathead, Blackfoot, Crow, and many other tribes, were furnished from the Shoshone of Southern Idaho."[98] "The Flatheads and the Cayuse Indians raised horses of a similar type [to the Nez Percé]. The Shoshones, or Snakes, however, had more horses and were the chief distributors of them all over the Northwest."[99] It will be noted that both enumerations include the very tribe, the Cayuse, whose notorious plenty has furnished the popular term for the Indian pony throughout the West,[100] as well as the Flathead, who stand supreme in the ancient Piegan informant's list. Yet at the very time under discussion, about 1833, Maximilian (who we must presume was quoting contemporary opinion, since he could have no data for an original pronouncement ex cathedra) says the Snake had not as many horses as the Blackfoot.[101] According to the same old Piegan, the Flathead had more horses than the Crow (circa 1865). Larocque seems to imply as much in 1805: they "have a great number of horses which they sell for a trifle, and give many for nothing."[102] We have cited testimony above to the position of the Crow as the "grand intermediaries" in Northern Plains horse distribution (1811, 1840, and after), and the ready thievery by which they augmented their capital stock in trade.[103] Maximilian tells us that about 1833 they were said to have nine thousand or ten thousand head, surpassing all other tribes.[104] Catlin, however, at the same precise period, awarded that distinction to the "Shiennes,"[105] whom the old Piegan did not even mention re 1865.

98 Haines, "Northward Spread of Horses," 436.
99 Dobie, "Indian Horses and Horsemanship," 272.
100 See Chapter VI *supra*.
101 Maximilian, *Travels*, in Thwaites, *Travels*, XXIV, 295.
102 Larocque, "Journal" (ed. by Burpee), 71.
103 See Chapter VI *supra*.
104 Maximilian, *Travels*, in Thwaites, *Travels*, XXII, 351–52; cf. the Pawnee "six thousand or eight thousand," and my remarks in note 11 *supra*.
105 Catlin, *Letters and Notes*, II, 2; cf. Henry, 1806, in Coues (ed.), *Henry-*

We have another striking relation in connection with Blackfoot horse numbers. According to the notable Jim Beckwourth, the
half-blood chief of the Crow, who was contemporary with Maximilian and Catlin, about 1833, the Crow stole 5,000 horses from
the Comanche, 2,700 from the Kootenay, and 800 from the Cheyenne. They lost 3,000 head to the Blackfoot, and retaliated by capturing 7,000 Blackfoot horses.[106] As I view the matter, the actual
authenticity of these figures is for the moment irrelevant, although
Lowie is prepared to consider Maximilian's foregoing figures possible.[107] This would in turn render Beckwourth's figures relatively
possible, even though Dobie, in recounting these details, says that
Beckwourth "was one of the West's most remarkable liars," which
is no light claim to put forth, and that his figures cannot be relied
upon.[108] Unless all these thieving episodes are lies cut out of whole
cloth (which the evil reputation of the Crow renders improbable),
we have here five large aggregates of horses, all associated with
well-attested horse tribes; and the largest single item of all is identified with *Blackfoot* horses. Even a liar has his limitations. Had
this been an unmitigated lie and nothing more, it is probable that
those 7,000 Blackfoot horses would have been gathered in without
the Crow's losing as much as a single hoof! It is incredible to me
that the most shameless liar, unless he were an even bigger fool—
which hardly seems true of Beckwourth, to give the devil his due—
would introduce any tribe as wealthy horse owners at an era when
it must have been notorious (on Ewers' premises) that they were
living from hand to mouth.

We have seen that after the severe losses arising from the hard
winter of 1876 and the epidemic of (possible) mange about 1880,
the young men were "encouraged" to recoup their losses at the
expense of the Crow, Assiniboin, and Cree. But it has already been
proved to us by Bradley's figures, which Ewers endorses, that their
horse numbers per lodge only averaged (about 1830) two-fifths of
those of the poverty-stricken Blackfoot themselves,[109] and we can-

---

Thompson Journals, I, 393. James, *Account of the Expedition under Long,* in
Thwaites, *Travels,* XV, 282.

[106] Dobie, *The Mustangs,* 80, 317.
[107] Lowie, *The Crow Indians,* xiv.
[108] Dobie, *Tales of the Mustang,* 18; *The Mustang,* 80, 317.
[109] Ewers, "Were the Blackfoot Rich in Horses?" 603, 607.

not suppose that this condition would be unknown to the vigilant Blackfoot scouts. With reference to the mid-nineteenth century (circa 1855), we find another very competent investigator stating that the Blackfoot "were better supplied with horses than were the Cree, who often attempted to replenish their stock from the plentiful Blackfoot herds."[110] Mandelbaum's conclusions are certainly much more in accordance with critical opinion at large; and also with the ascertainable facts. Ewers insists that "there is no proof that a rapid increase in the size of Blackfoot horse herds took place at any time during the nineteenth century buffalo days."[111] If that is true of the Blackfoot, who dwelt in one of the easiest regions of the Northern Plains area—the Chinook belt—it should a fortiori be even more true of the Assiniboin particularly, who dwelt in one of the hardest and were recognizably poorer horse masters to boot. And if they could be induced to do this "at a time when intertribal horse raiding should have become an anachronism," why could they not have recouped themselves, or attempted it, long before from better-equipped tribes? For illogical as it may seem, apart from four references to the Assiniboin and the Dakota, covering more than a century, (1773–1880), Ewers offers no evidence that these disastrous climatic extremes affected any Plains tribe but the Blackfoot; and aside from the three confederated tribes, no further data are indicated to connect the high and low figures in Bradley's table with the presence or absence of these adverse physical agencies. It is difficult to conceive how the Northern Plains area proper could have escaped them. It is equally difficult to conceive their devastating influence without its leaving a wealth of evidence similar to that which is considered to reveal the plight of the Blackfoot. There is some hint of what may have been an occasional or a normal winter mortality among the Crow and the Shoshone respectively, both dating 1805. Larocque says of the Crow: "He is reckoned a poor man that has not ten horses in the spring . . . many have thirty or forty."[112] Lewis and Clark observe concerning the Shoshone: "Notwithstanding their losses this spring, they have still at least 700 horses."[113] Beyond any inference deriv-

[110] Mandelbaum, "The Plains Cree," 184.
[111] Ewers, "Were the Blackfoot Rich in Horses?" 610.
[112] Larocque, "Journal" (ed. by Burpee), 64.
[113] Lewis and Clark, *Journals* (ed. by Coues), II, 558.

able from Larocque's language, nothing is said about this condition being normal or frequent. If it were the former in either of the two respective territories, this increases the high probability of the Northern Plains as a whole being even more acutely affected, and leaving fuller records of such ravages. The Blackfoot are not mentioned either as sufferers *in excelsis,* or as being exceptionally poor in consequence.

Actually, of course, we have seen that the Blackfoot did raid for horses, at a much earlier period and somewhat extensively; even as far south as the Río Grande.[114] On horse raiding, Ewers writes as follows:

In course of time, and at repeated risk of life and limb, energetic young men could amass new fortunes through capture of enemy horses. However, informants stated that raiding parties rarely succeeded in taking more than 60 horses in a single raid. The danger of being overtaken by the enemy while attempting to drive larger herds home was great. By the time the horses taken in a raid were divided among the participants, and after they in turn had distributed some of their shares as gifts to other people in the village, each warrior had but a few animals left to add to his own herd.[115]

One must certainly suppose that the party of 250 to 300 Assiniboin who in 1835–36 were preparing to make war on the Blackfoot ("who were very rich in horses") *expected* far more than the 300 or so which they got. One per man would not amount to much. Aside from any question of profit or loss in horse raiding, the numbers of the attacking party tend to confirm their conception—or Larpenteur's—of Blackfoot economic or social status in horse resources.[116] I am of the opinion, however, that the hypothesis which is implicit in Ewers' argument, of Blackfoot raiding as the last desperate resort of starving men, is untenable. He has underestimated the incentive of desire, the sheer love of raiding and of the aggrandizement it brought.[117] He says again:

[114] Thompson, *Narrative* (ed. by Tyrrell), 367 (see Chapter IV *supra*).
[115] Ewers, "Were the Blackfoot Rich in Horses?" 607.
[116] Larpenteur, *Forty Years a Fur Trader* (ed. by Coues), I, 91–93; cf. II, 372.
[117] "Lust for fame was axiomatically an end in all warfare"; a large herd of horses possessed "ostentation value" (Lowie, *The Crow Indians,* 219, 228). The horse was a feature in the emphasis on gift giving; "there is no reason to believe

Where horses were few in quantity they were rather sure to be poor in quality also among the nomadic plains tribes. . . . Horses with poor feet, saddle sores, or any of the many other ailments horses are heir to, could not be rested until they were completely recovered.[118]

Ewers in the foregoing adopts as his initial premise the very conclusion he is attempting to establish. The presence of 'sore backs' cannot be admitted as any proof of economic status; their explanation lies in temperamental variations. While it is true, as we have seen above, that the Crow, who could afford to, rested their sore-backed horses until they were well again, the Snake, who could even better afford it, did no such thing, but saddled their writhing animals with complete indifference.[119]

Ewers writes again regarding individual requirements:

Our Blackfoot informants . . . stated that the average household needed between 10 to 20 horses. A young childless couple could get along with 4 or 5 animals, but a large family consisting of more than five adults needed more than 20 horses. An average requirement of 15 horses per lodge throughout the camp would seem to be a conservative estimate.[120]

We have a few references to what may be regarded as ordinary individual totals, apart from the bloated plutocracy. The younger Henry (1809) remarks that "some of the Blackfeet own 40 to 50 horses. But the Piegans have by far the greatest numbers; I heard of one man who had 300."[121] This is purely a relative comparison; it contains nothing to indicate any positive lack among the Blackfoot. Ewers himself considers that at any time in the nineteenth century, 1809, 1830, 1850, or in the 1870's, a man who owned forty or fifty horses would have been considered well-to-do.[122] On the suggested estimate of fifteen per lodge (containing how many men

---

that the prevalence of horse stealing rested upon a purely economic motive" (Smith, "War Complex of the Plains Indians," 433). See also Grinnell, *The Fighting Cheyennes*, 43; Jablow, *The Cheyenne*, 78–89.

[118] Ewers, "Were the Blackfoot Rich in Horses?" 608.

[119] See Chapter XIII *supra*.

[120] Ewers, "Were the Blackfoot Rich in Horses?" 607.

[121] Coues (ed.), *Henry-Thompson Journals*, II, 526.

[122] Ewers, "Were the Blackfoot Rich in Horses?" 604.

or families?) as a requirement, this would no doubt be a sound conclusion. James Willard Schultz seems to imply a much higher maximum of individual standards of possession among the Piegan. He says of the period 1875–80: "There were individuals who owned from one hundred to three and four hundred [horses]."[123] At some period which is not entirely clear, but which appears to have been broadly contemporaneous, Gray-bull, with seventy to ninety horses, was apparently a man of some distinction among the Crow.[124] Farther west, among the still wealthier transmontane Nez Percé and Flathead (who must themselves have been the informants), Lewis and Clark noted that some men owned from twenty to as many as fifty, sixty, or even one hundred horses each.[125] On Ewers' premises, one could plausibly argue poverty in horseflesh among the Flathead from such figures. I believe a more correct explanation is the persistent Indian tribal diversity, almost their sole uniform characteristic, which defies reduction into averages and systems.

In the period circa 1833, which is our more immediate concern, the typical numbers mentioned by Maximilian may reasonably be taken to indicate his—or his informants'—standards of abundance. Concerning Blackfoot individual ownership, he writes at Fort McKenzie: "fifteen or twenty horses were grazing about the tent; but many Blackfeet possess a far greater number."[126] Maximilian also notes many "Sioux" with twenty horses each, and Tetons (Sioux) frequently with thirty or forty horses each; such men were "rich."[127] On the other hand, the Dakota at the Sioux Agency were 'indolent and poor,' seldom possessing more than two.[128] The personal equation was no doubt a significant factor. Among the Mandan, some had none, others several.[129] Catlin, in the same years, records the Mandans' turning a favorite horse loose, or the sacrificing of as many as seventeen by one individual owner.[130] This might imply plenty. Yet Maximilian tells us that at this time the two Mandan villages contained only about three hundred horses, and

123 *Ibid.*, 603; citing Schultz, *My Life as an Indian*, 152.
124 Lowie, *The Crow Indians*, 228, 262.
125 Lewis and Clark, *Journals* (ed. by Thwaites), V, 29, 31.
126 Maximilian, *Travels*, in Thwaites, *Travels*, XXIII, 121, 132.
127 *Ibid.*, XXII, 310, 327.
128 *Ibid.*, XXII, 306.
129 *Ibid.*, XXIII, 272.
130 *Catlin, Letters and Notes*, II, 247.

the neighboring Hidatsa villages even less—two hundred fifty to three hundred.[131]

There is one final crux which is perhaps the greatest of all; it certainly is not the least. Among all the various items of evidence by which Ewers seeks to establish his hypothesis, while we have an abundance of argument and some fact concerning comparative conditions as between the Blackfoot and other tribes, I have been unable to discover one single contemporary statement of those early times, circa 1830, that the Blackfoot were positively poor in horses. Ewers presents no evidence beyond post-dated (comparative) reminiscence, which we have seen to be in certain respects incomplete and faulty,[132] and modern critical inference therefrom. What is apparently the most direct notice we possess is from Duncan McGillivray, at Fort George, on the North Saskatchewan River, April 9, 1795: "This morning a Band of about 30 Blood Indians and 10 Blackfeet arrived: they have carried all their comodities on dogs their horses being too much exhausted by hunger to undergo the fatigues of the journey." He does not say that this was a normal condition, nor that Blackfoot horse poverty was a result of it.[133] And long before, Matthew Cocking had observed (December, 1772) that the Blackfoot were using horses for packing, instead of either dogs or their women.[134] Whatever inference may be drawn from McGillivray's notice, we have seen that late use of dog traction is recorded among many tribes, even including the Comanche,[135] and Ewers himself says "the presence of dog travois in the moving camp was not necessarily a sign of poverty in horses."[136]

In a large number of documentary sources from 1754 onward, from traders, travelers, explorers, missionaries, soldiers, and scientists, and culminating in modern anthropological students, I have

131 Maximilian, *Travels,* in Thwaites, *Travels,* XXIII, 272; cf. 235, 245.
132 See notes 71, 97 *supra.*
133 McGillivray, *Journal* (ed. by Morton), 69.
134 Cocking, "Journal" (ed. by Burpee), 111.
135 See Chapter I *supra.*
136 Ewers, "Were the Blackfoot Rich in Horses?" 609-10.

not found a single reference to this supposed condition in the Blackfoot. It is incredible to me that what would have been an amazing realization in such a tribe—as compared with the widespread popular suppositions to the contrary—would not have left some definite, positive record.

XVI

HORSES AND TRIBAL PSYCHOLOGY

Whether the coming of the horse introduced the Indians to anything fundamentally new, or whether this merely enlarged the field for the exercise of existing customs or characteristics, it scarcely seems possible to doubt that the new possession must have exerted a profound influence upon Indian psychology. We may take the analogous case of a sudden accession of wealth among our own peoples. The corrupting influence of money is proverbial. While this may or may not be true in individual cases, it is quite certain that the possession of more money induces *change* in many whom it does not corrupt. We shall have occasion in the following chapter to discuss the question of changes induced by the horse in the everyday subsistence—or subsistence processes—of the Plains tribes, and from two opposing angles of thought. Our present concern is with the influence of the animal upon the everyday thinking of the people in their relations one with another in the same tribe or band.

There can in my judgment be little doubt that the accession of the horse has exerted a very considerable influence in elevating the status of women in the horse tribes. In the opinion of competent students, the degradation of women in Indian societies at large has been much exaggerated.[1] It may perhaps be considered as a feature in the conventional conception of "Indians" as mere replicas of one another, turned out from the same mould. Anthropological study has certainly dispelled the once prevalent illusion of the "lazy hunter" stalking along in advance, too idle to carry anything but

[1] See Mooney, in Hodge, *Handbook*, I, 750; Henry W. Henshaw, *ibid.*, II, 282–86; J. N. B. Hewitt, *ibid.*, II, 968–73; etc.

his weapons, while his womenfolk toiled along behind. We realize that only by such instant preparedness could the man be ready at a moment's notice to defend those who looked to him for protection. We begin to realize also that the woman's admiration of such a competent lord was not altogether ill-bestowed.

Lewis and Clark note what was apparently an important distinction in this field, of high value as indicating that such variations were aboriginal, and not derived (they were little likely to be!) from white contacts. They write as follows:

> . . . the importance of the female in savage life has no necessary relation to the virtues of the man. . . . The Indians whose treatment of the females is mildest and who pay most deference to their opinions are by no means the most distinguished for their virtues.[2]

While Lewis and Clark have been criticized for the vagueness of some of their geographical references,[3] we must gratefully acknowledge a generally wide philosophical outlook, which included many phases of Indian life not always noted by later writers. If more attention had been paid to the variable features of Indian character and less to the comprehensive ignoramus-definition of the only good Indian as a dead Indian, the course of history might have been different. In the two important respects of the treatment of their women and the care of their aged we have one or two references in areas untouched by the horse, which again indicate such traits to be aboriginal. It is difficult to separate what we should term kindness per se from the men's sharing in the round of domestic routine; and for our present purposes we may class the two as phases of the same thing.

Lewis and Clark mention men of the Coast tribes as 'doing more of the domestic drudgery than had been expected.'[4] Franklin, in 1821, noted the 'exceptional kindness' of the Dog Ribs and of the Copper Indians toward their women.[5] It may well have been that the exceptional quality lay in its contrast with the common conventions on the subject, for we cannot regard Franklin as any

[2] Lewis and Clark, *Journals* (ed. by Coues), II, 781.
[3] Webb, *The Great Plains*, 142–44.
[4] Lewis and Clark, *Journals* (ed. by Thwaites), IV, 191–92.
[5] Franklin, *Journey to the Polar Sea* (1819–22), 289–90, 470–77.

particular authority in this field. It is of interest to note that the attitude of the foregoing tribes toward their women is neither to be attributed to any inherent qualities common to the Athapascan peoples as a whole, nor to the influences of the northern environment's rendering kindness easier (and hence more likely) among sedentary tribes than among nomads. For David Thompson speaks of the Chipewyan "treating their women like slaves, a conduct which the Nahathaways [Cree] detest." Yet the Chipewyan "exact chastity from their wives and seem to practise it themselves."[6]

The sympathetic attitude toward the aged is likewise found in widely sundered tribes; both prior to the advent of the horse and in areas where the horse never penetrated. Lescarbot records it among the tribes of New France, circa 1610, and a most competent student of the region considers this to be authentic.[7] George Keith, a Northwest Company trader, mentions it among the Beavers in the Athabaska country, about 1800.[8] We have to remember, also, that even the apparent opposite, the slaying or abandonment of old people, is not necessarily the unmitigated, wanton cruelty it has frequently been thought to be. The tribes in both the areas referred to above were largely or completely sedentary, and kindness to the old and feeble was much more easily practicable in their way of life than among the nomad hunters. Paul Kane, the artist, has recorded a conversation with Potika-poo-tis, an Assiniboin, at Fort Edmonton in 1846:

After relating various stories of his war and hunting exploits he, to my great astonishment, told me he had killed his own mother. It appears that, while travelling, she had told him that she felt too old and feeble to sustain the hardships of life, and too lame to travel any further, and asked him to take pity on her and end her misery, on which he unhesitatingly shot her on the spot. I asked him whereabouts he had directed his ball. His reply was, 'Do you think I would shoot her in a bad place? I hit her there'; pointing his finger to the region of the heart. 'She died instantly, and I cried at first; but after I had buried her, the impression wore off.'[9]

6 Thompson, *Narrative* (ed. by Tyrrell), 129–31.
7 Lescarbot, *History of New France* (ed. by Biggar), III, 146; citing note by W. F. Ganong.
8 Masson, *Les Bourgeois de la Compagnie du Nord-Ouest*, II, 70.
9 Kane, *Wanderings of an Artist*, 138–39.

It seems fairly clear from the foregoing that such acts cannot be ascribed wholly to "savagery" and the "fruits of heathenism," with all respect to some of those splendid pioneer missionaries who have done so.[10] For it would be illogical to suppose Paul Kane's Indian to be the only one to feel such compunction. It is not, however, until we review the situation among the horse Indians that we realize the wider application of this more liberal attitude toward their women which the possession of the horse rendered possible. Whether this arose from a truly active growth of benevolence per se, or from a calculated benevolence of sorts originating in mere self-interest, or from a contemptuous indifference which allowed the women to "help themselves" to an easier mode of life, really matters little. Our concern is with results.

Larocque has left us a most informative sketch of the Crow social atmosphere, as it appeared to him in 1805:

Like all other Indian nations the women do most of the work, but as they are not so wretchedly situated as those nations who live in forests the women do work here that is done by man among the Cree, Sauteux etc & yet have less work to do and are more at ease while the men are proportionally idle. . . . [the men] do not even saddle their own horses when their wives are present nor do they take off their [own] shoes and leggings when they come in to go to bed. In flitting[11] the women ride & have no loads to carry on their backs as is common among other nations though it is certain that had they no horses they would be in the same predicament as their less fortunate neighbours for though the men are fond of their wives and use them well, yet it is not to be supposed they would take a greater share of work than other Indians. The women are indebted solely to their having horses for the ease they enjoy more than their neighbours. . . .[12]

They are always on horseback . . . everybody rides, men, women, and children. The female[s] ride astride as the men do. A child that is

10 See Young, *By Canoe and Dog Train* (Lake Winnipeg tribes, 1868 *et seq.*), 46–48. Similarly, Rundle considered Indian couples' living together without marriage as sin, though who could have married them prior to his own coming is not clear. Certainly not the fur traders, who were commonly tarred with the same brush.

11 Either Larocque's tutor in English (if he had one) or his original translator must have been a North of England man. While "flit" as a noun (e.g. "moonlight flit" by a fraudulent tenant) is known in the South of England, I have never herd the verbal "flitting," for a change of home, from anyone born south of the Humber.

12 Larocque, "Journal" (ed. by Burpee), 59.

319

too young to keep his saddle is tied to it, and a small whip is tied to his wrist, he whips away and gallops or trots the whole day if occasion requires. Their saddles are so made as to prevent falling either backwards or forward, the hind part reaching as high as between the shoulders and the fore part of the breast. The women['s] saddles are especially so. Those of the men are not quite so high, and many use saddles such as the Canadians make in the N. W. Country. . . . They say that no equal number of other Indians can beat them on horseback, but that on foot they are not capable to cope with those nations who have no horses. They pass for brave and courageous among their neighbours. . . .[13]

This general description is borne out by certain incidental references in his daily jottings. He observes, regarding the party in whose company he traveled: "There were likewise many young children, but who could keep their saddles. . . . Two hours before daylight . . . they put all the young children on horseback and tied to the saddles, then they slept the remainder of the night."[14] Elsewhere Larocque says further: ". . . the Rocky Mountain Indians have so many horses, that they can transport their sick without trouble. Whether they did it or not before they had horses I do not know."[15]

We get a broadly similar picture among the Blackfoot, and also their confederates the Sarcee. The information respecting the latter tribe is of additional value, since in those particulars wherein we lack detailed knowledge we may perhaps reasonably infer a similarity of outlook in the great Southern Athapascan family of the Apache, such as has been found to persist in other psychological fields, despite their long separation.[16] In both tribes the general attitude of the men toward their women was one of outward disdain, especially with regard to giving any assistance in the camp-moving drudgery of a nomad life. Yet behind this ostentatious con-

[13] *Ibid.*, 60, 64, 65. The concluding remarks about war parties afoot may be compared with the supposition of Plains war parties for any long distances not being pre-equestrian. See Chapter XII *supra.*

[14] *Ibid.*, 39, 40 (August 24, 28, 1805).

[15] *Ibid.*, 57. Larocque's Rocky Mountain Indians are the Crow, but the term was rather loosely used by some. Larpenteur speaks of "Crows *and* Rocky Mountain Indians" (*Forty Years a Fur Trader* [ed. by Coues], I, 46).

[16] See John J. Honigmann, "Parallels in the Development of Shamanism among Northern and Southern Athapaskans," 512–14.

tempt the women appear to have possessed a considerable "backstairs" influence.

As we have seen, Matthew Cocking noted as early as 1772 that the Blackfoot were using horses instead of their women for packing their camp paraphernalia.[17] It is immaterial what the origin of their radical innovation was, whether it was demanded by the women or conceded spontaneously by the men (even if only to facilitate more rapid camp moving). It seems impossible for such a momentous advance to become a normal feature in community life without a corresponding psychological advance in the social status of women. It cannot be mere coincidence alone that similar advances were noted—and very possibly, if we knew everything, dating from proportionately early periods in their horse chronology —among such widely dispersed tribes as the Blackfoot, the Crow, and the Snake, who differed profoundly in many respects, and were frequently at active enmity one with another.

In the earlier pre-equestrian economy the Blackfoot women owned their own dogs and travois as their personal property. This right was transferred to the new regime. The Blackfoot woman owned her own horses and saddlery, and among the Piegans at least—perhaps with the other members of the Confederacy also— these were never gambled by the men. The unfortunate widow, however, lost this privilege at her husband's death.[18] In an intermittently federated tribe, the Atsina, the widow, if *persona grata,* might be given horses by her parents-in-law.[19]

Similar "woman's property rights" prevailed among the Cree. The Cree woman owned her dogs; though whether as a joint possession like the Hidatsa family or individually is not specified. The Cree woman also owned horses, and could freely dispose of them, but the men looked after them.[20] This very possibly carried with it a reciprocal right which Mandelbaum notes among the Cree men. Property such as horses or a gun was *owned* by one man, but could be used by his relatives.[21] The Cree woman's position as a horse

[17] Cocking, "Journal" (ed. by Burpee), 111. See Chapter I *supra.*
[18] Thompson, *Narrative* (ed. by Tyrrell), 361. This was confirmed by Kidd's native Siksika or Piegan informant ("Blackfoot Ethnography," 149–50).
[19] Kroeber, "Ethnology of the Gros Ventre," 181.
[20] Mandelbaum, "The Plains Cree," 182, 184, 196–97.
[21] *Ibid.,* 204–205.

owner may perhaps indicate a relatively very high status in a society which the same investigator and others consider was always poor in horses.[22] David Thompson's statement regarding the Cree disapproval of the Chipewyan harshness tends to confirm the supposition. We may note that the Reverend Egerton Young (Lake Winnipeg tribes, 1868 and after), amid much emphasis on the Cree woman's degradation, mentions a local chieftainess, apparently ruling in unquestioned security.[23]

We can scarcely doubt the existence of a broadly similar status among the Flathead, when we read that horse racing was their principal amusement, and was practiced by men, women, and children alike. The Flathead children came as near to being born on horseback as is humanly conceivable. The Reverend Samuel Parker, Marcus Whitman's missionary colleague, tells us that the Flathead women often suspended "the flat Indian cradle from their shoulders when on horseback," or from the pommel of the saddle.[24] Lewis and Clark observed that the Snake women were "seldom compelled (like those in other parts) to carry their burthens on their backs."[25]

It is with reference to the general transmontane area that those explorers draw the distinction noticed above, that there was no necessary connection between the treatment accorded to women and any higher degree of amiability in the men. Something was said among one of these bands in regard to the killing of old people, "yet in their villages we saw no want of kindness to old men."[26] Among the Blackfoot a very competent student says that the aged were not often abandoned, but were generally treated with respect.[27] With the Sarcee the ancient preceptor (in the most literal sense a pedagogue, and "Master of the Novices"), whose office "in every camp" was to instruct the growing boys in tribal ethics as well as in the manly arts of the warrior, inculcated respect for the aged and blind as part of the curriculum.[28] Gilbert Wilson, with reference to similar hygienic-disciplinary rituals among the Hi-

[22] See Chapters V, XV supra.
[23] Young, Canoe and Dog Train, 47–49, 148, 256–59.
[24] A. B. and D. P. Hulbert (eds.), Marcus Whitman, I, 129–30.
[25] Lewis and Clark, Journals (ed. by Thwaites), III, 41.
[26] Ibid. (ed. by Coues), II, 782, 783.
[27] Kidd, "Blackfoot Ethnography," 56–58; cf. 149–62.
[28] Jenness, The Sarcee Indians, 19.

datsa—including "the daily plunge in the river, winter or summer" —applies them to all Plains tribes.[29]

As long ago as 1897 the present writer had an opportunity of observing in a band of Mountain Stoney (Assiniboin) then encamped on Battle Lake, in the foothill country of central Alberta, that a chief's authority in their social polity was certainly not dependent upon his continued physical vigor. The old man could have been any age from sixty to seventy. He was crippled and bent with wounds or disease, perhaps both, and had to be assisted and supported by younger men of the band. Yet I have never seen a more utterly typical personification of authority. He was Shakespeare's incomparable phrase in flesh and blood: "every inch a king!"

Marcy noted a century ago an exception to the tribes we have been discussing. He states that the Comanche were kind to boys but not to girls, and treated their women cruelly and severely.[30] An inquirer of our own time, who has left few phases of Comanche life unexplored, says the precise opposite—that Comanche women were well treated.[31] It was stated by Gregg in the same general period that the Comanche, in contradistinction to some other tribes, never sold their women to visitors.[32] This was said of no other tribe to my knowledge except the Blackfoot, and in their case somewhat doubtfully,[33] although a contemporary historian considers that "all the tribes, except possibly the Cheyenne, were unchaste by white standards."[34] Marcy himself, moreover, observed that among the Comanche the impact of the horse had evidently favored the "emancipation of woman," to at least an equal degree with many other horse tribes, and their riding ("with a leg upon each side of the horse") was by no means limited to camp moving. Marcy watched two young Comanche women ride out with their lariats after a herd of antelope, maneuver them within striking distance, and rope two at the first throw.[35] In the same general period, Alfred

[29] Wilson, "Horse and Dog in Hidatsa Culture," 157–58.
[30] Marcy, *Exploration of the Red River*, 102.
[31] Richardson, *The Comanche Barrier*, 33.
[32] Gregg, *Commerce of the Prairies*, in Thwaites, *Travels*, XX, 344.
[33] See Chapter XIV *supra*.
[34] De Voto, *Across the Wide Missouri*, 98–99, 139.
[35] Marcy, *Exploration of the Red River*, 95; cf. Dobie, *The Mustangs*, 48.

Jacob Miller portrayed a Sioux girl on horseback, an Indian girl chasing a buffalo bull and others racing on horseback, and a Shoshone girl on horseback roping a wild horse.[36] These particulars suggest that the Comanche women were well up to standard in respect of freedom. If Marcy's general diagnosis respecting the Comanche women is correct, it may be considered a striking indication of change wrought in the tribe at large by the coming of the horse, that such a degree of feminine freedom had been achieved (or conceded) in so otherwise conservative a society. At the very time when Marcy was writing, a striking example to the contrary was flourishing among the Comanche, which might have given him pause had he heard of it. Richardson mentions the widow of Santa Anna, the Penateka (a southern band of Comanche) chief, who died in 1849. She was described in 1854 as "a fine-looking woman, a veritable 'Amazon,' and one of the best hunters in the tribe. She owned a good herd of horses and, according to Comanche standards, was therefore quite wealthy."[37]

In all these comparisons, however, there is one proviso that must constantly be borne in mind before making any glib pronouncements on these questions. We may be quite sure that in very few respects is the comprehensive term "Indians" equally applicable to every tribe. As I have remarked above with reference to "exceptional kindness" in some tribe, we cannot even be certain that some observed practice is uniform within that particular tribe, or which is the rule and which the exception. One of the earliest *resident* observers among a Canadian (or perhaps any) tribe has emphasized this for our instruction. Father Le Jeune writes as follows (1633):

I have observed that, after having seen two or three Savages do the same thing, it is at once reported to be a custom of the whole Tribe. . . . Add to this, that there are many tribes in these countries who agree in a number of things, and differ in many others, so that, when it is said that certain practices are common to the Savages, it may be true of one tribe and not of another. . . . It is indeed true that these people have not all the same idea in regard to their belief, which will some

36 Marvin C. Ross (ed.), *The West of Alfred Jacob Miller*, Plates 72, 90, 96, 137.
37 Richardson, *The Comanche Barrier*, 216.

day make it appear that those who treat of their customs are contra-dicting each other.[38]

So also the famous Pierre Esprit Radisson told a meeting of the "Honourable Adventurers to Hudson Bay" in London in 1671 that Indians "were of many races";[39] and careful scholars have stressed the fact in later times.[40] We have ample evidence of endless di-versities in tribal customs of long standing, and perhaps of remote aboriginal antiquity. Such diversity implies the possibility of simi-lar diversity in the readiness to adopt this or that modification. Wissler noted in 1911 that it was a disgrace among the Blackfoot to assist the women; and he makes no mention of any modernistic attitude on the question.[41] Jenness observed that in more recent years the reserve life has broken down many ancient customs in a federated (and neighboring) tribe. A Sarcee would assist his wife in erecting the tipi, which in former times they too would have scorned as utterly degrading.[42] Gilbert Wilson's native Hi-datsa informant, Wolf-chief, described his father's felling the cot-tonwoods from which the women and girls—"who were more ex-pert"—would strip the bark for their horses.[43] We may note that while there was no indication of social shame at the self-evident manner in which the women had acquired their skill, neither was there any sense of apology necessary for his father, as a lone de-linquent from tribal standards. While it seems more probable to attribute such an epochal change to the new epoch of the horse, it may possibly have been much older, since we find it coupled with a long-persistent pre-equestrian dog usage. In that case it would be an outstanding example of tribal diversity.

[38] Le Jeune, in Thwaites (ed.), *Jesuit Relations*, VI, 27, 101.

[39] Beckles Willson, *The Great Company*, 65.

[40] "Someone has truly said that between a Pueblo and an Apache or a Nez Percé and an Arapaho there is as much difference as between a Broadway merchant and a Bowery rough." (A. J. Fynn, *The American Indian as a Product of Environ-ment*, 45–59.) Cyrus Thomas: "One type is no more applicable to all Indians than it is to all whites": *The Indians of North America in Historic Times*, 417. Thomas and Swanton say that there is no single thing which can be stated with equal truth of *all* the Sioux (Hodge, *Handbook*, II, 577–79). For the Blackfoot, see Kidd, "Blackfoot Ethnography," 20–24.

[41] Wissler, "Social Life of the Blackfoot Indians," 27–28.

[42] Jenness, *The Sarcee Indians*, 13–24.

[43] Wilson, "Horse and Dog in Hidatsa Culture," 172–80.

If anything whatever could effect one modification, then some outside force or native social impulse (or the two in conjunction) may have effected others. Alexander Henry the younger has recorded the fact that in the trading operations of the Hidatsa with the Crow, Assiniboin, and Cheyenne, while the men dealt with such matters as guns and horses, the Hidatsa women negotiated the exchange of their own home-grown corn for such commodities as "leather, robes, smocks, and dried provisions, as if at a country fair."[44] Ferdinand Roemer, the German scientist, observed the Comanche women in 1849 making such articles as plaited rawhide lariats, and twisting ropes or halters of horsehair, in addition to more menial tasks, but apparently does not state whether the women had the trading of what they made or not.[45]

It seems not improbable that this advance in (Hidatsa) feminine status is ultimately traceable to the horse. For Charles Mackenzie noted the immense numbers of horses—whether actually "2,000" or not—brought by the Crow to the Hidatsa villages. While some 250 or so were offered in trade, in return for ammunition and 200 guns, it seems apparent that a large number were brought to carry back the more bulky agricultural produce which the Crow had obtained,[46] and that, *ipso facto,* such a type of commerce could scarcely have been carried on in pre-horse times on any such scale.[47]

Trade in agricultural produce was actually conducted on foot by Arikara women over half a century later. But their market was close at hand, and their total was probably less in bulk than a trade of tribe with tribe. F. V. Hayden writes thus concerning the Arikara (1863):

. . . they have two markets for their surplus produce. The first is the fort of the American Fur Company, located near their village, at which they trade from five hundred to eight hundred bushels [of corn] in a season. This trade on the part of the Indians is carried on by the women, who bring the corn by panfuls or the squashes in strings, and receive in exchange knives, hoes, combs, beads, paints, etc.; also am-

[44] Coues (ed.), *Henry-Thompson Journals,* I, 384–85.
[45] Richardson, *The Comanche Barrier,* 147–48.
[46] In Masson, *Les Bourgeois de la Compagnie du Nord-Ouest,* I, 345–46.
[47] See Jablow, *The Cheyenne,* 10–16, 41, 81, etc.

munition, tobacco, and other useful articles for their husbands. . . . The second market for their grain is with several bands of the Dakotas, who are at peace with them. These Indians make their annual visits to the Arikaras, bringing buffalo robes, skins, meat, etc., which they exchange for corn; and the robes and skins thus obtained enable the Arikaras to buy at the trading-post the various cloths and cooking utensils needed by the women, and the guns, horses, etc. required by the men.[48]

I do not consider the above particulars to invalidate my foregoing suggestion with reference to the Hidatsa women. For it is clear that the Arikara women could not have conveyed their produce 'by the panful,' etc., for any really long distance. Whereas the Dakota, who actually dwelt some considerable distance away, were (temperamentally, it would seem) more of a horse people, and being evidently but little versed in water lore even before their possession of the horse,[49] most probably could not have made such journeys for produce in large bulk in the pre-horse era.[50] I am deeply suspicious of the bullboat, as Alfred Jacob Miller depicts it, for large-scale transportation of bulky and perishable cargoes.[51] What the Arikara practice exhibits in my opinion is a conspicuous instance of that tribal diversity from which we can never escape for long. At this date they had had the horse for a century and a quarter, in the opinion of several critics;[52] and one, as we have

48 Cited by Jablow, ibid., 22.

49 La Vérendrye, 1738: "We were going among people who did not know how to kill the beaver, and who covered themselves only with ox-skin." ("Journal" [ed. by Brymner], 7; Journals [ed. by Burpee], 301.) On the absence of fishing in the bison area, see Wissler, The American Indian, 220; cf. also Coman, Economic Beginnings of the Far West, II, 77.

50 Jablow, The Cheyenne, 10–16, 41, 81, etc.

51 With unreserved acknowledgment of the artistic and dramatic merits of Miller's paintings, it must be recognized that they are not in all cases historically (i.e., photographically) accurate. Bernard De Voto (Across the Wide Missouri) notes more than one occurrence of practice depicted, "which Miller never saw." Among these are the crossing of a river in the night, and Indians inside the enclosure at Fort Laramie (both "against the rules"); and another to be noted in the following chapter, re buffalo hunting. His bullboat resembles no description I have read, of what was purely an emergency expedient. He depicts a large scow, requiring as many hides as a tipi, and loaded down with women and camp furniture. The "Crow Indians on the Lookout" would have put the Indians in full view of a lynx-eyed enemy two miles away! (Marvin C. Ross [ed.], The West of Alfred Jacob Miller, Plates 5, 150, 162, 180, 190, 200).

52 See Chapter V supra.

seen, would antedate that era by some sixty years.[53] Thirty years before Hayden, they were stated to have plenty.[54] About the same time they clearly valued their horses more than the lives of fellow tribesmen.[55] Doubtless they valued them more than the ease of their women.

Tribal diversity is unmistakably present amid the minutiae of social relationships, equestrian and otherwise. The horse or other war trophy captured by a young Sarcee on his first war party was presented to some male relative who had taken special interest in his welfare.[56] Whereas among the Mandan, all the horses a young man stole or captured in war belonged to his sister.[57] It is difficult to conceive of any *animal* predecessor to the horse in this particular connection. Quite probably the dog culture may have anticipated the horse in the field of marriage negotiations, but among the Assiniboin, gift horses from a suitor were appropriated by the girl's brother.[58]

With respect to psychological change induced in the horse tribes as a whole by any sensations of increased economic independence, or of tendencies toward a more exaggerated arrogance, insolence, haughtiness, or whatever form truculence may choose to adopt, we have seen that, while such conclusions appear so natural and logical as to be almost inevitable, they are scarcely borne out by historical fact. It has been shown that the potentially dangerous attitude of the Cayuse tribe toward Marcus Whitman (or what was asserted by tribal enemies to be such) cannot be ascribed to the horse, as Hulbert erroneously thought—somewhat fantastically, in reference to a people who had then possessed the animal perhaps 150 years, and of whose previous demeanor we know nothing.[59] For we have seen that similar evil propensities were at any rate charged against other tribes (and again by tribal enemies) both before and after their acquisition of the horse.[60] In the

[53] Hyde, "Mystery of the Arikaras," 190, 217 (Chapter V *supra*).
[54] Maximilian, *Travels*, in Thwaites, *Travels*, XXIII, 14, 387.
[55] *Ibid.*, XXIV, 104; De Voto, *Across the Wide Missouri*, 94–95.
[56] Jenness, *The Sarcee Indians*, 19.
[57] Maximilian, *Travels*, in Thwaites, *Travels*, XXIII, 281.
[58] Lowie, "The Assiniboin," 40.
[59] A. B. and D. P. Hulbert (eds.), *Marcus Whitman*, I, 71, 76–77, 234; cf. II, 1–20 (see Chapter XII *supra*).
[60] See Chapter XII *supra*.

case of the Iroquois it is difficult to conceive of any agency whatever that could add anything to the almost immeasurable arrogance and murderous hate that characterized the palmy days of their supremacy, and if by any interpretation they could ever have been termed horse Indians, their reign of blood certainly preceded that era.

One important psychological reaction has been attributed to the Nez Percé horses by the foremost authority on the horses of that tribe. Francis Haines emphasizes the influence of those fine animals in tending to establish friendly relations with Lewis and Clark, and the later beneficial effects of this in facilitating an important American expansion movement over a most difficult terrain where obstruction would have been easy for the Indians and disastrous for the immigrants.[61] While these latter facts are indisputable, we must not, however, overstress the horses at the expense of their owners. The attractiveness of the animals to Lewis and Clark would probably have accomplished little had the Nez Percé themselves proved unresponsive. Their historic recompense has been a hard and ungrateful one.[62]

While it seems the very beginning of wisdom to pronounce that the horse "*must* have produced" such and such changes, it proves difficult to put one's finger on them in cold fact. Apart from one possible exception which it will be the task of our following chapter to examine in detail, and the suggestions advanced in the present chapter with reference to an improved status of women resulting from the acquisition of the horse (for whatever that suggestion may be worth), I can find little or nothing which *in esse* or in full-blown actuality can reasonably be attributed *de novo* and unreservedly to its coming among the horse tribes.

There is, however, one psychological postulate which ought not to escape mention, in whatever category it is to be classed. Whatsoever may have been the distinctive features of the red man's paradise prior to the advent of the horse, one cannot feel surprised that later post-equestrian adjustments, among three notable Canadian horse tribes at least—and probably among many others—very fittingly included "fleet horses to catch the Bison and Deer,"

---

61 Haines, "Nez Percé and Shoshoni Influence on Northwest History," 379–93.
62 See Frank Dobie's summing up: *The Mustangs,* 55.

which creatures, most appropriately in a world of ideal perfection, were "always fat. . . ."[63]

Objection has been taken to the present chapter on the ground that, while professing to discuss the influence of the horse upon Indian psychology, it resolves itself in actuality into little or nothing more than a presentation of the status of women in post-equestrian tribal life. In so far as the present chapter itself is concerned, this criticism is entirely legitimate and just. It may be pointed out, however, that psychological changes induced—or otherwise—in the men are an essential and inseparable feature in the entire mass of evidence and comment which constitutes Part II of our study. The reader will have noted in more than one chapter that my own opinion, concurring with that of Wissler and certain other critics, is that the horse did little more than enable the men of the Plains tribes to do the same things more easily and to follow the same life *in esse* that they did before its coming. Whether this view commands critical support or not, those holding it are not required to enter upon detailed discussion of profound and widespread psychological change which they do not consider to have occurred.

With the Plains women the case was fundamentally different. Beyond varying phases of ownership (dogs, harness, etc.,) there was no forerunner in their pre-equestrian life of which the later liberties conferred by the horse could be regarded as merely an adaptation or extension. Greater or lesser possession of the dog, even under personal ownership, while it might ease their backs of the larger and heavier burdens such as tipis and bedding, could do nothing to reduce the toil of foot travel, or to enable them to share in the joys of the individual hunt, which beyond doubt would appeal temperamentally to many daughters of hunting sires quite as keenly as to their sons. In this respect the wealthiest woman dog

[63] For the Piegan: Thompson, *Narrative* (ed. by Tyrrell), 363; Kidd, "Blackfoot Ethnography," 190. Blackfoot: *ibid.*, 192; Coues (ed.), *Henry-Thompson Journals*, II, 528. Cree: Harmon, *Journal*, 316. While Maximilian's accounts of the Assiniboin and Mandan make no direct mention of horses, no doubt among an equestrian folk "the pleasures of the chase" mean the same thing (*Travels*, in Thwaites, *Travels*, XXII, 393; XXIII, 361).

owner in the tribe would be no better off than her poorest sister, for neither could ride her dog. I cannot conceive of any psychological change caused by or resulting from the coming of the horse at all comparable to this in importance, and I have so emphasized it.

It may at the same time be reasonably urged regarding the extension of the equestrian life to their women, quite apart from whether this arose from a spontaneous impulse *ab initio* in the men or as a mere grudging concession in response to the women's demand, that the existence of this condition purely as a *fact* following upon either free bestowal or half-sullen acquiescence must have marked or caused a profound psychological change in the male mind. This can scarcely be disputed, and it must undoubtedly be attributed to the horse since, as I have pointed out, there was no animal predecessor to which we could possibly ascribe it.

XVII

THE HORSE AND THE BUFFALO

The special topic which furnishes the title to our present chapter has been deferred until now for good and sufficient reason. The influence of the horse upon the animal from which the Plains tribes derived their title of "buffalo Indians" is the key topic of Part II of our study. It seemed well, therefore, first of all to place the reader in possession of every phase of such evidence as we have been able to collect concerning the horse on the North American continent at large. We thus avoid the confusion which might arise from referring the reader to parallel or comparative evidence with which he had not yet been made acquainted.

The influence of the horse upon the Plains world may be described as having been discussed hitherto from the angle of its relationship to mere *methods* of living in peace or war. Later pronouncements shift the ground to a more basic conception of the fundamentals of existence itself. It seems to be the considered conclusion of a certain section of archaeological opinion that it was not until the coming of the horse among the aborigines that the term "buffalo Indians" could possess any significance. For it was not (so they consider) until the Plains tribes had horses that they could—or in any event *did*—practice a mass slaughter of the buffalo. This appears inevitably to raise the question of subsistence itself, for if mass slaughter was actually wasteful in this or that specific instance, there must have been countless unrecorded examples, even in the short period since the horse came to them, when without this expedient of mass slaughter there would not have been enough buffalo meat or other products produced to serve their basic needs.

The opinion to which I refer is contained in an important paper by W. D. Strong,[1] to which reference has been made in an earlier chapter. Strong bases his conclusions upon archaeological field investigations, in which province he is a foremost authority for characteristic portions of the Plains area. As a result of his labors, Strong is of the opinion outlined above: that previous to their acquisition of the historic horse the Plains tribes—the "buffalo Indians" themselves—had not adopted and did not follow the most socially and economically important of the various practices that led, collectively, to that designation's being applied to them; that is, the mass slaughter of the buffalo in the various forms in which it was practiced in historic times. Or, to define the case in the phraseology of another American anthropologist of the very first rank: previous to the coming of the horse, the Plains Indians merely "nibbled at the buffalo."[2]

Before proceeding to discuss this hypothesis further, it may be pertinent to note here that Kroeber (unlike Strong) gives no detailed reasons for his pronouncement. They would have been of immense interest and, without doubt, of much value, coming from a scholar who is virtually the foremost authority on the pre-European aboriginal population of the North American continent.

Kroeber's statement could bear two separate meanings: (1) That buffalo were not a principal item of the Plains (prehistoric) diet (which is Strong's opinion *in esse*). (2) That there were not enough of the Plains Indians to materially affect the buffalo masses, however many they slew. General assertions are unsatisfactory without particularized elucidation. James Mooney estimated the pre-European population north of Mexico, about 1492, at approximately 1,153,000; of which some 800,000—approximately 69.5 per cent—were in the non-buffalo areas.[3] In his important discussion of the question, Kroeber reduces Mooney's total to 900,000. Subtracting 69.5 per cent of this number would reduce the buffalo users to about 280,000.[4] The buffalo aggregate has been estimated by Ernest Thompson Seton at 60,000,000 in 1830.[5] A co-ordination

[1] Strong, "Plains Culture in the Light of Archaeology," 271–87.
[2] Kroeber, *Cultural and Natural Areas in Native North America*, 88.
[3] Mooney, "Aboriginal Population of America North of Mexico," 1–40.
[4] Kroeber, *Cultural and Natural Areas*, 131–81.
[5] Seton, *Life Histories of Northern Animals*, I, 259–61, 292; also his *Lives of Game Animals*, III, 654–57.

of the various data, ratios of increase, natural causes of destruction, estimates of slaughter, statistics of hide shipments, etc., make it clear that there could scarcely have been less.[6] How could 280,000 horseless people do much more than "nibble" at such a tremendous aggregate of buffalo?

Strong's own conclusions are based very much upon the fact that the conditions revealed by excavation at the Pawnee villages on the lower Platte and the Loup Rivers, respectively (situated in Nebraska, not far above the junction of the Platte with the Missouri), are unfavorable to any other verdict. The contents of the kitchen-midden deposits, in the stratified layers which for other purposes of investigation are accepted as dating back to pre-equestrian eras, in his judgment reveal entirely too low a ratio of buffalo bones to justify the assumption that mass slaughter methods were then in use.[7]

In summing up his conclusions, Strong very justly emphasizes the importance of the "closely co-ordinated researches of historian, ethnologist, archaeologist, geographer, and geologist."[8] From the standpoint of the first of these categories, while it will not be suggested that historical inquiry possesses any inherent superiority over the other departments, it seems reasonably logical, in an examination working backward from the present to the past, to discuss the more recent evidence first. To this writer at least, it appears very strongly suggestive of paradox to proceed onward to archaeological inference—certainly in a widely generalized application—if direct historical testimony blocks the path. It appears therefore the more regrettable that Strong did not first give more adequate consideration to the available historical evidence.

Some attention has already been given to the question of what constitutes the vital test of a nomad.[9] Strong, by implication if not in so many words, prefers the horse. Wissler considers the dog travois to be the truer test.[10] The latter would of course, if generally accepted, automatically rule out the horse by purely chro-

[6] See Roe, *North American Buffalo*, 489–520; also App. G, "Estimates of Indian Populations Subsisting Wholly or Partly upon Buffalo" (*ibid.*, 742–803).
[7] Strong, "Plains Culture in the Light of Archaeology," 281.
[8] *Ibid.*, 286.
[9] See Chapter X *supra*.
[10] Wissler, "Influence of the Horse," 14.

nological priority. I have shown above, however, and quite conclusively, that, whether considered independently on their own
merits or consecutively because the one is the (Plains) successor
of the other, no form of transport can furnish a truly satisfactory
criterion of a nomad life. For either dog or horse could be utilized
for the conveyance of a completely *non-nomadic* people from one
fixed home or homesite to another at certain periodical seasons of
the year. Hence I consider the use of the portable dwelling to be
the more logical standard of classification in relation to the nomadic life.

For practical purposes, however, the movable home and the
dog travois upon which it was anciently transported are very closely
bound up together in a sense in which the horse is not. For the
horse, as with ourselves and numerous other peoples, could be ridden by wholly non-nomadic possessors, while the Indian dog could
not be ridden, and apart from occasional use for ritual or food purposes had no economic significance beyond "freight transport." As
Wissler asks unanswerably: "Why should the Plains people have
had the dog travois if they did not go on long journeys by land?"[11]

The pre-equestrian use of the dog travois appears to me
to bring forward another question of much significance.
Assuming the existence of a pre-equestrian nomad society in the Plains territory, which nevertheless did not "live on the
buffalo" (in the buffalo Indian sense) until the horse made mass
slaughter originally practicable, or easier, or popular, certain considerations follow. If that society did not live upon the buffalo, it
lived on something else. What "something else" was there in sufficient quantity in the same territory, and itself so utterly nomadic
that the inhabitants also had to become nomadic at an evidently
early era—as it is clear they did—in order to subsist upon it? A
Southwestern scholar makes mention of certain tribes of the Southwest who assembled for the pecan harvest, about 1530.[12] They
were probably nomadic at first from causes other than the pecans,
in relation to which they were really migratory. Nor is there any
indication that the pecan crop was sufficiently large or diffused to

[11] *Ibid.*, 14.

335

influence a really wide population area.[13] What appears to be the underlying supposition in itself, that the existence of stationary villages may be taken to indicate either that buffalo were not sufficiently plentiful or that the villagers did not utilize them to any material extent, is untenable. We find the plenty and the use given as the precise reasons why certain tribes were *not* nomadic. Fathers Dablon and Allouez say of the Northern tribes of the Illinois country in 1671: "[Buffalo] by their abundance, furnish adequate provision for whole Villages, which therefore are not obliged to scatter by families during their hunting season, as is the case with Savages elsewhere."[14]

Strong's hypothesis almost seems to involve the somewhat fantastic supposition that the buffalo themselves were at some remote period highly stationary in a fixed habitat distant from the Pawnee, and only became nomadic after the familiarization of the horse among the buffalo tribes. I use the term "familiarization" advisedly, rather than "appearance," "acquisition," or "possession," for some advanced degree of experienced use would surely be necessary before such a fundamental change in the life of the Indians (and of the buffalo) could be effected.

A great deal has been said about the profound mental change induced in the buffalo by the incessant persecution of their closing years of Plains freedom, although some of these postulates are not very well supported by the same writers' pronouncements elsewhere, or by their own or other incidental evidence at large.[15] We have in our own age evidence of considerable mental change noticeable in buffalo, but in this case the underlying causes are clearly biological, resulting from crossbreeding. The animals in question are those in the Northern Wood Buffalo Park at Fort Smith, Northwest Territories. Several late observers mention them as quite frequently 'stolidly ignoring' the human intruder, or even advancing *towards* him. Both are well-authenticated Plains characteristics, but quite alien to the aboriginal wood buffalo shyness, which is emphasized without exception by every observer from Samuel

12 Hallenbeck, *Journey and Route of Cabeza de Vaca*, 137–40.
13 *Ibid.*, at large; Bandelier (ed.), *Journey of Cabeza de Vaca*; Bishop, *Odyssey of Cabeza de Vaca*; etc.
14 Thwaites (ed.), *Jesuit Relations*, LV, 195–97.
15 See Roe, *North American Buffalo*, 119–53, etc.

Hearne (1771) to Rowan (1925), and perhaps later.[16] The latest classificationists write: "The true, pure-blooded woodland bison may be considered extinct as a result of the repopulation of their last wild range by the introduction of the plains bison in 1924."[17]

Whether in the abstract such change in Plains buffalo would or would not be possible under aboriginal conditions, the question of the time available for a process of this character is a highly practical one, and cannot be evaded. We have seen good reason to believe that many ultranomadic tribes were probably not acquainted with the horse before about 1700.[18] Historical data of this character have to be reckoned with in what may seem a pure problem in archaeology.

There are certain other factors involved in this hypothetical possibility of change which cannot be overlooked. While the "Great Trek" of the buffalo from Texas to Saskatchewan and back is a baseless rhetorical myth,[19] there seems to be some basis for a considerable amount of wandering for rather lengthy distances in some localities. We have fairly reliable evidence for northward spring movements from Texas roughly to the "Republican country" (i.e., along that river) in northern Kansas; but its actual times and character are vague and contradictory, as the Santa Fé caravan journals and later reminiscence reveal.[20] Furthermore, the essential identity of the "prairie type" of buffalo throughout the vast Prairie Plains habitat logically presupposes a degree of promiscuous intermingling sufficient to have precluded the development of local *Plains* varieties of the species. Entirely apart from the question of what are or are not accepted as varieties of *Bison americanus*, no variety has ever been suggested except from the eastern or western forest areas abutting on the Plains habitat.[21]

This requires that temperamental change in the buffalo would

[16] *Ibid.*, 35–53, also App. J, 829–41. See also J. Dewey Soper, "History, Range, and Home Life of the Northern Bison," *Ecological Monographs*, Vol. XI (1941), 396–401.

[17] Morris F. Skinner and Ove C. Kaisen, "The Fossil Bison of Alaska and Preliminary Revision of the Genus," *Bulletin of the American Museum of Natural History*, Vol. LXXXIX (1947), 166.

[18] See Chapters IV–VI *supra*.

[19] See Roe, *North American Buffalo*, 69–93, 543–600, etc.

[20] *Ibid.*, 541–52.

[21] *Ibid.*, Chap. III; cf. also Skinner and Kaisen, "Fossil Bison of Alaska," 157–68.

necessarily need to operate throughout the entire hosts of the species before its effects could have changed into nomads *all* those buffalo tribes who are so classed by experienced observers down to about 1800. For such tribes as the Plain Cree, the Assiniboin, or those Blackfoot whom Palliser in 1857 described as 'the Bedouin of the prairies,'[22] this allows a period of perhaps not more than seventy years after their acquisition of the horse for a succession of highly complex processes. These would comprise the mastering of the horse themselves, changing the buffalo consequently into a nomadic species, and being in turn similarly changed themselves by the reaction of the now nomadic buffalo upon their own conditions of subsistence.

We have no evidence of such change in the buffalo. The allusion above to the changes possibly effected in the buffalo by the bitter persecution of the final days can only—even if that be established—be taken to point an analogy, not a parallel. There is no parallel between the maddening holocausts of that evil time and the impact of the mounted Indian upon the species. We know (or can reconstruct) enough of the latter process to realize that, however soon the earliest of the tribes might inaugurate buffalo hunting on horseback, it would necessarily be a gradual innovation across the Plains habitat as a whole. This would be true both geographically and in the "tactical" sense of the numbers of mounted men available at the outset in any one tribe. In one important Northern buffalo tribe, this paucity is stated to have prevailed in much later eras. David G. Mandelbaum writes thus:

[Among the Plain Cree] only a few men owned horses which were swift enough for the chase and trained to hunt buffalo. Fineday stated that about one tipi in ten would have a good buffalo horse. A number of families would attach themselves to the owner of such a horse and follow him wherever he moved his camp. They shared in the buffalo he was able to secure by means of his horse. Since these families were dependent on the horse owner for food, they were naturally quick to carry out his wishes or orders.[23]

However reckless, sanguinary, wasteful (etc., etc.) the Indians

22 Palliser, *Journals,* 204.
23 Mandelbaum, "The Plains Cree," 195.

may be assumed to have been even by their severest critics, I can see no good reason to suppose that at the inception of mounted hunting they would even have the chance to adopt methods sufficiently drastic or severe to change the habits of the buffalo.

In respect to conscious or unconscious results of such a nature being likely to follow from mounted Indian contacts with buffalo, it is to be borne in mind that there is another side to the story of mass slaughter. The Indian has been the target for bitter and contradictory denunciation. According to Hornaday, whose dicta have been the standard history of the buffalo for sixty years or more, the Indians "killed in season and out of season";[24] but more experienced observers (including his own primary field authority, Colonel Dodge) pronounce differently.[25] Hornaday also says that the Indians "were too lazy to cure much buffalo meat," although he himself states elsewhere that "they formerly cured great quantities ... for use in winter";[26] and the recorded destruction of huge masses ('400,000 pounds in one village') by United States troops furnishes authentic confirmation.[27] There is abundant evidence to show that along with mass slaughtering methods at certain seasons, there went at other times a prudent restraint. The use of "soldiers" who regulated the buffalo hunting—and commonly with more than a chief's authority—is well attested in many tribes;[28] Hornaday himself notes them in the Omaha.[29]

Furthermore, there was, at all times a skilled "psychological" approach, born manifestly of an age-long study and a masterly knowledge of the buffalo mentality, such as won the grudging commendation of the fiercest censors of the Indian.[30] With regard to Indian reaction upon the buffalo as a whole, I know of no evidence either of fact or of informed opinion which indicates that prior to the "high-pressure" methods of the fur trade the buffalo were

[24] Hornaday, "Extermination of the American Bison," 506.
[25] See Edwin James (1820), Account of the Expedition under Long, in Thwaites, Travels, XIV, 301; Alexander Ross (1820–1855), Fur Hunters of the Far West, II, 126; Marcy (1852), Exploration of the Red River, 104; Dodge (1849–1883), Our Wild Indians, 287.
[26] Hornaday, "Extermination of the American Bison," 449, 499.
[27] See Roe, North American Buffalo, 658, for a large number of such.
[28] Ibid., 374, 658.
[29] Hornaday, "Extermination of the American Bison," 477.
[30] See Roe, North American Buffalo, 663, for numerous testimonies.

in any danger of extermination. Hornaday himself writes: "No wonder that the men of the West of those days, both white and red, thought it would be impossible to exterminate such a mighty multitude"; although, characteristically enough, he elsewhere castigates the Indians for *not* foreseeing it.[31]

Apart from the afore-mentioned opinions relating to the last days of the prairie herds, I have encountered nothing from any of the numerous chroniclers or generalizers relating to the buffalo which indicates the workings of any noticeable change from the time of their earliest European observer, Alvar Nuñez Cabeza de Vaca (circa 1530), onward. The supposition that mass slaughter by Indians is a post-equestrian procedure is pure assumption, wholly unwarranted by the historical evidence. There were at least three semi-independent discoveries of the buffalo by Europeans, at different eras and in widely sundered areas of the habitat. By "semi-independent" is meant that neither of the two latter discoverers crossed any known section of the great buffalo range in order to reach the territory with which his own name is particularly associated. He may even (in so far as his own account serves to inform us) never have heard of the reputed geographical haunts or limits of the species, nor where on his own projected route they might perhaps be encountered, if at all. It seems necessary to mention these circumstances, in order to demonstrate the original character of their several descriptions, and the virtual impossibility of copying or collusion. Each of these men testifies to the use of mass slaughtering methods by the Indian tribes in the region of his travels; and each man—the earliest one, Cabeza de Vaca, necessarily—describes a society in which the horse was unknown.

Concerning the aboriginal practice of impounding, Cabeza de Vaca writes as follows:

... when they had found a great multitude of these oxen, and would compasse them about and force them into certain inclosure or toiles,

31 Hornaday, "Extermination of the American Bison," 391, 480–82.

340

their enterprize prevailed but a little; they are so wild and so swift . . . they declared the wildnesse and innumerable number of these Oxen.[32]

It is possible that the silence of Coronado's chroniclers on this phase of Indian buffalo-hunting technique may have misled modern students into the supposition that it was not in use in 1541, in the regions somewhat more to the north of Cabeza de Vaca's route. This crux admits of a simple and logical explanation. Two principal facts may be noted. First, Coronado's party were well armed and well mounted. They traveled as a self-contained Spanish force, rulers of their own conduct. As they tell us, they 'slew the cows' for their own subsistence as mounted Europeans naturally would, on horseback and with firearms. Cabeza de Vaca on the contrary, was for most of the time a captive and in any case an unarmed stranger, compelled perforce to accompany the Indians in their wanderings. In this capacity he observed *their* methods. Secondly, the famous auxiliary expedition to "Quivira" took place in the summer time, from April to August, 1541. Indian slaughtering of buffalo in summer was almost everywhere reduced to the unavoidable minimum; and mass methods were not practiced at that season in any but exceptional circumstances.[33] Toward the closing days of the buffalo, mention is made of making up pemmican in the summer (this might be questionable, as the informant was eighty-six) by Norbert Welsh, an old half-blood trader on the Qu'Appelle (1845–1933).[34] The older contemporary accounts which give times all specify early spring. Henry (1809) complains of the hot fat not mixing well on the cold spring days. It was an important freight with the Saskatchewan (down-river) spring brigades.[35] These facts may serve to remind us that direct contemporary evidence (or its silence) may mislead.[36]

Our next example of ante-equestrian mass slaughtering prac-

[32] *Purchas His Pilgrimes,* XVIII, 78.

[33] See Roe, *North American Buffalo,* 116–18.

[34] Norbert Welsh, *The Last Buffalo Hunter* (ed. by Mary Weekes), 110.

[35] Coues (ed.), *Henry-Thompson Journals,* II, 593. See also Thompson, *Narrative* (ed. by Tyrrell), 432; Kidd, "Blackfoot Ethnography," 108. Vilhjalmur Stefansson's important and definitive work, *Not By Bread Alone* (1946), sums up everything that is known about pemmican. I am indebted to the author's kindness for a copy of this.

[36] See Chapter VI *supra* on completely unreliable reminiscence.

tice is from the Great Lakes territory. Father Hennepin was not actually the first European to encounter the buffalo in that region, as some writers have supposed.[37] That distinction very probably belongs to Father Ménard, the Jesuit missionary, who was slain by the Sioux apparently along the Black River in Wisconsin, in August, 1661.[38] But Hennepin's book was apparently the first contemporary account of travel in that area to be published, and since he almost certainly antedates the horse in the region by nearly a century,[39] the question of his literal priority in no way invalidates his testimony for our present purpose. Hennepin says of the Indians in the Illinois country:

Sometimes they send the swiftest among them . . . who would drive whole Droves of wild Bulls before them and force them to swim the River. Of these they sometimes kill'd forty or fifty, but took only the Tongues, and some other of the best Pieces.[40]

Also in the Illinois country (circa 1720; still prior to the horse), Father Sebastian Râle writes: "There is no year in which they do not kill . . . more than 2000 oxen [buffalo]."[41] The population of the Illinois tribe would presumably be the only sound criterion which could determine whether such figures indicate mass slaughter methods in use by the tribe, or mere "nibbling." As they stand they simply suggest a considerable annual consumption by a semi-agricultural people who are known to have followed a varied diet.[42]

[37] As Hornaday, "Extermination of the American Bison," 375. Fathers Dablon, Allouez, Marquette, also Joliet, Daniel Greysolon Duluth, not to say Radisson and Groseilliers—if they were there—all antedate Hennepin.

[38] Emma Helen Blair, *Indian Tribes of the Great Lakes and Mississippi Valley Region*, I, 172.

[39] See Chapter V *supra*.

[40] Hennepin, *New Discovery* (ed. by Thwaites), I, 242. See another description of the surround and its methods (lasting some twelve hours) in the same general area, by a contemporary, Nicholas Perrot (1670–1699): Blair, *Indian Tribes of the Great Lakes*, I, 120–24. Wissler wrote, 1910: "The surround was evidently a method developed after the introduction of the horse." ("Material Culture of the Blackfoot," 50; so also Lowie, "Material Culture of the Crow Indians," 210.) But Wilson, 1924, notes Mandan tales of its pre-equestrian use ("Horse and Dog in Hidatsa Culture," 141, 155). Cabeza de Vaca is strangely ignored.

[41] Thwaites (ed.), *Jesuit Relations*, LXVIII, 169.

[42] The Illinois proper (not the Confederacy) were estimated by Hennepin, 1680, at some six thousand souls, and by Father Râle, about 1690, at approximately nine thousand. "Perhaps excessive"; so Mooney and Thomas, in Hodge, *Handbook*,

Hennepin also speaks of "encompassing the Wild Bulls with fire" as a custom among the Miami and Illinois tribes.[43]

Henry Kelsey, our third European discoverer, who encountered the buffalo very probably on the Carrot River prairies of northern Saskatchewan (about 53° N, 103° W), writes under the date of August 23, 1691:

This Instant [today] ye Indians going a hunting Kill'd great store of Buffilo. Now ye manner of their hunting these Beast on ye Barren Ground is where they see a great parcel of them together they surround them with men wch done they gather themselves into a smaller Compasse K eping ye Beast still in ye middle & so shooting ym till they break out at some place or other and so get away from ym.[44]

Certain other examples are also of importance. The first of these antedates not merely the horse but the buffalo in that particular territory,[45] and the others refer to areas where the aboriginal inhabitants never became horse people. In reference to Virginia, circa 1607, the renowned Captain John Smith mentions a native practice there of "environing the Deere with fire."[46] In a region of northern British Columbia where the historic buffalo never penetrated, Father Morice mentions the use of pounds for taking the indigenous (gregarious) game species.[47] Jenness notes the ancient use of buffalo pounds among the Beaver Indians (Tsattine) of the Fort Chipewyan territory, where buffalo were formerly much more plentiful than is now the case.[48] The same authority also records (from personal observation) the use of drives for the mass slaughter of caribou among the Copper Eskimo of Coronation Gulf.[49] These accounts confirm the assertions of earlier travelers. Samuel

I, 598. Father Claude Allouez, 1677, mentions fourteen roots and forty-two fruits eaten by the Illinois, who were also in part agriculturists: Thwaites (ed.), *Jesuit Relations*, LX, 161.

[43] Hennepin, *New Discovery* (ed. by Thwaites), I, 147.

[44] *The Kelsey Papers* (ed. by Doughty and Martin), 13.

[45] On the absence of buffalo from Virginia before 1625, see Roe, *North American Buffalo*, 212–19.

[46] Smith, "Description of Virginia," 1607, in *Purchas His Pilgrimes*, XVIII, 444.

[47] Morice, *History of the Northern Interior of British Columbia*, 38.

[48] Jenness, *Indians of Canada*, 383. D. W. Harmon, about 1800, notes that these Indians "were formerly clothed with the skins of the buffalo" (*Journal*, 149); cf. Hodge, *Handbook*, II, 822.

[49] Jenness, *The Copper Eskimo*, 124, 136, 148–50.

Hearne describes the Chipewyans impounding of deer, in pounds made upon 'regularly frequented paths.' One was so made, March, 1771, "but the deer did not keep on it."[50] Alexander Mackenzie in 1793 also mentions "snares" (pounds) made for elk in what was broadly the same territory covered by Father Morice.[51]

In the case of Henry Kelsey's Indians, noted above, it might very conceivably be argued that such a failure as he mentions perhaps tends to indicate a rather recent acquaintance with buffalo hunting in 1691, and by the nomad method of the surround, particularly; an acquaintance which had not yet advanced these Indians very far beyond the greenhorn stage. As we have seen, however, Cabeza de Vaca alludes to such occasional failures.[52] Cabeza de Vaca's territory is contiguous to—perhaps actually identical with —that where less than ten years later the buffalo tribes visited by the Coronado expedition exhibited a buffalo economy which is indistinguishable in everything but the horse from that of the nineteenth century.[53] And precisely similar occasional failures are recorded by Matthew Cocking (1772),[54] Alexander Henry the younger (1809),[55] Rundle the missionary (1841),[56] and John McDougall (1862 and after).[57] At least the last three failures belong to eras when expert Indian proficiency had become a truism; and while naturally disappointing at the moment, they are in no sense treated as an occurrence so rare as to be almost unheard of except with novices. Cocking, being a newcomer himself, is the only one who feels it necessary to explain their ill luck. His "Asinepoet" (Assiniboin) companions were "perhaps not so expert" as the "Archithinue" (Blackfoot).[58]

50 Samuel Hearne, A Journey from Prince of Wales Fort in 1770, 1771, and 1772 (ed. by J. B. Tyrrell), 120, 126, 193, 309. Compare this occurrence with the conventional claptrap about "never deviating"!

51 Mackenzie, Voyages, 121–22, 131.

52 Note 32 supra.

53 See on this, Hallenbeck, Journey and Route of Cabeza de Vaca, 57, 129, 269–70; also on Quivira, Chapter III supra. For the manifold uses of buffalo, see evidence collected in Roe, North American Buffalo, 602–607.

54 Cocking, "Journal" (ed. by Burpee), 108–10, 116.

55 Coues (ed.), Henry-Thompson Journals, II, 517–20.

56 Rundle, "Journal" (ed. by Berry and Roe), January 16, 1841.

57 McDougall, Saddle, Sled, and Snowshoe, 271–81. Perhaps the most intimate of the many descriptions I have seen.

58 Cocking, "Journal" (ed. by Burpee), 108–10, 116.

In speaking of the "nomad method" of the surround on foot, I use the expression deliberately and advisedly. This particular expedient must be carefully distinguished from the "pound" proper. The latter was in some cases a fixed and permanent institution; these instances were generally a "jumping-pound" over a cliff or "cut-bank." The practice is commemorated (in translation) in Western place names. There are Dog Pond and Jumping Pond (properly "pound"), Alberta. The latter in Blackfoot is "nina-piskan," and contains the great Algonquian buffalo-root "pisik" ("peecheek"), which has spread into many tribes.[59] Hind has recorded Buffalo Pound Hill Lake, in the Qu'Appelle country in Saskatchewan.[60] McClintock mentions a double jumping-pound, at a river confluence, known as Two Medicine Piskan[61]—"piskan" or "piskun" being the term for an ordinary pound. Poundmaker, the Cree chief in the "Rebellion" of 1885, derived his name from this contrivance.

In all cases the pound was on a predetermined site.[62] Those which were not jumping-pounds necessitated much preliminary labor since an enclosure, corral, or yard had to be built of logs and brush, high and strong enough to prevent the entrapped buffalo from escaping before they could be slain. In addition, all pounds must be provided with the "markers." These were of any material available: piles of brush, or failing those, perhaps merely an old buffalo hide, behind or beneath which the auxiliaries to the drive crouched unseen. The markers were placed very far apart at first, like a "squeezer" on a ranch (which may very possibly have copied the buffalo-pound technique in this particular), converging gradually to a narrow bottleneck at the mouth of the pound, which in some tribal practices involved a drop of two feet or more from the gateway into the enclosure. As the oncoming herd passed each suc-

[59] *Place-Names of Alberta,* 43, 69. Rundle speaks of going to visit Fort Edmonton's winter meat camp at "Buffalo Pond,". eastward from the fort ("Journal," January 16, 1841).

[60] Hind, *Report, 1858,* 53.

[61] McClintock, *Old North Trail,* 438, 520.

[62] Mandelbaum says: "Hunters did not plan such drives beforehand, but simply exploited the natural advantages of the terrain" ("The Plains Cree," 192). This may have been obtained from inaccurate later informants. Beyond the basic distinction between built-up and jumping-pounds, it is grossly incorrect. Jenness's description of the Sarcee pound includes a sketch-plan, apparently indicating a fixed tribal design (*The Sarcee Indians,* 14–17).

cessive pair of markers, those hidden behind them rose up and by forming a cordon across the rear assisted to block the retreat, yelling and gesticulating to frighten the animals forward, until the mouth of the pound or the edge of the cliff entrapped or engulfed them. In the latter case they were too badly injured by the fall to be able to get away. In the ordinary pound the entrance was hastily closed with a buffalo hide or the like, and the animals were slain with lances and arrows. None were allowed to escape—unless by some evil chance the corral proved faulty.[63] As we shall have occasion to note later, this was not waste. It had deeply rooted religious (and perhaps other) sanctions behind it.

It seems contrary to all logical probability to suppose that this luring to a previously selected and prepared situation followed any other sequence since its first inception than as the complex, highly developed, evolutionary outcome and finale of later times, of which the surround in the open with such facilities as they might chance to possess at the moment was the rudimentary beginning. The methods of the open surround unmistakably reveal its origin in a nomad society. The surround was clearly for entrapping the herds of buffalo or other animals *wherever they might be found.* So far from being post-equestrian, as Wissler appears at one time to have held,[64] we have seen that it was practiced in regions where neither horse nor buffalo had then penetrated, and white visitors who never saw the Plains witnessed its use for buffalo in localities whose native tribes never became horse Indians in any Plains acceptation of the term. A young English visitor to Kentucky writes thus (May 24–28, 1775): "Surrounded 30 Buffaloes as they were crossing the river."[65] A learned anthropologist sums up the evolutionary process:

The climax of this first class [taking game with the hand, poacher's lore, etc.] was the communal game drive, in which a whole band or tribe

[63] If this happened with a new pound, the "bringer-in" was humiliated, the new pound made unlucky, and the camp sadly disappointed. It was thought unlucky to burn up an old pound among the Cree, as John McDougall once did when in straits for a fire (*Saddle, Sled, and Snowshoe,* 19, 28, 279); so also among the Piegan, about 1857 (John C. Ewers, "The Last Bison Drives of the Blackfoot Indians," *Journal of the Washington Academy of Sciences,* Vol. XXXVIII (1949), 358).

[64] Strong, "Plains Culture in the Light of Archaeology," 271. See note 40 *supra.*

[65] A. G. Bradley (ed.), *The Journal of Nicholas Cresswell,* 78, 80.

would surround a herd of animals and coax or force them into a gorge, corral, or natural *cul de sac*.[66]

I am completely unable to comprehend how the relics of a fixed pound on a permanent site, or any other accepted evidences of mass slaughter at a sedentary village situation, can be thought to indicate a (relatively) recent adoption of the nomadic life by those who accumulated them. Even if "nomads" *in villages* were not paradox per se, the mere circumstance in itself of a historically-late nomadic tribe's having evolved the stationary game trap would to me be very strong evidence that, however completely nomadic they might seem to be today, they had progressed far from a stage in which the surround in the open represented their ultimate achievement in procuring subsistence from the large game of their habitat. I should be prepared, rather, to rank such people as sedentaries *in esse*, confined willingly or unwillingly in the nomad class by the character of their principal food supply. An American anthropologist of high standing (now deceased) considered the term "nomadic" not properly applicable to any Indian tribe.[67]

I have shown what appear to be reasonably satisfactory grounds for considering the surround to be the elementary and perhaps much earlier predecessor of the fixed pound of any character. Yet this later development itself seems clearly to have been of a material and, not impossibly, of an immense antiquity. Sir Cecil Denny, who was one of the original Northwest Mounted Police force of 1874 (Alberta, 1874–1928), mentions an ancient deposit of buffalo bones found on the Elbow River in 1875, some ten miles above its junction with the Bow at Calgary, Alberta. These were believed to mark an old pound site. They were covered with many feet of soil, and flint arrowheads were found among them.[68] Henry Youle Hind refers to something

[66] Otis T. Mason, in Hodge, *Handbook*, I, 580.
[67] Henry W. Henshaw, *ibid.*, II, 283.
[68] Denny MS., 42. Denny left two MSS. containing overlapping material. The one here cited contained a chapter on the buffalo. While his generalizations are of little value, owing to an entire lack of comparative criticism, his firsthand buffalo reminiscences are most interesting and some experiences are almost unique in the

similar at the Forks of the Assiniboine River and the Little Souris, in southern Manitoba, in 1858.[69]

Not being a trained archaeologist, it is with great diffidence that I venture to comment upon archaeological field data—but flint arrowheads viewed in this connection seem to possess a distinct significance. As native artifacts, they are sufficiently early that their presence in conjunction with 'many feet of soil' logically precludes them as any proof of the argument for the essential lateness of buffalo pounds. Considered in relation to the probable chronological eras of iron or steel arrowheads among the Plains Indians prior to the importation of manufactured ones, flint-headed arrows remained in use down to times sufficiently "modern" that these are similarly unsatisfactory as evidence for an antiquity, in the case of this pound, so remote that it could only be associated with some long-extinct fossil species of bison. Of this last, no instances of any nature have thus far been found in or near the locality, down to 1947.[70] A flint arrowhead was discovered in association with fossil bison remains in Kansas many years ago. An eminent paleontologist was disposed to consider this as evidence for a higher antiquity for man on this continent.[71] A later student prefers to regard it rather as indicating an exceptional, late survival of a generally extinct species. But even his "lateness" is purely archaeological and relative, and implies an age of several centuries.[72]

It is of course regrettable that the identification as an old pound site does not rest upon recognized archaeological or geological authority. It may be noted, however, that the accepted recognition by scientific observers of more superficial or surface deposits as being such was not unknown to plainsmen at that time. Charles

buffalo literature. I was kindly permitted by the author to make extensive notes from this. The other MS. has since been printed (*The Law Marches West* [ed. by W. B. Cameron]). The buffalo chapter, which should have been collated, is most deplorably omitted.

[69] Hind, *Report, 1858,* 42.

[70] There is no mention of such in Skinner and Kaisen's exhaustive monograph, "Fossil Bison of Alaska," which goes far beyond its title. I am greatly indebted to the authors for a copy of this. For data on importation of arrowheads and some dates, 1626–1671, see Thwaites (ed.), *Jesuit Relations,* IV, 207; Innis, *Fur Trade in Canada,* 14–18, 31, 99, 127, 139, 274, 290, etc.; Garretson, *The American Bison,* 179–80.

[71] Henry Fairfield Osborn, *The Age of Mammals,* 463, 464, 483, 497.

[72] Kroeber, *Cultural and Natural Areas,* 88; cf. Roe, *North American Buffalo,* 20–23, for various views.

N. Bell, then (I believe) of the Canadian Geological Survey, writes as follows:

I saw such a structure south of the Battle River, in Saskatchewan, in October, 1872, and the quantities of bones left in the neighbourhood were amazing. . . . I saw another buffalo trap . . . the piles of skulls and bones left at the foot of the cut-bank must have represented tens of thousands of animals.[73]

Palliser noted some spot (possibly the very same one) in the same general region, south of Carlton, in 1857.[74] With respect to Denny himself, moreover (who was personally known to the present writer), while no specialist, he was not an unread man; and Hind was a trained geologist.[75] In any event, the dissenting critic cannot have it both ways. Such masses of bones *ipso facto* denote large numbers of buffalo slain in one place. This must either be effected by repeated slaughterings at the same spot—in short, the pound—or by a single supermassacre at one time, which itself is hardly compatible with "nibbling." It may be fairly argued also, I believe, that the antiquity of the historic buffalo-impounding practices (in every feature but the use of the horse) is good presumptive evidence of the parallel case for necessity, discussed above. A similarity of methods logically favors, though it does not *prove*, the interpretation of a similarity of circumstances.

Another phase of anthropological evidence for the probably high antiquity of pre-equestrian buffalo impounding calls for our attention. It may be noted that in a rather considerable volume of buffalo literature, which includes most of the original Western travel relations in print and much yet in manuscript form, one very striking feature stands out conspicuously. While the various mount-

[73] Charles N. Bell (ed.), *The Journal of Henry Kelsey*, 24. This is very near to where Matthew Cocking saw a similar pound exactly a century before (October, 1772), and may even have been the identical spot (notes 54, 58 *supra*). See also Joel A. Allen, *The American Bisons, Living and Extinct* (1876), 51; Wissler, "Material Culture of the North American Indians," 492; also his *The American Indian*, 272; Jenness, *The Sarcee Indians*, 14–17; Ewers, "Last Bison Drives of the Blackfoot Indians," 355–60.

[74] Palliser, *Journals*, 57.

[75] Ewers ("Last Bison Drives of the Blackfoot Indians," 356) speaks of "local enthusiasts" drawing unwarrantable inferences. That term could hardly apply to Hind or Henry Fairfield Osborn.

ed expedients were frequently employed beyond doubt for driving or turning the herd toward the general vicinity of the (permanent) pound—more particularly, perhaps, when the animals were some distance away—the final "luring" or "decoying" into the mouth of the pound was (in my reading) invariably done on foot. The buffalo were not driven in, but *led*.[76] It is of course self-evident that to a horseless tribe no other course was really practicable.

Even if we had not the direct evidence already cited concerning the very earliest recorded tribes in the extreme northern and southern portions of the horse-and-buffalo territory to show a preequestrian—and probably very high—antiquity for buffalo mass slaughter, I believe the consideration of the decoy, the "bringerin," as the Plain Cree called him,[77] would go far to establish the case. The persistence of the foot practice would tend a priori to indicate a technique of perhaps even enormous antiquity, so deeply rooted as a phase of an orthodox ritual in what was plainly quite as much a sequent series of rites as a mere logical succession of practical expedients, that even the phenomenal innovation of the horse had failed to eradicate it. And it may pertinently be emphasized that Cabeza de Vaca, the earliest European chronicler who noted the mass slaughtering usages, recorded also the nomad society of which this mass slaughtering is considered even on Strong's own principles to be an essential manifestation or corollary.

There are certain salient details in what I have suggested as the ritual of impounding which in my opinion tend strongly to support the view of considerable antiquity for the practice as a whole. The denunciations of the wastefulness of buffalo impounding are familiar to everybody: 'the slaying of whole herds down to the last animal!' We are supposed to have learned somewhat more of comparative anthropology than was available a century ago to Gregg[78]

[76] James Willard Schultz, *Apauk, Caller of Buffalo;* cited by Roe, *North American Buffalo,* 649; see also 880–84 ("Buffalo Pounds"). In the Alfred Jacob Miller collection there is a picture of Indians "Driving Buffalo over a Bluff," which is (presumably) meant to depict an impounding drive into a jumping-pound. De Voto, who reproduces this (*Across the Wide Missouri,* Plate LX) says this is something "which Miller never saw." If descriptions by experienced observers are of any value, neither did anyone else. They might be trying to drive the buffalo over the American Fall at Niagara! (*The West of Alfred Jacob Miller* [ed. by Ross], Plate 190).

[77] "O-noh-che-buh-how" (Cree, "Who Goes After Them," or "Who Brings Them In": McDougall, *Saddle, Sled, and Snowshoe,* 275, 276).

or Frémont;[79] yet professed men of science within the last half-century have not been ashamed to repeat these diatribes, or to continue to hold up as oracles other scientists who did so.[80] Actually of course the explanation has nothing whatever to do with what in our societies is termed waste. To apply the expression to buffalo slaughter was meaningless to the Indian mind. To the Indian, the perpetual continuance of buffalo did not depend upon vital statistics, the ratio of births to deaths. The Manito sent them at His good pleasure. He could take them away if it should seem good in His sight, and again restore them in due season.[81] The impounded herds were to be slaughtered to a finish lest escaping survivors should warn other herds to shun the dangerous neighborhood. Such beliefs were not confined to buffalo Indians. Many tribes believed this. The "Neutrals" of Ontario slew any animals they met, whether needing them for food or not, for fear of this contingency.[82] In our own day, Ernest Thompson Seton tells us: "I had offended Chief Snuff . . . he now gave it out that I was here to take out live Musk-Ox, which meant that all the rest would follow to seek their lost relatives."[83] It seems not impossible also that some of these practices may at times have been actuated by a "scorched earth" policy against tribal enemies. In case of later alliances with former foes, such an ostensible reason would obviate any need for inconvenient explanations.[84]

There is a further phase of this total slaughtering which is of a less mystic and more utilitarian character. It has frequently been asked why could not the Indians have been content to drive into their pounds only such numbers as were necessary to meet their daily (or periodical) needs; the failure to do so was commonly

[78] Gregg, Commerce of the Prairies, in Thwaites, Travels, XIX, 243–44; XX, 260–64.

[79] Frémont, Narrative, 142, etc.

[80] See notes 99–100 infra.

[81] For much evidence on this, see Roe, North American Buffalo, 642–49. My friend E. A. Corbett, Director of Adult Education for Canada, was told in 1933 by the grandson of an old Hudson's Bay Company man that the buffalo 'were not exterminated by man. It would have been an impossibility; they went back into the earth whence they came.' In the "Rebellion" of 1885, 'if the white men could be driven out, the buffalo would return' (Katherine Hughes, Father Lacombe, 304).

[82] J. N. B. Hewitt, in Hodge, Handbook, II, 60.

[83] Seton, Arctic Prairies, 144; cf. also Warburton Pike, The Barren Ground of Northern Canada, 183.

[84] Jablow, The Cheyenne, 73–74, on the Great Peace of 1840.

attributed to their insane and incurable wastefulness. The buffalo are believed by some students of their history to have been composed of small "families" of some fifty or sixty head, whose leader was their own sire, or perhaps grandsire. According to this hypothesis, these smaller "clans" made up the enormous aggregates of the great herds, and even if separated, would rejoin their own close kindred when the larger masses disintegrated and scattered.[85]

Any man who (like the present writer) has driven anything wilder than a bunch of milking cows, and over the open range, will recognize the enormous difficulty of trying to "cut out" four or five from fifty or sixty head. I believe any Western cowman would agree with me that the Indians probably impounded an entire small herd or "clan" because that was the only way they could impound any. And once the buffalo were entrapped, I suspect the sternest rationalistic economist would discover in the case of the simple (non-jumping) pound that only by slaying all the herd was it safe or even practicable to enter to secure the meat.

In view of the clear convergence from many angles of a mass of evidence pointing to a considerable antiquity for mass impounding practices, it is of interest to note that the reminiscent and traditional evidence procurable from the Blackfoot and intermontane tribes is contradictory and somewhat adverse. John C. Ewers cites testimony from a number of those tribes. Lemhi Shoshone informants told Robert H. Lowie in 1906 that the Blackfoot method of buffalo impounding was unknown to their people, which may imply that they had methods of their own.[86] The Flathead and Coeur d'Alêne formerly stampeded buffalo over cliffs (jumping-pounds), but the ethnologist who obtained this information could not determine whether the practice prevailed before the coming of the horse. Harry Turney-High's Flathead informants denied that their forefathers drove buffalo over cliffs or into pounds. To the same scholar, the modern Kutenai (or Kootenay) denied that members of that tribe drove buffalo over cliffs in the pre-equestrian era, despite mention of that method in tribal folklore.[87]

[85] On "clans," see Roe, North American Buffalo, 69–70, 114–15, 144, etc.

[86] It is not clear whether this refers to the jumping-pound, or to the ledge or drop of three or four feet into the simple (level) pound of the Blackfoot, which was also a Cree feature (McDougall, Saddle, Sled, and Snowshoe, 274).

[87] Ewers, "Last Bison Drives of the Blackfoot Indians," 356.

As I have previously had occasion to point out, I am deeply sceptical concerning the advisability of treating Indian tradition, or counterassertion concerning it, as authentic historical testimony. The Canadian Blackfoot denied that the tribe had ever followed the ancient Plains practice of drinking the juices from the buffalo stomach when in extremities from thirst,[88] an occurrence which was first recorded by Pedro de Castañeda.[89] Yet it was in the Canadian Blackfoot territory where Daniel W. Harmon learned of this.[90] The same native informants denied strenuously that the Blackfoot had ever eaten dogs, though Kidd himself (the recorder) feels dubious.[91] Several contemporary witnesses affirm (as did the Indians to Hector in 1857) that the trapped buffalo in the ordinary pound always "ran with the sun"—following the decoy.[92] Kidd's Blackfoot informant (born about 1900) considered the "sun-turning" absurd.[93] Such details do nothing to strengthen a very feeble faith in reliable (remote) historical information from nonliterate sources. There is a tendency which is found in more than one race which is on what we ourselves like to think is the upward path toward civilization to repudiate features in their former life which now seem derogatory to their more advanced selves. I suspect this attitude is not without influence in these disclaimers. Then too, comparative knowledge, the vital source of sound conclusions, is a closed book to tribal tradition, of which the Kutenai just mentioned present an acute example even in their own sphere. Whatever the data cited by Ewers may be thought to prove or disprove concerning the tribes in question, they cannot in my judgment outweigh a mass of cumulative evidence extending back over four centuries and more, and spanning a continent. I note that Ewers himself (whose very recent essay I did not see until long after forming the foregoing opinions) reaches a similar conclusion *in esse*.

There is little doubt that in its common historical "apologetic" form—to prevent surviving animals from warning others—the total-

---

[88] Kidd, "Blackfoot Ethnography," 108, 170.
[89] Castañeda, in Winship (ed.), *Journey of Coronado*, 112.
[90] Harmon, *Journal*, 279.
[91] Kidd, "Blackfoot Ethnography," 103–104.
[92] See Roe, *North American Buffalo*, App. AA, 880–84.
[93] Kidd, "Blackfoot Ethnography," 98.

slaughter practice is age-old. In the latter days of the wild herds, realists were not lacking among the Plains tribes who could pierce through the clouds of a mystical fatalism and discern the approaching end.[94] There were others—including even old men in both categories—who had remained aloof from the "wasteful" expression of such beliefs by practicing prudence and moderation in killing, which could be done even more effectively after they acquired the horse.[95] Yet for the great majority these credos were so embedded in the Indian mind, either from psychological-religious sanctions or from a compulsion enforced by the habits of the herds themselves, that even the visible approach of the final tragedy was powerless to uproot them. Cowie mentions 'wasteful slaughter' by Cree young men around Gull Lake (Saskatchewan) in 1868, 'despite the warnings and entreaties of the elders.'[96] But after all, why *should* they school themselves to a hitherto needless frugality in order to leave more for other people?

Old as I consider these "articles of faith" to be, if it were possible to recover the beginnings of things in this field, I should not be surprised to find beyond them an older inhibition still. It is conceivable that in the remote eras of first contacts with buffalo the more scrupulous or more prudent—possibly with sad traditional memories of a tribal past less bountifully supplied—who shrank from the holocausts which the buffalo temperament probably made inevitable, were silenced and quelled by the force of a cult which transformed a disagreeable expedient (to them) into a ritualistic injunction. There can be little doubt that the Mosaic law is full of such transmutations.[97]

If we assume for the moment the soundness of the conclusion that the nomadic mass-slaughter methods are a product of the Plains horse culture, I confess myself unable to comprehend why

[94] Jablow cites the case of Yellow Wolf, a Southern Cheyenne, to Lieut. J. W. Abert in 1846 (Jablow, *The Cheyenne*, 84–85). Similarly, an Assiniboin chief to Father De Smet, about 1850 (*Life of De Smet* [ed. by Chittenden and Richardson], III, 935).

[95] See examples, Roe, *North American Buffalo*, 42, 652–58.

[96] Cowie, *Company of Adventurers*, 297.

[97] The constant reiteration of the terrific injunction "Thus saith the Lord" in the case of extermination massacres was probably intended to justify (to many) an atrocity at which their humanity shuddered; so also, no doubt, with the ordinances re hygiene, etc., in their tropical camp life.

the horse was not used for the complete process of buffalo impounding. On Strong's own showing—it is the very essence and keynote of his argument—there was no ancient ante-equestrian corpus juris of deeply rooted buffalo-pound usage to be overthrown and abrogated before the new agency could operate. Or are we to suppose that this complete utilization of the horse *was* attempted, was found to be impracticable, was discarded, and was then replaced by semi-occult or "psychological" processes never before tried (as we must necessarily assume), and which would certainly require some lengthy period of development for their well-attested degree of expert and effective use? In view of the very limited space of time available for such a series of experiments, perhaps not more than from 1567 in the extreme south to 1730 in the extreme north of the prairie buffalo range—where expert horsemen and mounted buffalo driving toward the camp are well authenticated in 1754[98]—it is quite evident the situation would call for some quick work to be done.

I am of the opinion that Strong, in advancing the hypothesis of the post-equestrian origin of the buffalo drive en masse, has fundamentally misconceived the influence of the horse upon the Indian mind. His analysis of the aboriginal response to this new asset is purely along quantitative lines; the possibility even of a qualitative appeal is not mentioned. One is driven to the conclusion that the conventional concept of the improvidence, wastefulness, extravagance, recklessness (etc., etc.) of the Indian was his basic assumption and starting point. This comprehensive postulate was emphasized abundantly by Hornaday, and it must be acknowledged that when Strong was writing (1933) the infallibility of Hornaday (the term is not too strong) was still an article of scientific faith. The uncritical endorsement of Hornaday's essay by Ernest Thompson Seton in 1910, and again in 1929, virtually without modification[99]—even extending to points where Seton himself possessed superior knowledge—obscured recognition

[98] Henday, "Journal" (ed. by Burpee), 335–51.
[99] *Life Histories of Northern Animals* (1910); *Lives of Game Animals* (1929). Garretson, *The American Bison* (1938), is even more extravagant.

355

of the fact that in 1929 Hornaday had become a landmark in the history of scientific opinion and little more. The earliest discoverable criticism of Hornaday is not until 1933,[100] the actual year of Strong's above-mentioned publication.

Hornaday adopted *in toto* the average nineteenth-century plainsman's attitude toward the red man; well summed up in Sheridan's classic definition—'the only good Indian is a dead Indian.' Starting from this datum, it was not difficult to find early expressions of opinion from like-minded plainsmen which represented the Indian in buffalo relationships to be utterly wasteful and worthless. Contrary opinion was ignored, except in the one instance of George Catlin. Catlin, whose twenty pages give the best field description of the buffalo ever written, sympathized with the Indians.[101] He was therefore derided and denounced as half liar and half fool. Hornaday's Indians, depicted from this angle—he scarcely ever mentions one without contempt—became the standard buffalo Indian of scientific knowledge.

Given an "Indian" of this character, a murderous, ungovernable predator against man or beast, it was not difficult to explain his slaughterings of the buffalo. Whether he indulged his propensities prior to the coming of the horse or not becomes almost a matter of academic indifference. If he did, the horse enabled him to do so more freely than before. If he did not, the horse gave him the opportunity to "go off at the deep end" and show what he really could do with such a ready helper! As the Indian was assumed to be an insatiable temperamental slayer to begin with, the further assumption follows automatically: once he had the horse, all that he could or would think of would be to slay more buffalo and yet more! Evidence in abundance indicates that, speaking broadly, the horse resulted in the Indians' killing less and less individually; that is to say, prior to the intensive era of the fur trade, from about 1830 onward.[102] But for the first time in their age-long history, in all probability, they were under no compulsion to take an entire

100 This is mild enough: "Part of his [Hornaday's] account of the wood buffalo is somewhat confused because he treated it as being identical with the so-called mountain buffalo." (Hugo M. Raup, *Range Conditions in the Wood Buffalo Park of Western Canada*, 46.)

101 For Catlin, see Roe, *North American Buffalo*, 7–9, 530–33, 803, etc.

102 This is Hornaday's classification: "Extermination of the American Bison," 484–86.

small herd, good and bad alike, but could kill, as I have said, qualitatively. They were able at last to pick their beasts. We shall review some of the evidence to which I have referred in support of these conclusions.

We have noted above the great attachment of the Indians of many tribes to their cherished "buffalo runners," and also the alleged or relative rarity of these super-steeds, which is probably one explanation of the high prices men were willing to pay to obtain one. It is idle to suppose that an especially fast horse (or stallion?) was necessary in order merely to *surround* a small herd, which eyewitnesses (in about 1530, 1680, and 1691 respectively[103]) tells us was done by men afoot, perhaps with some difficulty at times, but done nevertheless. The buffalo *running* which gave these horses their name is familiar in outline at least to most readers, for it has often been described in fact and done to death in fiction.[104] Horse and buffalo raced neck-and-neck, and afforded the rider an unequalled opportunity to plant a fatal arrow or bullet in that most vulnerable spot behind the shoulder, which commonly brought the great beast down, while the well-trained horse jumped aside to avoid being crushed beneath the fallen giant. Man after man has told us how the good hunters could pick their animals at full gallop. John McDougall mentions a Cree (1862) who slew sixteen buffalo in this manner with seventeen arrows.[105]

It was quite probably the running of buffalo that developed the superlative archery of the foregoing character among the Plains Indians. The bow retained its favor and also its expert use down to the very last days of the Indian buffalo hunt.[106] About 1800 the gun was prohibited by the Assiniboin for buffalo; and while the Mandan and Hidatsa were less rigid, they much preferred the bow.[107]

Beyond dispute, it is the running of buffalo, and certainly not the surround, which explains the activities of the well-known "soldiers" or "Dog Soldiers" in regulating the tribal hunting move-

---

[103] Notes 32, 40, 44 *supra*.

[104] See on this, Roe, *North American Buffalo*, 401, 630.

[105] McDougall, *Forest, Lake, and Prairie*, 144.

[106] See Roe, *North American Buffalo*, App. T, "Late Survival of Indian Archery," 868.

[107] Jablow, *The Cheyenne*, 18.

ments. Prohibitions against individual hunters setting forth alone or in advance of the general body are meaningless in reference to the surround, in which single men or even a small number would wear themselves out vainly. While there is no reason to doubt that the psychological sense of greatly enlarged powers would be fully present to the Indian mind, it would in my opinion express itself in terms of quality, not quantity.

So far from the equestrian era inaugurating mass slaughter, it seems to be more correct, historically, to suggest that the advent of the horse terminated it, or at least marked the beginning of the end. I do not of course refer to aggregates composed of individual "kills" in buffalo running, but to co-operative drives or surrounds. Working progressively northward from the Spanish country, it appears to have been the case that as the Plains tribes acquired a sufficient strength in horseflesh—which process must probably include the selection or development of the buffalo runners—the communal hunt fell into disuse, and its place was taken by the semi-communal or aggregated movement of later historic times. This was still very much organized, but it was made up of independent actors, who in respect of *slaying* (though not of claiming each animal they slew) did whatever their own resources or capabilities permitted. Perhaps the Pawnee summer hunts, or the Red River hunt—apart from its transport system—are *in esse* the most familiar examples, for it seems fairly evident that the restrictive rules of the latter were largely modeled on the Indian "soldiers'" regulations.[108]

It is noteworthy that in all the early references to mounted hunting by Indians, from Tonty (1682) onward, there is no allusion to impounding of any character. Neither have any Southwestern counterparts of the "pound" place names proved discoverable. We have noted several incidental allusions, in Northern travel journals more particularly, to pounds or enclosures prior to 1800. The earliest historical notice known to me, treating them as a notorious practice, is not until 1818. William Faux, then in North Carolina, writes as follows:

Buffaloes . . . are thus decoyed and taken; but not alive. A man

108 Roe, *North American Buffalo*, 374, 658.

dresses himself in one of their skins, and walks on all fours to the brink of a stupendous precipice, so concealed as to be unobserved by the hurrying animals. The decoy steps aside, and down rush and tumble the herd, and break their necks or legs in falling. The skins and tongues are then taken, and the carcasses left.[109]

Faux neither specifies any tribes, nor the sources of his information. The latter probably reached him, or his informant, via St. Louis, which was then the great entrepôt for far western travel, and about 1818 was actually more in touch with Missouri River than with Southwestern points. Faux's region is most probably northern, for it is a curious fact that with one exception, the Pawnee—who are described as "wasteful"[110]—all other general denunciations are applied to Northern tribes, the Sioux and Crow,[111] or the Blackfoot, Cree, and Assiniboin.[112] Men as far away as Gregg had heard of the last-named and their unholy deeds.[113] Gregg is an unsparing censor of Indian buffalo depredations, which he only witnessed in the south. He says: ". . . for every one killed by the whites, more than a hundred, perhaps a thousand, fall by the hands of the savages." Yet Gregg has not one word about impounding.[114] On the supposition of its continued use among the Southern tribes, such a silence would be unthinkable. The farthest southern mention I have found is from Edwin James (1820), then in the South Park region or the upper Colorado River country: "Our guide informed us that the Indians, a few years ago, destroyed every individual of a large herd of bisons, by driving them over the brink of one of these precipices."[115] The very latest description of a surround known to me is of one which was witnessed by "Buffalo Jones" among the Pawnee in 1872. This herd, of "at least two thousand buffalo," furnishes an instructive commentary on some of these glib round numbers. Jones says: "After the Indians had de-

---

[109] William Faux, *Memorable Days in America, 1818–1820*, in Thwaites, *Travels*, XI, 86.

[110] Dodge, *Our Wild Indians*, 576, 577. See also Roe, *North American Buffalo*, 484, 637, 640, 885, etc.; Allen, *American Bisons, Living and Extinct*, 207.

[111] Dodge, *Our Wild Indians*, 291, 576, 577.

[112] Hornaday, "Extermination of the American Bison," 478, 480.

[113] Gregg, *Commerce of the Prairies*, in Thwaites, *Travels*, XX, 268.

[114] *Ibid.*, XIX, 244.

[115] James, *Account of the Expedition under Long*, in Thwaites, *Travels*, XV, 282. See also Dodge, *Our Wild Indians*, 291, 577.

parted, I counted up their day's work. I supposed, of course, from their demonstrations and hurrahs, I would find at least a hundred dead buffaloes, but imagine my disgust when the total numbered only forty-one!"[116] In my view, however, this would not justify any inference of the unbroken continuance of the impounding practice down to that date. The southern extermination-massacre was then at its height, and included the Pawnee country. The Pawnee may quite probably have been forced into what was really a late manifestation of a long-abandoned practice.

In an essay already cited in the present chapter, Ewers presents conclusions reached from a totally different angle of inquiry, which appear to confirm the foregoing hypothesis very strongly. By a careful collation of his own research with evidence collected by scholarly predecessors, he considers that the last buffalo drive of the Blackfoot was in 1872 also. As long ago as 1910 no known living (Piegan) informant remained who had taken part in a buffalo drive. In 1921 two 'very old men' were discovered to have done so. In 1943, again, there were none.[117] Ewers brings some very strong contemporary testimony in support of his argument. We have two early testimonies to the use of impounding among the Blackfoot: Maximilian in 1833;[118] and Audubon, the naturalist, in 1843.[119] These are the last contemporary allusions.

In describing impounding among the Assiniboin in 1854, Edwin T. Denig wrote as follows: "We know of no nation now except the Assiniboin and Cree who practice it, because all the rest are well supplied with horses that can catch the buffalo, therefore, they are not compelled to resort to these means to entrap them."[120]

Ewers also emphasizes Lt. James H. Bradley's use of the past tense in describing Blackfoot hunting in the mid-seventies: "The usual manner of hunting buffalo was by making pens at the edge of a precipice and driving the animals over, sometimes killing them by hundreds and even thousands."[121] The past tense is also used

[116] Inman (ed.), *Buffalo Jones's Forty Years of Adventure*, 97–102.
[117] Ewers, "Last Bison Drives of the Blackfoot Indians," 358.
[118] Maximilian, *Travels*, in Thwaites, *Travels*, XXIII, 108.
[119] John James Audubon and (Rev.) John Bachman, *The Quadrupeds of North America*, II, 49–50.
[120] Ewers, "Last Bison Drives of the Blackfoot Indians," 357.
[121] Cited by Ewers, *ibid.*, 357.

by another commentator (1887) whom Ewers does not mention. Hornaday writes:

> ... such wholesale catches were of common occurrence among the Plains Crees of the South Saskatchewan country, and the same general plan was pursued, with slight modifications, by the Indians of the Assiniboine, Blackfeet, and Gros Ventres, and other tribes of the Northwest. ... Strange as it may seem to-day, this wholesale method of destroying buffalo was once practiced in Montana.[122]

The persistence of the practice among the Plain Cree and Northern Assiniboin virtually to the very last—for it was found necessary to forbid impounding by statute as late as 1877[123]—has commonly been attributed to the Indians' "senseless destructiveness." The facts as given above by Denig put the case in another aspect. As in the pre-equestrian era, these Northern Indians slew 'whole herds at once' from necessity, not choice. Short of "still-hunting," which neither Indians nor half-bloods favored,[124] it was the only way they could get any. These facts and the figures, cited by Ewers in another essay, and showing the Cree and the Assiniboin to have had the lowest ratios of horses among the northwestern Plains tribes,[125] throw a complementary light each upon the other. In view of Ewers' strenuous insistence upon the *positive* as well as relative poverty of the Blackfoot in horses, it might be wished that he had given some information showing why the Blackfoot were able to abandon impounding as early as 1843–1854, for he makes no mention of any sudden accession of additional wealth in horses which at last enabled them to join the freer class in 1872. It seems not improbable that some contingency arising from the influx of white invaders that poured into the territory over the Bozeman Trail from the middle sixties onward[126] forced the Blackfoot to resort to a practice which had fallen into

[122] Hornaday, "Extermination of the American Bison," 470.

[123] See Morris, *Treaties with the Indians of Manitoba*, 175–272; Black, *History of Saskatchewan*, 196, 247; Edmund H. Oliver (ed.), *The Canadian North-West*, II, 1046, 1051; Denny MS, 273 (an eyewitness).

[124] Hornaday, "Extermination of the American Bison," 470.

[125] See Chapter XV *supra*.

[126] See Roe, *North American Buffalo*, App. H, 811–16.

disuse—according to Denig's testimony, quite manifestly—years before.

In a final summing up, what I consider to be the more correct interpretation, as against Strong's contention, cannot be better presented than in Ewers' own summary, which I quote:

In the use of bison drives by the Blackfoot tribes we observe the survival of traditional, prehistoric bison-hunting techniques among the historic peoples. Undoubtedly the drive was devised in prehistoric times as a method of cooperative hunting by pedestrian Indians armed with bows and arrows and/or lances which were most effective at short range. After the Blackfoot acquired firearms and horses in the eighteenth century they possessed more efficient and sure means of killing bison. Nevertheless, they rarely used guns in hunting bison on horseback. They employed the surround and individual chase on horseback in bison hunting during the spring and summer seasons. However, all the Blackfoot tribes continued to make use of the traditional drives in collecting their winter meat supply late in fall. The Piegan abandoned the use of drives in the middle of the nineteenth century. The North Blackfoot, poorest of the three Blackfoot tribes, continued to employ drives until bison were nearly exterminated in their territory.[127]

In more than one relationship, the problem of the bones of the formerly vast buffalo hosts of the Great Plains is a difficult one. I attach little value to the argument from bone ratios in the ancient Pawnee kitchen-midden deposits as proof of a (proportionately) low buffalo consumption in the pre-equestrian era. It is open to grave doubt whether the respective quotas of deer and buffalo bones found in early village sites can be considered such clear evidence as to support the conclusions regarding the nomadic hunter's life which appear to be implied in Strong's references to them.[128] The bones of one wild species, deer, would seem, a priori, to furnish equally weighty evidence with those of another. A hunter is equally as likely to be a nomad if his favorite or principal food were venison as if it were buffalo meat. In fact, if the conventional jargon about the "regular migrations" of the

[127] Ewers, "Last Bison Drives of the Blackfoot Indians," 360.
[128] Strong, "Plains Culture in the Light of Archaeology," 261.

buffalo were sound he would almost necessarily be more so. And of course as a denizen of a village which has accumulated kitchen deposits of this nature, he is equally unlikely to be a nomad in either event.

There are one or two historical references in the earlier times to large quantities of buffalo bones seen in what were apparently exposed and level situations. Pedro de Castañeda writes (re 1541):

> Another thing was a heap of cowbones [i.e., buffalo in general], a cross-bow shot long or a very little less, almost twice a man's height in places, and some eighteen feet or more wide, which was found on the edge of a lake in the southern part.[129]

Father Hennepin, on the Illinois or Mississippi River, 1679, says: "There must be an innumerable quantity of Wild Bulls in that Country, since the earth is covered with their Horns." "Wild Bull" (*taureau sauvage*) is Hennepin's generic term for buffalo, and does not here indicate sex any more than Castañeda's "cows."[130]

There are also a number of references to what were very probably old jumping-pound sites, as discussed above, but by far the greater proportion have probably left no trace. It has been thought that on the level Plains areas of Kansas, for example, huge quantities must simply have been stamped and ground into the earth, and a chemical analysis of virgin soil tracts might yield some instructive results. Colonel Henry Inman states that between the years 1868–1881 the bones of 'over thirty-one million' buffalo were *sold* from Kansas alone![131] Inman is seldom reliable, and his prices and aggregates differ widely from those of others who were on the ground at the same time, but the bare mention of such figures testifies to enormous masses.[132] In relation to our own immediate discussion, have we any guarantee—and if so, what?—that the ratios of buffalo bones found in the Pawnee kitchen middens, in proportion to bones of deer (or even of vegetal remains, if such

---

[129] Castañeda, in Winship (ed.), *Journey of Coronado*, 140. This heap of bones may be compared with Wascana Lake, Regina, Saskatchewan. Regina's earlier name was "Pile o' Bones" (Sioux: "Wascana"). G. H. Armstrong, *The Origin and Meaning of Place-Names in Canada*, 238.

[130] Hennepin, *New Discovery* (ed. by Thwaites), I, 146.

[131] Inman, *Old Santa Fé Trail*, 203.

[132] See Roe, *North American Buffalo*, 511–20, 862.

could survive), represent their actual ratio in the food resources or food habits of the early denizens?

Treating the surround as the earliest manifestation of wholesale buffalo capture, and the fixed pound as the later, more advanced development, certain considerations follow. The fixed and permanent pound enabled the tribe to entrap their buffalo where they would. This need not necessarily be *at* their permanent or semi-permanent village. That might very conceivably be inconvenient or impracticable by reason of various considerations such as fuel supplies or tribal camping idiosyncrasies, which were frequently very pronounced. There may quite probably have been such "village pounds," sufficiently near to the home sites for all purposes of practical everyday convenience; yet far enough away that village-site excavations would not disclose them. Waldo R. Wedel notes that the (historic) Pawnee village fields or gardens were sometimes 'several miles' from the village home sites.[133] Such places might contain an abundant number or volume of bone-deposit vestiges, perhaps fully sufficient to necessitate a recasting of conclusions based upon their present paucity.

The wolves are also to be considered. If the prehistoric Plains wolf possessed the cunning of his later successor the coyote (*canis latrans*)—which there is probably little reason to doubt—such remains would be far more exposed to wolf depredations than any kitchen garbage which was more closely adjacent to the abodes of man, or than vegetal rubbish of any character. They would, in fact, from their larger, more solid, and more meaty content, be the prime attraction long after abandoned carcasses or portions thereof had been consumed. The gnawings of wolves were generally conspicuous enough on the tips of the bone vestiges that could be seen quite plentifully on the central Alberta prairies fifty or sixty years ago—I am speaking from personal experience. These gnawings were commonly and reasonably considered an important accelerating cause of decay. The very usual "spreading" or splitting, and the resultant drying of the laminal structure of the horns, together with the tendency of vegetal growth to occupy the interior cavities of the bones, have both greatly facilitated destruction by prairie fires. In addition to such causes of disappearance, there are

133 Wedel, "Cultural Sequences in the Central Great Plains," 340.

probably many bone deposits still in existence which are covered with superimposed layers of soil, as Denny's was. Jenness records a discovery of such a deposit in 1920, on the present Sarcee reserve southwest of Calgary, Alberta, from which the Sarcee sold several tons of bones.[134] It is unthinkable that such a deposit could have lain bare to view since 1880 or before. A deposit of this type could occur, not only by natural sedimentation in the course of centuries, but also by sudden slips, particularly at old jumping-pound sites on the edges of cut-banks, which were characteristically selected for impounding purposes. The term "cut-bank" itself is derived from such landslides. Although it is the precise nature of such hypothetical factors that they can leave no visible evidence, I do not think they can safely be ignored.

From another angle of approach, the implied evidence which is thought to be derivable from the paucity of buffalo bones about the early Pawnee village sites is in my view highly precarious, and needs the most careful particularization. The buffalo were much larger and heavier animals than the deer, particularly the commoner Southern Plains species of the latter. Transportation of whole buffalo carcasses intact, or even of half-carcasses[135] or sides from the open plains to the village must have been in most cases impossible with no larger draft animal than the dog. Once they were compelled to resort to cutting up their buffalo at the scene of the slaughter, certain other features must almost inevitably develop. Our direct historical analogies, such as the Red River hunt and the common Indian custom of cutting the meat into thin strips for drying (which has even given rise to Western place names),[136] point clearly to certain fundamental limitations and practices, beyond doubt of long standing. In addition to preserving unsalted meat from going bad in the heat, the drying reduced a given bulk very materially in weight and size.

[134] Jenness, *Indians of Canada*, 58; *The Sarcee Indians*, 14.

[135] According to Garretson (*American Bison*, 97, 117), the hide hunters' standard practice was to split the skin lengthwise. I have not found this elsewhere, but I note a band or division of the Sisseton Sioux, the "Basdecheshni": "those who do not split the buffalo" (Hodge, *Handbook*, I, 132). This can only indicate that the Gentiles in the outer courts *did* split the buffalo.

[136] Dried Meat Lake, Alberta, so originating (*Place-Names of Alberta*, 44). Frémont notes a Dried Meat Camp, 1842 (*Narrative*, 56), and Palliser another, 1857 (*Journals*, 87, 90). Either of these might, by mere chance, have become a permanent place name.

Even without this evidence as demonstration, one may suggest that sheer common sense would also induce the horseless Pawnee to leave the bones behind, apart from that relatively small proportion (in the annual "kill" of a tribe or village) which might be required for the various practical or ceremonial uses. It has been labeled "Indian wastefulness," a crime of immemorial standing, according to the Hornadays *et hoc genus omne*, that the Indians' 'took only the very best parts.' While Hornaday's resultant conclusions of wastefulness follow neither necessarily nor historically,[137] the general fact of Indian selectiveness is correct enough in itself. It seems fantastic to suppose that Pawnee (or Indian) conceptions of the very best parts would include a large and burdensome annual tonnage in bones. In the case of the partly-sedentary tribes, the explanation might lie in either of two alternatives: (1) That they conserved their limited transportation resources for the carriage of meat proper (and in this connection a learned anthropologist urges the improbability of the Plains Indians of the pre-equestrian era 'packing large quantities of useless bones.'[138]). (2) That a portion—perhaps even a very considerable portion—of their yearly consumption of buffalo meat was not *eaten* at their villages. Both of these suggestions find the very strongest probability of confirmation from the available historical evidence. More than that, the particular tribe more especially under discussion, the Pawnee, furnish some of its most significant items, as we have seen.

The narrative of Juan Jaramillo mentions the Coronado party's meeting, on the way to Quivira in 1541, ". . . some Indians who were going hunting, killing the cows [buffalo] to take the meat to their village, which was about three or four days still farther from us."[139] In 1835, Maximilian noted that the Arikara hunters did not load their horses with the buffalo meat, but carried it themselves, often for a considerable distance.[140] The same observer tells us that at this time the Arikara had many horses,[141] and they are believed to have possessed horses, at the latest, since about 1738.[142] Al-

137 See authorities collected in Roe, *North American Buffalo*, 484, 860, 885, etc.
138 Wedel, "Cultural Sequences in the Central Great Plains," 300.
139 Jaramillo, in Winship (ed.), *Journey of Coronado*, 234.
140 Maximilian, *Travels*, in Thwaites, *Travels*, XXIII, 391.
141 *Ibid.*, 14, 387.
142 See Chapter V *supra*.

though the tribe were apparently rather miserly both in exchanging and sacrificing their horses, that is not precisely the same thing as saving the horses at their own expense; though they were quite willing, it would seem, to save them at the expense of their women.[143] Indians in general have not been especially remarkable for a purely humanitarian treatment of their horses, although even this varied.[144] It seems more probable, since there is no mention of the horses being incapacitated for any reason, that the Arikara practice was a survival of long-standing pre-equestrian usage. Be this as it may, however, it is inconceivable, either in 1541 or 1835, that the Indians would load their dogs or their own backs with a superfluous weight of bones.

In relation to our second proposition, the cases of the Miami in the seventeenth century and of the Pawnee in the nineteenth have been already noticed. These instances lift the proposition from the realm of probability—however convincingly strong—into that of historical fact. In both societies, much of their annual quota of buffalo consumption for subsistence would be utilized elsewhere than at their villages. Unless due attention is paid to this historical proviso, the ratios of buffalo bones found at their village sites might lead to very incorrect and misleading conclusions.

The absence of supposedly adequate ratios of bone remains does not entirely exhaust the question. Even the *presence* of relatively large buffalo bone deposits, if such were found to be the case, may require to be interpreted with great caution. Edwin James, the secretary and historian of Stephen H. Long's Plains expedition of 1819–1820, has recorded a really remarkable incident in the history of the Pawnee themselves, which occurred in the springtime of the year previous to Long's visit. After wandering around for some weeks following the annual vacation of their villages, in a vain search for buffalo, the tribe found themselves in the vicinity of their own homes, and on their arrival there actually encountered a large herd among their earth lodges![145]

[143] See Chapter XVI *supra*.
[144] See Chapter XIII *supra*.
[145] James, *Account of the Expedition under Long*, in Thwaites, *Travels*, XV, 256.

While I have found no parallel record of a precisely identical character—the nearest approach was a single buffalo's doing this[146] —it would be fundamentally absurd to suppose that *anything* in the age-long contact of Indian and buffalo occurred only once. The Pawnee experience is really only an extreme example of what is actually not an uncommon feature in the buffalo literature: the discovery of herds close at hand after unavailing search by experienced hunters over wide areas for some considerable time. Maximilian notes the Mandan hunters scouring the Missouri plains far and wide for buffalo in January, 1834, during a characteristic demonstration of Dakota's terrible winter, for over a week without success, and then finding them only some six miles distant.[147] It was probably similar weather, in the kindred climate of Manitoba in the bitter January of 1803, that explains Alexander Henry the younger's finding "Mr. McDonnell, junior, at Manitoba House almost starving with buffalo at his door."[148] In the second winter following this, 1804–1805, Patrick Gass records the experiences, which were very similar to those described by Maximilian, of the Lewis and Clark expedition at the Mandan villages.[149] Gass is corroborated by Charles Mackenzie, the Northwest Company trader, both for the same winter of 1804–1805 and the winter following.[150] Catlin, during the same years as Maximilian and at the closely adjacent villages of the Minataree (Hidatsa), mentions the sudden appearance of an unsuspected herd when the Minataree were actually starving.[151] About the same time (1833), experiences very similar to Maximilian's are related by John K. Townsend near Fort Hall (Pocatello, Idaho),[152] and also by Bonneville.[153] On the Saskatchewan, John McDougall describes how in autumn, 1864, the local Crees hunted vainly over their own utterly familiar home

[146] Paul Kane, *Wanderings of an Artist*, 89.

[147] Maximilian, *Travels*, in Thwaites, *Travels*, XXIV, 55; cf. XXIII, 274; XXIV, 45, 53, 57, 63, 89, 94.

[148] Coues (ed.), *Henry-Thompson Journals*, I, 208.

[149] Gass, *Journal of the Lewis and Clark Expedition* (ed. by Hosmer), 55, 62.

[150] Mackenzie, in Masson, *Les Bourgeois de la Compagnie du Nord-Ouest*, I, 331, 366.

[151] Catlin, *Letters and Notes*, I, 199.

[152] Townsend, *Narrative*, in Thwaites, *Travels*, XXI, 212–19.

[153] Irving, *Captain Bonneville*, 311.

territory and finally gave up in despair after a fruitless month—only to find the buffalo in the close vicinity on their return home.[154]

Reasoning in the absence of direct evidence, along purely inductive channels from other known facts, we might quite fairly and not illogically conclude, in the case of a sedentary or semi-sedentary people, that a relatively large deposit of buffalo bones discovered in their kitchen middens represented a herd or herds for whose possible coming these sedentary folk had waited, declining or fearing to leave their village (as did the Mandan at one early period),[155] and that such herds had been slain near by when they made such a chance appearance.[156] Yet in the case of Long's Pawnee, such an entirely rational and seemingly probable (if not positively flawless) chain of reasoning would be completely wrong in point of fact. It was in their summertime role as "nomads" that the Pawnee encountered this particular herd. It is difficult to see how we can eliminate the possibility of other similarly imperceptible, yet perhaps cardinal or crucial, errors.

The cumulative result of these various considerations in detail appears to me to concentrate and focus itself upon one supreme and vital factor—the time element. This, in its application to primitive peoples, and perhaps pre-eminently in its relationship to the chronology of change, has commonly been insisted upon as the very keynote of anthropological study. We must also, I believe, bear in mind that in the Indian world we are not, in general, dealing with social polities in which the edict of a despot could change the life of a people overnight. This apparently could only come in Indian tribal communities through the slow permeation of ideas. This fact makes the time element of greater significance than ever. The Indian, like most primitive peoples aboriginally but little exposed to the insistent methods and disintegrating influences of what we term civilization, was essentially a conservative. We have noted above (in the case of the Sar-

---

[154] McDougall, Saddle, Sled, and Snowshoe, 117.

[155] La Vérendrye, Journals (ed. by Burpee), 312, 355, 366. Coues (ed.), Henry-Thompson Journals, I, 336.

[156] Ibid., I, 336; Catlin, Letters and Notes, I, 199, 256.

cee cooking-pots)[157] the difficulty of our employing what seemed to them to be a fairly definite innovation in their community life as a satisfactory basis for chronological estimates, or even for the general acceptance of the new article itself. Yet the last feature seems essential in any conception of *tribal* change.

I do not consider that my view of the Indian in general as a conservative is invalidated by the ready adoption of such novelties as the horse, the firearm, the repeating rifle, or even the iron cooking-pot. In the final analysis, these articles were facilities and nothing more. They only enabled their possessors to do *the same things* more easily or conveniently. In my judgment there is a fundamental difference between the utilization of such facilities and what would be a basic and fundamental change in habits of thought. This is not to dismiss the influence of the horse, but simply (as I view it) to appraise it in its proper degree. J. Frank Dobie puts the case very succinctly:

If the horse did not create traits in the Indian but only intensified those he already had, its effect was no less upon him than the effect the automobile and other material acquisitions have had upon his conquerors. As far back as history can scrutinize, man's intellectual and spiritual potentialities have not changed.[158]

We have noted above, with reference to the supposed influence of the horse in the inception of war *de novo* and as a basic mental concept in the Indian (which seems to be the kernel of the hypothesis), that (1) such wars were a deeply rooted, virtually instinctive element in the Indian psychology long before the horse was known, and that (2) in some most important features the horse did not change the approved methods of Indian tactic. These factors—the latter one particularly—point to a stubborn conservatism of mind which it would be illogical to overlook elsewhere.

Let us for the moment, if we can, dismiss from our minds the array of evidence which has been reviewed in these pages and consider the inherent likelihood (or unlikelihood) of Indian readiness to change. The hypothesis which it has been the purpose of this

[157] See Chapter V *supra*.
[158] Dobie, "Indian Horses and Horsemanship," 265.

chapter to examine is basically an assumption of a facile readiness to alter a way of life. The period allowable for this change varies. In the case of the Northern tribes, Cree, Assiniboin, or Blackfoot—tribes as completely "changed" in this particular as any other tribes—this allowable time may have been as brief as twenty years, or possibly even less. The way of life which the horse supposedly altered in this short space had without doubt endured— whatever it may have been—for centuries, and not impossibly with some tribes for tens of centuries.

Since the disappearance of the buffalo herds from various quarters of the Plains area, dating roughly from seventy to one hundred years ago, administrators, educationists, agriculturists, and missionaries have been endeavoring to change the Indian way of life once again. The change which they are seeking to inculcate has, broadly speaking, almost every conceivable urge of *visible* self-interest to commend it to the Indian. On the very principles of those who contend for the post-equestrian origin of the characteristic practices of the buffalo Indian, the irresponsible nomad instincts which the various agencies are striving to eradicate and supplant have no aeon-long sanctions of crystallized use and wont behind them to bed them deep in the Indian mind. Yet the almost unanimous testimony of those who are working to effect this change emphasizes the slowness, difficulty, and some would say impossibility, of accomplishing anything really material.

It is somewhat unfortunate that we are apparently compelled to employ the rather vague and unsatisfactory generalization, "the Plains." Strong's and other discussions indicate important local and territorial variations, geographical, topographical, geological, and ecological, which are not implicit in their titles, any more than they are in my own. In relation to the fact that the field excavations under discussion appear to have been conducted principally in the Pawnee home area, it is conceivable that the reaction of a partly-agricultural and partly buffalo-using people to the acquisition of the horse might differ from that of the non-agricultural nomads in the more arid regions of the Plains. Such difference might make the former more like what the latter had always been, or it might not. But unless the semi-agriculturists deliberately adopted horse agriculture, it seems probable that the horse might accentuate more noticeably the hunter element in their lives, rather than the farmer element. Certainly neither tribal diversities (which were endless) nor tribal animosities appear to have prevented the Plains tribes from adopting many extraneous innovations; decidedly they have not at any rate rejected such innovations merely on the foolish principle that "no good thing could come out of Nazareth." The distribution of the horse itself and also of such features as Spanish saddlery and the Spanish practice of mounting from the right side came from European enemies to begin with; and no doubt, as with the Blackfoot noted above, such practices were passed on by many tribes to bitter foes.

It is perhaps not irrelevant to point out that in the Canadian horse Indian territories, where topographical variations are perhaps more widely prevalent than those described by Strong between the Pawnee terrain and the surrounding regions, the reactions toward the horse appear to have been broadly the same throughout. Any noticeable variations were seemingly tribal and temperamental. We have seen above that neither the possession of the horse nor the removal into more favorable buffalo territory changed the Kickapoo into nomads.[159] I know of only one instance where pronounced differences of temperament in the same tribal kin coincide with the Plains (or prairie) "horse frontier." This is between the Wood and Plain Cree, the latter of whom are generally recognized as much wilder, and more warlike, vindictive, and uncontrollable. I believe this to be far older among them than the horse. It is much more probably traceable, in my opinion, to the Plain Cree's having been for centuries, as the "advance guard," in more direct contact with the hated Blackfoot. It should perhaps be made clear that in so far as the southern ranching areas of the Canadian West and the better-watered agricultural regions farther north are concerned, the resident tribes of the latter portion were rather hunter-fishermen than hunter-agriculturists, if that is thought likely to favor any definite distinctions in their respective horse reactions.

[159] See Chapter XI *supra*.

There is one final consideration, which has apparently been overlooked or insufficiently emphasized. As we have seen, it is the ancient Pawnee village economy from which, evidently, the archaeological evidence has principally been taken. This raises a fundamental question. Can the Pawnee be said to have ever become true nomads? After some two centuries of horsemanship—perhaps considerably more, to Parkman's time at least—they were still semisedentary, leading a life not materially different, in their winter village environment at least, from that which is thought to be established by the archaeological evidence. Looking backward, in my judgment we must consider them a most unhappy choice by which to confirm any sort of hypothesis of a *former* non-nomadic state, to be later changed by any process or influence whatever. They would, one feels, have been far more weighty evidence for that innate conservatism in the Indian which I have emphasized above; a conservatism in their case so strong that even the tremendous impact of the horse wrought only a partial change, enabling them *in esse*, one may say, simply to live their former life more easily. Having regard also to the close resemblance between the "true" buffalo Indians of the Southern Plains areas who 'lived upon the cows' in the time of the Spanish *Conquistadores*, and the tribes of the same regions in the nineteenth century—exhibiting a virtual identity apart from the one particular of the horse—I consider that in their case likewise the two pictures reveal the conservative much more clearly than they do the innovator.

Concerning the antecedent probability that the fixed buffalo practices noted in 1541 were then ancient, Waldo R. Wedel notes the very early "Folsom peoples" of New Mexico (found in connection with fossil bison vestiges) as nomadic hunters. Wedel observes that the "Dismal River complex" (Kansas and Nebraska) reveals a heavy emphasis on hunting, but no indication of the horse.[160] Julian H. Steward notes that the Promontory Cave culture (of Utah), where bison vestiges were found, exhibits no trace of horticulture, but great reliance on hunting. I do not understand Steward's emphasis that the use of the tipi by the Northern Shoshone and Ute was conditional upon the acquisition of the horse,

[160] Wedel, "Cultural Sequences in the Central Great Plains," 298–301, 323, 326–30, 338, 343.

in the face of clear historical testimony to its pre-equestrian use on the Plains, unless he adduces this not as a necessary factor, but simply as an incidental historical fact. How this was ascertained he does not say. He also makes communal bison hunting a *post-equestrian* feature among peoples whose customs "were completely re-vamped by the coming of the horse."[161] This seems dangerously like using one assumption to prove another. Wedel states that among the corn-growing village peoples it is not known whether communal bison hunts antedated the horse or if the chronology were reversed.[162] Neither scholar defines precisely what is meant by a communal hunt, whether drive, surround, or running. In Steward's instance it could even mean the last.

For the Plains area, Strong (with apparent approval) cites Wissler on 'a lack of permanent habitation-sites,' and Kroeber on 'an intermittent population,' both of them features of pre-equestrian societies.[163] What can these phenomena signify but broad indications, to say the least, of a nomad economy?

Certain practices have been noted which, in the historic era, were characteristic features or at least accompaniments of nomadic societies among the typical horse-and-buffalo Indians of the Plains. These same practices were beyond any reasonable doubt, of considerable and probably of great antiquity. Therefore, it is indeed difficult to understand with just what degree of logical authority we can pronounce these practices to be anything other than concomitants and evidences of a similar society which existed at the very commencement of the historic period. The horseless nomads of about 1530 possessed both the inclination and the capacity to practice mass-slaughtering methods of hunting buffalo, and their social economy was to all appearances as dependent upon the buffalo resources as it was in the early nineteenth century (in proportion to population figures, which are more likely to have fallen than risen since 1530.[164] In accordance with these facts, I cannot

---

161 Steward, "Native Cultures of the Intermontane Area," 472–74, 475–87, 494–95.

162 Wedel, "Cultural Sequences in the Central Great Plains," 330.

163 Strong, "Plains Culture in the Light of Archaeology," 273.

164 See on this, Roe, *North American Buffalo*, App. G, "Estimates of Indian Populations Subsisting Wholly or Partly on Buffalo," 742–803; with special reference to epidemic outbreaks.

comprehend upon what grounds such intensive utilization of the buffalo is to be postdated, for the Plains buffalo tribes at large, until the equestrian era.

XVIII

THE INDIAN AND THE HORSE

In an inquiry of the present character, it is obviously impossible to separate facts from theorizings. Our information is fragmentary to begin with. So much that is now of the highest historical interest and value was utterly commonplace to the men who could best (or perhaps solely) have enlightened us. So much more, the cream of all our potential information, was locked away in the minds of a race which, for the most part, did not possess the art of writing, and whose treatment at the hands of the conquerors—the tragedy of our continent—did not conduce to the revelation of knowledge while there was yet time. In these circumstances, the inquirer can do little else beyond following the principle laid down by one who was himself an eminent anthropologist-historian: "Disciplined imagination, working upon a basis of ascertained fact. . . ."[1] This I have endeavored to do throughout.

Since information and comment must inevitably go hand-in-hand, as they have done in these pages, the reader is already in possession of my general conclusions. There is little to be added to them in a formal summary. As I have suggested, in my view the most profound influences exerted by the coming of the horse into Indian life were in the spiritual realm.[2] The sense of possession was a psychological tonic in itself; perhaps our nearest approach to a realization of this may be seen in a boy who is given a pony or a dog. It widened the Indian's spiritual horizon. This I think is to be seen in the rapidity with which the red men mastered the

[1] The reference is to Rice Holmes (*Ancient Britain* [1907], 48).
[2] Compare Dobie, "Indian Horses and Horsemanship," 265, 266.

376

equestrian arts. With less sentimental attachment, race for race, than our own people, the Indian set himself to *discover* the combined potentialities of horse and rider. The *act* of riding was a joy to him, as it is to most people whose fortune it has been to ride in conditions of untrammeled freedom such as the Indian's Plains environment bestowed. In this field of achievement (and for very practical ends) the Indian may be said to have begun where the circus trainer (for money) left off.

So too with the Indian women. It appears impossible to doubt that the coming of the horse, and the enormously enlarged facilities which it brought into their lives (as a sex), must have contributed immensely to a consciousness of greater equality, freedom, and what we term a sense of position. In one phase the women surpassed the men. After all, the man only rode where formerly he had walked. The woman rode where formerly she had trudged with a burden on her back, most commonly. We have seen in the Comanche, the Flathead, and the Crow, that the women vied as expert riders with the men; and we have no reason to doubt that this would be a common condition among the other tribes. We have also seen that with the Blackfoot Confederacy and the Mandan the right of women's ownership was recognized.[3] These tribes belonged, respectively, to two important family stocks, which argues a possibility at least that such recognitions were widely prevalent. If this, in the case of the Blackfoot—as of course it may have been with the Mandan also—was merely an extension of a long-existent right in dog ownership,[4] it none the less contributed to a psychological self-consciousness of a higher status. For we have seen that ownership in severalty was a feature in many tribes, and that among the pre-equestrian Crow this expressed itself in "rich" and "poor" possessions in dogs.[5] A woman owning only one or two dogs would secure little relief from the toil of camp moving; and in summertime—when camp moving was commonest—the wealthiest woman of them all could not *ride* her dogs. So also when the buffalo were "far out" and famine attacked the camp. Human nature being what it is, very probably the women's horses would

[3] See Chapter XV *supra.*
[4] See Chapter XV *supra.*
[5] See Chapter XIII *supra.*

be the first to be sacrificed for food. But one horse, fat on the pasturage which the absence of buffalo made all the richer, would outweigh half a dozen trains of starving dogs. A famine of any long duration could wipe out the entire dog resources of a camp. As with ourselves, such a descent into poverty would carry inevitable psychological repercussions. Here, too, the horse exerted a considerable indirect influence.

When we descend from the high realms of spiritual exaltation to the prosaic department of plain, everyday use, in my judgment the horse also descends from the superlative to the comparative status. We are not at the moment contrasting the historic period with remote archaeological eras. We are dealing with the Plains world as it was when the horse appeared upon the scene. In my view the horse merely widened the stage on which the Indian had always moved, and enabled him to do more easily the things he had always done. To seize upon later trade expansions after white traders appeared upon the Indian scene as evidences of the much greater influence of the horse than had been allowed by earlier critics (and simply because the horse transported and paid for this more extended commerce) seems in my judgment untenable.[6] This is much like crediting George Stephenson with the giant diesel locomotives of today. In addition to a trade in horses themselves, there is some evidence of earlier trade movements in certain regions, of an intertribal character, which dealt in native products; some which could scarcely have been handled very conveniently in any bulk prior to the horse. But the ratios of increased bulk are only proportionate, broadly, to the difference between dog and horse, precisely like the same ratios in a tribe's own internal transport, and such movements fall within that broadening which I affirm.

It is of course quite true that in many fields, perhaps preeminently in those of scientific knowledge, "time makes ancient good uncouth." But we have no right to assume that *because* a thesis is of the day before yesterday it is therefore outworn and discredited. This would be to reduce knowledge to the intellectual

---

[6] Jablow's fine study appears (in my judgment) to somewhat overemphasize the changes "produced by the horse" in an era which, according to his title, commences about 1795 (*The Cheyenne in Plains Indian Trade Relations, 1795–1840*).

plane of the automobile business ethic. In the precise field of our present topic, there is one scholar of the day before yesterday whose verdicts are still much more valid than are some among critics who would undertake to amend him.[7] With reference to controversy on the era, character, and causes of the nomad society in Plains life, amid an endless wealth of learned anthropological dissertation, no one, so far as I have been able to discover, has even attempted a solution to Wissler's crux: "Why should the Plains people have had the dog travois if they did not go on long journeys by land?"[8] And why indeed should they have had the movable dwelling which was thus transported? It seems to be unanswerable.

Wissler's final verdict still seems in my judgment to be in every respect as sound as ever: "As an intensifier of original Plains traits, the horse presents its strongest claim."[9]

This pronouncement finds support from two particularly competent scholars. The first is accepted as the foremost historical authority on the Great Plains.[10] The second is an outstanding plains man-author, who combines in an extraordinary degree the philosophy of the saddle and of the study.[11] I really do not see what other broad general conclusion can be reached from a careful review of the historical evidence.

[7] *Ibid.*, 10–18. See Chapter XIII *supra*.
[8] "Influence of the Horse," 14.
[9] *Ibid.*, 18; "Material Culture of the North American Indians," 484–86.
[10] Walter Prescott Webb, *The Great Plains*, 52–59, 62, 83, etc.
[11] J. Frank Dobie, "Indian Horses and Horsemanship," 265–75, and throughout all of his works about the horse.

APPENDIX A

TRIBAL IDENTIFICATIONS

It is with great diffidence that one ventures to dissent from such an authority as the late Clark Wissler. He identifies a reference of 1724 to the "Padouca" as being the Comanche. "[They] seemed to be on good terms with the Spaniards, from whom they obtained their horses by barter. . . ." (Wissler, "Influence of the Horse," 21.) In view of the varied evidence that has been reviewed in the foregoing pages, these alleged good relations between Spaniards and Comanche at that era arouse suspicion.

I am aware that the identity of Padouca with Comanche has weighty support (Hodge, *Handbook*, I, 327–29, 339; Thwaites, *Travels*, XVIII, 375; etc.). But Lewis and Clark, in 1804, mention the Castahana (1,500 souls), Cataka (300 souls), and Dotame or Dotami (120 souls), in the upper Tongue River country, Wyoming. These were "supposed to be remnants of the great Padouca nation, now lost, even by name" (Lewis and Clark, *Journals* [ed. by Biddle], I, 75). On the expedition's return in 1806, the Castahana are "a small band of Snake Indians" (*ibid.*, III, 232). The *Handbook of American Indians* (I, 212) says that the Castahana themselves may be Arapaho, who are Algonquian. But the others remain. It seems extraordinary that the identity of Padouca with Comanche would not have been mentioned to Lewis and Clark. Were the Shoshonean affinities of "Snake" and Comanche recognized in their day, or in that of their early editor, Nicholas Biddle (1814) ? Following on the common principles of territorial tribal nomenclature, one would have looked for the Padouca somewhere near Paducah, Kentucky, about the mouth of the Tennessee or Wabash River;

and there seems no warrant for connecting the Comanche with that region in historic times.

Our knowledge of the southward movement of the Comanche is fragmentary and inconsequential. They were "driven south" by Sioux pressure (Hodge, *Handbook*, I, 327–29). A later specialist on this particular tribe denies this, however (Richardson, *The Comanche Barrier*, 19, 24–28, 55, etc.), and considers they advanced or were "lured" south (see Dobie, "Indian Horses and Horsemanship," 265) to obtain the horse, or more horses. The "driving south" appears to involve an incredibly early era for the Sioux west of the lower Missouri, or an incredibly late era for the Comanche trek to the horse country. Gregg *(Commerce of the Prairies*, in Thwaites, *Travels*, XX, 342) speaks of the Comanche's ranging north of the Arkansas River, about 1790; and Richardson mentions them on the upper Missouri in 1802 (*The Comanche Barrier*, 49); but that proves nothing at any era for equestrian nomads with as wide a range as theirs (*ibid.*, 47–53). Wissler elsewhere considers the *Gens des Chevaux* of the sons of La Vérendrye, 1741–42 to have been, "evidently the Comanche" ("Influence of the Horse," 3, 15). On his own showing, it is very unlikely those explorers ever reached the Comanche country of 1740; and Wissler himself, as we have seen, stresses the infrequency of permanently changed habitats among the Plains tribes after about 1680 (*ibid.*, 13). This last factor in itself seriously imperils the driving south by the Sioux. We may note further that other scholars who have given much attention to these problems classify the *Gens des Chevaux* respectively as Arikara (Worcester, "Spanish Horses among the Plains Tribes," 410) and Cheyenne (Scott, "Early History and Names of the Arapaho," 546; La Vérendrye, *Journals* [ed. by Burpee], 407). Whoever is right, such identifications cannot *all* be self-evident.

There is another possible confusion with the Comanche. Father Douay, 1687, mentions the Cenis (Coeni, Asinai, Hasínai) as being allies of the Chouman (Comanche?) (Cox [ed.], *Journeys of La Salle*, I, 233). Isaac Joslin Cox (editor's note, *ibid.*, I, 286) considers the Cenis to be the same tribe as the Teyas of Castañeda, who were themselves identified with the Comanche by Winship (*Journey of Coronado*, 104, editor's note). Wissler seems to identify the Teyas as Gattacka and Manrhoat (Kiowa-Apache and Kiowa)

("The Influence of the Horse," 2); while a very recent commentator, John P. Harrington, classes them as Lipanan Apache ("Athapaskawan Origins, Divisions, and Migrations," 512); and the latest of all considers the Manrhoat "a mystery" (George E. Hyde, "Mystery of the Arikaras," 197). The Gattacka, and Lewis and Clark's "Cataka"—who were Padouca (Comanche) to them—are both classed as Kiowa-Apache by the *Handbook of American Indians,* II, 1037, 1038, 1056. The same work classifies the Kiowa-Apache as Athapascan, while the Comanche are Shoshonean, and the Hasínai are Caddoan (*ibid.,* II, 1028, 1038, 1060). Hyde speaks of "the Gatakas or Padoucas" (about 1680), but elsewhere states that Padouca was the name given by the French to the Apache (of the nineteenth century) ("Mystery of the Arikaras," 190, 217–18). These are also of course Athapascan. Thus, linguistic family classifications and tribal identifications are sometimes quite irreconcilable.

Similar difficulties confront us in the case of La Vérendrye's "Pananas and Pananis" of 1738. His editor, Lawrence J. Burpee (*Journals,* 335), notes that these tribes are thought to be the Arikara. This presumably goes *pari passu* with Wissler's (and Webb's) dating the Arikara as horse Indians, 1738. The only apparent foundation offered for this identification of Arikara with Pawnee lies in the classification of the Kaninavish or "Ka-ne-na-vish" by Lewis and Clark as a "Ricara band" of emigrants from the Pawnee; and in their further statement that the Mandans "called all the Ricaras by the name of Pawnees, 'Ricara' being their own native name" (Lewis and Clark, *Journals* [ed. by Biddle], I, 73, 142, 155–95). This would make the Ricara or Arikara, Caddoan, like the Pawnee; but the Kaninavish are classed as Arapaho, and hence Algonquian (Coues [ed.], *Henry-Thompson Journals,* I, 384; Wissler, *The American Indian,* 403, 405).

Furthermore, on Lewis and Clark's map, the same Kaninavish are shown near the Forks of the Platte, not far from where Wissler put the true Arapaho (about Julesburg, South Platte). I am not aware of any general migration of the Arikara about 1735–1820; and Wissler, as we have seen, discounts such movements generally, in that era. About 1820, the Arikara were certainly upper-central Missouri River Indians, as they are on Wissler's map (see Chittenden, *American Fur Trade*, II, 588–607; Dale [ed.] *Ashley-Smith Explorations*, 70–87, 182). Pending further evidence, it would seem that if the Pananas and Pananis were Southern Indians, they cannot be considered as Arikara with much probability.

On the other hand, is it certain that the horse Indians were southern? Burpee speaks of white buffalo skins being brought in trade to the Mandan villages as Bismarck, North Dakota, in 1739 (Burpee, *Search for the Western Sea*, 378; La Vérendrye, *Journal* [ed. by Burpee], 366). Now Catlin, an eyewitness, mentions the Blackfoot's bringing one to the Mandan (*Letters and Notes*, I, 133). These Blackfoot might conceivably, from the locality, have been Blackfoot Sioux (Sihasapa or Etasapa). But some of the Sioux prized white buffalo skins too highly to part with them, and some of the Sioux also were bitter enemies of the Mandans, although the Yanktonais (? having no horses before about 1770) brought white buffalo skins to the Mandan and Hidatsa (Maximilian, *Travels*, in Thwaites, *Travels*, XXIII, 289, 321, 371; XXIV, 48). Catlin knew of and probably signified the Blackfoot proper (Siksika).

Burpee thinks the Siksika had horses about 1700 (see his edition of Antony Henday's "Journal," 318; and also see Wissler on this, Chapters IV–V *supra*), perhaps from the transmontane Kutenai and Shoshone, which would obviate any implied necessity that early horse Indians on the Missouri about 1738 were *ipso facto* Southern Indians. It seems rather strange, also, that if the tradition, or whatever it is, referred to some tribe which had not long possessed the horse it did not include some allusion to such a stupendous factor in their tribal life. These considerations make me rather skeptical of any very precise dating for the Arikara horses, and also—in so far as the foregoing evidence is concerned—of the identification of the Pananas as Arikara. Each assumption appears to rest upon the other.

But why should not these "Southern" Indians be what their name and geographical proximity (if they were really southern) might logically imply—the Pawnee proper? Bancroft long ago considered them to be such (*History of Arizona and New Mexico*, 236). The most recent contributor to the question (Hyde, "Mystery of the Arikaras," 187–218) considers the Pananas, Panas, or Padanas of La Vérendrye to be the Arikara, and the Pananis, Panis,

383

or Padanis to be the Pawnee. He discusses distinctions between the two tribes, sufficient to justify their separate designation as two by the Mandan. As we have seen (Chapter V *supra*), he puts the Arikara possession of the horse as early as 1680, by trade with the "Gatakas or Padoucas" (Apache). This dating appears to present certain obstacles. It is difficult to imagine the horse's having not yet penetrated to a neighboring tribe in the course of nearly sixty years. On the other hand, sixty years' possession would readily explain the failure of the Mandan (noted above) to make any reference to La Vérendrye about the horse's being a recent acquisition by those Southern Indians.

There is another terminological confusion with the Pawnee also, although this could scarcely affect the Mandans' Pananis. The Lipan are one of the sixteen divisions of the Apache, 1894, (Coues [ed.], *Expeditions of Pike*, II, 748; Wissler, *The American Indian*, 404, and given on his map, 1922, as in Mexico, near the Río Grande and Pecos forks). Pike designated them in 1807 as *Lee Panes, Le Panis, Lee Pawnees* (Coues [ed.], *Expeditions of Pike*, II, 697, 746, 778). Pike also mentions the true Pawnee as *Panis (ibid.,* II, 567–74, 581, 590, etc.), and as *Pawnees (ibid.,* II, 582). Coues himself has the true Pawnee as *Les Panis (ibid.,* II, 697).

APPENDIX B

A PERSONAL EXPERIENCE

Over fifty years ago, in what was then northern and is now called central Alberta, I was reduced to only two horses, as a result of the devastating epidemic of "swamp fever" (gleet) and glanders which ravaged the territory during the excessively wet cycle of 1899–1903 inclusive. The saturated condition of the country rendered prairie fires, with their purifying action on the miasmic rotting vegetation, an impossibility for six years; and as the popular name indicates, the foul swamps were undoubtedly the cause (or occasion) of the plague. Since I have elsewhere discussed the question of epidemic disease among Indian horses from another angle, I need only say here that while the pestilence wrought havoc among the valuable imported horses of all breeds and from all regions and countries, it affected the native Western horses much less, and the cattle not at all. It was particularly fatal in the rich, well-watered, "black soil" scrublands in the Red Deer district, halfway between Calgary and Edmonton. Large numbers of farmers suffered crippling losses. We ourselves were reduced to one horse, to which we were able to add another.

The two in question were a middle-aged gelding and a somewhat younger mare. The gelding was a bright bay of Cleveland Bay siring, out of a dam that came from Blackfoot buffalo-runner ancestry. He had a white star between the eyes, rather smaller than a golf ball, and a white diamond on the muzzle somewhat over an inch across; together with one hind "white stocking" and black mane and tail. He was in fact the horse I have mentioned in Chapter VIII in another connection.

385

The mare was of a type known among us as "French-Canadian," a type whose distinctive features are a dark bay or rich brown coloring (I have heard both terms used), with a very heavy and *wavy* black mane, tail, and forelock, and a pronounced tendency to a darker dapple on flanks and rump. There was not a white hair on her; and in general appearance and build she bore a very noticeable resemblance to Ariel, a renowned forebear of the American Quarter Horse (pictured in Denhardt, *Horse of the Americas,* 134; see also an admirable paper, R. Leslie Jones, "The Old French-Canadian Horse," *Canadian Historical Review,* Vol. XXVIII [1947], 125–55). The mare was with foal to a heavy Clydesdale stallion of almost the same color, but with two rather long hind "white stockings," and a broad white blaze down the entire length of his face, over three inches in width.

No practical horseman needs to be told how close is the attachment between two stablemates living entirely to themselves. Such is most emphatically a case where "two's company and three's none," and this was a very typical example. Since both were equally handy as saddle beasts, I used them indifferently on my not very heavy saddle work as occasion required during the mare's earlier months; and the pathetic whinnyings at separation and the correspondingly triumphant, affectionate greetings at reunion were spectacles not soon to be forgotten (See Dobie, *The Mustangs,* 117–20).

When the foal was born we noticed that her general appearance with respect to markings and (probable adult) coloration bore little resemblance either to sire or dam. Owing, probably, to our seeing her frequently, and perhaps also to the somewhat pronounced differences which often appear at the adult stage, we gave little marked attention to the young filly. It was not until I broke her to light team work—she was broken to familiar handling, like all my young horses, at three days—that the full significance of her general appearance was brought home to me.

I broke her to harness principally with the old gelding, who was quieter and less excitable in emergencies than her own mother. I well remember this particular occasion in the summer of 1908, though I have forgotten its precise purpose. It was some community affair, election, school meeting, or the like, and many of the neighborhood were there. Their teams were "nosed up" against the schoolhouse fence, automobile fashion, and tied there. I came out of the building with some half-dozen of my neighbors, Canadians and Western Americans. These were all men who had been reared among horses from infancy, knowing the distinctive points and markings of the neighborhood stock as some old seamen know a ship they have seen once. They were, moreover, quite well acquainted with my old gelding, who was a bit of a local "character." My neighbors were, furthermore, like most men of their type, men of strong upright natures and sound integrity, but without the smallest vestige of imagination; not in the least likely, in Shakespeare's phrase, to see "Helen's beauty in a brow of Egypt."

As we came toward the gate my two horses were directly facing us, looking over the fence. It was the oldest and closest among all my friends who spoke first: "Which is which, Frank? I can't tell t'other from which!" The two faces were almost replicas, one of the other; star and diamond were indistinguishable a few feet away. The old gelding's rather Roman nose—what is sometimes termed in England a "furrow-bred"—was perhaps not quite so pronounced in the young mare, and had her other markings been similar to either parent, might have attracted little attention. As it was, the otherwise complete lack of facial resemblance to either sire or dam made the contrast with the latter's straight nose and very full, square nostril stand out the more conspicuously. The young mare's adult coloration also resembled that of neither parent. It was just a faint shade darker than the old gelding's bright, rather tawny bay. My other friends joined in the chorus of astonishment; and in the guessing match which followed, to decide which animal was really "old Jim," two of them actually picked the wrong one!

Perhaps I may add that the foregoing has been read by an anthropological critic who discredits the relevance of "childish recollections" for evidential purposes. At the time I was exactly thirty years of age. I had read Darwin's two great works very shortly before; this fact without doubt contributed to brand the occurrence in my mind. I committed the episode to writing while the details were still fresh.

There is only one final consideration to be added concerning this phase. In respect of fact, entirely apart from any questions of interpretation, one can in the nature of things cite no other authority than his own. Had this testimony of fact been adduced by myself at secondhand, as coming from some aged and illiterate informant in a tribe whose culture I had been investigating, and the only real authority for which would in the final analysis be my honesty and good faith, I have no reason to suppose that their authenticity as facts told *to* me, whatever their value might be estimated to be, would have been questioned for a moment. Facts told *by* me, and deliberately vouched for as such, should be at least equally acceptable. The scrupulous documentation of every statement of fact in these pages which is susceptible to questioning by the reader entitles the author to anticipate this, whatever the final conclusions respecting interpretation may be.

Certain criticisms have been directed against my remarks in Chapter VII on the possibility of "parental influence" as a factor in pinto coloration on the North American continent. More has been read into them than was present in the writer's mind, or than is in my opinion to be logically inferred from the language. The rejection by my critics is based upon a declared failure of such a hypothesis to conform to the requirements of genetic law. This hypothesis was not insisted upon. It was merely suggested that it might be an explanation of the problem. So far from insistence, I offer in the following chapter what might possibly have been thought to be another principal or contributory solution of the problem, as it was related by old Julián (see Chapter VIII).

I am permitted to quote the following correspondence, from an eminent geneticist, Laurence H. Snyder, Dean of the Graduate College, the University of Oklahoma, and here given verbatim:

The concept of 'maternal impressions,' or 'prenatal influence,' as it is sometimes called, has been thoroughly discredited by scientists. Twenty years ago textbooks on genetics devoted many pages to the reasons why scientists could not accept such a concept; today the subject is not even mentioned in most texts, because it is not considered worthy even of passing reference. No proven example of this superstition has ever been presented. Some experiments have been designed to test it, and have always given negative results.

Most supposed examples of maternal impression are due either to coincidence, where the explanation was invented to account for the observation, or to selection. It is easy to devise an explanation for an event after it has occurred, but the explanation, to be acceptable, must have a rational basis. There is no rational basis for maternal impressions. The embryo foal, for example, is not connected to its mother in any physical way which could permit such effects. No nerves run from the mother to the embryo. No blood from the mother passes through the embryo. The developing embryo is as remote from the mother, even though physically inside her body, as if it were growing in a different region entirely.

Selection, however, can rapidly change the characteristics of a population. The key to the whole argument about pintos is most probably to be found right here. The author is undoubtedly right in pointing out that pintos originally reached both North and South America. [In] . . . Chapter VII he says: 'The ancient Hispano-Arabian dislike for the pinto was not shared by the Indians of North America. Actually, he was rather their favorite.' In other words, the North American Indians undoubtedly practiced selective breeding in favor of pintos. The South American Indians, on the other hand, did not share the preference for broken colors, as witnessed by the author's statement (. . . Chapter VII) that 'while the natives of the South American horse regions painted themselves in various manifestations, I have failed to discover any evidence or even a suggestion either in history or fiction, of their having painted their horses.'

The gene for pinto spotting is a dominant gene, and would therefore be rather difficult to get in a pure, or 'homozygous' condition. In other words, some of the progeny of two pinto horses would often be solid colored. Nevertheless even a slight selective breeding in favor of pintos would markedly increase the proportion, whereas even a slight selection against them would even more markedly decrease [it].

The only acceptable explanation of the different proportions of pintos in the two Americas is this obvious difference in preference, and consequently in selection.

One last point should be mentioned. In Chapter VIII . . . the author raises the possibility that the crossing of white horses with solid colored ones might eventually result in pintos. This simply does not happen. White is a unit character, and segregates out as white, never spotted. Spotting is also a unit character, dependent upon a gene for spotting, and can never be caused by a blending of a white gene and a colored one.

In the present state of our knowledge, the foregoing particulars must be accepted by a non-geneticist inquirer as definitive. Yet even a non-geneticist may ask questions, despite his incompetence to furnish answers. There are certain historical facts to which a historian, whose conclusions must be determined by such data, is entitled to draw attention. A contributory critic, who writes an endorsement of Dean Snyder's comments, considers that possibly "one of the most important contributions yet offered in this [present] book will be the conclusion that, after all, the prevalence of Pintos and the existence of Appaloosas in North America are due in large part to a higher degree of selective breeding than has yet been realized, and to the possession by the Indian of more basic genetics information than we thought possible."

The acceptance of the portion of the latter critic's suggestions relating to pintos necessarily requires the acquisition of genetic lore *(de facto* if not *de jure)* by Indians at a very early date in their horse history. It is furthermore a case in which it seems inconceivable that their only domesticated animal, the dog, could furnish any general or abstract knowledge of genetic law which could be profitably, if at all, applied to the horse. For with the dog it must have been characteristics regardless of color that counted—if the Indian had anything to do with the matter—whereas in the pinto supposition the desideratum would be color regardless of characteristics. It has been pointed out in more than one application that down to the virtual extinction of the unimpaired native culture—say not later than 1865, with the beginning of the first railroad across the Plains—the historical evidence, more generally and acutely the earlier the period, indicates very little selective breeding among most of the tribes, apart from the Nez Percé, and among some tribes none whatever. Among the Southern Indians, the most specific accounts we possess relate to the Pawnee in Pike's time. While these mention careful and prudent treatment of breeding mares, there is no allusion to *selection* among either sex; and to judge from the data we have, the (early) quality of the horses among such tribes as the Pawnee and the Osage was probably traceable more to their nearer proximity to the Spanish sources of supply than to any selective care of their own. Historically it appears to have been the case that as era followed era the term "Indian horse" sank lower and lower in general estimation.

With reference to the Appaloosa, its foremost authority, Francis Haines, certainly applies the term "selective breeding" to the Nez Percé in relation to this type. But his particulars appear to indicate that the Nez Percé desideratum was to retain unimpaired (by degeneracy from contact with other strains) a breed they already possessed. This in my judgment is very different from selective breeding to raise a typical breed of a certain coveted coloration which they did *not* already possess, or not in sufficient numbers to meet their wishes. In conformity with my remarks in the preceding paragraph on a general Indian ignorance of selective breeding, Haines notices the degeneracy and virtual disappearance of the Appaloosa among the two actually leading Southern Plains horse tribes. Haines writes thus:

Other Appaloosas were stolen from time to time by the Kiowas and Comanches, and were taken to the Great Plains, but they never formed an appreciable part of the horse herds there because their new owners did not understand the principles of selective breeding, and had difficulty in raising any colts (*The Appaloosa Horse,* 37).

It is difficult to conceive from what quarter we can expect any further evidence of fact—as distinct from opinion—regarding *early* Indian knowledge of selective breeding. For we must bear in mind that the time element here is equally as vital as in any other phase of Indian horse-mastery as a whole, to say the least. It would have to be acquired rapidly to fit with recorded recognitions of "Indian horses" in various regions from about 1770 onward. I have noted in Chapter IV a learned critic's opinion that the horse had not yet reached the Platte by 1720. Assuming the existence, perhaps in "a higher degree ... of genetic information than we thought possible," we are facing something of a dilemma. We cannot eat our cake and have it. We can scarcely extol this advanced Indian one moment, and relegate his practices and beliefs to superstition and old wives' folklore the next. I have referred to the lack of any historical evidence for the Indian's knowledge or practice of what could really deserve the name of selective breeding. It should be noted that in the one (asserted) instance which the lay mind might include in that category—that of old Julián, in Chapter VIII—expert biological opinion pronounces the supposition to be an untenable fallacy, impossible under genetic law.

In relation to the exceptionally advanced proficiency attributed to the Nez Percé in this province, we may note the description by Francis Haines of the veteran horse breeder, Sam Fisher, and his "prenatal technique" for securing the correct and much coveted Appaloosa markings. Sam Fisher was himself a Nez Percé, and a renowned expert in that expert tribe. Haines and his collaborator apparently do not reject the *factual description* of Fisher's methods (Haines, *The Appaloosa Horse*, 42, 46). This case is of some significance. Sam Fisher himself "did say that the medicine worked better when spotted horses were used for the breeding stock" (Haines, *ibid.*, 42). It has yet to be shown what the 'more favorable' condition of a *spotted* horse could do to facilitate the reproduction of the much desired *five-finger* markings. If spots were all that were sought, or could be achieved, they already had these on the spotted animal in question.

Everyone will agree that it is easy to devise an explanation for an event after it has occurred. We cannot very well devise one before. Since these discredited phenomena "do not happen," because they cannot, it is perhaps less easy to comprehend why an explanation of any character was thought necessary. We have been told that Kelly's hair is red and his eyes are blue, but the most crassly superstitious devotee feels no need of any explanation simply because a red-haired and blue-eyed baby has appeared at the Kelly's home.

To the lay intelligence, the foregoing particulars respecting the embryo foal reduce the mother's function before birth to that of a mere sac or container in which the embryo achieves its own destiny. The critic's words are: "There is no rational basis for maternal impressions." Using that term as the preferred alternative for "prenatal influence," this may be correct. But the lay mind again finds itself wondering how the mother (presumably any mother of the mammalian order) contrives to convey, imprint, transmit—or what you please—any trait whatever to her offspring, whether of the visibly physical or of the more subtly characteristic order. While the subject was under discussion, this process might have been mentioned, if it is known. If it is not known, what guarantee have we that other processes may not also remain unknown, including some whose course of operation is thought to have been correctly demonstrated?

Dean Snyder, apropos of the North American preference for the pinto as against the South American dislike, writes: "The only acceptable explanation of the different proportions of pintos in the two Americas is this obvious difference in preference, and consequently in selection." Without prejudice to a learned authority's pronouncements on genetic law per se, the present writer must be permitted to demur to this identification of *preference* with *selection*. I may have a strong preference for a thing, while at the same time possessing neither the means, the desire, nor the competence to enter upon any course of selection or action to make it mine. Selection, in the connotation here being discussed, is no doubt an operation of (or under) genetic law, but it is also a historical event *in esse* or *in posse* in its relation to a course of tribal action. It either occurred or it did not. If its employment here rests upon the argument—"What else could it be?" that seems a very insecure basis upon which to rest a definitive statement; and in relation to the suggested possibility as expressed in Chapter VII, it would be to assume the final issue at the outset.

The suggestion discussed in Chapter VIII, of the possibility that the Great White Horse—the legend of which has not been found in South America—is in its collective capacity the ancestor of the North American pintos raises one of those questions which even a layman may ask, but which none but a geneticist can hope to answer. Dean Snyder, who speaks on the subject with authority, states (as we have seen above) that this "simply does not happen," since white "is a unit character, and segregates out as white, never spotted." In regard to the *first* pinto that ever existed, it seems inescapable that one of two things must have occurred. This first pinto was born as a pinto from (necessarily) non-pinto ancestry, of either solid white or solid non-white coloration. I cannot comprehend how we can evade the conclusion that (1) white *could* split up into a white motley, or that (2) white could spontaneously "appear" without recognizable or identifiable antecedent cause, ancestral or otherwise. One may doubt whether anything in the world ever occurred only once, but if a thing occurred once in nature it could occur again. In some future day later knowledge may furnish answers to these questions.

APPENDIX C

ROUND NUMBERS

It may be of interest and possibly of some use to the reader to present, in a convenient, collected form, some of the "round numbers" to which reference has been made. I cite the sources, but of course I do not imply that the writers mentioned necessarily endorse these figures.

There can be little doubt that in these general assertions by early plainsmen, taken as a whole, their authors did not pretend either to count the numbers deliberately, or even to apply such rough tests as the area of the ground or the like, which might be used by two men whose estimates differed. Such methods were frequently employed in the same broad era with regard to masses of buffalo (see Roe, *North American Buffalo*, 354–65). The fact of such wide discrepancies as are noted below would have brought these criteria into play had the witnesses (or disseminators) been more scientifically minded. We may take it that the round numbers are guesses pure and simple, governed principally by the temperamentalisms of the observer. In the very few instances where horses were *counted* we find a significant shrinkage in the numbers. We may fairly assume that Thomas James's three hundred Comanche horses were counted in 1823, since he had to buy them (Dobie, *The Mustangs*, 71). A century earlier, Du Tisné actually did count three hundred horses bearing Spanish brands at the Pawnee villages. He described them as being "scarce" at this time; highly valued and not for sale (Wissler, "Influence of the Horse," 2, 5–6; Haines, "How Did the Indians Get Their Horses?" 433). It is not impossible that this may have meant scarce in relation to the masses he had been led to anticipate. J. Frank Dobie, who maintains a healthy skepticism in this rather fevered atmosphere, notes another case which tends to support that suggestion. Ross Cox, in the Nez Percé country in the Columbia Basin in 1816, estimated from seven hundred to one thousand in one band. "Some of his fellow explorers reported bands of from three thousand to four thousand head in the Snake Indian country; one of two hundred head verified by Cox sounds more realistic." (Dobie, *The Mustangs*, 106.) Dobie mentions a traveler in Texas in 1846 who "estimated one aggregation of mustangs at five thousand head, though his companions put the number at seven thousand" (*ibid.*, 103). In 1550, a monk in Paraguay was likewise cautious. It was asserted that "one thousand died from hostilities and famine," but Fray Alonso Baptista "does not swear to their being more than eight hundred and fifty, or slightly more or less" (Nichols, "The Spanish Horse of the Pampas," 121). Buffalo Jones speaks of a surround of buffalo by a band of Pawnee, which he witnessed in 1872. There were "at least" two thousand in the herd; and after all the yelling and commotion he expected "at least" a hundred slain. To his disgust (he says) the total was only forty-one! (*Buffalo Jones' Forty Years of Adventure*, 97–102). Zenas Leonard is quoted as saying, about 1839, that the Crow killed seven hundred in a single surround (Lowie, "Material Culture of the Crow Indians," 212). Bernard De Voto, however, says that Leonard "must be used with care," and finds him exaggerating or positively wrong in almost every statement cited (*Across the Wide Missouri*, 76, 422, 432). Even apart from deliberate desire at times to surpass some rival raconteur, we must not forget that this is the familiar colloquial verbiage of the evening campfire, when tongues as well as muscles relaxed and the long-bow yarn was the staple entertainment. J. Frank Dobie, who has met plenty of it, says truly enough that "exaggeration is an unvarying means for being interesting" (*The Mustangs*, 66). Given below are some of the examples of this class of "evidence."

1691 (Texas) "St. Denis, the romantic Frenchman who reported lead mines never seen by anybody else, testified that 'thousands of cows, bulls, stallions and mares, covered the surrounding ranges.'" (Dobie, *The Mustangs*, 98.)

1694 (Mexico) "One hundred thousand stolen in Sonora and Sinaloa." (Bancroft, *North Mexican States and Texas*, I, 255.)

1758 (Texas) "An official inspector reported thousands of mares, horses, mules and burros in herds between Reynosa and Laredo." (Dobie, *The Mustangs*, 100.)

1758 Two thousand Comanche warriors at San Saba River mission, all mounted (Richardson, *The Comanche Barrier*, 67).

1767 (Texas) Four hundred horses driven off; pursued "one hundred leagues" (about two hundred and sixty-five miles; Dobie, *The Mustangs*, 65).

1774 (Texas) Three hundred out of four hundred driven off by Comanche and others (*ibid.*).

1777 (Texas) Fray Morfi estimated that "one congregation of wild horses along the route numbered three thousand head" (*ibid.*, 101).

1790 (South America) The naturalist Azara reported "congregations of *baguales* amounting without exaggeration to ten thousand." During the first quarter of the nineteenth century "as many as five hundred thousand of the superfluous feral and semi-feral mares in Argentina were slaughtered annually" (*ibid.*, 106; citing official [?] records).

1800–1850 Concentrations of Comanche horses and mules running up to three thousand and even five thousand head. Successful warriors owned fifty to two hundred each (Dobie, *Mustangs*, 71). One Comanche reputed to have owned one thousand at one time (E. Adamson Hoebel, "Political Associations and Law-Ways of the Comanche Indians," 15).

1805 (Shoshone) "At least seven hundred horses." (Lewis and Clark, *Journals* [ed. by Coues], II, 558.)

1807 Two thousand driven off in one raid from Ojo Caliente (Coues, [ed.], *Expeditions of Pike*, II, 537, 600).

1813 (Texas) "About fifteen hundred Comanches." "About seven thousand horses were gathered nightly into San Antonio." Two weeks later the Comanches "took all the horses away" ("too many horses": Dobie, *The Mustangs*, 66).

1816 "Three thousand to four thousand head in the Snake Indian country [or two hundred: Ross Cox]. . . ." (Dobie, *ibid.*, 106.)

1819 "Six thousand to eight thousand Pawnee horses" (Long, or Edwin James, *Account of the Expedition under Long*, in Thwaites, *Travels*, XV, 207–208, 215).

1821 (Arkansas River) ". . . about twenty thousand horses" (Fowler, *Journal* [ed. by Coues], 61).

1823 Sixteen thousand Comanche horses (Thomas James: Dobie, *The Mustangs*, 71).

1826 One thousand Snake Indians going annually to the Spaniards to steal horses (Peter Skene Ogden: Dobie, *ibid.*, 80).

1831 "Ten thousand Crow horses" (from a local fur trader, "corroborated," i.e., repeated, by Maximilian, *Travels*, in Thwaites, *Travels*, XXII, 351–52).

1833 "Four thousand to five thousand," owned by one Blackfoot chief (*ibid.*, XXIII, 121).

1834 At least three thousand Comanche horses (Catlin, *Letters and Notes*, II, 62).

1835 "Several thousand" Pawnee horses (cited by Dobie, *The Mustangs*, 57).

1835 (circa) Jim Beckwourth "stole five thousand Comanche horses . . . fellow-tribesmen lifted twenty-seven hundred horses from the Kootenays. Soon the Crows lost twelve hundred horses to raiding Blackfeet, but promptly took two thousand from them. Next the Blackfeet took three thousand; the Crows recovered twenty-five hundred and picked up thirty-five hundred from other sources." ("Jim Beckwourth should have kept a ledger": Dobie, *ibid.*, 80.)

1840 "Three hundred thousand horses" owned by one Mexican woman; one thousand white ones of one year's foaling (Dobie, *Tales of the Mustang*, 40).

1843 "Some thousands" of Comanche near Bent's Fort (trader's report, in Richardson, *The Comanche Barrier*, 180).

1846 "Upwards of ten thousand head of horses and mules have already been carried off" (that year) by the Comanche (George Frederick Ruxton: Dobie, *The Mustangs*, 70).

1847 "Thousands and tens of thousands" in Texas (Thomas A. Dwyer: Dobie, *ibid.*, 104).

1849 "About a thousand" Comanche horses (Ferdinand Roemer: *ibid.*, 72).

1853–1860 Thousands probably taken in Comanche horse raids in Texas and Mexico (Richardson, *The Comanche Barrier*, 193–205, 243, etc.).

1855–1860 (?) ". . . thirty thousand to forty thousand horses in one herd" ("Bigfoot Wallace," whose relatives disbelieved him: Dobie, *The Mustangs*, 105).

1867 "Fifteen thousand horses and three hundred or four hundred mules in Comanche camps in Texas" (an Indian Agent, Labadi: Dobie, *ibid.*, 71).

1874 "Towards one thousand" at Adobe Walls (battle, June 27–30: *ibid.*, 45).

1875 (Texas) Estimated that fifteen thousand horses came together, Mission Prairie, San Antonio River (*ibid.*, 141).

1876 "Ten thousand Sioux and Cheyenne; twenty thousand to forty thousand horses" (*ibid.*, 41).

1877 "About three thousand horses" (Chief Joseph, Nez Percé: *ibid.*, 55).

1881 (Texas) "Fully one thousand" (Nueces River country: *ibid.*, 107–108).

Apropos of the weighty contribution of the Comanche to the foregoing, a leading authority on that tribe considers that Comanche horse traditions are negligible (Richardson, *The Comanche Barrier*, 25). With all our advantages of the written word in regard to Western history, we ourselves have little enough to boast about. I have noted in the Introduction the respective estimates of Charles Goodnight and John Hitson concerning losses of Texas livestock during certain periods, in which the one computation exceeds the other by fifteen to one. J. Frank Dobie sums up as follows, with respect to the final residue of the mustangs:

No scientific estimate of their numbers was ever made. Plainsmen in the '70s guessed the number between the Palo Duro in the Texas Panhandle and the Salt Fork of the Brazos at 50,000 head. The guess was not based on any system of computation. All guessed numbers are mournful to history. My own guess is that at no time were there more than a million mustangs in Texas and no more than a million others scattered over the remainder of the West. Wherever they ranged, they were exceedingly visible. Mention of them by travelers over the plains is frequent, but the total number enumerated by many a chronicler during a month's time is surprisingly low (*The Mustangs*, 108–109).

Dobie supports this conclusion by a citation from the journal of a United States Army officer, who in ten weeks in the Southwestern Plains area (midsummer, 1843) saw "one herd" of wild horses, and less than fifty other horses; never more than twelve at once (*ibid.*, 109).

One is irresistibly reminded of Herodotus and the five millions invading Greece under Xerxes, and also of the "Magpie and Stump," which contained "500,000 barrels of double stout in the cellars of the establishment" (*Pickwick Papers*, Chap. XX). Dickens had without doubt seen this somewhere; but only a Dickens notices such things. It is still believed by some people that in the War of the Roses 110,000 men met on a Yorkshire hillside about the size of a nine-hole golf course at Towton (Palm Sunday, 1461) and fought there for twelve hours, during which time 38,000 of them were slain—fifty-three every minute; the Christian burial of whom apparently devolved upon and was carried out by the energetic benevolence of *one man*, a neighboring squire or yeoman, with (let us hope!) the assistance of some of his friends or dependents.

BIBLIOGRAPHY

Adair, James. *History of the North American Indians* (ed. by Samuel Cole Williams.) Johnson City, Tennessee, 1930.

Aiton, Arthur S. "The Later Career of Coronado," *American Historical Review*, Vol. XXX (1924), 298–304.

———. "The Muster-Roll of Coronado," *American Historical Review*, Vol. XLIV (1938), 556–70.

Alexander, Hartley B. "The Horse in American Culture," *So Live the Works of Men* (*q.v.*).

Allen, Joel A. *The American Bisons, Living and Extinct* (*Memoirs of the Museum of Comparative Zoology*, Vol. IV, No. 10). Cambridge, Mass., 1876.

Armstrong, G. H. *The Origin and Meaning of Place-Names in Canada.* Toronto, 1930.

Audubon, John James, and John Bachman. *The Quadrupeds of North America.* 2 vols. New York, 1846, 1854.

Bancroft, Hubert Howe. *Works.* 38 vols. San Francisco, 1883–1890.

———. *History of Arizona and New Mexico, 1530–1888.* San Francisco, 1889.

———. *History of California, 1542–1890.* 7 vols. San Francisco, 1890.

———. *History of Nevada, Colorado, and Wyoming.* San Francisco, 1890.

———. *History of the North Mexican States and Texas, 1531– 1889.* 2 vols. San Francisco, 1884, 1889.

———. *History of the Northwest Coast, 1511–1866.* 2 vols. San Francisco, 1886.

———. *History of Oregon, 1834–1888.* 2 vols. San Francisco, 1886, 1888.

———. *History of Pastoral California, 1769–1849.* San Francisco, 1888.

———. *History of Utah.* San Francisco, 1889.

———. *History of Washington, Idaho, and Montana, 1845–1889.* San Francisco, 1890.

———. *Native Races of the Pacific States.* 5 vols. San Francisco, 1883.

Baraga, Bishop. *A Grammar and Dictionary of the Otchipwe* [Ojibwa] *Language.* Montreal, 1879.

Bartram, William. *The Travels of William Bartram, 1773–1778* (ed. by Mark Van Doren). New York, 1928.

Bieber, Ralph P. (ed.). *Exploring Southwestern Trails* (*Southwestern Historical Series, No. VII*). Glendale, 1938.

Bishko, Charles Julian. "The Peninsular Background of Latin-American Cattle Ranching," *Hispano-American Review,* Vol. XXXII (1952), 491–515.

Bishop, Morris. *The Odyssey of Cabeza de Vaca.* New York, 1933.

Black, Norman Fergus. *A History of Saskatchewan and the Old Northwest.* Regina, Saskatchewan, 1913.

Blair, Emma Helen. *Indian Tribes of the Great Lakes and the Mississippi Valley Regions.* 2 vols. Cleveland, 1911.

Blakiston, (Lieut.) Thomas. "Report on the Exploration of the Kootanie and Boundary Passes of the Rocky Mountains in 1858," *Occasional Papers of the Royal Artillery Institution,* 118–20, 237–54. Woolwich, England, 1860.

Boller, Henry A. *Eight Years in the Far West, 1858–1866.* Philadelphia, 1868.

Bolton, Herbert Eugene. *Coronado, Knight of Pueblos and Plains.* New York and Albuquerque, 1949.

———. "Odoesmades," *Handbook of American Indians North of Mexico* (*q.v.*), II, 106.

———. (ed.). *Spanish Exploration in the Southwest, 1542–1706.* New York, 1916.

Borrow, George. *The Bible in Spain.* London, 1906.

Brackenridge, Henry Marie. *Views of Louisiana; Together with a Journal of a Voyage up the Mississippi River in 1811* (Vol. VI in Reuben Gold Thwaites [ed.], *Early Western Travels, q.v.*).

Bradbury, John. *Travels in the Interior of North America* (Vol. V in Reuben Gold Thwaites [ed.], *Early Western Travels, q.v.*).

Bradley, (Lieut.) James H. "Affairs at Fort Benton," *Contributions to the Historical Society of Montana,* Vol. III (1900).

———. "Characteristics, Habits, and Customs of the Blackfeet Indians," *Contributions to the Historical Society of Montana,* Vol. IX (1923).

Brittain, Alfred. *Discovery and Exploration* (Vol. I in Guy Carlton Lee and Francis Newton Thorpe [eds.], *The History of North America, q.v.*).

Bryce, George. *The Remarkable History of the Hudson's Bay Company.* Toronto, 1904.

Buchanan, Angus. *Wild Life in Canada.* London, 1920.

Burlingame, Merrill G. *The Montana Frontier.* Helena, 1942.

Burpee, Lawrence J. *The Search for the Western Sea.* New York, 1908.

Burton, Sir Richard. *The City of the Saints.* New York, 1862.

Butler, Sir William F. *Autobiography.* London, n.d.

———. *The Great Lone Hand.* London, 1910.

———. *The Wild North Land.* London, 1878.

Byington, Cyrus. *A Dictionary of the Choctaw Language* (ed. by John R. Swanton and Henry S. Halbert), Bureau of American Ethnology, *Bulletin 46.* Washington, 1915.

Byrne, P. E. *The Red Men's Last Stand.* London, 1927.

Cabeza de Vaca. *The Journey of Alvar Nuñez Cabeza de Vaca and his Companions from Florida to the Pacific, 1528-1536* (tr. by Fanny Bandelier and ed. by Adolf F. Bandelier). New York, 1922.

Catlin, George. *Letters and Notes on the North American Indians.* 2 vols. London, 1851.

Champlain. *The Voyages and Explorations of Samuel de Champlain, 1604-1616, Narrated by Himself* (tr. by Annie Nettleton Bourne and ed. by Edward G. Bourne). 2 vols. Toronto, 1911.

———. *The Voyages and Explorations of Samuel de Champlain, 1604-1616* (ed. by H. P. Biggar). 6 vols. Toronto, 1922-1936.

Chard, Thornton. "Did the First Spanish Horses Landed in Florida and Carolina Leave Progeny?" *American Anthropologist,* Vol. XLII (1940), 90-106.

Chittenden, (Gen.) Hiram M. *The History of the American Fur Trade of the Far West.* 3 vols. New York, 1902.

Cocking, Matthew. "The Journal of Matthew Cocking" (ed. by Lawrence J. Burpee), *Proceedings and Transactions of the Royal Society of Canada,* 3rd. Series (1908), Sec. II, 89-121.

Coman, Katherine. *Economic Beginnings of the Far West.* 2 vols. New York, 1912.

Coronado, Francisco Vásquez de. *The Journey of Coronado, 1540-1542* (ed. by George P. Winship; including the accounts of Coronado and his followers: the History of Castañeda; Coronado to Charles V and Viceroy Mendoza; Narrative of Jaramillo; the *Relación del Suceso;* the "Anonymous Document" [*Traslado de Las Nuevas*] and the Report of Hernando de Alvarado). New York, 1922.

Coues, Elliott (ed.). *New Light on the Early History of the Greater Northwest: The Henry-Thompson Journals.* 3 vols. New York, 1897.

Cowie, Isaac. *The Company of Adventurers*. Toronto, 1913.

Cox, J. Charles. *The Royal Forests of England*. London, 1905.

Cox, Ross. *The Columbia River*. 2 vols. London, 1832.

Cresswell, Nicholas. *The Journal of Nicholas Cresswell, 1774–1777* (ed. by A. G. Bradley). New York, 1928.

Cumberland and Hudson House Journals, 1775–1782 (First and Second Series). 2 vols. London, 1951, 1952.

Cunninghame Graham, R. B. *The Conquest of the River Plate*. London, 1924.

——. *The Horses of the Conquest*. London, 1930.

Dale, Harrison C. (ed.). *The Ashley-Smith Explorations, and the Discovery of a Central Route to the Pacific, 1822–1829*. Cleveland, 1918.

Darwin, Charles. *The Descent of Man*. New York, 1898.

——. *Journal of the Voyage of the Beagle*. London, 1891.

——. *On the Origin of Species by Means of Natural Selection*. New York, 1898.

Davis, W. W. H. *The Spanish Conquest of New Mexico*. Doylestown, Pa., 1869.

De La Grasserie, Raoul. *Cinq Langues de la Colombie Britannique*. Paris, 1902.

Denhardt, Robert Moorman. *The Horse of the Americas*. Norman, 1947.

Denig, Edwin T. *Indian Tribes of the Upper Missouri* (ed. by J. N. B. Hewitt), *Forty-sixth Annual Report of the Bureau of American Ethnology*. Washington, 1930.

Denny, Sir Cecil. *The Law Marches West* (ed. by W. B. Cameron). Toronto, 1938.

——. Manuscript of personal reminiscence (Alberta, 1874 *et seq.*), in Alberta Provincial Legislative Library, Edmonton.

De Smet, Father Pierre-Jean. *Letters and Sketches, with a Narrative of a Year's Residence among the Indian Tribes of the Rocky Mountains* (Vol. XXVII in Reuben Gold Thwaites [ed.], *Early Western Travels, q.v.*).

——. *The Life, Letters, and Labors of Father Pierre-Jean De Smet, 1801–1873* (ed. by Hiram M. Chittenden and A. T. Richardson). 4 vols. New York, 1905.

——. *Oregon Missions and Travels over the Rocky Mountains, 1845–1846* (Vol. XXIX in Reuben Gold Thwaites [ed.], *Early Western Travels, q. v.*).

De Soto, Hernando. *Narrative of the Career of Hernando de Soto, in the Conquest of Florida, 1539–1542* (ed. by E. G. Bourne; including the Narrative of the Gentleman of Elvas; the *Relación* of Luys Hernandez de Biedma; and Oviedo's account from the *Historia General,* based upon the Diary of Rodrigo Ranjel, De Soto's secretary). 2 vols. New York, 1922.

De Voto, Bernard. *Across the Wide Missouri.* Boston, 1947.

Díaz del Castillo, Bernal. *The Conquest of New Spain* (tr. and ed. by A. P. Maudslay). 5 vols. London, 1908–1916.

A Dictionary of the Kalispel or Flathead Language (compiled by the Missionaries of the Society of Jesus). St. Ignatius Mission, Montana, 1879.

Diller, Dorothy. "Early Economic Development of Alberta Previous to 1905," unpublished M. A. thesis, University of Alberta, 1923. MS. in Provincial Legislative Library, Edmonton, Alberta.

Dixon, Roland B. and John R. Swanton. "Numeral Systems of the Languages of California," *American Anthropologist,* Vol. IX (1907), 663–90.

Dobie, J. Frank. *The Flavor of Texas.* Dallas, 1936.

——. "Indian Horses and Horsemanship," *Southwest Review,* Vol. XXXV (Autumn, 1950), 265–75.

——. *The Mustangs.* Boston, 1952.

——. (ed., with others). *Mustangs and Cow Horses.* Austin, 1940.

——. *Tales of the Mustang.* Austin, 1936.

Dodge, (Col.) Richard Irving. *Our Wild Indians.* Hartford, 1885.

——. *The Plains of the Great West.* New York, 1877.

Donkin, John G. *Trooper and Redskin in the Far Northwest.* London, 1889.

Dorsey, J. O., and John R. Swanton. *Dictionary of the Biloxi and Ofo Languages,* Bureau of American Ethnology, *Bulletin 47.* Washington, 1912.

Douglas, George M. *Lands Forlorn.* New York, 1914.

Drannan, William F. *Thirty-one Years on the Plains and in the Mountains.* Chicago, 1900.

Early Western Travels, 1748–1846 (ed. by Reuben Gold Thwaites). 32 vols. Cleveland, 1904–1907.

Essays in Historical Anthropology in North America (Swanton, Memorial Volume), Smithsonian Miscellaneous Collections, Vol. I. Washington, 1940.

Ewers, John C. "The Last Bison Drives of the Blackfoot Indians," *Journal of the Washington Academy of Sciences,* Vol. XXXIX (1949), 355–60.

——. "Were the Blackfoot Rich in Horses?" *American Anthropologist,* Vol. XLV (1943), 602–10.

Farnham, Thomas J. *Travels in the Great Western Prairies, 1839* (Vols. XXVIII–XXIX in Reuben Gold Thwaites [ed.], *Early Western Travels, q.v.*).

Faux, William. *Memorable Days in America, 1818–1820* (Vol. XII in Reuben Gold Thwaites [ed.], *Early Western Travels, q.v.*).

Fenton, William N. "Problems Arising from the Historic North-Eastern Position of the Iroquois," *Essays in Historical Anthropology in North America* (*Swanton Memorial Volume*), *q.v.*

Fiske, John. *The Discovery of America.* 2 vols. New York, 1892.

Ford, Richard. *Gatherings from Spain.* London, 1907.

Fowler, Jacob. *The Journal of Jacob Fowler* (ed. by Elliott Coues). New York, 1898.

Franchère, Gabriel. *A Voyage to the Northwest Coast of America, 1811–1814* (Vol. VI in Reuben Gold Thwaites [ed.], *Early Western Travels, q.v.*).

Franklin, Sir John. *Narrative of a Journey to the Shores of the Polar Sea in the Years 1819, 1820, 1821, and 1822.* London, 1825.

———. *Narrative of a Second Journey to the Shores of the Polar Sea in the Years 1825, 1826, and 1827.* London, 1828.

Frémont, John Charles. *Narrative of the Exploring Expedition to the Rocky Mountains in the Year 1842; and to Oregon and North California in the Years 1843 1844.* London, 1846.

Fynn, Arthur John. *The American Indian as a Product of Environment.* Boston, 1908.

Galbraith, J. S. "The Hudson's Bay Company under Fire," *Canadian Historical Review,* Vol. XXX (1949), 322–35.

Garretson, Martin S. *The American Bison.* New York, 1938.

Garrioch, (Rev.) Alfred C. Manuscript: Beaver-Cree-English Vocabulary.

Gass, Patrick. *Journal of the Lewis and Clark Expedition* (ed. by John K. Hosmer). Chicago, 1904.

Gates, Charles M. (ed.). *Five Fur Traders of the Northwest* (comprising the Narrative of Peter Pond; and the Diaries of John McDonnell, Archibald N. McLeod, Hugh Faries, and Thomas Connor). Minneapolis, 1933.

Ghent, W. J. *The Road to Oregon.* London, 1926.

Gibbon, Edward. *The Decline and Fall of the Roman Empire* (ed. by H. H. Milman). 5 vols. New York, n.d.

Gilmore, Raymond M. "Fauna and Ethnozoology," *Handbook of South American Indians* (*q.v.*).

Gilmour, (Rev.) James. *Among the Mongols.* London, 1885.

Glazebrook, G. P. de T. *A History of Transportation in Canada.* New Haven, 1938.

———. "Roads in New France," *Canadian Historical Association Annual Report, 1934,* 48–56.

Glover, Richard. "The Difficulties of the Hudson's Bay Company's Penetration of the West," *Canadian Historical Review,* Vol. XXIX (1948), 240–55.

Goodwin, George G. "Buffalo Hunt–1935," *Natural History* (Sept., 1935), 156–63.

Gordon, D. H. "Swords, Rapiers, and Horse Riders," *Antiquity,* Vol. XXVII (1953), 67–78.

Greater America (Essays in Honor of Herbert Eugene Bolton). Berkeley and Los Angeles, 1945.

Gregg, Josiah. *The Commerce of the Prairies* (Vols. XIX–XX in Reuben Gold Thwaites [ed.], *Early Western Travels, q.v.*).

Grinnell, George Bird. *Blackfoot Lodge Tales.* New York, 1900.

———. *The Fighting Cheyennes.* New York, 1915.

———. "Horses," *Handbook of American Indians North of Mexico* (*q.v.*), I, 569–71.

———. *Indians of Today.* New York, 1911.

Haines, Francis D. *The Appaloosa Horse.* Lewiston, Idaho, 1951.

———. "How Did the Indians Get Their Horses?", *American Anthropologist,* Vol. XL (1938), 112–17.

———. "Nez Percé and Shoshoni Influence on Northwest History," *Greater America* (*q.v.*).

———. "The Northward Spread of Horses among the Plains Indians," *American Anthropologist,* Vol. XL (1938), 429–37.

———. "The Westward Limits of the Buffalo Range," *Pacific Northwest Quarterly,* Vol. XXXI (1940), 389–98.

Hakluyt, Richard. *The Principal Navigations, Voyages, Traffiques, and Discoveries of the English Nation.* 8 vols. London, 1907.

Hallenbeck, Cleve. *The Journey and Route of Alvar Nuñez Cabeza de Vaca.* New York, 1940.

Hammond, George P., and Agapito Rey (eds.). *The Expedition into New Mexico Made by Antonio de Espejo, 1582–1583, as Revealed in the Journal of Diego Perez de Luxán, a Member of the Party.* Los Angeles, 1929.

———. (eds.). *New Mexico in 1602.* Los Angeles, 1938.

Hancock, Samuel. *The Narrative of Samuel Hancock, 1845–1860* (ed. by A. D. Howden Smith). New York, 1927.

Handbook of American Indians North of Mexico (ed. by Frederick

Webb Hodge), Bureau of American Ethnology, *Bulletin 30*. 2 vols. Washington, 1910.

Handbook of Canadian Indians (National Geographical Board of Canada). Ottawa, 1913.

Handbook of South American Indians (ed. by Julian H. Steward), Bureau of American Ethnology, *Bulletin 143*. Washington, 1946 *et seq.* (in progress).

Harmon, Daniel Williams. *A Journal of Voyages and Travels in the Interior of North America*. New York, 1922.

Harrington, John P. "Athapaskawan Origins, Divisions, and Migrations," *Essays in Historical Anthropology in North America* (*Swanton Memorial Volume*), *q.v.*

———. *Vocabulary of the Kiowa Language*, Bureau of American Ethnology, *Bulletin 84*. Washington, 1928.

Havighurst, Walter. *The Land of Promise*. New York, 1946.

Hawkes, John. *Saskatchewan and Her People*. 3 vols. Chicago, 1924.

Hayden, F. V. "On the Ethnography and Philology of the Indian Tribes of the Missouri Valley," *Transactions of the American Philosophical Society*, Vol. XII (New Series; 1863), 231–461.

Hearne, Samuel. *A Journey from Prince of Wales Fort in 1770, 1771, and 1772* (ed. by J. B. Tyrrell). Toronto, 1911. *See also* Tyrrell, J. B.

Hebard, Grace R., and E. A. Brininstool. *The Bozeman Trail*. 2 vols. Cleveland, 1922.

Henday, Antony. "The Journal of Antony Hendry [Henday]" (ed. by Lawrence J. Burpee), *Proceedings and Transactions of the Royal Society of Canada*, 3rd. Series (1907), Sec. II, 307–54.

Hennepin, Father Louis. *A New Discovery of a Vast Country in America* (ed. by Reuben Gold Thwaites), 2 vols. Chicago, 1903.

Henry, Alexander (the elder). *Travels and Adventures in Canada and the Indian Territories between the Years 1760 and 1776*. New York, 1809.

Henry, Alexander (the younger; nephew of the elder). *See* Coues, Elliott.

Hewett Anniversary Volume. See *So Live the Works of Men*.

Hewett, Edgar Lee. *Ancient Life in the American Southwest*. Indianapolis, 1930.

Hewitt, C. Gordon. *The Conservation of the Wild Life of Canada*. New York, 1921.

Hilzheimer, Max. "The Evolution of the Domestic Horse," *Antiquity*, Vol. IX (1935), 133–39.

Hind, Henry Youle. *Report on the Assiniboine and Saskatchewan Exploring Expedition of 1858.* Toronto, 1859.

History of North America (ed. by Guy Carlton Lee and Francis Newton Thorpe). 20 vols. New York, 1903–1907.

Hoebel, E. Adamson. "The Political Association and Law-Ways of the Comanche Indians," *Memoirs of the American Anthropological Association, No. 54* (1940).

Honigmann, John J. "Parallels in the Development of Shamanism among Northern and Southern Athapaskans," *American Anthropologist,* Vol. LI (1949), 512–14.

Hornaday, William T. "The Extermination of the American Bison," *Smithsonian Report, 1887,* Part II, 367–548.

Hughes, Katherine. *Father Lacombe, the Black-Robe Voyageur.* New York, 1911.

Hulbert, Archer Butler. *The Historic Highways of America.* 16 vols. Cleveland, 1902–1905.

———. (ed.). *Forty-Niners.* Boston, 1931.

———, and Dorothy Printup Hulbert (eds.). *Marcus Whitman, Crusader.* 3 vols. Denver, 1936–39.

Hyde, George E. "The Mystery of the Arikaras," *North Dakota History,* Vol. XVIII (1951), 187–218.

Inman, (Col.) Henry. *The Old Santa Fé Trail.* New York, 1898.

——— (ed.). *Buffalo Jones' Forty Years of Adventure.* London, 1899.

Innis, Harold A. *Peter Pond, Fur Trader and Adventurer.* Toronto, 1930.

———. *The Fur Trade in Canada.* New Haven, 1930.

Irving, Washington. *Complete Works.* 12 vols. New York, n.d.

———. *Adventures of Captain Bonneville.* Vol. XI in *Complete Works.*

———. *Astoria.* Vol. VIII in *Complete Works.*

———. *A Tour on the Prairies.* Vol. VII in *Complete Works.*

Jablow, Joseph. *The Cheyenne in Plains Indian Trade Relations, 1795–1840 (Monographs of the American Ethnological Society, No. XIX).* New York, 1951.

James, Edwin. *An Account of an Expedition from Pittsburg to the Rocky Mountains, Performed in the Years 1819, 1820, under the Command of Major Stephen H. Long* (Vols. XIV–XVII in Reuben Gold Thwaites [ed.], *Early Western Travels, q.v.*).

Jenness, Diamond. *The Copper Eskimo* (Vol. XII in *Report of the Canadian Arctic Expedition, 1913–1918*). Ottawa, 1923.

———. *The Indians of Canada,* National Museum of Canada, *Bulletin 15.* Ottawa, 1932.

——. *The Sarcee Indians of Alberta,* National Museum of Canada, *Bulletin* 90 (Anthropological Series, No. 23). Ottawa, 1938.

—— (ed.). *The American Aborigines, Their Origin and Antiquity.* Toronto, 1933.

Johnson, Charles W. "Protein as a Factor in the Distribution of the American Bison," *Geographical Review,* Vol. XLI (1951), 330–31.

Johnson, John J. "The Spanish Horse in Peru before 1550," *Greater America (q.v.).*

Jones, L. R., and P. W. Bryan. *North America.* London, 1928.

Jones, R. Leslie. "The Old French-Canadian Horse," *Canadian Historical Review,* Vol. XXVIII (1947), 125–55.

Kane, Paul. *Wanderings of an Artist among the Indians of North America.* Toronto, 1859.

——. *Ibid.* (ed. by Lawrence J. Burpee). Toronto, 1925.

Kelly, L. V. *The Rangeman.* Toronto, 1913.

Kelsey, Henry. *The Journal of Henry Kelsey* (ed. by Charles N. Bell). Winnipeg, 1928.

——. *The Kelsey Papers* (ed. by A. G. Doughty and Chester Martin). Ottawa, 1929.

Kendall, George Wilkins. *Narrative of the Texas Santa Fé Expedition* (ed. by Milo Quaife). New York, 1929.

Kenton, Edna. *Simon Kenton, His Life and Period.* New York, 1930.

Kidd, Kenneth E. "Blackfoot Ethnography," unpublished M. A. thesis, University of Toronto, 1937.

Kroeber, Alfred L. *Cultural and Natural Areas in Native North America.* Berkeley, 1939.

——. "Ethnology of the Gros Ventre," *Anthropological Papers of the American Museum of Natural History,* Vol. I (1908), 142–281.

Lacombe, Father Albert. *Dictionnaire et Grammaire de la Langue des Cris.* Montreal, 1874.

La Flesche, Francis. *A Dictionary of the Osage Language,* Bureau of American Ethnology, *Bulletin* 109. Washington, 1932.

Larocque, François Antoine. "The Journal of François Antoine Larocque" (ed. by Lawrence J. Burpee), *Publications of the Canadian Archives, No. 3.* Ottawa, 1910.

Larpenteur, Charles. *Forty Years a Fur Trader on the Upper Missouri: The Personal Narrative of Charles Larpenteur* (ed. by Elliott Coues). 2 vols. New York, 1898.

La Salle. *The Journeys of Robert René Cavelier, Sieur de la Salle* (ed. by Isaac Joslin Cox; including the accounts of Henri de Tonty, Fathers Zenobius Membre, Anastasius Douay, Christian Le Clercq, and Louis Hennepin; La Salle's brother, Jean Cavelier, and his trusted subordinate, Henri Joutel). 2 vols. New York, 1922.

La Vérendrye. *Journals and Letters of Pierre Gaultier de Varennes, Sieur de la Vérendrye, and His Sons* (ed. by Lawrence J. Burpee). Toronto, 1927.

———. "La Vérendrye's Journal of 1738" (ed. by D. Brymner), *Report of the Canadian Archives, 1889.*

Legardeur de Saint-Pierre, Jacques Repentigny. *See* Saint-Pierre.

Lescarbot, Marc. *A History of New France* (ed. by H. P. Biggar). 3 vols. Toronto, 1907–1914.

Lewis, Oscar. *The Effects of White Contact upon Blackfoot Culture* (*Monographs of the American Ethnological Society, No. VI*). New York, 1942.

Lewis, Meriwether, and William Clark. *Journals of the Expedition of 1804–1806* (ed. by Nicholas Biddle). 3 vols. New York, 1922.

———. *Journals of the Expedition of 1804–1806* (ed. by Elliott Coues). 4 vols. London, 1893.

———. *The Original Journals of the Lewis and Clark Expedition* (ed. by Reuben Gold Thwaites). 8 vols. New York, 1904–1905.

Lewis, Francis J., Eleanor S. Dowding, and E. H. Moss. "The Vegetation of Alberta," *Journal of Ecology*, Vol. XIV (1926), No. 2; Vol. XVI (1928), No. 1; Vol. XVII (1929), No. 1; Vol. XX (1932), No. 2.

Long, John. *Voyages and Travels, 1768–1782* (Vol. II in Reuben Gold Thwaites [ed.], *Early Western Travels, q.v.*).

Long, Morden H. *A History of the Canadian People.* Toronto, 1942.

Long Lance, Chief Buffalo Child. *Long Lance.* New York, 1929.

Lowie, Robert H. "The Assiniboin," *Anthropological Papers of the American Museum of Natural History*, Vol. IV (1909), 1–270.

———. "Ceremonialism in North America," *American Anthropologist*, Vol. XVI (1914), 602–31.

———. *The Crow Indians.* New York, 1935.

———. "Material Culture of the Crow Indians," *Anthropological Papers of the American Museum of Natural History*, Vol. XXI (1922), 205–70.

MacInnes, C. M. *In the Shadow of the Rockies.* London, 1930.

MacKay, Douglas. *The Honourable Company.* Indianapolis, 1936.

Mackenzie, Sir Alexander. *Voyages from Montreal, on the River St. Lawrence, through the Continent of North America to the Frozen and Pacific Oceans, in the Years 1789 and 1793* (including the *General History of the Fur Trade*). New York and Philadelphia, 1802.

Macoun, John. *Autobiography.* Ottawa, 1922.

——. *Manitoba and the Great Northwest.* Guelph, Ontario, 1882.

MacRae, A. O. *History of Alberta.* 2 vols. Calgary, 1912.

McClintock, Walter. *The Old North Trail.* London, 1910.

McDougall, (Rev.) John. *Forest, Lake, and Prairie.* Toronto, 1910.

——. *In the Days of the Red River Rebellion.* Toronto, 1911.

——. *On Western Trails in the Early Seventies.* Toronto, 1911.

——. *Pathfinding on Plain and Prairie.* Toronto, 1898.

——. *Saddle, Sled, and Snowshoe.* Toronto, 1910.

——. Unpublished MS. in the Provincial Legislative Library, Edmonton, Alberta.

McGillivray, Duncan. *The Journal of Duncan McGillivray* (ed. by A. S. Morton). Toronto, 1929.

McGuire, Joseph D. "Trails and Trade Routes," *Handbook of American Indians North of Mexico* (q.v.).

McLean, John. *Notes of a Twenty-Five Years' Service in the Hudson Bay Territory* (ed. by W. S. Wallace). Toronto, 1932.

McLean, (Rev.) John. *Canadian Savage Folk.* Toronto, 1896.

——. *The Indians of Canada.* London, 1892.

——. *McDougall of Alberta.* Toronto, 1927.

Mandelbaum, David G. "The Plains Cree," *Anthropological Papers of the American Museum of Natural History,* Vol. XXXVII (1940), 153–316.

Marcy, (Gen.) Randolph B. *Exploration of the Red River of Louisiana, in the Year 1852.* Washington, 1854.

——. *The Prairie Traveller.* New York, 1859.

Masson, L. R. *Les Bourgeois de la Compagnie du Nord-Ouest.* 2 vols. Quebec, 1889, 1890.

Mawer, Allen. *The Chief Elements Used in English Place Names.* Cambridge, 1924.

Maximilian, Prince of Wied. *Travels in the Interior of North America, 1833–1834* (Vols. XXII–XXIV in Reuben Gold Thwaites [ed.], *Early Western Travels, q.v.*).

Mereness, Newton D. (ed.). *Travels in the American Colonies, 1690–1783.* New York, 1916.

Merriam, C. Hart. "The Bison in Northeastern California," *Journal of Mammalogy,* Vol. VII (1926), 211–14.

Milman, (Rev.) Henry H. *History of the Jews.* 2 vols. London, 1906.

Milton, Viscount, and W. B. Cheadle. *The North-West Passage by Land.* London, 1901.

Minutes of the Council, Northern Department of Rupert's Land, 1821 (ed. by R. Harvey Fleming). Toronto, 1940.

Mommsen, Theodor. *The History of Rome.* 4 vols. New York, 1929–31.

Mooney, James. "The Aboriginal Population of America North of Mexico" (ed. by John R. Swanton), *Smithsonian Miscellaneous Collections,* Vol. LXXX, No. 7. Washington, 1928.

———. "Calendar History of the Kiowa Indians," *Seventeenth Annual Report of the Bureau of Ethnology,* Part I. Washington, 1898.

Morice, Father A. G. *Fifty Years in Western Canada.* Toronto, 1930.

———. *History of the Catholic Church in Western Canada.* 2 vols. Toronto 1910.

———. *History of the Northern Interior of British Columbia.* Toronto, 1906.

Morris, Alexander. *Treaties with the Indians of Manitoba and the North-West Territories.* Toronto, 1880.

Morris, (Capt.) Thomas. *Journal, 1764* (Vol. I in Reuben Gold Thwaites [ed.], *Early Western Travels, q.v.*).

Morton, Arthur S. *A History of the Canadian West to 1870–71.* New York, 1939.

Myres, John Linton. *Who Were the Greeks?* Berkeley, 1930.

Nichols, Madaline W. "The Spanish Horse of the Pampas," *American Anthropologist,* Vol. XLI (1939), 119–29.

Nuttall, Thomas. *A Journal of Travels into the Arkansas Territory, 1819* (Vol. XIII in Reuben Gold Thwaites [ed.], *Early Western Travels, q.v.*).

O'Callaghan, Mary A. "An Indian Removal Policy in Spanish Louisiana," *Greater America (q.v.).*

Ogden, Adele. "New England Traders in Spanish and Mexican California," *Greater America (q.v.).*

Oliver, Edmund H. "The Beginnings of Agriculture in Saskatchewan," *Proceedings and Transactions of the Royal Society of Canada* (1935), Sec. II, 1–32.

———. (ed.). *The Canadian North-West (Publications of the Canadian Archives, No. 9).* 2 vols. Ottawa, 1914, 1915.

Osborn, Henry Fairfield. *The Age of Mammals.* New York, 1910.

Osgood, E. S. *The Day of the Cattleman.* Minneapolis, 1929.

Palliser, (Capt.) John (*et al.*). *Journals, Detailed Reports, and Observations, Relative to Palliser's Exploration of British North America, 1857, 1858, 1859, 1860.* London, 1863.

Palmer, Joel. *Journal of Travels over the Rocky Mountains, 1845–1846*

(Vol. XXX in Reuben Gold Thwaites [ed.], *Early Western Travels, q.v.*).

Parkman, Francis. *A Half-Century of Conflict.* 2 vols. Boston, 1910.

——. *La Salle and the Discovery of the Great West.* Boston, 1910.

——. *The Oregon Trail.* Boston, 1892.

——. *Pioneers of France in the New World.* Boston, 1910.

Pattie, James Ohio. *Personal Narrative, 1824–1830* (Vol. XVIII in Reuben Gold Thwaites [ed.], *Early Western Travels, q.v.*).

Pike, Warburton. *The Barren Ground of Northern Canada.* London, 1917.

Pike, Zebulon M. *The Expeditions of Zebulon Montgomery Pike, 1805–1807* (ed. by Elliott Coues). 3 vols. New York, 1895.

Place-Names of Alberta (National Geographic Board of Canada). Ottawa, 1928.

Post, Christian Frederick. *Journals, 1758–1759* (Vol. I in Reuben Gold Thwaites [ed.], *Early Western Travels, q.v.*).

Prescott, William H. *History of the Conquest of Mexico.* 2 vols. London, 1906.

——. *History of the Conquest of Peru.* 2 vols. New York, n.d.

——. *History of the Reign of Ferdinand and Isabella.* 3 vols. Philadelphia, 1872.

Purchas, (Rev.) Samuel. *Hakluytus Posthumus, or Purchas His Pilgrimes: Contayning a History of the World in Sea Voyages and Lande Travells by Englishmen and Others.* 20 vols. Glasgow, 1905–1907.

Radin, Paul. *The Indians of South America.* New York, 1942.

Raup, Hugo M. *Phytogeographic Studies in the Peace and Upper Liard River Regions, Canada.* Cambridge, Mass., 1934.

——. *Range Conditions in the Wood Buffalo Park of Western Canada, With Notes on the History of the Wood Bison.* New York, 1933.

Ravenhill, Alice. *The Native Tribes of British Columbia.* Victoria, B. C., 1938.

Richardson, Sir John. *Arctic Searching Expedition through Rupert's Land and the Arctic Sea in Search of Sir John Franklin, 1847–1850.* London, 1852.

——. *Fauna Boreali-Americana.* 4 vols. London, 1829–1837.

——. *The Polar Regions.* London, 1861.

Richardson, Rupert Norval. *The Comanche Barrier to South Plains Settlement.* Glendale, Cal., 1933.

Riddell, Francis A. "The Recent Occurrence of Bison in Northeastern California," *American Antiquity,* Vol. XVIII (1952), 168–69.

Rodnick, David. "An Assiniboine Horse-Raiding Expedition," *American Anthropologist*, Vol. XLI (1939), 611–16.

Roe, Frank Gilbert. "The Extermination of the Buffalo in Western Canada," *Canadian Historical Review*, Vol. XV (1934), 1–23.

———. "From Dogs to Horses among the Western Indian Tribes," *Proceedings and Transactions of the Royal Society of Canada* (3rd Series), Vol. XXXIII (1939), Sec. II, 209–75.

———. *The North American Buffalo*. Toronto, 1951.

Rogers, J. E. Thorold. *The Economic Interpretation of History*. New York and London, 1909.

———. *A History of Agriculture and Prices in England*. 7 vols. Oxford, 1866–1902.

Rogers, Joseph. *Thomas Hart Benton*. Philadelphia,.1905.

Rollins, Philip Ashton (ed.). *The Discovery of the Oregon Trail* (Robert Stuart's Narrative). New York and London, 1935.

Roosevelt, Theodore. *Hunting Trips of a Ranchman*. New York, 1885.

———. *The Winning of the West*. 4 vols. New York, 1889–1910.

Ross, Alexander. *Adventures of the First Settlers on the Oregon or Columbia River, 1810–1813* (Vol. VII in Reuben Gold Thwaites [ed.], *Early Western Travels, q.v.*).

———. *Fur Hunters of the Far West*. 2 vols. London, 1855.

———. *The Red River Settlement*. London, 1856.

Ross, Marvin C. (ed.). *The West of Alfred Jacob Miller*. Norman, 1951.

Rowan, William. "Canada's Buffalo," *Country Life*, Vol. LXVI (1929), 358.

———. *The Riddle of Migration*. Baltimore, 1931.

Rundle, (Rev.) Robert Terrill. "Journal" (ed. by [Rev.] J. P. Berry and Frank Gilbert Roe), unpublished MS. in the McDougall Memorial Museum, Edmonton.

Saint-Pierre, Jacques Repentigny Legardeur de. "Journal" (ed. by D. Brymner), *Report of the Canadian Archives, 1886*.

Saunders, Richard M. "The First Introduction of European Plants and Animals into Canada," *Canadian Historical Review*, Vol. XVI (1935), 388–406.

Scharff, R. F. *Distribution and Origin of Life in America*. London, 1911.

Scholes, France V. "Juan Martinez de Montoya, Settler and Conquistador of New Mexico," *New Mexico Historical Review*, Vol. XIX (1944), 337–42.

———. "Troublous Times in New Mexico," *New Mexico Historical Review*, Vol. XII (1937), 137–74.

Schultz, James Willard. *Apauk, Caller of Buffalo*. New York, 1916.

———. *My Life as an Indian*. New York, 1907.

Scott, Hugh Lennox. "Early History and Names of the Arapaho," *American Anthropologist*, Vol. IX (1907), 545–60.

Seton, Ernest Thompson. *The Arctic Prairies*. New York, 1911.

———. *Life Histories of Northern Animals*. 2 vols. New York, 1910.

———. *Lives of Game Animals*. 4 vols. New York, 1929.

Setzler, Frank M. "Archaeological Perspectives in the Northern Mississippi Valley," *Essays in Historical Anthropology in North America* (*q.v.*).

Shaler, N. S. *Nature and Man in America*. New York, 1900.

Simpson, Sir George. *Fur Trade and Empire* (ed. by Frederick Merk). Cambridge, Mass., 1931.

———. *Narrative of a Journey Around the World in the Years 1841 and 1842*. 2 vols. London, 1847.

– ––. *Simpson's Athabaska Journal, 1820–1821* (ed. by E. E. Rich). Toronto, 1938.

Skinner, Alanson. "The Culture of the Plains Cree," *American Anthropologist*, Vol. XVI (1914), 68–87, 314–18.

———. "Notes on the Eastern Cree and Northern Saulteaux," *Anthropological Papers of the American Museum of Natural History*, Vol. IX (1911), 1–177.

Skinner, Morris F., and Ove C. Kaisen. "The Fossil Bison of Alaska and Preliminary Revision of the Genus," *Bulletin of the American Museum of Natural History*, Vol. LXXXIX (1947), 123–256.

Smith, Marian W. "The War Complex of the Plains Indians," *Proceedings of the American Philosophical Society*, Vol. LXXVIII (1938), 425–64.

Snyderman, George S. "Behind the Tree of Peace: A Sociological Analysis of Iroquois Warfare," *Pennsylvania Archaeologist*, Vol. XVIII (1948), 2–93.

Solanet, Emilio. "The Criollo Horse" (tr. and ed. by Thornton Chard), *Journal of Heredity*, Vol. XXI (1930), 451–80.

So Live the Works of Men (Essays in Honor of Edgar Lee Hewett). Albuquerque, 1939.

Soper, J. Dewey. "History, Range, and Home Life of the Northern Bison," *Ecological Monographs*, Vol. XI (1941), 347–412.

Southesk, Earl of. *Saskatchewan and the Rocky Mountains*. Edinburgh and Toronto, 1875.

Stanley, George F. G. *The Birth of Western Canada*. London, 1936.

Steele, (Gen.) Sam B. *Forty Years in Canada*. London, 1915.

Stefansson, Vilhjalmur. *Not by Bread Alone*. New York, 1946.

415

———. "Pemmican," *The Military Surgeon,* Vol. XCV (1944), 89–98.

Steward, Julian H. "Native Cultures of the Intermontane (Great Basin) Area," *Essays in Historical Anthropology in North America* (*q.v.*).

Strong, W. D. "From History to Prehistory in the Northern Great Plains," *Essays in Historical Anthropology in North America* (*q.v.*).

———. "Plains Culture in the Light of Archaeology," *American Anthropologist,* Vol. XXXV (1933), 271–87.

Swanton, John R. "Ethnological Positions of the Natchez Indians," *American Anthropologist,* Vol. IX (1907), 513–28.

———, and Roland B. Dixon. "Primitive American History," *American Anthropologist,* Vol. XVI (1914), 376–412.

Swanton Memorial Volume (*Essays in Historical Anthropology in North America, q.v.*).

Taylor, Isaac. *Words and Places.* New York and London, 1911.

Thomas, Alfred Barnaby. *After Coronado.* Norman, 1935.

Thomas, Cyrus. *The Indians of North America in Historic Times* (Vol. II in *History of North America, q.v.*).

Thompson, David. *Narrative of Explorations in Western America, 1784–1812* (ed. by J. B. Tyrrell). Toronto, 1916. *See also* Coues, Elliott.

Thwaites, Reuben Gold (ed.). *The Jesuit Relations and Allied Documents, 1610–1791.* 73 vols. Cleveland, 1896–1901.

Tolmie, W. Fraser, and George M. Dawson. *Five Comparative Vocabularies of Indian Tribes of British Columbia.* Montreal, 1884.

Townsend, John K. *Narrative of a Journey across the Rocky Mountains, 1833–1834* (Vol. XXI in Reuben Gold Thwaites [ed.], *Early Western Travels, q.v.*).

Turner, Frederick Jackson. *The Frontier in American History.* New York, 1920.

Turner, G. J. *Select Pleas of the Forest.* London, 1901.

Turney-High, Harry. "The Diffusion of the Horse to the Flatheads," *Man,* Vol. XXXV (Dec., 1935), 183–85.

Tyrrell, J. B. (ed.). *The Journals of Samuel Hearne and Philip Turnor.* Toronto, 1934.

Umfreville, Edward. *The Present State of Hudson's Bay.* London, 1790.

Villagrá, Gaspar Pérez de. *History of New Mexico.* (tr. by Gilberto Espinoza and ed. by Frederick Webb Hodge). Los Angeles, 1933.

Vocabulary of the Navaho Language (compiled by the Franciscan Fathers). 2 vols. St. Michaels, Arizona, 1912.

Watkins, (Rev.) E. A. *A Dictionary of the Cree Language* (ed. by [Rev.] R. Faries [*et al.*]). Toronto, 1938.

Webb, Walter Prescott. *The Great Plains.* New York, 1931.

———. *The Texas Rangers*. New York, 1936.

Wedel, Waldo R. "Culture Sequences in the Central Great Plains," *Essays in Historical Anthropology in North America* (*q.v.*).

Wellman, Paul I. *The Trampling Herd*. New York, 1939.

Welsh, Norbert. *The Last Buffalo Hunter* (ed. by Mary Weekes). New York, 1939.

Willson, Beckles. *The Great Company*. Toronto, 1899.

Wilson, Gilbert L. "The Horse and the Dog in Hidatsa Culture," *Anthropological Papers of the American Museum of Natural History*, Vol. XV (1924), 127–311.

Winsor, Justin (ed.). *A Narrative and Critical History of America*. 8 vols. Boston and New York, 1884–1889.

Wissler, Clark. *The American Indian*. New York, 1922.

———. "The Influence of the Horse in the Development of Plains Culture," *American Anthropologist*, Vol. XVI (1914), 1–25.

———. "Material Culture of the Blackfoot Indians," *Anthropological Papers of the American Museum of Natural History*, Vol. V (1910), 1–175.

———. "Material Culture of the North American Indians," *American Anthropologist*, Vol. XVI (1914), 477–505.

———. "The Riding Gear of the North American Indians," *Anthropological Papers of the American Museum of Natural History*, Vol. XVII (1915), 1–38.

———. "The Social Life of the Blackfoot Indians," *Anthropological Papers of the American Museum of Natural History*, Vol. VII (1911), 3–64.

Worcester, D. E. "Spanish Horses among the Plains Tribes," *Pacific Historical Review*, Vol. XIV (1945), 409–17.

———. "The Spread of Spanish Horses in the Southwest," *New Mexico Historical Review*, Vol. XIX (1944), 225–32.

Wyeth, John B. *Oregon, 1832* (Vol. XXI in Reuben Gold Thwaites [ed.], *Early Western Travels*, *q.v.*).

Young, (Rev.) Egerton R. *By Canoe and Dog Train*. London, 1892.

INDEX

The dates attached are broadly those to which the entries refer.

The Indian and the Horse

has been printed directly from slugs cast on the Linotype composing machine, in the eleven-point size of Caledonia, with two points of space between lines. The face was designed by W. A. Dwiggins, who began his thinking about these letter forms by noticing the "lively curves" and sturdy practicality of a type cut by William Martin for William Bulmer around 1790. But there are no specific historical or esthetic reasons for selecting this particular type face for a book about Indians and horses. One may rationalize that horses have "lively curves," but there is no connection between Martin's 1790 and the latest date (1770, only twenty years earlier) on the "Dispersion Map" in this book. The principal reason for using Caledonia is that it makes a legible type page in a readable piece of literature.

 NORMAN

UNIVERSITY OF OKLAHOMA PRESS